Urban Development

WALLACE F. SMITH

URBAN

DEVELOPMENT

THE PROCESS
AND
THE PROBLEMS

University of California Press
Berkeley · Los Angeles · London

UNIVERSITY OF CALIFORNIA PRESS
BERKELEY AND LOS ANGELES, CALIFORNIA

UNIVERSITY OF CALIFORNIA PRESS, LTD.
LONDON, ENGLAND

ISBN 0–520–02780–9
LIBRARY OF CONGRESS CATALOG CARD NUMBER: 74–79772
PRINTED IN THE UNITED STATES OF AMERICA
DESIGNED BY HENRY BENNETT

CONTENTS

V

CONTENTS   vii

FIGURES

TABLES

PREFACE

THIS BOOK describes in a generalized way how people make the kinds of decisions that produce cities—decisions that determine how cities will evolve physically and economically, and how their benefits and cost will be distributed among the people who share the same urban environment. It was written as a textbook for an introductory course in real estate and urban land economics which I have taught at the University of California in Berkeley and at the University of British Columbia. The book and the course are both moderately interdisciplinary, though focused clearly on business and economic behavior. The purpose of the book is to introduce students with a variety of interests to the types of motivations and constraints that govern decision-making about the development and use of urban land.

This is not a theoretical book, and it makes no effort to produce policy recommendations from a quantitative model. There is no lack of recent books on "urban economics" that are theoretical and policy-oriented, books concerned about the decisions that *should* be made. This book is about the way decisions *are* made, about the way people conduct the day-to-day business of urban resource management—making the housing inventory go around, paying for streets, getting a shopping center started, finding room for another factory, or adjusting when an industry leaves town, and so on. These decisions are not coherent or consistent. Objections can be made to almost every option that an individual or a community exercises, but the whole course of events in the formation and use of the urban environment is not under anyone's control. This situation is not likely to change, but it is not impossible to live with. This book begins to tell us how.

ACKNOWLEDGMENTS

This book responds to a need for instructional material in courses which integrate the principles of urban land economics and contemporary real estate business activity. In the early decades of this century real estate education tended to be narrowly vocational, while urban land economics occupied only a tiny cluster of concerned intellectuals. The relevance of each of these subject matter areas for the other was brilliantly demonstrated in Richard Ratcliff's *Urban Land Economics*, published in 1949 by McGraw–Hill. That book served as a pre-eminent text for many years, defining the subject with clarity and cohesion, though the practical context—issues associated with the use of urban land and with the evolving forms of real estate business—changed greatly. To a major extent the present book rests on Ratcliff's concept of a new, integrated discipline; the presentation of that concept is amplified and brought more nearly current.

The challenge of the classroom environment in the School of Business Administration at the University of California in Berkeley required that amplification and updating, as well as ever more searching re-examination of underlying ideas. Students have been, and are, the most important part of that environment. In turn, the opportunity to have students in courses on real estate and urban land economics arose because of the interest and consent of the School's deans and faculty and the indirect assistance of the State of California's Department of Real Estate. It is particularly important in this subject matter area that students from beyond the precincts of the Business School itself were permitted and encouraged to participate in these courses, adding so much to their scope and interest.

The author is indebted to present and former colleagues at the University of California and at the University of British Columbia to a degree that precludes exact definition, and to a now wonderfully varied and distinguished array of people elsewhere in the intellectual community who have helped this subject matter mature.

Among these are the following, whose works are drawn upon specifically in the pages of this book: Ralph Turvey, author of *The Economics of Real Property* (George Allen and Unwin, Ltd.); John Dyckman, Abel Wolman, and the late Charles Abrams, contributors to the remarkable issue of *Scientific American* in September, 1965, from which certain material has been reproduced by permission of W. H. Freeman, publishers; Constance M. Green, author of *American Cities in the Growth of a Nation*; Wilbur Thompson, *A Preface to Urban Economics* (copyright in the name of The Johns Hopkins University Press); the late Larry Smith, whose article "Space for the CBD's Functions," appeared in the February, 1961, *Journal of the American Institute of Planners*; Hugh O. Nourse, *Regional Economics* (McGraw-Hill Book Co.); Sherman J. Maisel, *Financing Real Estate* (McGraw-Hill Book Co.); O. A. Davis and A. B. Whinston whose stimulating article appeared in *Urban Renewal: The Record and The Controversy*, James Q. Wilson, ed. (M.I.T. Press), and from which material has been used with the permission of the editor and the publisher; Constantinos A. Doxiadis, *Ekistics: An Introduction to the Science of Human Settlements*, from which material has been used with the permission of Doxiadis Associates International Co., Ltd. for Hutchinson Publishing Group, and of Oxford University Press; Larry S. Bourne, *Internal Structure of the City*, from which material has been used with the permission of Canadian Geographer and of Oxford University Press; Martin Beckman, *Location Theory* (Random House, Inc.); Jane Jacobs, *The Economy of Cities* (Random House, Inc.), from which illustrative material has been excerpted and paraphrased; Emmanuel Tobier, whose article "Economic Development Strategy for the City," appeared in *Agenda For A City: Issues Confronting New York*, by L. C. Fitch and A. H. Walsh, eds., pp. 27–85 (Sage Publications, Inc., 1970); D. A. Turin, author of "Housing in Africa," *The Economic Problems of Housing*, A. A. Nevitt, ed. (St. Martin's Press, Inc., and Macmillan & Co., Ltd.), which was paraphrased with the permission of the publishers; Jean Gottman, author of *Megalopolis* (The Twentieth Century Fund, 1961); J. H. Niedercorn and E. F. R. Hearle, authors of "Recent Land-Use Trends in Forty-Eight Large American Cities," *Land Economics*, February,

1964, from which tables in this book were taken with the permission of the University of Wisconsin Press; Robert H. Carey, President of Thompson–Brown Company, Realtors, Farmington, Michigan, whose subdivision plan appearing in this book was reprinted with permission from ULI, The Urban Land Institute, 1200 18th St. N.W., Washington, D.C. 20036, as well as from Thompson–Brown Company, Realtors; F. S. Chapin and S. F. Weiss, *Urban Growth Dynamics* (John Wiley & Sons, Inc.), from which an illustration was reproduced with the publisher's permission. Permission to reproduce material from the author's own previous works was granted by Hong Kong University Press, *The City as a Centre of Change in Asia* (1972); The Town Planning Institute of Canada–Plan, *Canada*, Vol. 13, No. 2; and the Center for Real Estate and Urban Economics, University of California, Berkeley–several monographs.

This manuscript was first typed by Gillian O'Mara in Vancouver, Canada, for use as a text at the University of British Columbia; subsequently a revised manuscript was typed by Ellen McGibbon. The index was prepared by Naomi Steinfeld. It takes much more than typing skill to type a manuscript, and the author considers himself fortunate indeed to have had the help of both typists. The experience of indexing, though it comes rather late in the game to affect the text itself, can be a creative reflection that helps an author recall his own flow of ideas–or recognize that there was a flow; the author will use this book more effectively in time to come because of the thoughtful indexing effort.

A number of the drawings were done by Adrienne Morgan, who has helped the author in the past and who clearly seems able to interpret what is on his mind. Mary Lou Pung assisted in the matter of permissions correspondence. Editorial advice and assistance provided by the University of California Press was as gentle and encouraging as any book writing professor could ask.

The author says thanks also to his wife, Mi–Ja, without whose help and understanding this book would have remained no more than a file of miscellaneous class notes, an assortment of mislaid books and journals with scraps of paper marking things I must not forget to work into that book I was going to write someday.

1

WE LIVE IN CITIES

THE TIME is fast approaching when half the world population will be living in cities of 100,000 or more. In many major nations, the proportion of population classified as "urban" was well above the fifty percent mark by 1970—83.2 percent in Japan, 79.1 percent in the United Kingdom, and 75.2 percent in the United States, for example. A few places such as Hong Kong and Singapore are properly called "city states" because they have no rural population at all. East Germany's population was 84.2 percent urban in 1970, higher than Japan and just above the 82.2 percent figure for the Federal Republic of Germany. Israel was 81.3 percent urban. Australia was the most completely urbanized major nation in 1970, with 88.5 percent of its population living in urban areas. The urban population of mainland China was estimated to be 177 million in 1970.

The direction is clear, but the reasons for increasing urbanization are still obscure. A city, after all, does not produce its own food, nor does it usually have within its boundaries significant supplies of natural resources. If a city is effectively besieged in wartime, it must soon collapse because it is not self-sufficient. Even in peacetime, there are signs that a city can collapse of its own weight and diminishing ability to function, with New York heading the list of examples. The physical crumbling of Calcutta is manifest to any visitor, though its population rose from 5.2 to 7.4 million between 1950 and 1970.

Why, then, do urban populations rise both relatively and absolutely, all over the globe? Is the city merely a refuge for surplus rural population, or is it a beckoning frontier which holds out the promise of a better life? Is

1

it inevitable that cities should "self-destruct" at some point, or can they be built and managed in a way that allows them to survive and prosper? Does urbanization tempt us to squander our resources or help us to conserve them? How much population can any one city or a world of cities accommodate, and what new modes of work and living does urban life require of the people who come to share it? What new economic, political, and social arrangements are needed to allow mankind to flourish in cities as we like to think he once flourished in the country, living at peace with nature as a tiller of the soil? In short, are cities viable? Is urbanization fundamentally consistent with the laws and constraints of nature and with the inherent capabilities and motivations of human beings?

This book will argue that the answer is yes. But it is a qualified yes. Cities are artificial environments, in the physical, economic, and social sense, not unlike the giant spaceships that may someday roam for ages among the stars. Their structure and missions require much thinking and rethinking. Thus far, cities have evolved without benefit of much understanding of how they grew or what their growth implied, and perhaps this evolutionary process has served human beings well enough. But there is nothing to be lost by understanding something we are confronted with, and there is a possibility that something can be gained. Since we now live or expect to live primarily in urban environments, it makes sense to learn how to control them.

DEFINING "URBAN"

Statistics about urbanization must, of course, be based on a definition of "urban." The statistics, such as an increasing rate of world urbanization, are not meaningful or useful unless we know the underlying definition. It means one thing, for example, if a given city's population grows because that city keeps extending its boundaries, and quite something else if the growth represents increasing density within a fixed geographic area.

Beyond statistics, any useful statement we might make about urbanization or cities could turn out to be incorrect under some reasonable definition of the terms which had not occurred to us. For example, we may think that particular cities are becoming more "crowded" because their population has risen; but in fact most urban areas in the United States became "less crowded" between 1950 and 1970, despite much higher nose-counts and relatively stable geographic boundaries, in the sense that the number of residents in the suburban fringes increased very rapidly and the population of the central cities actually fell. People were not so tightly bunched up in the center. So, what do we mean by "crowded"? And if we want to call what happened "crowding," does it call for more investment in rapid transit?

There are many definitions of "urban" to choose from, and any one of them might be appropriate for certain kinds of inquiries. The following list of definitions does not imply a preference ranking, though comments are attached, mostly to call attention to points that are not so obvious.

Minimum size.— Demographers often classify a "place" as urban if its population is greater than some arbitrary level, such as 1,000 or 2,500. This begs the question somewhat, for someone must first make a list of "places," some of which may be groupings of villages, no one of which alone would come up to the minimum "urban" size. Nevertheless, most statistics on urbanization rely chiefly on minimum size classifications, despite the fact that the population figure that makes a place "urban" differs from country to country.

Political status.— In most of the world, a "city" is a semiautonomous political unit for which precise legal-geographic boundaries exist and consolidated statistical information is available. Once designated a city, a community rarely loses its separate statistical identity, even though its population may fall or its identity become lost within a contiguous metropolis, as is the case with the many "cities" that make up greater Los Angeles, for example. At the other extreme, a tiny rural community may be given the status of a city so that it can function as a regional administrative center for the national government.

Density of population.— The most familiar definition of "urban" is probably one that rests on population density, a large number of people living and working in a small area. Density permits contact, and it may be this exposure to large numbers of other people that makes a person "urbanized." There is no agreement, however, on how many persons per square mile make an area urban, and probably there can be none for the world as a whole. In 1970, the rural areas (political definition) of South

Korea had an aggregate population density of 199 persons per square kilometer, or about .8 per acre; many affluent urban neighborhoods in the United States are less densely populated than that.

Nonextractive occupations.— Farming, ranching, mining, and fishing are occupations which extract resources from the earth or water and thus require the people regularly engaged in them to live close to those resources. By the same token, they must live far enough from each other so as not to overburden the natural resources they are working with—particularly in the case of farmers and ranchers. On the other hand, manufacturing, commerce, government, education, and entertainment require workers to congregate and to live in close proximity. Recreation and transportation business may fall in either category. Since cities grew up very often as administrative centers or as places of manufacturing, and since clustered living is incompatible with extractive economic activities, it seems natural to frame a definition of "urban" in terms of occupations—that is, to say that a cluster of people engaged almost wholly in nonextractive occupations is a "city". This definition is the basis for "economic-base" theory, which will be examined in a later chapter; the purpose of that theory is to facilitate predictions about the growth of a particular city. It is a very useful concept, but it has a few important weaknesses. A mining firm, for example, may be headquartered in a city quite remote from the ores it is extracting. Similarly for logging, petroleum, fisheries, and corporate farming—the administration of extractive industries, representing a large part of their total employment, can be and increasingly is carried on in urban centers. Retirement or recreation communities, which are "urban" to the common man, may also be extractive, in a sense, since their basic product is the surrounding natural environment.

Mechanical infrastructure.— When a large number of people live and work in a confined district, they can no longer obtain water from individual wells or safely dispose of sewage and other wastes by burying them close by. The water table would soon disappear and the ground would be polluted (not that these things don't happen!). In the long run, some substantial collective investment in water supply and waste disposal systems will pay off. Electric power and natural gas fuel can also be secured more efficiently through large systems, used and paid for jointly by a densely populated community. And when a city reaches a certain geographic size, it is no longer feasible for workers to walk to and from work, the way farmers do in rural areas; capital investment in streets, buses, trains, or automobiles becomes imperative. Provision of collective capital equipment—such as streets, water supply, waste disposal, and even schools, hospitals, and libraries—is one of the principal functions of an urban government, so it makes some sense to say a place is urban when it has and requires this type of infrastructure. This definition anticipates a discussion of problems in providing an infrastructure.

A symbol of wealth.— A city is something physically recognizable, a cluster of tall buildings with an occasional monument. Paris has its Eiffel Tower and San Francisco its Golden Gate Bridge. All cities represent masses of building material, so archeologists in search of lost civilizations look for mounds (called "tells") of compacted rubble which stand out on flat plains and betray the fact that more physical material was once brought into those places than was ever carted, blown, or eroded away. Thus a city is a large heap of durable capital goods, much of which is consumer capital—houses, palaces, temples, stores, and so on. It stands as testimony to the productivity of people who have inhabited it—the most conspicuous form of consumption. Many Asian cities are dotted with curious, windowless buildings called "godowns," in which wealthy families put their treasures for safekeeping. The number of godowns a family has is a measure of its wealth—even though misfortunes might have left the godowns empty. Perhaps that fate awaits cathedrals and universities in western countries. In part, a city is an architectural monument to wealth, if not always to wisdom or taste, and to some people that's almost all it is—an artifact.

A life style.— At the opposite extreme we can think of "urban" as referring to a point of view. City people have wider and less personal relationships with each other than rural people do. In a city you can shop in many stores for a pair of shoes before doing business with one, and then never see or be concerned with any of the people you talked with again. You can strike up a casual conversation in an elevator or you can turn your back. You can seek information or make a business deal without first establishing personal rapport with the other human being. The bigger the city, the more you are constrained to be selective in all that you do, and the

Table 1

Rural and Urban Populations of Selected Nations, 1950 and 1970

(Figures in Thousands)

Nation	Total 1950	Total 1970	Rural 1950	Rural 1970	Urban 1950	Urban 1970	1970 Percent urban
USA	151,761	206,985	54,637	51,352	97,124	155,633	75.2
Brazil	52,022	93,545	33,239	43,520	18,783	50,025	53.5
Mexico	25,791	50,624	14,808	21,156	10,983	29,468	58.2
Argentina	17,070	24,089	6,270	7,111	10,800	16,978	70.5
Canada	13,737	21,673	5,257	5,489	8,480	16,184	74.7
Colombia	11,334	21,168	7,135	9,520	4,199	11,648	55.0
Peru	8,319	13,581	5,366	7,325	2,953	6,256	46.1
Venezuela	5,092	10,390	2,791	2,456	2,301	7,934	76.4
U.S.S.R.	180,050	244,125	103,550	92,125	76,500	152,000	62.3
West Germany	50,774	61,796	13,958	10,969	36,816	50,827	82.2
United Kingdom	50,616	56,065	11,389	11,724	39,227	44,341	79.1
Italy	46,769	53,648	26,213	26,042	20,556	27,606	51.5
France	41,736	51,402	19,138	16,515	22,598	34,887	67.9
Poland	25,008	32,980	15,249	14,571	9,759	18,409	55.8
Spain	27,977	32,958	14,339	13,589	13,638	19,369	58.8
Yugoslavia	16,346	20,649	13,535	12,663	2,811	7,986	38.7
Romania	16,311	19,701	12,140	12,047	4,171	7,654	38.9
East Germany	18,388	16,999	5,362	2,685	13,026	14,314	84.2
Czechoslovakia	12,338	14,577	7,147	6,993	5,191	7,584	52.0
Netherlands	10,114	13,110	2,984	3,648	7,130	9,462	72.2
Hungary	9,338	11,064	5,906	6,343	3,432	4,721	42.7
Nigeria	30,500	66,000	26,500	52,174	4,000	13,826	20.1
U.A.R.	20,461	33,283	13,946	18,739	6,515	14,544	43.7

Ethiopia	16,000	24,754	15,050	23,111	950	1,643	6.6
South Africa	12,458	20,044	7,582	9,949	4,876	10,095	50.4
Congo (Dem.Rep.)	11,390	17,405	10,540	14,405	850	3,000	17.2
Sudan	8,950	15,631	8,382	14,328	568	1,303	8.3
Morocco	8,959	15,519	6,887	10,035	2,072	5,484	35.5
Algeria	8,920	13,663	6,737	8,446	2,183	5,217	38.2
Tanganyika	7,733	12,878	7,498	11,959	235	919	7.1
Kenya	6,018	10,861	5,706	9,861	312	1,000	9.2
China	560,000	750,665	498,310	573,940	61,690	176,725	23.5
India	354,931	544,621	294,148	442,188	60,783	102,433	18.8
Indonesia	76,000	118,184	66,663	97,048	9,337	21,136	17.9
Pakistan[a]	75,053	114,191	67,417	96,013	7,636	18,178	15.9
Japan	83,419	102,795	52,216	17,286	31,203	85,509	83.2
Philippines	20,275	38,290	16,246	29,423	4,029	8,867	23.2
Thailand	19,635	35,898	17,666	31,239	1,969	4,659	13.0
Turkey	20,800	35,225	16,207	24,218	4,593	11,007	31.2
South Korea	20,513	32,168	16,763	19,621	3,750	12,547	39.0
Iran	16,276	28,805	11,929	17,499	4,347	11,306	39.3
Burma	18,766	27,447	16,341	23,115	2,425	4,332	15.8
North Vietnam	12,000	22,079	11,069	16,802	931	5,277	23.9
South Vietnam	10,500	18,380	8,799	13,584	1,701	4,796	26.1
Afghanistan	12,000	16,715	11,306	15,587	694	1,128	6.7
Taiwan	7,619	14,402	3,642	5,130	3,977	9,272	64.4
North Korea	9,700	13,685	8,439	10,685	1,261	3,000	21.9
Ceylon	7,678	12,685	6,529	10,585	1,149	2,100	16.6
Australia	8,257	12,404	2,300	1,424	5,957	10,980	88.5
Nepal	8,000	11,143	7,808	10,591	192	552	5.0

Source: Kingsley Davis, *World Urbanization, 1950–1970* (Berkeley: Institute of International Studies, University of California, 1969), pp. 57–82.
Notes: 1970 figures are estimates. The definition of "urban" underlying these statistics is that of separate national classification – the country's own classification of its populated areas. Nations included are those with 1970 population greater than ten million.
[a] Includes the new state of Bangladesh, formerly East Pakistan.

quicker you must move out of the way when your business is done. There is more action and less heart, more choice and less conscience. To the jet-age executive, the nation or the world is just one city, a setting for contracts, a realm of anonymous opportunities. City people have families, but the city itself, unlike the village, is not a family. City dwellers can put the pieces of their lives together cafeteria-style. They can walk past each other like visitors to a social zoo, without getting more involved than they wish to be. They can abruptly change what they do, how they do it, and the persons they do it with.

URBAN POPULATION MAGNITUDES

Table 1 lists the fifty nations in the world that had a population of ten million or more in 1970. It shows the total population of each nation in 1950 and in 1970 and breaks these totals down into rural and urban, using each nation's separate classification of "urban places." The countries are grouped by broad geographic regions.

With the sole exception of East Germany, all these nations experienced increases in total population between 1950 and 1970. The percentage increase varies sharply: 36.4 percent for the U.S., 10.8 percent for the U.K., 96.3 percent for Mexico, and 104.0 percent for Venezuela, to mention a few. The population of the U.S.S.R. rose by 35.6 percent.

Without exception, these countries show increases in urban population. Mainland China's urban population rose by 186.4 percent from 1950 to 1970, Japan's by 174.0 percent, Brazil's by 166.3 percent, and Canada's by 90.8 percent. The United Kingdom's cities grew only 11.4 percent in population, while those in the U.S. rose 60.2 percent. South Korea's rate of urban expansion was 234.6 percent, and North Vietnam's increase was 466.8 percent. It must be kept in mind, of course, that the basis for classifying places as urban varies among countries, and also that statistical information is much less reliable or exact for some countries than for others. Percentage increases should also be interpreted in conjunction with absolute figures, lest a country with a rather small proportion of its population in cities at either point in time seem to be leading the globe in the race to urbanize (e.g., North Vietnam).

Most of the countries listed also show absolute increases in rural population between 1950 and 1970. In Turkey, for example, the rural population rose by 8 million, or 49.4 percent, while the urban population rose by 6.4 million, or 139.6 percent. Thus, it is easy to misinterpret rapid increases in urban population as somehow indicating a shift away from rural economic activities accompanied by mass migration to the cities. The number of people living in rural areas may increase, as in the case of Turkey, by a larger absolute amount than the number of city dwellers, even though the percentage increase in city population is much higher. At the same time that nations are becoming more urbanized, they may experience growing rather than diminishing population pressure in the rural areas.

On the other hand, several of the countries listed had absolute decreases in rural population between 1950 and 1970. The most precipitous decline was in Japan, where rural population fell by 34.9 million, a figure that represents 41.9 percent of Japan's total population at the beginning of the twenty-year period. The other countries whose rural populations decreased between 1950 and 1970 are: the U.S., Venezuela, the U.S.S.R., West Germany, Italy, France, Poland, Spain, Yugoslavia, Romania, East Germany, Czechoslovakia, and Australia. This list includes many of the economic frontrunners in the world community, and nations on either side of the iron curtain. For these countries, the march of urbanization probably reflects the pull of economic opportunity in the city rather than the push of rural overpopulation. For the world as a whole, though, the picture is mixed. Some urban expansion is attributable to redundancy of rural population, but not all and perhaps not typically.

Table 2 lists the fifty largest cities in the world in 1970, based on their estimated populations. There is a certain amount of wrangling over just what is included in the geographic areas identified as "New York," "Tokyo," "London," and so on, because population rank carries with it an inexplicable prestige; the reader is cautioned against getting into arguments based on the rankings shown here. One safe statement that can be made is that there are some fifty cities in the world today with populations of 2.5 million or more. In 1950, the fiftieth ranked city, Montreal, had a population of 1,354,000, and there were only 19 cities above the 2.5 million mark. From a longer list in the same source we find that there were at least 100 cities in 1970 with populations exceeding 1.5 million.

If there were a proportional representative form of world government, the cities listed in Table 2 would each have a significant block of votes. Several of them already have notable political and economic significance in their respective nations. London has 20.6 percent of the entire population of the U.K., Paris has 17 percent of the population of France,

Table 2

Fifty Largest Cities by 1970 Population
(Figures in thousands)

New York	16,077	Port Arthur–Dairen	4,000
Tokyo	12,199	Leningrad	3,850
London	11,544	Mukden	3,750
Los Angeles	9,473	Mexico City	3,541
Buenos Aires	9,400	Chungking	3,500
Paris	8,714	Osaka	3,307
Shanghai	8,500	Teheran	3,250
Sao Paulo	8,405	Karachi	3,246
Peking	8,000	Delhi	3,100
Calcutta	7,350	Madrid	2,990
Rio de Janeiro	7,213	Birmingham (U.K.)	2,981
Chicago	6,983	Rome	2,920
Essen-Dortmund-Duisburg	6,789	Harbin	2,750
Moscow	6,750	T'ai-Yuan, Yu-Tz'u	2,725
Cairo	5,600	Sydney	2,720
Bombay	5,100	Washington, D.C.	2,666
Seoul	4,661	Warsaw	2,664
T'ientsin	4,500	Istanbul	2,600
Djakarta	4,500	Madras	2,600
San Francisco–Oakland	4,490	Boston	2,600
Detroit	4,447	Santiago	2,600
Philadelphia	4,355	Manchester	2,541
Wu-Han	4,250	Toronto	2,511
Hong Kong	4,105	Bogota	2,500
Manila	4,100	Lima–Callao	2,500

Source: Kingsley Davis, *World Urbanization, 1950–1970* (Berkeley: Institute of International Studies, University of California, 1969), pp. 239–240.
Note: 1970 population figures are based on projections. Figures given are for urban areas rather than for political units, in most cases.

Sydney has 21.9 percent of the population of Australia, Cairo has 16.8 percent of the population of the U.A.R., and 39 percent of the population of Argentina lives in the Buenos Aires area (all based on 1970 figures in Tables 1 and 2). The eight U.S. cities in Table 2 have a combined population of 51.1 million, 24.7 percent of the entire nation. Within a particular country and among the nations of the world we can reach an increasingly significant proportion of humanity by stopping off at just a few urban centers. It is probably not too soon to start envisaging the world as a cluster of cities rather than a family of nations; London has more in common with Tokyo than it has with Stratford-on-Avon. It may be hard to say what New York and Los Angeles share that makes them "American," but they are certainly both "cities."

SIZE DISTRIBUTION OF CITIES

Despite the size and dominance of Paris, there are other cities in France. The same can be said of New York in the U.S., of Tokyo in Japan, of Warsaw in Poland, of Seoul in South Korea, and so on down the whole list of cities and nations. There are very big cities, medium-sized cities, and small urban centers in any nation where urbanization has reached significant proportions. Demographers and economic geographers have observed two interesting facts about the size distributions of urban places within particular nations. One is that the biggest cities grow the most; lesser cities may hold their own or even shrink as a proportion of total population. That is, an ever larger percentage of a nation's population is accounted for by its largest city (or, as in the case of the U.S., by the several largest cities). The second fact is that there is an approximately constant relationship between the size of an urban place (its population) and its numerical ranking in a list of all the urban places in the same nation. That is, if we have a ranked listing of 100 cities in a country, we can expect that the fiftieth city on the list has one-fiftieth of the population of the largest city.

A few illustrations of the first point are shown in Table 3. In the U.S. the percentage of total population in cities of a million or more rose from 25 percent in 1950 to 37.6 in 1970. Similar shifts in the distribution of population toward the largest cities occurred in France, Poland, and South Korea. In fact, in the study from which the numbers in Table 3 were drawn, there was not a single nation in the world that showed a decline in this proportion. (There are many, of course, in which there is no city as large as a million.) Not only are nations becoming more urbanized, as the proportion living in rural areas drops, but urbanization is becoming more intensive as well, with ever more of the people living in the very largest of the cities.

It is significant that the proportion of population living in smaller

Table 3

Percent of Population in City-Size Categories, Selected Countries

Country	Date	Percent rural	Percent in cities with population of			
			Under 100,000	100,000– 499,999	500,000– 999,999	1,000,000 or Over
U.S.A.	1950	36.0	20.1	12.8	6.1	25.0
	1970	24.8	16.9	13.3	7.5	37.6
France	1950	45.9	27.9	8.8	3.0	14.4
	1970	32.1	27.5	16.9	2.0	21.4
Poland	1950	61.0	15.9	8.1	3.1	11.9
	1970	44.2	25.0	7.0	5.3	18.6
South Korea	1950	81.7	3.1	5.4	2.6	7.2
	1970	61.0	6.6	6.4	6.7	19.4

Source: Kingsley Davis, *World Urbanization, 1950–1970* (Berkeley: Institute of International Studies, University of California, 1969), pp. 112–138.
Note: 1970 figures are estimates.

cities (less than one million) has risen less than that for the largest cities, or has even fallen, despite increases in total national population and major shifts of population away from rural areas. In 1950, about one person in five in the U.S. lived in a city of 100,000 or less; in 1970 only one person in six lived in such a place. It is not clear whether this means that people in smaller cities moved to bigger cities, or that the smaller city itself ascended the size-category scale through population growth, but the result is that the typical person had many more close neighbors in 1970 than he had in 1950. There has been an upward shift in the scale of communities, and this may be associated with changes in modes of economic organization, in local government, and in urban life styles and urban problems.

Empirical research reveals a relationship between the absolute size of a city's population and its rank relative to other cities in the same nation: as we look at cities farther down in a list of cities arranged in descending order by size of population, the sizes of cities diminishes very rapidly at first and then less rapidly. This implies that there are many cities in the smaller-size categories, several intermediate-sized cities, and only a few giants. Illustrative data for the U.S. in 1960, in Table 4, support the approximate validity of the rank-size rule. There are about twice as many cities with more than 250,000 people as there are cities with more than 500,000, and about twice as many cities with 25,000 or more people as there are cities with 50,000 or more. The numbers do not conform precisely to the "rule," but this is attributable, in part, to arbitrary definitions of city limits as well as to historic or geographic factors relating to the growth of particular cities that would not be expected to conform to a general statistical regularity.

Over the years, sufficient information has been collected about the size distribution of cities to convince geographers and demographers that there really is such a rule. Urban and regional economists have advanced theories to explain this regularity in the size distribution of cities, in the sense that it can be considered an efficient spatial allocation of economic activities. Attention will be given in a later chapter to this "central place theory," but some suggestion of its principles is appropriate here.

For example, in a "typical" metropolis we might expect to find one downtown area providing offices, entertainment, and some retail services for the whole community, and three or four shopping centers, located almost equidistant from each other, each serving one slice of the urban area. Within each of these slices we might find a dozen or so supermarkets, again approximately equidistant from each other and serving a defined subsector of the urban map.

By the same token, we might expect to find in the national landscape a set of equally spaced small market towns serving the daily needs of the rural population, with several of these small towns surrounding a somewhat larger community where hospital, governmental, and business facilities are available. In turn, several of these moderate-sized communities are grouped about a larger city, where a wider range of retail shopping, financial services, medical care, and so forth is available.

Such a system of urban places was identified in southern Germany by Walter Christaller. Basic information from his study is shown in Table 5, which tells the same story as Table 4. He found that rural market towns were about 7 kilometers apart, had populations of about 800 people, and served areas of some 45 square kilometers having 2,700 inhabitants. For every three of these market centers (roughly) there was a township center

Table 4

United States Urban Places, by Size, 1960

Population size	Number of places with at least this population
1,000,000	5
500,000	21
250,000	51
100,000	131
50,000	334
25,000	761
10,000	1,907
5,000	3,233
2,500	5,022

Source: U.S. Bureau of the Census, *Statistical Abstract of the United States*, 1966, p. 15, cited in Hugh O. Nourse, *Regional Economics* (McGraw-Hill, 1968), p. 48.

of about 1,500 people which served 8,100 people—and so on up the hierarchy. The regional capital city served an area containing about 750 market hamlets, 250 township centers, 84 county seats, and so on. Since Christaller's study, similar observations have been made in other countries.

MEGALOPOLIS AND THEN SOME

In 1961 Professor Jean Gottmann, a distinguished French geographer, completed a twenty-year study of urbanization along the eastern seaboard of the United States. He found "an almost continuous stretch of urban and suburban areas from southern New Hampshire to northern Virginia and from the Atlantic shore to the Appalachian foothills," and he labeled the vast area "megalopolis."[1] In 1960, this slice of the U.S. had a population of 37 million.

In his perceptive and nearly exhaustive study of how megalopolis

1. Jean Gottman, *Megalopolis* (Cambridge, Mass.: MIT Press, 1961), p. 3.

emerged, Gottman makes it very clear that the distinguishing feature of the region, quite apart from its size, is its lack of traditional urban structure. There is no integrated "downtown" and no regional separation of industrial, residential, and commercial land uses. There is no department of public works in charge of maintaining and extending a coherent system of roads, water supply, or sewage. Initially, there were many separate cities and towns, and they remain politically distinct, by and large. But they have fused together geographically, snuffing out the open spaces between and within them. Life in Megalopolis is abundant, and Gottman shows that the region, by virtue of compactness and size, has been a generator of economic progress for the remainder of the nation. But he cautions against a

Table 5

System of Urban Places in Southern Germany, from Christaller

Type of Urban Place	Towns		Tributary Areas	
	Distance apart (kilometers)	Population	Size 2 (kilometers)	Population
Market hamlet	7	800	45	2,700
Township center	12	1,500	135	8,100
County seat	21	3,500	400	24,000
District city	36	9,000	1,200	75,000
Small state capital	62	27,000	3,600	225,000
Provincial head city	108	90,000	10,800	675,000
Regional capital city	186	300,000	32,400	2,025,000

Source: Edward L. Ullman, "A Theory of Location for Cities," *The American Journal of Sociology* (May 1941), 853–864; reprinted in *Urban Economics*, W. H. Leahy, D. L. McKee, and R. D. Dean, eds. (New York: The Free Press, 1970), p. 108.

continued "muddling through" process of public administration and planning for the region, warning that communities so extensively bound together in all their functions require coordination if they are to continue to flourish.

Gottmann concluded his study by noting the emergence of other megalopolitan areas whose growth might benefit from the experience and problems of the eastern seaboard. A few years later Herman Kahn and Anthony J. Wiener identified two other such areas in the United States, one called "Chipitts" because it extends from Chicago to Pittsburgh, and another called "Sansan" for its terminal points of San Diego and Santa Barbara—perhaps ultimately San Francisco—along the southern coast of California.[2] "Chipitts" might have 40 million people by 2000 A.D. and include Toronto, Detroit, Toledo, Cleveland, Akron, Buffalo, and Rochester, thus extending indifferently across several state boundaries and one international boundary as well. "Sansan" could have 20 million people by the end of the century, and the original megalopolis, which Kahn and Wiener called "Boswash" (for Boston and Washington, D.C.), might reach a population of 80 million.

In Japan, the development of another megalopolis is well advanced, linking Tokyo and Osaka. It has been called the Tokaido Megalopolis, after the ancient road joining these once widely separated cities; it had a population of 49,650,000 in 1970, or about 47.9 percent of the entire population of Japan.[3]

Every continent has at least an incipient megalopolis, and it is now the forecast of some urbanologists that these megalopolitan areas themselves will fuse together in the not-too-distant future. Then we shall need a new term, already coined, which is "Ecumenopolis" or World-City.[4] By the end of the twenty-first century, the continents will be laced with broad bands of dense urban settlements, according to the internationally famous Greek planner, Constantinos Doxiadis. The Peking-Canton district of China will be linked by rail and air transport to one end of a European

2. Herman Kahn and Anthony J. Wiener, *The Year 2000* (New York: Macmillan, 1967), p. 61.

3. Minoru Tachi, "The Inter-Regional Movement of Population as Revealed by the 1970 Census," *Area Development in Japan, No. 4–1971* (Japan Center for Area Development Research, 1971), p. 15.

4. Constantinos Doxiadis, *Ekistics—An Introduction to the Science of Human Settlements* (London: Hutchinson, 1968).

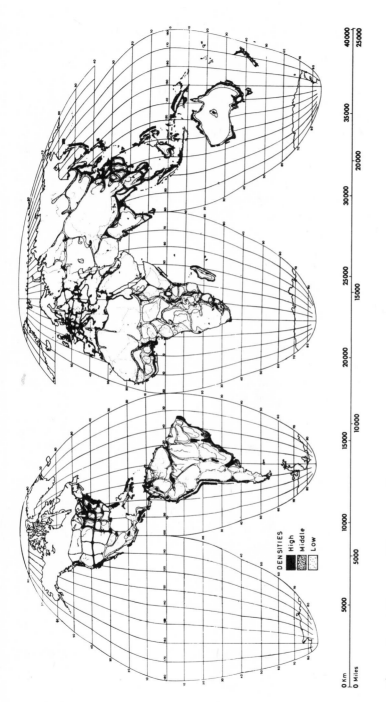

Figure 1. A Forecast of Ecumenopolis.

Source: Arnold Toynbee, *Cities on the Move* (New York: Oxford University Press, 1970), p. 204, taken from Constantine Doxiadis, *Ekistics.*

settlement stretching from the Donetz Basin through Upper Silesia, Saxony, and the Ruhr Basin to Düsseldorf on the Rhine. Thence it will branch northwestward through Belgium, northern France, and Britain, and southward along the Rhine and Po rivers to the Adriatic. Jumping the Mediterranean, it will continue along the Nile into western Africa.[5] Figure 1 suggests the World-City pattern that Doxiadis predicts.

Urban development is easier to chart and predict than it is to explain or evaluate. We are urbanized to a great extent already, and we can reasonably expect this characteristic to become more important in our lives as time goes on. If this is true, then there seems to be a strong presumption that urbanization makes economic sense, that it enhances out capacities to produce useful things from limited resources—but we have yet to explain why this may be true. There is also our realization that a truly urbanized race will not be the product of natural evolution. Our social, cultural, and political traditions were shaped by long centuries of largely agricultural existence. Perhaps human psychology and even religious or moral values are also resistant to the modes of organization and behavior which intensive urbanization will require. As the twentieth century draws to a close, we already sense that certain urban problems are nearly out of control, and yet we know that urbanization is not about to go away. Before we can devise better methods of sharing life in cities, we need to look much more closely at how cities grow and function.

DISCUSSION QUESTIONS

1. Will the trend toward urbanization ultimately be reversed? (Be sure to define "urbanization" before you decide.)

2. Is the "rank-size rule" inconsistent with the relatively greater expansion rate of the largest cities?

3. Based on your general knowledge of world geography, cultures, politics, technology, and trade, which, if any, of the figures in the "1970 percent urban" column of Table 1 comes as a surprise to you? Why?

5. See Arnold Toynbee, *Cities on the Move* (New York: Oxford University Press, 1970), pp. 205–206.

4. If the quality of life in a city depends on the size of its population, why are people content to live in each of the various sized cities represented by the distribution in Table 4?

5. Does the concept of a "megalopolis" require a new definition of "city"? Of "urban"?

6. Which of the cities in Table 2 are national capitals? Which are ports? If you were to make a list of the fifty "most important" cities in the world, how would it differ from Table 2? How about a list of the "best cities to live in"—how would it differ?

SELECTED REFERENCES

Abrams, Charles. *Man's Struggle for Shelter in an Urbanizing World*. Cambridge, Mass.: MIT Press, 1964.
Well-illustrated account of urban housing problems in many developing nations, based on the author's extensive consulting surveys for international organizations.

Davis, Kingsley. *World Urbanization, 1950–1970*. Berkeley: Institute of International Studies, University of California, 1969.
Demographic information for all the nations of the world, extended and adjusted for comparability, with analysis of trends for urban population.

Kahn, Herman, and Anthony J. Wiener. *The Year 2000*. New York: Macmillan, 1967.
Scenarios of possible economic, social, political, technological, and demographic patterns at the end of the century, prepared by a leading research institute.

Hall, Peter. *The World Cities*. New York: McGraw-Hill, 1966.
A well-illustrated description of seven of the largest metropolitan centers in the world, with emphasis on urban problems and planning approaches.

Nourse, Hugh O. *Regional Economics*. New York: McGraw-Hill, 1968, Chapter Three.
Theory of size and distribution of cities.

Scientific American. *Cities*. New York: Knopf, 1966.

A set of essays by urban scholars, covering the origin of cities, problems of land use and transportation, and their internal economies.

Toynbee, Arnold. *Cities on the Move*. New York: Oxford University Press, 1970.
The renowned historian examines the experiences of ancient cities for clues about the future of modern urban society.

United Nations. *Statistical Yearbook*.
A careful compilation of economic and demographic information for the various nations of the world.

2

THE ECONOMIC
BENEFITS
OF CLUSTERING

THOMAS JEFFERSON believed that cities would be the ruination of American democracy. He wrote in 1784: "let our workshops remain in Europe. . . . The loss by the transportation of commodities across the Atlantic will be made up in happiness and permanence of government. The mobs of great cities add just so much to the support of pure government, as sores do to the strength of the human body."[1] Historian Arnold Toynbee's recent book on cities takes a pessimistic view of the coming World-City; he foresees that the future increase in world population will "silt up in urban slums."[2] Across the ages, men of considerable intellectual stature have expressed a dread of urbanization. To be sure, there have been city enthusiasts among men of letters in ancient Athens and modern Paris, but the general tendency of writers seems always to have been to deprecate the city.

To reconcile an adverse view of urbanization with the incontrovertible growth of cities, we would have to maintain either that people live in

1. *Notes on Virginia*, cited in Morton and Lucia White, *The Intellectual Versus the City* (New York: Mentor, 1962), pp. 25–26.
2. Toynbee, *Cities on the Move*, p. 211.

21

cities because there is no other place for them to earn a livelihood, or that they irrationally and incorrectly believe that their economic opportunities will be better in the city. Certainly in the streets of Calcutta there are hundreds of thousands of desperately underemployed people who were literally driven off the land by recent religious and civil wars. In prosperous California it appears that only one out of three persons who migrates into the state succeeds in finding the primarily urban job and the sort of life he believed he could get there—the other two are disappointed.

URBANIZATION AND GNP

Gloomy views notwithstanding, as a nation urbanizes, its real standard of living rises. That is, there is a statistical relationship between per capita gross national product and the proportion of the population living in cities, as is shown in Figure 2. The data for that figure include all nations with a population of at least ten million in 1960, exclusive of communist nations (for which reliable GNP figures are not available). The GNP figures, expressed in U.S. dollar equivalent, per capita, are for 1963, and they are shown on a logarithmic scale.

Pakistan, for example, is 12.8 percent urban in this data and has a 1963 per capita GNP of $94. Mexico was 50.7 percent urban, with a per capita GNP of $493. Australia was 81 percent urban and its per capita GNP was $1,812. For the thirty-six nations included in this comparison, there is a linear relationship between the logarithm of GNP per capita and the percent urban, with a coefficient of determination of 0.88. If we know the proportion of its people that lives in cities, we can make a very good guess about a nation's average income.

Statistical relationships such as this do not prove that a causal relationship exists, that living in cities necessarily causes average incomes to be high. We might find a close relationship between good scholarship in college and going to bed after midnight, but that would not mean you could improve your marks by staying up late. Nor can you turn yourself into a successful businessman by developing an ulcer, despite the fact that those two things are frequently found together. So the statistical relationship in Figure 2 does not mean that gathering all the people of Nepal together in Katmandu would make them wealthy.

If there is a causal relation between urbanization and income, it could conceivably work the other way; that is, after a nation achieves a higher income, people move into cities to enjoy their money. Wealthy ranchers in

1963 PER CAPITA GNP (S)

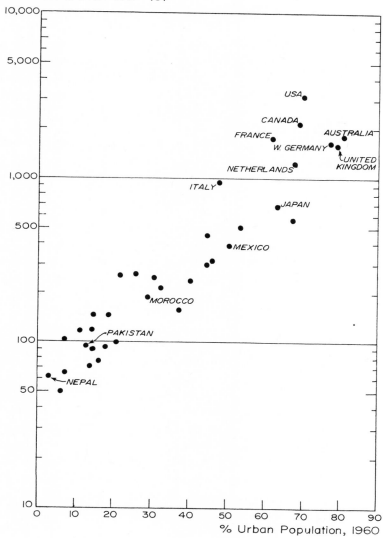

Figure 2. Urbanization and per capita GNP.

Source: Percent Rural : *World Urbanization, 1950–1970*, Vol. I, Kingsley
Davis, Population Research Monograph Series, No. 4 (Berkeley:
University of California). GNP Distribution of National Income:
U.N. Statistical Year Book, Tables 191 and 186. Taken from W. F.
Smith, "Is Urban Land a Factor of Production?" in *Land Using
Activities*, W. F. Smith, ed. (Berkeley: Center for Real Estate and
Urban Economics, University of California, 1970), pp. 58–59. *Note:*
Data limited to those nations with total populations of more than
ten million in 1960.

South America and oil-rich Middle Eastern potentates live in town. Kings of France pushed the peasantry to greater and greater productivity so that the surplus rural output could be converted into urban opulence (although this stopped abruptly in 1789). Agrarian philosophers have long believed in their bones that it was the countryside and the labor of farmers that supported all that frivolity in the cities.

But Figure 2 does not establish that kind of causal relationship either. What it does come close to proving is that urbanization and economic progress can be compatible, or that factors which bring about economic improvement probably induce the growth of cities as well. The data are also consistent with the hypothesis that cities result from the exploitation of new technologies, or with the stronger hypothesis that urbanization is itself a kind of technological discovery that allows us to get greater amounts of useful commodities from given resources. Our next job is to build up a deductive argument in support of these hypotheses.

BENEFITS OF CLUSTERING

In a population-dot map for an agricultural region, the dots are pretty well spread out and, depending on the geology, may appear roughly equidistant. The same kind of map for a region with substantial nonextractive employment will show some clustering: there will be perceptible bunching of the dots, and some degree of bunching can be taken to define a city. Spatial clustering is the principal physical attribute of urbanization—some would say that it is the attribute from which all others stem—and this clustering has obvious economic consequences. It means that people in the region can do business with each other with less difficulty and expense. That is, their aggregate transportation costs can be reduced.

Four abstract levels of clustering are illustrated in Figure 3. The first is called "scatter," which here means that individuals are as far from their neighbors as possible. The eight little squares in the rectangular "map" represent the amount of land each of the eight persons uses. This kind of spatial arrangement maximizes the aggregate cost or potential cost of an exchange of visits, messages, or commodities by the people involved.

There are not too many situations in which "scatter" makes sense. A field army that is under aerial attack or artillery bombardment (but not immediately engaged by enemy infantry) may minimize its losses by

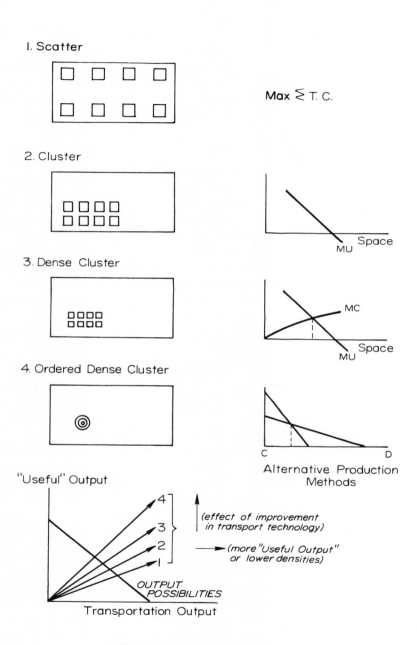

Figure 3. Economics of density.

spreading out. Students in a reading room preparing for an exam often tend to maximize their physical separation. Pioneering farmers or nearly self-sufficient communes may also have a positive preference for the shield of distance. Early manufacturing, under the so-called domestic system, required entrepreneurs to make the rounds of widely separated farmsteads where spinning, weaving, or some other simple manufacturing process was carried on as supplementary employment, resulting in a very considerable transportation cost factor for manufacture.

Suppose, however, that the preference for isolation is not strong and there is some amount of interaction between the people of the region—they have a postal service, or a church to go to on Sunday. Then it makes sense to draw individual landholdings together into the pattern called a "cluster." The diagram to the right of the schematic map indicates that each person occupies all the land that he can use, for which his marginal utility is positive. There is such a thing as a farmer with more land than he can work with efficiently, and there is also such a thing as having too large a front or back yard to be responsible for in the city. Our definition of "cluster" in Figure 3 means that space to use is a "free good"—a person can have as much as he wants—but all the holdings are consolidated within the minimum convenient perimeter.

To achieve most of the goals that human beings have, "cluster" is more efficient than "scatter." The cost of getting together is less, and this includes the time spent going from one of these separate plots of ground to another, the cost of making roads and stringing telephone wires or power lines. The savings can be considerable, but it is interesting and important that they are not attributable to any of the individuals involved, nor to pieces of land, whether within or outside the cluster. The benefit of clustering is a social product, and it is not self-evident who is entitled to it or what should be done with the resources it saves.

The next concept is that of a "dense cluster." Here we recognize that space is not a free good in a community that must allow for interaction. If we compare two communities, both circular in shape and with even density, but with each household occupying one-quarter acre in one while in the other each household occupies an entire acre, the radius of the less dense community will be twice that of the more dense community. In the less dense community the average household is farther from the center than his high-density counterpart; thus all the costs associated with regular trips to the center are greater in the one-acre community. Just how rapidly these costs grow with increasing lot size (falling density) depends on a great many practical factors, such as the technology of the transportation, but as the density of the city falls there is almost certain to be an increase in a community's aggregate "transportation" costs (all costs associated with movement of commodities, messages, and persons). The marginal cost of lower density to the community (the increase in total cost) is represented by the *MC* line in the diagram next to the "dense cluster" map in Figure 3.

This marginal cost intersects the marginal utility function for greater space or dispersion, establishing the optimum density for the community. This optimum density is necessarily greater (the amount of space consumed is less) than the density based on zero marginal utility. Consequently, "cluster" gives way to "dense cluster," which is represented in Figure 3 by a group of squares that are smaller than their counterparts in the "cluster" map.

This is once again a surrender of isolation or control over space in the interest of conserving transportation resources. A dense cluster is more efficient than a cluster, as these terms have been defined, and the saving is attributable to the process by which users of space are persuaded to recognize that space in a community is not a "free good." The saving is not attributable to the individual users of space nor to any particular pieces of land. It is a form of wealth not unlike the discovery of new natural resources or an accidental breakthrough in technology, and it raises interesting problems in distribution. Left to themselves, individuals in the community will simply pocket the saving—that is, they will spend less on transportation—but that does not mean the saving is not real or appreciable. Indeed, most of the advantages we all associate with living in cities are derived from clustering, yet there is no common means of assuring that this benefit gets used the way the community as a whole wants it used.

The fourth stage of clustering is the "ordered dense cluster." If an urban community includes several categories of land users—retail merchants, manufacturers, apartment dwellers, single-family home owners, and so on—then there is a further economy in aggregate transportation resources to be achieved by arranging these various uses in a specific pattern. A spatial order in which retail stores (and perhaps factories) are located in the center, surrounded by a belt of apartments that is, in turn, encompassed by districts of single-family homes, is more efficient in its use of resources for transportation than a pattern in which the stores are strung out along the periphery and the apartments are scattered through single-family-home areas.

That fact may be nearly obvious. Less obvious, and far more important, is the fact that an urban land market trends to create an efficient ordering of land uses, given certain plausible conditions. In later chapters we shall look carefully into the operation of an urban land market—its requirements, results and problems—so we need only see at this point that urban land market processes are extensions of the principle of clustering. In the diagram to the right of the "ordered dense cluster" map in Figure 3, the center of the city is labeled C and the horizontal axis measures radial distance from this center. The horizontal axis measures the value of land resulting from the saving in transportation costs by people who reside there as an alternative to residing on the fringe (where land would be free). The steeper line shows the amounts that apartment dwellers, for example, would be willing to pay for land at various distances from the center. The other line is the value of land to single-family house dwellers, and it is less steep because there are fewer such families per acre than there would be among apartment dwellers. In the center the apartment dwellers outbid single-family home dwellers for land, while in the ring of land beyond the intersection of these two sloping lines the opposite is true. Thus, within the city, the transportation-saving characteristic of particular pieces of land is translated into a structure of land prices, and these prices allocate land among competing categories of users.

This final benefit of clustering, unlike the first two, is attributable to specific pieces of land and is reflected in the price of land that landowners will be able to demand. Perhaps we should acknowledge that the saving is realized only if a number of business functions having to do with land are performed. There must be developers and investors, and there will probably have to be brokers, appraisers, and lawyers at work to bring economic order to the pattern of land uses in a city and to maintain that order in the face of constantly changing circumstances—the growth of population, for example. The economic benefit resulting from the spatial ordering of urban land uses is thus shared by landowners and people who engage in land-related business. Much of the benefit, however, can be construed as a social product rather than the result of skill, labor, or investment.

At the bottom of Figure 3 is a "guns and butter" diagram, such as we find in an introductory economics textbook, on which the four clustering concepts are brought together. Given all the economic resources of a community, the greater the amount of transportation output, the less "useful output" it will be possible to enjoy. The diagonal line shows the maximum combinations of the two types of output that a fixed supply of resources makes possible. The arrows labeled 1, 2, 3, and 4 show how total output will be divided between transportation and useful output under the four degrees of clustering illustrated by the abstract maps. As we move from scatter to cluster, for example, we can obtain from our limited resources a greater amount of useful output. Similarly, a dense cluster and then an ordered dense cluster moves us farther up the scale of useful output.

What happens if transportation itself becomes cheaper as a result of an improvement in technology? (The electric streetcar was such an improvement, and it had a major impact on the form and growth of many cities in the late nineteenth and early twentieth centuries.) All the arrows from the origin in this diagram would swing upward, and they would probably lie closer together. The economic payoff of clustering would be reduced, and we might therefore choose to have less spatial order in our cities, or lower densities, or both. Los Angeles and other twentieth-century North American cities seem to bear witness to a pronounced reduction in per-mile urban transportation costs relative to other things. The "energy crisis" more recently upon us implies that clustering is becoming more important, rather than less, and that the long-run effect on the spatial arrangement of cities can be substantial.

INTERNAL AND EXTERNAL ECONOMIES TO THE FIRM

The benefits of clustering together in urban areas arise because people have a need for interacting. Once clustering has occurred, however, people may be able to avail themselves of other technological economies. That is, they may be able to reorganize what they individually do for a living in such a way that they can provide goods or services at less cost. This is a supplementary benefit of urbanization and not just another way of looking at the obvious benefit, the direct economy of burning up less resources for intracommunity transportation.

Under the old "domestic" system of manufacture, there was a large transportation cost in distributing raw materials to the scattered workers and later going back to gather up their finished products. If all of these workers could have been brought together—perhaps in adjacent cottages along a single street—the expense of transportation could have been greatly reduced. That would be a benefit of clustering.

Having all the workers within easy walking distance of some central building, however, means that a distinctively new kind of cost reduction is possible. The workers can specialize more completely and they can make use of power-driven machinery. As a result, the unit cost of production will fall. Economies of large-scale production are generally achievable only if production takes place in one location. Spatial concentration is an implicit requirement of most mass-production technology.

This kind of cost reduction is called an "internal economy of scale" by economists, who illustrate it by means of a downward-sloping average cost curve, as in Figure 4. If output in a given place can be expanded from OA to OB, AC will fall. If output OB can be sold at a price that covers this lower unit cost, then the promise of the new mechanical technology can be realized.

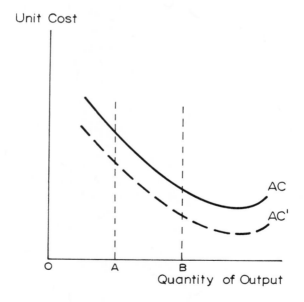

Figure 4.   Internal and external economies to the firm.

This is actually quite a string of assumptions. We must have the new technology, we must have the investment in machines, there must be a clustered labor force, and there must be an expanding market for the product. Clustering, or urbanization, is a necessary but not a sufficient condition for this form of economic progress. Where progress occurs in this fashion, it is difficult to say how much urbanization contributed to it. We can say with some assurance, however, that it was not the supplier of machinery alone who brought about the progress, nor was it the group of workers alone. And it was not entirely the combination of workers and machines that caused the promise of the new technology to be realized, because urbanization was a precondition. The city helped, and the city is a social product in a far deeper sense than Marx's famous "labor theory of value" suggests. The benefits offered by a city are attributable to social organization, not to the physical exertions of laborers.

Early machines were driven by water power, which could be transmitted only a very short distance from a waterfall or swift stream. Many machines had to be placed together, and thus workers had to live, in substantial numbers, within walking distance of the factories. Thus there had to be a city: houses, shops, and streets; means of distributing food, water, and fuel; and systems of public safety. Steam power encouraged factories to move close to coal fields, but it did not otherwise change the urbanization requirement. Electric power is much easier to transmit, but the assembly-line method of production still ties machines and their operators into such aggregations that an urban settlement is required as the location for manufacturing. That is, urbanization was a technological requirement in the factory era.

A manufacturing business located in a sufficiently large city may benefit from additional cost-reducing opportunities which the economist calls "external economies" because they arise out of the expansion of the community rather than from expansion of the individual firm. For example, if there are a number of similar manufacturing firms within the same city, they can share the cost of long-distance transportation facilities. Many factories make fuller use of a rail line or port than a single firm can. One firm in a large city can purchase parts from a local supplier who has several other local customers and who, as a result, may enjoy significant internal economies of scale. A number of relatively small businesses in an urban community can share the services of an accounting firm, a law firm, a power supply company, or a machinery repair firm. They can also tap a local reservoir of trained labor, already housed, educated, and supplied with customary social services such as access to hospitals, whereas a solitary firm in a "company town" finds itself responsible for providing all of these things. Having provided them for an expansion of its labor force, the company town employer is at a grave disadvantage in economic and moral terms if his market falters and production must be curtailed.

This phenomenon, which some writers have called "agglomeration economies," is represented in Figure 4 as an average cost curve, AC', lying below that of the solitary firm. Throughout the range of possible output for the firm, unit costs are lower if the firm is situated in a large community.

For those of us who have always lived in fairly large cities, the difficulties an enterprise faces in a small community may be difficult to appreciate. In her thought-provoking book *The Economy of Cities*, Jane Jacobs describes an instance in which these difficulties became painfully clear:

The Rockefellers, early in the 1960's, decided to build a factory in India to produce plastic intrauterine loops for birth control. At the same time they were undertaking to combat the Indian birth rate, they also wanted to curb the migration of rural Indians to cities. A way to do this, they thought, was to set an example of village industry, placing new industry in small settlements instead of cities. The location they chose for the factory, then, was a small town named Etawah in highly rural Uttar state. It seemed plausible that the factory could as well be located in one place in India as another and the loops were to be exported throughout India. The factory was to be small, for with modern machinery even a small factory could begin by turning out 14,000 loops a day. The work had been rationalized into simple, easily taught tasks; no pre-existing, trained labor pool was required. The problem of hooking up to electric power had been explored and judged feasible. Capital was sufficient, and the scheme enjoyed the cooperation of the government of Uttar.

But as soon as the project was started everything went wrong, culminating in what the *New York Times* called "a fiasco." No single problem seems to have been horrendous. Instead, endless small difficulties arose: delays in getting the right tools, in repairing things that broke, in correcting work that had not been done to specifications, in sending off for a bit of missing material. Hooking up to the power did not go as smoothly as expected, and when it was accomplished the power was insufficient. Worse, the difficulties did not diminish as the work progressed. New ones cropped up. It became clear that—even in the increasingly doubtful event the plant could get into operation—keeping it in operating condition thereafter would probably be impractical. So after most of a year and considerable money had been wasted, Etawah was abandoned and a new site was chosen at Kanpur, a city of some 1,200,000 persons, the largest in Uttar, where industry and commerce had, by Indian standards, been growing rapidly. Space in two unused rooms in an electro-plating plant was quickly found. The machinery was installed, the workers hired, and the plant was producing within six weeks. Kanpur possessed not only the space and the electric power, but also repairmen, tools, electricians, bits of needed material, and relatively swift and direct transportation service to other major Indian cities if what was required was not to be found in Kanpur.[3]

This is what is meant by "agglomeration" or "external economies." The surrounding urban settlement affects the feasibility and efficiency of an individual business undertaking because a larger and more diversified community is more likely to have the things that meet unanticipated needs of enterprises. In this additional way, urbanization benefits not only the entrepreneur but the consumer and the economy as a whole. The development of urban centers is not merely a passive consequence of industrialization and national economic development, but an active agent in bringing such changes about.

MOBILIZING LABOR

The concept of "external economies" can include the benefits of urbanization arising from the formation of substantial pools of labor on which individual enterprises may draw. However, "labor mobility" is a somewhat larger concept and merits separate recognition.

The larger the urban area in which we work, the greater is the probability that we can find the kind of work for which we are best suited. There is no need for a research chemist in a small agricultural market town, and in such a town a person with latent skills or even extensive education and experience in chemical research may find himself doing clerical work in a feed and grain store. A student seeking part-time work as a taxi driver is likely to find there is not much turnover in taxi-driving jobs in a small town. In a small town a schoolteacher whose training and talents lie in the area of modern languages may have to handle geography, bookkeeping, and shop. Being in a large community does not guarantee that a person's

3. Jane Jacobs, *The Economy of Cities* (New York: Random House, 1969), pp. 186–187.

abilities will not be wasted, but it does expose him to ranges and levels of opportunities. Labor, in the twentieth century, is highly differentiated on both the demand and the supply side, and it is only when labor becomes highly mobile that the community and the individual can realize the full potential in this resource.

Labor mobility resulting from urbanization is more than a matter of letting a factory expand its work force without being obliged to teach new workers arithmetic or construct housing for them. That kind of benefit is real and important, but the benefits arising from making the best possible match of personal abilities with economic and technological requirements is also significant. Without it, the complex technology and the vast diversity of consumer goods that characterize economic life in the late twentieth century would not be possible. Nevertheless, many nations in the world have adopted policies that would sacrifice this kind of labor mobility, by decentralizing urban populations in collections of "new towns."[4] And it must certainly be acknowledged that a number of institutional factors, such as barriers to technical education and the vesting of private pension rights, deter the optimal allocation of labor. The full benefits of urbanization, in this respect as in many others, cannot be realized unless a long list of conditions is met.

ENLARGING CONSUMER CHOICE

Thus far, urbanization has been considered mostly from a "business" or production point of view, with a focus on its cost-reducing and efficiency-enhancing potential. But urbanization also has a powerful effect on consumption patterns. The diversity of a city—the number of different kinds of shops, medical specialists, restaurants, schools, entertainment and cultural facilities, and so on—allows the city dweller to get more for his consumption dollar than he can get in a small town.

It is really a very old principle. Adam Smith pointed out that "the division of labour is limited by the extent of the market."[5] In his famous example, ten men who divide up the work of making pins can make 4,800 pins every day, while one man working alone could probably not make more than twenty. But unless there is a market for 48,000 pins per day—the

4. The arguments for and against "new towns" will be examined more fully in Chapter Ten.
5. *The Wealth of Nations*, Book One, Chapter Three.

output of the group of ten men—the great technological economy of specialization cannot be realized. **1887683**

Smith was talking about specialization in processes of production. The principle applies with equal force, however, to consumption, for things that cannot be offered at a reasonable price or cannot be produced at all because of the limited size of a market are obviously not available to the consumer. And a further corollary is that the greater the extent of the market, the greater the extent of possible specialization.

Suppose a market population of 1,000 people is necessary to support a restaurant of minimum feasible size. A population of 2,000 could then support two restaurants, but in order for each of them to survive they would have to divide the market exactly in half. They could do this either by offering identical kinds of food at the same prices or by offering two different kinds—"American" and "Chinese," for example—for which demand among the people in the community was equally divided. If people in a community would patronize the Chinese restaurant only once for every five meals away from home, then they would not have the choice of American or Chinese unless there were 5,000 people living in that town. If they wanted to try Mandarin instead of Cantonese cooking, they might be out of luck until the town grew to a population of 50,000.

A person living on a farm or in a small town is probably just as likely to be afflicted with leukemia as someone living in a big city, but facilities for treating leukemia are practically available only in a large urban center, where the number of cases justifies them. Computer programming schools find it necessary to be in major cities, and a person who wants to read up on the fashionable subject of ecology won't get very far in a small textile mill town, as a rule, because not enough other people are asking for books on ecology.

The great attraction of "downtown" is comparison shopping. Unless it is convenient for us to walk through several clothing stores, or jewelry stores, and so on, we may never even be aware of major differences in styles or prices. Shopping is a species of education, crass though that might seem to some people. In the economist's language, we get more utility for the money we spend if we have a large number of choices, and we do not have choices unless we become aware of alternatives.

Figure 5a uses the "indifference curve" concept of elementary economics to illustrate the effect of options on utility or welfare. If we have a certain amount of money to spend on shoes and spend it all on black shoes,

a)

Pairs of Black Shoes

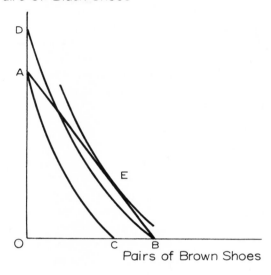

Pairs of Brown Shoes

b)

Number of Consumer Options

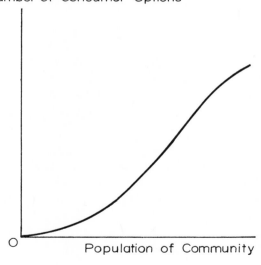

Population of Community

Figure 5. Consumption choices.

we get quantity OA. If we buy brown shoes instead, in the quantity OC, we could feel just as well off as with OA black shoes—because the brown shoes were more durable or because they went better with our brown suit, or whatever. Because of the relative prices of black and brown shoes, however, the amount of money we have to spend would be enough for OB brown shoes. That is, we could purchase any combination of black and brown shoes along the straight line AB, while combinations along the curving line AC would provide us with equal amounts of utility. So, if we know about brown shoes and have the option of buying them instead of black shoes, our money will go farther in obtaining utility. We can achieve a level of satisfaction equivalent to having OD black shoes even though our budget would not allow us to purchase that many. Combinations along the curve DB are all preferable to combinations along the curve AC.

But combination E, with some of each kind of shoes, is better still, and it is also feasible because it lies on budget line AB. The benefits of having options do not rest on all-or-nothing choices, but upon the opportunity to experience—not merely to contemplate—variety.

The availability of options manifestly depends on the scale of the community—for shoes, dresses, medical specialists, restaurants, theater performances, and so on through the entire list of goods and services in which modern people have interest. This is represented in Figure 5b, making the degree of diversity a function of community size. The shape of the function suggests that specialized types of goods and services become available only slowly at first, as a community grows in size; but then availability accelerates and finally decreases at a lower and lower rate. By the time a community is big enough to support a Chinese restaurant—5,000 people in the earlier hypothetical case—it is probably almost big enough to support still another type, say a French restaurant, without eliminating the previous options of American and Chinese. On the other hand, when a metropolis achieves a certain very great magnitude, there is not much unrealized potential for diversity and choice. Virtually any type of automobile can be purchased in San Francisco, a city of only some 700,000 people, and there are probably almost as many different kinds of restaurants in San Francisco as in New York City, which has well over ten million inhabitants.

Two important points remain to be mentioned. Urban size is a necessary but not a sufficient condition for diversity of consumer goods and services. The gourmet is probably better off in little San Francisco than in big Detroit, but a really small community is not able to enter the competition at all.

The other point is that the consumer benefits of urban diversity do not show up in the GNP, at least not fully or explicitly. Figure 2 understates the economic importance of urbanization in this respect; GNP does not measure how much satisfaction people get from the things they spend their money on—merely how much money they have to spend and the physical quantity of what they get, weighted essentially by cost.

FOSTERING INNOVATION

During the nineteenth century, cities in Europe and North America grew very rapidly as manufacturing centers. The economies of scale in factory production, both external and internal, pulled population into very sizeable clusters and created the impression that urbanization was no more than an inevitable, perhaps regrettable, concomitant of industrialization.

But manufacturing requires much more than factories and labor and raw materials. What is produced must be sold, and the prodigious expansion of industrial output forced nineteenth-century entrepreneurs to scour the world for markets, to introduce new products, and to make unremitting efforts to improve their technology in order to cut costs. In short, the application of industrial technology is not a static, repetitive process. The questions of what to produce, how much, for whom, with which kinds of capital equipment, and how to secure money to finance both capital equipment and the process of manufacturing must be answered anew almost every day. Decisions have to be made constantly, and decisions require information, much of it from outside the enterprise itself.

Urbanization facilitates communication. A banker in a textile manufacturing town soon learns much about the world markets for textiles, about likely technological changes in the textile industry, and about the comparative advantage or disadvantage of the textile industry in his own town. The banker transmits this information to entrepreneurs who come to him in search of financing. Companies supplying power to local factories have to plan ahead for the expansion of their facilities, so they, too, need information about the prospects of local industry, and they are nearly obliged to make systematic efforts to gather such information. Machine repairmen or mechanical engineers who are called in to fix machines in several local factories soon become aware of common problems and promising solutions. New entrepreneurs can learn enough about the operation of successful, existing manufacturing companies in town to avoid costly mistakes in joining the competition.

The urban environment thus becomes as much a place for constructive thinking about how and why things are made as it is a place for making them. By the mid-twentieth century, more people in the prosperous industrialized countries were engaged in thinking about manufacturing things than in directly manufacturing them. When white-collar occupations expand, blue-collar jobs contract.

One of the first to call attention to this fact and to examine its significance was the geographer Jean Gottmann, in his justly famous book *Megalopolis*. Gottmann also called particular attention to the rapid expansion of information-supplying occupations, "those supplying services that require research, analysis, judgment—in brief, brainwork and responsibility."[6] This brainwork can be done, and continues to be done, within the confines of the factory itself by people in "back offices" doing the accounting or product development and research, and in "front offices" putting internal and external information together to formulate decisions.

Increasingly, however, white-collar occupations have been spatially separated from manufacturing operations. It is in the towering downtown office buildings that most decisions concerning business activity are made today. Not only have these brainwork functions migrated out of factory buildings and even out of factory towns, but they have increased greatly as a proportion of all occupations. Today, the smoking factory has ceased to epitomize urbanization; it has been replaced by the skyline of tightly clustered, tall office buildings.

It is not immediately obvious that this change increases the productive capacity of the national economy. Paperwork strikes most people as inherently less useful than physical work with tangible objects. It is easier to count widgets coming off the assembly line than to estimate the contribution of a legal secretary or a specialist in operations research to the GNP. Once a machine is invented or a new product like nylon or transistors is in production, it is easy to forget that much intangible creativity went before.

Creativity—the discovery of new products and new processes—is an urgent requirement of the twentieth-century economy. Mass production of staple commodities is a first stage in economic growth, but in our time an increasing proportion of jobs depends on satisfying less basic and thus more volatile consumer demands. Stereo tape decks and nonpolluting detergents

6. Gottmann, *Megalopolis*, p. 580.

characterize the present economy the way cotton textiles and steel rails characterized the end products of the nineteenth-century economy. The higher the plane of consumption, the more changeable its composition.

This is a very difficult race to be in. Continuous, finely honed innovation is imperative for the survival of the business firm, the local economy, and even for nations. This is an age in which millions of people in underdeveloped parts of the world depend for their livelihood on a world market for hairpieces and wigs, plastic battery-operated toys, and other "trivial" kinds of consumption goods. A misjudgment about the kind of chrome trim for a new automobile model can mean financial disaster for thousands of factory workers. It may seem regrettable that good work-manship and useful products without frills are no longer a guarantee of a place in the world market, but these things do eventually lose their importance. Ever-increasing diversity of consumer goods, leaving a thinner and less-assured market for one and all, is what the twentieth-century world economy is asked for, not just a larger quantity of familiar goods.

In the center of Seoul, South Korea, there is a long, wide street lined with innumerable tiny shops that stock sheets of stainless steel, vats of various kinds of chemicals, slabs of foam rubber, assortments of small electric motors and roller bearings, plastic tubing, and many other indus-trial products produced elsewhere and brought together along that street, the name of which is Chung-e-Chung Ro. All day long, Chung-e-Chung Ro is a bedlam of people chasing up and down, back and forth, from shop to shop with freight-carrying bicycles, baskets, wheelbarrows, or with an A-frame tied to their backs for carrying things—picking up something here, something there, and something else in another place before return-ing to their little workshops somewhere else. They are innovators, trying recipes for new products in which they place their hopes for business success or survival. Chung-e-Chung Ro is their parts inventory and their assembly line. What they are putting together is, in every case, something new, something the world has not exactly seen before because that is what the world wants, what the world will buy from a country that lacks significant quantities of natural resources or large, modern factories.

On the streets of Seoul, at the same time that this frenetic activity along Chung-e-Chung Ro could be observed, hawkers were selling strings of little plastic ducks on wheels. They were doing pretty well. It was a new product. It struck the fancy and fitted the pocketbook of the local consumer. It probably had some acceptability in the world market. It was a product of the bustling, almost chaotic experimentation of Chung-e-Chung Ro, a product of the urban nexus. A trivial, cheap, unsophisticated product, we would have to admit, but it reflects the strange new exigencies that man confronts. A pocket-sized computer or a chemical for congealing oil spills might appeal to us as more dignified examples of twentieth-century progress, but the plastic duck is just as truly a case of making a living with one's brains.

New products, processes, marketing techniques, and other management innovations are required of the vast white-collar labor force assembled in metropolitan centers. It is essential that they be assembled, not just in huge, single-firm office buildings, but in clusters of office buildings surrounded with supplementary facilities such as photocopy shops, stationary supply stores, technical libraries, and coffee shops. The coffee shop is not a whimsical addition to the list. Urban man seems to do some of his best communicating in informal environments: neutral ground with distractions that somehow make it easier to get to the heart of a problem. A recent book on the urban economy puts it this way: "Finally, the metropolis, with its universities, museums, libraries, and research laboratories, becomes one big, spatially integrated 'coffee house,' where bright minds out of diverse cultures clash and strike sparks that ignite the fires of new products and processes—new export industries."[7] Another urban scholar has demonstrated a relationship between the amount of information to which a person is exposed by virtue of living in an urban environment and the average income in his community.[8]

Jane Jacobs relates the factors that encouraged a research physicist to carry on his work in New York City, even though the firm he was doing the work for was not located there. He needed many items for his experiments, items he could purchase from suppliers. For the most part they were fairly common items, but their diversity was such that New York was the most convenient place to obtain them quickly. His shopping list for one month included:

From an electronics supply store: one voltage reference diode, five precision resistors of three different sizes, ten alligator clips, one ordinary resistor, a published

7. Wilbur R. Thompson, *A Preface to Urban Economics* (Baltimore: The Johns Hopkins Press, 1965), p. 15.
8. Richard L. Meier, *A Communications Theory of Urban Growth* (Cambridge: The Joint Center for Urban Studies of MIT and Harvard University, 1962), Chapter Two.

collection of electronic industrial circuits, a quantity of insulated copper wire, a dry cell, a small potentiometer;

From a store selling surplus electronics equipment: two precision resistors of still other sizes, and a double-pole, double-throw switch;

From a laboratory supplier: a quantity of aluminum sulphate, a specimen jar for crystal growing, glass rod, glass capillary tubing, vacuum grease, epoxy glue;

From a surplus tool store: a screw-threading die;

From a hardware store: two drill bits; a quantity of braided steel wire, silicone sealing cement, screw eyes, two dry cells;

From another hardware store: brass bolts and turnbuckles;

From an industrial hardware store: a drill bit, a hacksaw blade, two fine-threaded large steel bolts and a stainless-steel machinist's rule;

From a plastics supply house: plexiglass sheets of two different thicknesses;

From the factory of a small manufacturer of specialty wire: a two-foot length of extra-fine stainless-steel wire;

From a machine shop: a soft-iron cone, made to order;

From a scientific supply house: two first-surface mirrors and a special lens;

From an aircraft supply house: rubber 0 rings of three different sizes.[9]

It is worth noting that most of the several suppliers were themselves so specialized that they could not exist except in a rather large city, and also that the research physicist probably could not anticipate all of his requirements at the outset of his work. He needed access to the largest array of possible sources for research materials, which means not only that they had to be there, but that he had to have a way of finding out about them. No doubt, the yellow pages of the New York telephone directory were among the most important tools in his research work. What he did was no different in principle from the search and assembly process that produced the plastic duck in Seoul.

To foster innovation successfully, a city must have great diversity and devices for letting people know who and what is available. This goes for consumers as well as for toy manufacturers and research physicists. When there is a wealth of consumer choices available, the market will quickly get an idea of what sells and what doesn't. From successes and failures in the urban market, entrepreneurs can get valuable information about promising new directions of further innovation, whether in shapes of men's neckties or nightclub comedy routines.

9. Jacobs, *The Economy of Cities*, p. 189.

If we buy the idea that innovation is important in the modern economy and acknowledge that communication is essential as a stimulus to innovation, it follows that cities can be organized in such a way that communication is encouraged. The most obvious example is the down-town comparison-shopping district. Less obvious is the office-building complex of the financial district. Still less obvious are spatial, legal, and financial arrangements that will allow neophyte entrepreneurs to see what they can do. What kind of permit do you need to manufacture costume jewelry, and what rent would you have to pay for a place to do it in? Least tangible of all, perhaps, is the capacity of the city as a whole to attract a sufficiently large and diverse population to generate demands for new products and services, as well as to supply the imagination and skills those things require.

THE COSTS OF CLUSTERING

So far in this chapter, we have made a case for the following advantages of urbanization: it saves transportation resources through various forms of spatial clustering; it lowers the costs of producing goods (and services) by permitting large-scale producing and by giving rise to certain economies of agglomeration; it makes better use of people in the labor force by matching their diverse abilities against the widest range of things to be done; it stimulates innovation of every kind; and it allows the consumer to get the most benefit from each dollar spent by maximizing his choices. But this would be a one-sided view of what cities mean to the economy, and would be open to criticism on two principal points.

The first one is that it is based on deductive arguments. Although it seems logical to say, for example, that clustering should reduce total trans-portation costs, the fact is that no tidy, real-life experiments have been made to prove it. Experimentation in the social sciences, particularly in eco-nomics, is largely unfeasible because too many factors that are presumably important cannot be held constant. Perhaps the people who live in a very spread-out community value their privacy, or the quiet, or something else, so much that they are more than compensated for their "inefficient" transportation costs. It might seem reasonable to argue that the clustering of automobile factories would stimulate innovation, but how could we prove that Detroit "caused" automatic transmission to be developed? Even if we did, could we properly infer from the case that cities are a significant factor in bringing about innovation across the board? As knowledge about cities, communication, and innovation accumulates, the constructive economic role of urbanization may become easier to believe in, but there is still much room for skepticism.

The second reservation about the economic benefit of urbanization is that it is by no means a net benefit. In the earliest cities there were problems uniquely urban – public health dangers, noise, congestion, and disorders. A later chapter will examine these diseconomies of urban scale with greater care, but it will be useful as well as honest to take note of them here:

Involuntary contacts. – A city exposes us to people, sights, and forms of organization that we might prefer to avoid. We are fair game to dishonest merchants, to panhandlers, and the like. We have to tolerate parties and trombone lessons in our neighbor's house. We have to worry that drug pushers will get to our children in school, or that our spouse will succumb to advertising for an extravagant new car or fur coat. We have to submit to the community will, however formulated, about shopping on Sunday or what we wear when sunbathing in the park.

Supporting the infrastructure. – Because cities need streets, museums, fire-fighting equipment, and schools, people who live in cities must pay for these things whether they as individuals use them or not. Conversely, individuals might be more than willing to pay their share of the cost of an opera house or a ballpark, but they might not be able to do so because the community in some way decides against these things.

Interdependence. – An orthodontist who treats the children of retail store merchants in Detroit finds that his livelihood is directly affected by market researchers at Ford and General Motors who have made serious mistakes about the demand for compact cars in the recent past. University professors in Seattle were laid off because environmentalists in the United States won political support in their campaign against the supersonic transport, to which the Boeing Company was heavily committed. A newspaper strike in San Francisco caused a slump in the entertainment business and in retail stores because new attractions and sales could not be advertised. It is in the nature of urban life that most people are indirectly dependent on most other people; we are not our own masters in the way that a homesteading farmer might be.

Specific scale diseconomies.— The larger the city, the higher the average cost of commuting, in general, and the greater the congestion in the central area. The supply of water and disposition of sewage and other wastes may be costlier per capita for large urban centers than for small ones. Levels of noise and of air pollution, to which every resident is about equally exposed, rise as the population rises. Amenities such as parks are harder to provide in the large city, and the accumulation of unsightly housing, shops, and old factories is greater.

Anonymity.— In a small town people know each other and know what others are doing. This can be reassuring to some people, but oppressive to others. Many migrants to big cities hope to escape the confining mores and unbounded responsibilities of the family and the small community by being among strangers in the city. Anonymity might be listed among the benefits of urbanization—if it were not for the fact that so many people dislike it. Either they feel that urban anonymity makes their own lives less meaningful or they blame it for allowing more and more of the human race to become dissolute and unfeeling. The term "anomie" has come into wide use among urban sociologists and political scientists, who feel that the citizens in a large community become so distant from their government that they despair that personal problems requiring the help of sympathetic public agencies will ever be dealt with—or worse, that the action of public agencies, such as police in dealing with a low-income neighborhood, will be positively unsympathetic. The best that can be said about urban anonymity is that it is a questionable virtue, and so we list it among the defects that urbanization should be held accountable for.

DISCUSSION QUESTIONS

1. Do you agree with the common "intellectual" bias against cities? Do you think most people feel the same way? Is it a matter of "economics" versus something else?

2. Does GNP reflect the economic benefits of "cluster"? Of "dense cluster"? Of "ordered dense cluster"?

3. Suppose a technological breakthrough greatly reduces the cost of intraurban transportation. Would it be better to consume more

space per capita or to allow the land-use pattern of the city to become less efficient? Who would decide how to use the savings?

4. Distinguish between internal and external economies of scale. How does urbanization allow each to be realized? Suppose that the largest employer in your community were the only employer; would its costs of production be greater because of this?

5. Is Jane Jacob's report on the Etawah experiment a completely valid illustration of urban agglomeration benefits?

6. How many job categories are used by government employment services in your area?

7. What is the most "exotic" restaurant in your community? How many stores did you visit when you last shopped for a pair of shoes?

8. Do you agree that consumer benefits from urban diversity are not reflected in GNP? Does a community of homogeneous consumers enjoy a higher real standard of living than one where people's tastes are heterogeneous?

9. Are business decisions likely to be more creative if more people are involved in making them? Does the principle of "division of labor" apply? Can the urban land market affect the quality of (non-real estate) business decisions?

10. Is urban anonymity a plus or a minus as far as you are concerned?

SELECTED REFERENCES

Dantzig, George B., and Thomas L. Saaty. *Compact City*. San Francisco: W. H. Freeman and Co., 1973.
A team of engineers describes an urban megastructure design which minimizes the consumption of ground space and other natural resources.

Isard, Walter. *Location and Space Economy*. Cambridge, Mass.: MIT Press, 1956, Chapter Eight.
The theory and concept of urban agglomeration economies.

Jacobs, Jane. *The Economy of the Cities.* New York: Random House, 1969.
Lively description of the growth of many business enterprises which benefited from urban agglomeration economies, tied together with a set of theoretical perceptions.

Meier, Richard L. *A Communications Theory of Urban Growth.* Cambridge, Mass.: The Joint Center for Urban Studies of MIT and Harvard University, 1962.

Samuelson, Paul. *Econmics*, Seventh Edition. New York: McGraw-Hill, 1967, Chapter Twenty-Two.
The theory of consumer demand, including the concept of utility and indifference curves.

Smith, Adam. *The Wealth of Nations*, 1776 (reprinted by Modern Library and others), Book One, Chapters I, II, III.
Description of the division of labor, and the increase in productivity which it allows.

Thompson, Wilbur, R. *A Preface to Urban Economics.* Baltimore: The Johns Hopkins Press, 1965, Chapter One.
Examination of the factors which attract labor and capital to new urban locations.

White, Morton, and Lucia White. *The Intellectual Versus the City.* New York: Mentor, 1962.
A survey of the opinions of leading ancient and modern opinion-makers concerning the disadvantages of city life.

3

A GOOD PLACE
FOR A CITY:
ECONOMICS OF
LOCATION

BOTH INTERNAL and external economies of production, which were described as benefits of urbanization in the preceding chapter, are subject to certain locational constraints. That is, in choosing a location for a factory, the manufacturing firm must consider whether raw materials are available at various alternative sites, what it will cost to transport other raw materials that are not available, and what it will cost to transport the finished product from factory to market. Internal economies of large-scale production cannot be achieved if raw material, market, or transportation factors limit the size of a manufacturing firm in a particular location. Unless these same factors are conducive to efficient operation by a number of different firms, external or agglomeration economies will also go by the board.

So, the question is: What is an efficient location for a manufacturing firm? Thanks to many theoretical, mathematical, and empirical studies by economic geographers, we have several useful answers to this question.

WEIGHT-GAINING PROCESSES

There are several answers because there are several possible situations. One is a type of manufacturing process that results in an increase in the cost per mile of transporting the commodity. A familiar example is a soft-drink bottling plant. Here the manufacturing process consists largely of adding water to a syrup concentrate which is produced elsewhere. Sufficient quantities of suitable water for this purpose are almost always available in an urban community which is, at the same time, the market for the bottled product. The total transportation costs of a soft-drink business are minimized if the bottling is done at the market rather than at the source of the ultimate raw materials (sugar and flavorings) or even at the place where the syrup is produced (a separate kind of manufacturing process with distinct locational criteria).

This is illustrated in Figure 6a. The horizontal axis links the raw material location (RM) to the market (Mkt). The vertical axis measures transportation cost per unit of final product. The line sloping up from RM to Mkt indicates that, as we consider processing plant locations farther from RM in the direction of Mkt, the transportation cost of the inputs (the syrup, for example) rises at a certain rate, which can be measured by the slope of the line. The line sloping down from RM to Mkt measures the transpotation cost of getting the product, (the bottled drinks) from the factory to the market, and this is naturally lower the nearer the plant is to the market.

Adding the cost of transporting inputs and the cost of transporting outputs, for all the possible places between RM and Mkt at which the processing plant might be located, gives us the dashed line at the top. In Figure 6a, this total transportation cost is lowest when the plant is located at the market, and that gives us the first of our answers. For a weight-gaining process, the optimum location is at the market.

There are several assumptions behind this conclusion. One is that the nontransportation costs of production are identical in any location. Recognizing that labor may be less costly in one place than another, that water costs may differ, and so on, we have to qualify our first answer, but it does not become less informative when we do that.

Another assumption is that transportation cost is a simple function of weight and distance. In reality, the cost of transportation is affected by bulk, fragility, and perishability. Bread baking is an example of a market-oriented processing activity that is not so much weight-gaining as it is

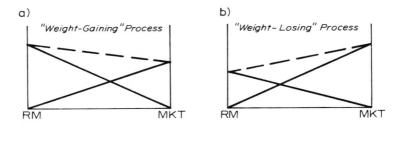

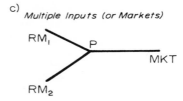

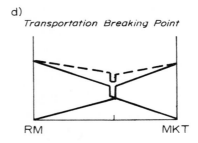

Figure 6.   Location of processing activities.

bulk- and perishability-creating. Again, recognizing this assumption makes the simple locational answer more informative.

Still another assumption is that we are talking about the transport costs that the manufacturing firm itself bears, and not the real or "resource" cost to the economy. If suppliers of raw materials decide, for competitive reasons, to bear some of the cost of getting their output to users, or if they employ a delivered pricing schedule that obscures the effect of distance, this will encourage processing firms to locate near markets. If publicly regulated freight rates discriminate against certain raw materials, so that processing firms have to pay more per mile to get those materials to their plants than it really costs, processing activities will be pulled toward the raw material location. What it "really costs" to move a ton of X from place A to place B is a terribly complex problem for which transportation economists can seldom provide convincing answers; we must realistically presume that there is a degree of social undesirability in the transportation costs that form the basis of decisions by business firms. Hence, the pattern of industrial location is probably inefficient to some degree for the economy as a whole.

The last principal assumption embodied in Figure 6a is that location choices are continuous—that is, that the firm is free to locate anywhere along the line between RM and Mkt. In reality, only certain locations are feasible, and they do not necessarily lie along a straight line connecting the two points. Generally, there must be a town, a labor force, power and water supplies, available land and buildings, access to long-distance transportation systems, and so on. This may not seem to matter if the choice finally is one of locating either at RM or Mkt, but if other production costs are considered in the location equation—as they should be —intermediate points might well be selected. Another considerable type of cost problem arises when raw material sources or market locations (or both) change for a manufacturing firm that has already taken root some-place. Then there is a major opportunity cost of the investment in existing facilities and the roster of trained employees who cannot readily move to accommodate dynamically changing transportation factors.

WEIGHT-LOSING PROCESSES

Early steel mills consumed three or four tons of coal for every ton of steel produced. The manufacturing process eliminated the weight of the coal, so the weight of the inputs greatly exceeded the weight of the outputs, for each unit of output. Using the principles of Figure 6a, but altering the slopes of the two cost functions, we have in Figure 6b a location diagram for a weight-losing process. Clearly, total transportation cost, per unit of final product, is least when the plant is located at the raw material source. And, in fact, coal fields were the principal locational magnets for steelmaking in the nineteenth-century period of industrialization, notably in Pennsylvania in the U.S. and in the Lorraine area in western Europe. Somewhat earlier it had been water power—used directly to turn factory wheels rather than indirectly to generate electric power—which had attracted manufacturing. The city of Holyoke, Massachusetts, was laid out over a large tract of farm land in 1847 by Boston financiers, who hoped to build the world's greatest cotton manufacturing city around the falls in the Connecticut River at that point.[1] Water power, like coal, disappears in the process of production, while it is, itself, very difficult to transport.

The second answer to the manufacturing-location question, then, is that weight-losing processes tend to locate near the source of raw materials. This statement is subject to the same reservations made in connection with weight-gaining processes.

In particular, the significance of "other factors" overshadows transportation costs in many real-world situations. In the 1970s, Japan is the world's third largest producer of steel, though it has virtually no coal. Almost all the fuel used by Japan's steelmakers must be imported from enormous distances, but that cost is offset by economies accruing from low wage levels and highly efficient plants. In many parts of the United States, communities offer new manufacturing plants such inducements as property-tax exemptions and low rents in industrial parks. In other sections, labor unions and local governments exert the powers they have to prevent manufacturing plants from "running away" to lower-cost locations. Transportation cost considerations often seem to get lost in the shuffle.

MULTIPLE SOURCES AND MARKETS

Steelmaking requires iron ore as well as fuel. Most industrial processes, for that matter, involve several inputs that are taken originally from separate places. And most manufacturing output is sold in more than one

1. Constance M. Green, *American Cities in the Growth of a Nation* (New York: Harper and Row, 1957), pp. 80–81.

market. Can the general principle of Figures 6a and 6b be applied in the case of multiple raw material sources and multiple markets? The answer, illustrated in Figure 6c, is yes; but once again a number of assumptions should be kept in mind.

Suppose, for example, that iron ore is found at RM_1 and a supply of coal is located at RM_2, while the market for steel products is at Mkt. There is a point, P, connecting these three locations, at which the aggregate transportation cost per ton of steel product is least. At that point, the weight times the distance in each of the three directions is equal, and the point can be found by various algebraic, geometric, and analog methods.[2] It is a general solution that applies to any number of inputs or markets and that can be adapted to differences in wage rates or other processing costs at the various locations.

The reader may wonder whether this kind of theory is in very wide use, and the realistic answer is no. The present city of Gary, Indiana, is said to have been created as a result of an analysis like Figure 6c, because it lay conveniently close to iron ore, coal, and the market for steel products that Gary was to make. Present-day industrial location consultants give considerable weight to the concept of a transportation-cost-minimizing location for a client's new factory, but they are likely to emphasize other factors such as local tax rates, the quality of the community environment as a place for employees to work, the adequacy of electric power, and the attractiveness of a new industrial park.

In any case, new industrial facilities are not likely to be set down in a wilderness with the expectation that a town will eventually grow up around them. New factories are strongly attracted to communities where secondary industry (manufacturing) is already well established. One reason for this, of course, is the external economies of agglomeration, already discussed. Another relates strictly to transportation costs, to a variation on Figures 6a, 6b, and 6c, and it is one of the most important ideas we have about the economics of urbanization.

TRANSPORTATION BREAKING POINTS

Going back to Figures 6a and 6b, consider what happens to the two diagonal lines and the dashed line at the top if there is some point along the

---

2. See Martin Beckmann, *Location Theory* (New York: Random House, 1968), pp. 15–19.

route from *RM* to *Mkt* where it is necessary to change the mode of transportation—from ship to rail, for example. Handling costs have always been a major component in freight transportation cost and continue to be so even in the age of containers. If a factory is located at *Mkt*, raw materials from *RM* must be handled once at the transportation breaking point because of the change in transportation mode and again when they are unloaded at the factory. The same is true if the factory is located at *RM*. Both of the diagonal transportation cost lines—for getting raw materials to the factory and for taking finished goods to market—jog upwards at the transportation breaking point.

At that point, however, the total transportation cost line has a notch in it. One handling of the materials or products can be avoided by locating the processing plant at the transportation breaking point. Hence, the port attracts industry, and this simple fact goes a long way in explaining the location, activity, and growth of most of the major cities in the world. London, New York, Tokyo (with Yokohama), Chicago, Calcutta, San Francisco, Rio de Janeiro—and many other cities—owe their existence to this relationship between transportation modes and industrial location. A look at the list of cities will also suggest that the juncture of ocean and rail transportation systems has been more significant than any other combination of transportation modes.

Buffalo, New York, began as a flour milling city, processing wheat from the American midwest into flour for the markets of New York City and the world beyond, for Great Lakes wheat carriers had to be unloaded at Buffalo, the western terminus of the Erie Canal and later of railroads. Chicago processed livestock from the midwest into meat products for the East because it was at the juncture of overland and water transportation. Chicago also processed ores and other materials, brought by water, into manufactured products such as farm tools for the midwest. Vancouver, B.C., and Seattle, Washington, both got started as processers of timber that abounded in the hinterland but which distant markets needed in the form of cut lumber or other wood products.

When we look beyond the physical handling and manufacturing that converts raw materials into usable commodities, it becomes even more apparent why ports attract business enterprise. "Processing" wheat into flour involves not only physical milling but also the business functions of contracting with wheat growers or their agents, financing the delivery of wheat and possibly the distribution of flour, developing and managing markets for flour, insuring goods in transit, and, of course, raising capital for the flour-milling enterprises. These are interrelated activities requiring constant communication, and each has to be located somewhere. As is generally true for administrative, "white-collar" kinds of economic activities, they neither import nor export bulky materials, so they are reasonably free of transportation-cost constraints which can be significant for the physical side of manufacturing. It is practical and logical for these administrative activities to settle down adjacent to the port and the manufacturing plants. In time, as we shall discuss in Chapter Five, these administrative activities may come to overshadow both the port and the manufacturing processes themselves.

Figure 6d, which illustrates the transportation breaking point idea, is drawn in such a way as to suggest that the breaking point is attractive for either a weight-losing or a weight-gaining process. With relatively small differentials in freight rates for inputs and outputs, the transshipment point does have the advantage. But in extreme cases—for example, where the cost of sending finished goods to market is negligible—it can pay to locate away from the breaking point, despite the extra handling costs. Ore smelting and food processing are likely to stay pretty close to the sources of their raw materials.

FOOTLOOSE INDUSTRIES

As time goes by, the cost of transportation and even the expense of handling goods at transshipment points seems less and less effective as an explanation for the location of specific industries and business firms. This is because transportation costs are becoming smaller, relative to other costs of production, for a number of significant kinds of products. This, in turn, is due to technological improvements in transportation and to the emergence of new kinds of industry.

The airframe industry is a case in point. William Boeing was a resident of Seattle when he built an experimental seaplane, mostly of wood and canvas, and more as an expression of personal interest than as a business venture. This was in the early 1920s. In successive efforts, Boeing was able to develop a kind of airplane for which there was a market. He opened a factory in Seattle in 1929, manufactured both commercial and military planes, and gradually absorbed the changes in aircraft technology so that his output during the Second World War consisted of all-metal planes, including the famous "Flying Fortress" and the B-29.

The raw materials for aircraft had to be imported into Seattle and, of course, the planes produced had to be delivered hundreds or even thousands of miles away. Today the Boeing 707 and 747, fabricated from parts and materials brought in from many parts of the U.S., are sold to nations all over the world. The factory complex, however, remains in Seattle (there is a branch factory in Kansas, established during World War II as an industrial decentralization measure). The location is a historical accident, but there are no compelling transportation cost economies that would be achieved by moving it. Other major producers of aircraft frames in southern California have a similar story. Wichita, Kansas, became a center of airplane manufacturers as early as the First World War because the surrounding flat, wheat-growing area makes things a bit safer for test pilots.

Scientific research requires certain materials and much information for which transportation costs per se are nearly insignificant. The result of the research can be delivered with a postage stamp. Research facilities have sprung up mostly in high amenity areas, as a consequence, because the personnel can be attracted to the pleasant living environments in Santa Barbara, California, and in the San Francisco area, for example. The existence of major universities seems to attract research laboratories, but the universities themselves are a kind of footloose industry.

Diamond cutting is a classic example of an enterprise in which transportation costs are very small in relation to the value added. Rough diamonds are flown from South Africa to Holland, and recently to the Island of Mauritius in the middle of the Indian Ocean, and cut diamonds are sent to market by air freight. The presence of skilled labor and managerial know-how outweighs the relatively small factor of transportation.

Electronic goods, such as transistor radios, can be put together, mostly from imported parts, in Hong Kong, Puerto Rico, and other places and shipped to markets around the world. Fashion clothing became an important industry in the Los Angeles area because good designers lived there, despite the cost of transporting materials to that area and shipping the finished product to market in other parts of the U.S.

The list could be extended without difficulty, and it is constantly growing. The ever more sophisticated nature of industrial output, coupled with technological progress in various kinds of transportation, diminishes the importance of transportation costs in determining the location of manufacturing or, more broadly, of production. This does not mean there is no more employment for economic geographers or that all industry is up for grabs, for we are becoming more aware of the significance of resources that cannot be transported at all. The Florida climate, the easy-going atmosphere of San Francisco, the Chinese-speaking refugees in Hong Kong, the enthusiasm of Japanese workers for their companies, financial know-how that oozes from the business warrens of Manhattan—these are the ore deposits and the timberlands of the twentieth century. People and business go to them, not because they are weight-losing or weight-gaining kinds of businesses, but because the key resources cannot be budged. It is something of a misnomer to say that these activities are "footloose," but the term may be excusable because it emphasizes the relative freedom from ton-mile costs which characterizes more and more of economic life.

DISTRIBUTION CENTERS

An increasing proportion of all jobs is accounted for by "trade"—retail and wholesale businesses. In the distribution of goods and services there are clear geographic patterns that conform to nearly intuitive economic theories. Basically, because distribution activities locate at the center of their respective trade areas, the question becomes one of defining the limits of the trade areas.

Figure 7a is an adaptation of Figure 6, with goods to be distributed obtained from RM but at negligible cost. Since supermarkets throughout a metropolitan area obtain their inventories at about the same delivered cost, the geographic source of those inventories does not influence the location of the store. Essentially the same is true of department, hardware, drug, and furniture stores in the cities of a given region of the country. As far as services go, the "cost" of a doctor, teacher, or lawyer does not depend on how far he has come from the place he got his degree. So the transportation cost of inputs fades away in Figure 7a.

Also, in this figure the line sloping upward from Mkt has a new meaning. Not all consumption takes place at this market, but rather Mkt is the point of distribution, and the sloping line indicates the cost of transporting commodities from Mkt to a wider and wider region, assuming that potential customers or clients are distributed across the landscape. The trade area for the distribution or service firm at Mkt extends to point L, for beyond that point the cost of obtaining the product or service from competing Firm X is less.

The distance from Mkt to L is the radius of a circle, so that our first

a)

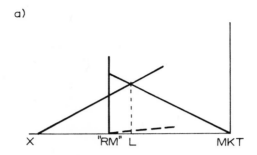

b)

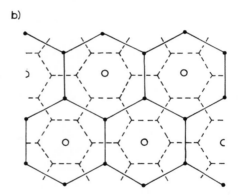

Figure 7. Distribution center locations.

approximation to the definition of a trade area is a circle surrounding the point of distribution, on the perimeter of which delivered prices are equal to the delivered prices of the nearest competitor. This suggests a commercial landscape made up of nonintersecting circles, which happens to be a geometric impossibility. If the circles do not intersect, there must remain spaces between them. When the concept of equal delivered prices is extended into these spaces, or interstices, the result is a patch of hexagons, as in Figure 7b. In a landscape of competitive distribution and service firms, trade areas are therefore basically hexagonal.

The small hexagons in Figure 7b are equal in size and their centers are equidistant. This suggests that these several firms differ only with respect to location, that is, that they are equally efficient in what they do and their products are considered to be homogeneous. Since these things are unlikely to be true for many kinds of distribution and service activities—for example, department stores, supermarkets versus mom and pop grocery stores, and lawyers and dentists—we have to allow that the real pattern of trade areas will not resemble the regular geometry of our illustration.

While we are doing that, we might as well take into account something else that affects the radius over which a business firm can compete, namely, the internal economies of large-scale production. The larger the market, the lower the unit cost of production (not considering the cost of transportation), at least up to some scale of output where the AC curve turns up. Retail stores and dentists have significant scale economies, just as factories do.

Even adding in the cost of transportation, the delivered price of the commodity or service being distributed may fall for a time or rise only slowly as a wider and wider area is served. The more efficient the firm and the greater its potential economies of scale, the farther back it can push the trade area of is neighboring competitors, even to the point of putting those competitors out of business. If marginal transportation costs associated with serving remote customers are absorbed in one fashion or another by the distribution or service firm, the effective trade grows even larger.

Ultimately, a trade area pattern will emerge that reflects the competitive strength of individual firms and the incidence of transportation costs. We will then have a map showing the location of distribution and service firms. The same principle can be extended to manufacturing activities where raw materials are to be found in sufficient quantities in a great many places and the question is how many such manufacturing plants are required in the nation as a whole. In this sense, steelmaking is a distribution activity, and automobile assembly is another example.

The larger hexagons in Figure 7b represent higher-order distribution facilities than the smaller hexagons. Because of economies of scale, a supermarket, for example, may serve a larger area than a drugstore. There will be fewer supermarkets (shown by the small circles in Figure 7b) than drugstores (shown by the black dots *and* the small circles). The efficiency of the supermarket may lie in its quantity discounts or in the great variety of items its large trade area allows it to stock.[3] "Industry structure," by which economics textbooks mean whether a line of business is perfectly competitive, oligopolistic, discriminatory, cartellized, and so on, is also reflected in the map of market jurisdictions and hence in the locations of trading businesses.

WAY STATIONS

The Inca empire was a long-strung-out affair, needing swift communication but lacking horses (and writing). The solution was a system of foot runners, called *chasqui*, and impressively engineered mountain highways for them to run on. The distance between Quito and Cuzco, about 1,250 miles, could be covered in five days.[4]

Not by one man, of course. Though the runners ran a mile in six and a half minutes, at altitudes ranging from 6,000 to 17,000 feet, the system was really a series of relay stations one and a half miles apart, where verbal messages, knotted strings that served as Inca accounting records, and some types of commodities were passed on to a fresh runner. The relay stations were not much, just two beds and a hearth.

The American Pony Express operated on a similar system of relays, as did couriers in the ancient Roman Empire. The Franciscan padres who labored to convert the Indians of California built twenty-one missions one day's journey apart so that travelers would be sure of a secure resting place. Many of these missions became hubs of urban communities. Elsewhere in California, the present cities of Danville and Vacaville were originally way stations on wagon routes linking north and south. People have to get off their horses now and then—and off their Greyhound buses, too.

The way-station function may be added to a community that has come into existence for some other reason. Market towns, as we have said earlier, tend to be spotted at roughly equal distance through an agricultural region, though not necessarily at distances that travelers find ideal. In the spring of 1972, President Nixon stopped over in Vienna on his way to major negotiations in Moscow, in order to get adjusted to the time difference first.

3. For a careful theoretical statement of all the concepts in this section, see Beckmann, *Location Theory*.

4. V. W. von Hagen, *The Ancient Sun Kingdom of the Americas* (Cleveland, Ohio: World Publishing Company, 1957), pp. 557ff.

Many remote islands in the Pacific were settled and fought over because they could be used as coaling stations for old-time ships. The city of Trinidad, Colorado, began as a railroad coaling station. Honolulu, besides its other attractions, draws trans-Pacific airliners because there is gasoline there for their empty tanks; the same is true of Anchorage, Alaska.

There always have been way stations, and there probably always will be. One function of any urban settlement is to accommodate people who are just passing through. In one sense or another, that is a big job. The way-station function alone, however, is not a very promising rationale for an urban settlement, because it is subject to technological obsolescence.

DISCUSSION QUESTIONS

1. What transportation cost factors are involved in setting up a regional automobile assembly plant? Is it a weight-gaining or a weight-losing process?

2. Where in North America are most shoes manufactured? What are the apparent reasons for those locations?

3. What effect will freight containers have upon the location of processing activities? Why?

4. Do you think that a community with high unemployment should offer subsidies to new manufacturing companies to offset the community's locational disadvantage? Explain.

5. What is the clearest example in your area of a processing firm established in accordance with the simple location concepts presented in Chapter Three?

6. If you were the leasing agent for a large industrial park, would you prefer as tenants firms that were raw-material oriented, market-oriented, or "footloose"? Explain.

7. The trade area of an urban mom and pop grocery stores is very small, while a similar store in a rural area draws customers from a much wider area. Identify all the factors that account for this difference.

8.   Is there a processing firm in your community that located there because of "artificial" transportation costs for its raw materials or its finished products?

SELECTED REFERENCES

Beckmann, Martin. *Location Theory*. New York: Random House, 1968.
A summary of the mathematical theory of industrial, retail, and residential location in a market economy.

Green, Constance M. *American Cities in the Growth of the Nation*. New York: Harper & Row, 1965.
Historical accounts of the establishment and growth of a number of U.S. urban centers, illustrating location economics concepts and the evolution of both basic and service sectors of local economics.

Hoover, Edgar M. *The Location of Economic Activity*. New York: McGraw-Hill, 1948.
A treatise on industry location, integrating theory and empirical information.

Nourse, Hugh O. *Regional Economics*. New York: McGraw-Hill, 1968.
A summary of the main theoretical concepts of regional economics —industry location and industry structure, land use allocation within cities through the price mechanism, central place theory, and systems of cities.

4

THE ECONOMIC BASE: TOWN BUILDERS AND TOWN FILLERS

THE SPECTER that haunts city hall in any but the very largest urban community is that Company X will lose a major contract or will move out of town. Company X is not a McDonald's hamburger outlet or a TV repair shop. It is not a law firm and, except under unusual circumstances, it is not the city's major department store.

Company X is an "export industry." It sells goods and services primarily to people beyond the borders of the city itself. This brings in money which is eventually used to pay for goods and services that are imported by the residents of this community. Without this inward flow of funds, the existence of the city as a whole is threatened; and only certain types of business (or, more broadly, economic) activities bring money in. These activities make up the community's "economic base."

There can be many firms like Company X in a city, but each is important to the city's prosperity. An export firm with ten employees is more important to a community in many ways than a nonexport firm with 100 employees. It is the export function, not the size, that is critical. It is not the capital investment, the property or payroll taxes the firm pays, nor its attitude on pollution, that creates this special concern in city hall, but the fact that it sells things to the rest of the world.

THE ECONOMIC BASE MULTIPLIER

When the dollar earned by export is spent locally, it creates non-export jobs in the community. Eventually, this export dollar is used to pay for imports, so it leaves the community. But first it circulates in town. And it is the circulation that does the trick. The automobile factory worker spends his dollar in the grocery store, and some of that dollar goes to pay the wages of clerks in the store. The grocery clerk gives some of his dollar to a dentist, and the dentist in turn uses it to pay his phone bill. The telephone operator gets her hair done in a beauty shop. And so on. Some part of every dollar goes directly to guy things from out of town—to pay for the supermarket's inventory, the clerk's federal taxes, the dentist's gold, the interest on telephone company bonds, the hair spray used in the beauty shop. Finally, the last cent has been re-exported, but in the process local firms have rung up sales, paid their city taxes, and met their payrolls. Tomorrow's sales, taxes, and payrolls depend on new exports of goods and services by the firms that make up the town's economic base.

Because the spending habits of consumers are so predictable, we can anticipate that a given number of jobs in export industries will result in a specific number of jobs in nonexport industries. As a general average, there are two jobs in town for every one in the export base. Local consumption spending multiplies the employment of the economic-base component of the city's business. Not only can we say that the multiplier for the average city is two, but we can also say, with confidence, that the multiplier is lower for a relatively young (more recently established) community and higher for a large city regardless of age. Each city, at each point in time, has its own numerical economic base multiplier. From it, the people in the banks, the stores, and in city hall can forecast changes in their volumes of deposits and loans, their sales, their need for schoolteachers and policemen, and many other important things that need to be predicted in the interest of running the city and its businesses well. Knowing that Company X is going to lay off or take on a specific number of workers, and knowing the numerical value of the local economic base multiplier, means that such changes in the general economy of the city can be anticipated with reasonable accuracy. Even if we don't know precisely what the multiplier is, we still can translate information about Company X's plans into plans and expectations for almost every locally oriented business and, of course, for local government.

The concept of the economic base multiplier is shown graphically in Figure 8. Because many readers are probably familiar with the "Keynesian investment multiplier"—which in economics texts is defined as the relationship between an increase in investment spending and the consequent increase in overall national income—these two multiplier concepts are shown side by side. Their derivations are similar, but their differences have some important implications.

The horizontal axis in Figure 8a measures tht total number of jobs in a community. The vertical axis measures, alternatively, the number of jobs in export businesses (E) or in local, nonexport businesses (L). The latter is often called "service" employment, but there are a few difficulties with the idea that export employment involves the production of goods while local employment means the service industries. These difficulties of classification will be taken up later.

The vertical axis also measures the number of jobs lost because of

Figure 8. Part (a): Economic Base Multiplier.

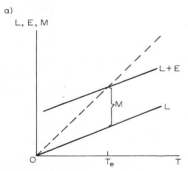

$$T \equiv L + E$$
$$T \equiv L + M$$
$$L/T = g$$
$$1 = g + E/T$$
$$T(1 - g) = E$$
$$T = E \cdot (1 - g)^{-1}$$

But: $\quad g = L/T = (1 - M/T)$ increases as T grows because M can be replaced with local production (L).

b) Part (b): Keynesian Investment Multiplier.

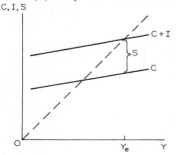

$$Y \equiv C + I,$$
$$\Delta Y = \Delta C + \Delta I$$
$$Y \equiv C + S,$$
$$\Delta Y = \Delta C + \Delta S$$
$$\Delta C/\Delta Y = k$$
$$1 = k + \Delta I/\Delta Y$$
$$\Sigma Y(1 - k) = \Delta I$$
$$\Delta Y = \Delta I \cdot (1 - k)^{-1}$$

imports (M), which turns out to be just equal, numerically, to the number of export jobs, for the same reason that saving and investment are equal in the Keynesian scheme.

Beneath Figure 8a is an algebraic summary of the economic base multiplier's derivation. To begin with, we define total employment as the sum of local and export employment. Then, since E and M are numerically equal (in equilibrium), total employment can also be expressed as the sum of local employment and employment created elsewhere by the community's imports.

The next step, which is crucial to the economic base concept, is the assumption that people in a community spend their money in such a way that the relation between the total number of jobs in the community, T, and the number of nonexport jobs, L, is a constant (g). This may sound a bit complicated, but all it really means is that housewives spend x percent of their budget at the grocery store and y percent for the house, and so forth, while the grocery store pays out a percent of its receipts for goods, b percent for wages, and so on. In fact, these percentages do show great consistency in the aggregate. As long as we are dealing with a narrow range of variation in T, it is reasonable to assume that L/T is constant, though some of the more interesting things we can say about economic base theory involve looking at wider variations in T.

Now, if we divide each of the terms in the equation at the top by T, we get $T/T = L/T + E/T$, which simplifies into $1 = g + E/T$. What we are looking for is an algebraic statement that explains the level of total employment in a community, so we bring T over to the left-hand side and put everything else on the right-hand side of the equal sign: $T = E \cdot [1/(1-g)]$.

The result is that T is shown to be equal to E, the number of export jobs, times a constant term (a multiplier) involving g, which is itself a constant. Suppose $g = 1/2$; then $(1/(1-g) = 2$, which means that total employment in the community is twice the number of jobs in the economic base. Recalling that $g = L/T$, if people in the community have spending habits that make this fraction $3/4$ instead of $1/2$ (if they spend more of their money on local goods and services), then the economic base multiplier is 4 instead of 2. Thus, the multiplier's numerical value, and the consequent sensitivity of total employment to changes in export employment, are derived from customary household expenditure patterns among the people in the community. The more these people want to spend their money outside the community, the smaller the total employment in the community will be.

The reader might well object to the inference that people in the community can expand and contract job opportunities in their city, more or less at will, by changing the way they manage their household budgets. It smacks of the "bootstraps" argument, for which something is to be said on both sides. On the one hand, it certainly is possible for Mr. and Mrs. Urbanite to spend all the money allotted for a new automobile on sending their children to a local, private school, thus creating some fraction of a job for a local teacher and eliminating about the same fraction of a job in Detroit. On the other hand, if jobs in Detroit and other outside cities are reduced, then the market for hometown exports will shrink. The gain in local teacher employment may be offset by a reduction in factory work in the same community. It is also possible that the number of public schoolteachers in town will be reduced as the number of private school-teachers rises, so that the objective of raising local employment is frustrated.

The bootstraps discussion can become very complex. But there is one basic objection that people uncomfortable with the bootstraps idea can always make: a person cannot buy something from a local producer if the commodity or service is not produced locally. It makes no sense to suppose that household food budgets can be shifted around so as to create more local employment, because people need certain quantities of food and virtually all of this food must be imported into the city. Early goldminers in California are said to have sent their laundry to China (a round trip of six months to a year in those days before air freight) because there was no one around who preferred doing laundry to panning for gold.

When the argument is raised in this way, we are forced to consider a very useful amalgamation of location theory, discussed in the previous chapter, and the economic base idea, because the issue is one of the dynamics of employment expansion in a community. After all, when a primary industry—such as goldmining or logging—or a secondary industry—such as steelmaking or food processing—takes root in a frontier or agricultural region, there may well not be any tertiary industries—laundries, dentists, schools, haberdashers, and the like—which the workers in the new export industry can patronize. Why should there be? (This is not a rhetorical question.)

How, then, will tertiary industries emerge? The goldminer and his like have an economic base multiplier of one—unity—because they spend all of their money outside the community. L/T is zero, which makes g also zero, and $(1-g)^{-1}$ equal to one. The number of jobs in town is just those jobs in the export industry. If L/T really were constant, then a town, in the sense that we know it, would not come into being. The parameter g, and with it the economic base multiplier, must change over time until it reaches a stable level. This will be recognized as the "maturing" of the local economy, a process which ends when the local component of employment in the new community has approximated the share of T that we find in other communities, long established and mature, a process that influences the culture of the new settlement.

The process is one of substituting local services and goods for things that are imported. Eventually there will be more miners in the gold fields than there are promising claims, so some will be looking for other kinds of work. At the same time, even the successful miners, loggers, and factory workers will wish they could get their laundry done a little faster, or that they didn't have to live with their toothaches until they could make a trip to the dentist in Philadelphia, or that they could buy factory-made axes or furniture which was imported in carload lots and was thus cheaper or better than the alternative. People with no intention of digging for gold or felling trees will come to the gold fields and logging camps because they believe there will be a market for service-type skills.

In this kind of scenario, L and g are initially zero, and the economic base multiplier is one. As time goes by, L becomes a positive number because M is reduced, and then L grows at a faster rate than T. At some point, however, the opportunities for substitution of L for M are exhausted. This point comes when the people in the community, as consumers, feel that imported goods and services are preferable to those that might be added to the list of items locally produced, or that additional local services would be inefficient. Thus, most communities, including even New York City, stop short of manufacturing their own automobiles, growing their own food, or making all their own movies. Many communities are too small to support a full-line department store or a symphony orchestra.

In terms of Figure 8a, the scenario is only slightly different. Beginning with a number of export employees, measured vertically by the distance M, local employment grows as these export employees spend some fixed fraction of their wages on local goods and services. Local employees, in turn, spend the same fraction of *their* wages on local goods and services, generating successive rounds of expansion in local employment. Equilibrium in total employment is reached, at T_e in the diagram, when the aggregate amount of employment still imported, in the form of goods or services actually secured somewhere else, is equal to the amount of export employment (assumed unchanged from the beginning). Until this point is reached, the *capacity* to import—measured by E—exceeds the *desire* to import—measured by the vertical distance between the L function and the 45° line—the surplus purchasing power being transformed into higher and higher levels of local employment. Beyond T_e, the demand for imports would exceed the level of exports, both expressed in employment terms, and the local economy would be obliged to retrench in some way.

Figure 8a is not the dynamic case. The influence of time or of the scale of population on the slope of L, (that is, L/T, or g), is not represented. To be sure, T is a good proxy for the total population of the community, and since we have good reason to believe that the larger a community gets the more nearly self-sufficient it becomes (the greater is the ratio of L to T or of L to E), we could draw the L function with an upward curve. Most likely, it would be a rather elongated S-curve, rising slowly, then quite rapidly, then less rapidly, and finally leveling out.

Figure 9 contains some empirical information about the relationship of city size to the ratio of export and local employment (E to L). Nonexport employment makes up about 30 percent of the total for cities of 10,000 population and about 45 percent for cities of 100,000. If these lines are extrapolated, they indicate a "local" employment ratio of zero for a population of four people—about the size of a family, all of whose employment is "outside"—and a ratio of 90 percent for a population as large as that of the United States as a whole, which just happens to derive about 10 percent of its national income from trade with other countries. Limited as this statistical information is, it corresponds with our natural supposition that the larger a community, the more nearly self-sufficient it is likely to be. The economic base multiplier is an index of this self-sufficiency.

The effect of time, or the maturing of a community, on the economic base multiplier would have to be shown by adding another dimenson to Figure 8a. Visualize an axis perpendicular to both the horizontal and vertical axes of this diagram, projecting backwards through the page. As we look farther along that axis, the slope of the L-curve (or its position, if we are talking about a line that is no longer straight) rises—slowly at first, then

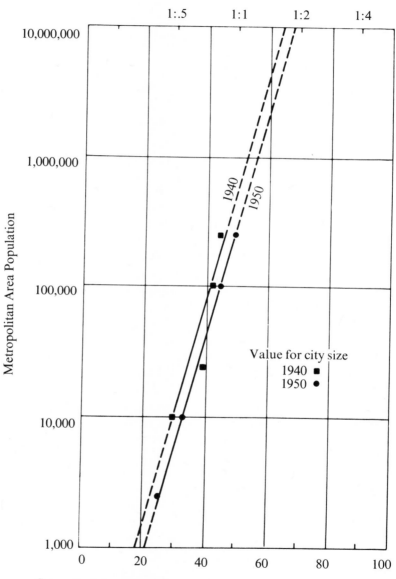

Export–Internal ratio

rapidly, then gradually leveling out, again in the fashion of a stretched-out letter *S*. This happens because a new community, being less well served by merchants, doctors, and other nonexport employment groups, simply spends less than normal cities do on locally produced goods and services. But, gradually, the local economy fills up as doctors, lawyers, hairdressers, TV repairmen, tax accountants, and the great variety of other service purveyors that we expect to find in a city decide to take up residence. At length, these activities are about as well represented as they are in the country as a whole, or at least in mature communities of the same population size.

It is important to remember that the *L*-curve from which the economic base multiplier is derived is not a straight line, but rather a surface that curves in at least three dimensions. We are speaking loosely, then, when we define L/T–and hence both g and the economic base multiplier–as a constant. Nevertheless, given the time and place, it is usually close enough to being a constant that it can be applied in practical ways. If a factory employing 1,500 people shuts down, for example, and the multiplier of the community is in the neighborhood of 2, we can be rather certain that another 1,500 people in the nonexport sector are going to lose their jobs (or that a greater number will go on short hours). We also know that a city which has seen a rapid increase in factory employment, and which has only 1.3 total jobs to export jobs, is probably going to witness a major increase in retail store construction, in the building of hospitals and schools, in addition to the fire and police forces, and so on, for the next several years as the town fills up.

LOCAL ECONOMIC STABILITY

The reason for interest in an economic base is that a city's economy is a magnification of its export businesses. If Company X flourishes, so do a

---

Figure 9.   City size and nonexport employment.

Source: Edward L. Ullman, "The Nature of Cities Reconsid-
ered," Papers and Proceedings of the Regional Science
Association, 9(1962), 7–23. *Note:* This study employed
the "minimum requirements" method of measuring
economic base. See text for description of this and
alternative methods.

wide range of other firms. If Company X has to cut back its payroll, many other companies in town will have to follow suit. When Company X sneezes, the town can get pneumonia.

But something can be done about this, and the theory of the economic base multiplier suggests the answer. Cities do have some degree of control over the kinds of industries that make up their economic base, and it is possible to use this influence to minimize the risk of economic instability for the city's merchants, public employees, doctors, house-builders, and other nonexport categories of working people. Granting that the economics of location, discussed in the preceding chapter, may indicate that City A is the best place for Company X to locate its factory, City A can effectively deter Company X from coming in, by means of zoning, taxes, withholding of necessary permits, and other means, including verbal dissuasion, while encouraging Company Y by opposite policies. Location economics indicate general regions in which a firm should operate, not necessarily the precise city. Four separate strategies are available to cities:

1. Preferring a firm with stable, long-run prospects to one whose market is likely to fluctuate. Denver, Colorado, counts as part of its economic base the regional offices of the U.S. Reclamation Service, the Forestry Service, the Bureau of Internal Revenue, and the Veterans Administration, all functions of the national government which are nearly immune to retrenchment. Seattle, Washington, looks primarily to Boeing Aircraft, which in turn depends heavily on enormous but often unpredictable contract awards by the U.S. Department of Defense. Flour milling is more stable than steelmaking, which in turn is more stable than the manufacture of automobiles. San Francisco's tourist business may well be a growth industry, but its restaurants and nightclubs respond rapidly and sharply to national economic reverses.

2. Encouraging diversity. A town with a large collection of relatively small firms in its economic base will almost certainly enjoy greater overall stability than a city of the same total size that depends on just one or two major export industries. If the diverse firms represent separate industry classifications—apparel, food processing, machine tools, plastics, pharmaceuticals, and so on—then an unfavorable trend in one area is likely to be offset by expansion in another. This is an application of the insurance principle—the law of large numbers—which says that we can predict what is going to happen in the aggregate—i.e., the overall mortality rate—even though we cannot hope to predict whether a particular Mr. A or Company

X will survive the year. The idea is not to put all of the community's economic eggs in one, single-industry, export basket.

3. Achieving diversity through size. Just because they are large communities, Los Angeles, New York, and Chicago are protected from massive economic instability—to some extent, anyway. Size is likely to bring with it the diversity of economic base activities that such cities enjoy, because agglomeration economies serve as a magnet that draws enterprises unselectively. Other location factors aside, export-type businesses are prone to favor a community where a large labor pool already exists, where there are numbers of specialized business services, where banking institutions are broadly informed about all categories of industry, and so on, regardless of just what it is that these businesses export.

4. Continuous promotion. When a secretary or a salesman quits, the personnel director of a company is supposed to be able to find a replacement right away. When the marketing director quits, it may take some time to replace him. When an export-employment company leaves town, it may be quite impossible to replace, but it behooves the town to have someone who knows how to look. In the same ways that a community may entice a more stable export firm to locate in its midst, the community can hope to induce Company Y to come in when Company X packs up and leaves. There will, after all, be vacant industrial space, a labor force, supplies of power and water, and a transportation terminal. The town searching for a firm to shore up its economic base may decide to offer some property tax concessions or other benefits. In any case, it seldom happens that a town has no hope of getting a new firm to take the place of an old one; the problem is usually whether there will be costly delays.

Most communities engage in continuous industrial promotion efforts, partly in the hope of overall expansion, perhaps, but also to make the inevitable turnover of firms within the economic base a smooth and efficient process. The better this function is performed, the less the community is likely to be aware of it, even though it is not clear whether it is properly a function of local government or of the local business community. Indeed, we could take the view of Dickens's Mr. Micawber that "something will turn up"; believing that our home town is inherently attractive, we could be content to let nature take its course. Promotional activity, however, is unlikely to do any harm (to the economic base) and may pay off once in a while, so most communities engage in it.

There is an apparent paradox in associating large community size with economic stability. The larger the community, as we have shown above, the more nearly self-sufficient it is, and the higher is the numerical value of its economic base multiplier. Therefore, the loss of an export job will put more nonexport people out of work in a large city than it will in a small city—which seems to say that the larger city will have a less stable economy than the smaller one. Does this contradict or offset what we have just said about the stabilizing effect of diversity-inducing urban size?

The answer is no. Let us compare two cities, one with a population of 50,000 and one with 500,000, and with the following economic characteristics:[1]

Population	50,000			500,000		
Employment type	T	L	E	T	L	E
Payroll ($ millions)						
before	100	50	50	1,000	750	250
after E loss	90	45	45	900	675	225
after E gain	110	55	55	1,100	825	275
Econ. base multiplier		2			4	
$(1/1-L/T)$						

In the smaller city, there is only one nonexport job for each export job (letting the size of the payroll stand for the number of jobs), but in the larger city there are three nonexport jobs for each one in the economic base. Thus, the multiplier is 4 in the larger city—total employment will decrease by 4 for every export job that is lost—while the smaller city's multiplier is 2.

Suppose, first, that each city suffers a decline of 10 percent in its export employment, a loss of 5 million payroll dollars in the small city and 25 million in the large city. True to the definition of the multiplier, the decline in total payrolls is 2 × $5 million = $10 million in the small city, and 4 × $25 million = $100 million in the large city. The *proportionate* loss is the same in each place, however—10 percent. The larger city is not less stable because of its higher multiplier. Man for man, it has more to lose from a decrease in export employment, but it starts out having proportionately fewer men engaged in export businesses.

The same conclusions appear when there is an expansion of 10 percent in the export employment of both places. Despite the disparity of

1. From Thompson, *A Preface to Urban Economics*, pp. 144–145.

the multipliers, the end result is an expansion of 10 percent in total employment. The small export tail of the larger urban economy does not really wag the dog.

THE NONEXPORT SECTOR: ACTIVE OR PASSIVE?

The Keynesian counterpart (see Figure 8b) to the theory of the economic base multiplier happens to be relevant to this question of stability. It is not just the algebraic similarity that warrants putting the two multiplier concepts side by side.

Referring back to Figure 8b, note first that Y, total national income (or GNP) is defined as the sum of consumption, C, plus investment, I. It is also defined as the sum of consumption plus savings, S. The two equations are also written in incremental form, which means that an increase in Y is made up of an increase in C, and an increase in I or S, for example. At the level of Y for which savings equals the amount that is being invested, equilibrium exists—Y_e in the diagram.

An increase or decrease in the level of investment, from one year to the next, results in a multiplied change in Y. The logic is very similar to the economic base idea that additional factory workers go out and spend their wages in grocery stores, thus giving rise to additional employment in the retail sector. In the Keynesian scheme, people who earn money making the new investment goods—machine tools, housing, and so on—go out and spend most of it, giving rise to new jobs and new income in other sectors of the economy.

The Keynesian multiplier, $1/(1-k)$, in Figure 8b, is based on an incremental constant and not on a simple ratio of absolute quantities such as L/T on the economic base side. That is, the constant term, k, is the ratio of a *change* in consumption spending to a *change* in total income, Y. Thus, although people may always spend 75 percent or so of any additional money they might receive, it does not follow that they spend 75 percent of all the money they receive. There is a distinction between the incremental or marginal propensity to spend on consumption, and the average propensity.

In the economic base diagram, Figure 8a, the average and incremental ratios of local employment to total employment are the same. This is be-

2. Since it is a chief preoccupation of economics professors to explain just why Savings and Investment are as equal as this set of equations says they are, we will not encroach on that domain in this book. Readers who are disinclined to take the equality on faith are referred to the nearest available economics major.

cause the L-function starts from the origin. In Figure 8b, the C-function intercepts (if extrapolated) the expenditure axis at some positive quantity, which means that even if total income were zero, some money would be spent on consumption—presumably from savings of some kind. Perhaps the most interesting question about economic base is whether the L-function should in fact have a similar positive intercept. That is, should we assume that in the absence of any export employment a community can exist in economic terms? Can people live by taking in each other's washing?

Another way of putting it, which is much more practical and which gets us back immediately to the question of local economic stability, is to ask whether the L-function is reversible. Does local employment really fall by the same proportion as export employment drops when problems appear in the economic base? People do have savings to draw on; they have fixed obligations with respect to mortgages and property taxes, for example; and there is only so much cutting back they can do in buying groceries. At least in the short run, the response to a drop in export employment may be considerably milder than the simple concept of the economic base multiplier would suggest.

Figure 8a might be a reasonable explanation of how Seattle grew from a population of 20 in 1851 to 531,000 in 1970, but Figure 8b might be more appropriate for describing how Seattle reacted to the laying off of many thousands of Boeing workers in 1968, 1969, 1970, and 1971.

To go back still further in our discussion, a city is a large collection of durable consumer goods—houses, schools, streets, hospitals, restaurants, police stations, water mains, and so on. An urban population does not readily pick up and move, and it is even less likely to do so if job conditions in other cities around the country are not much different. Ghost towns can be found scattered throughout the American West, mostly in the vicinity of worked-out mineral resources. Even in this century, small communities occasionally perish because of the extinction of a factory or government activity, or because young people just move away to the larger cities. But a community big enough to be called a city simply does not go out of business, because factors exist that tend to keep the L-function in Figure 8a irreversible.

The most important of these factors is the city itself—the physical city and, in particular, the existence of nonexport activities. New industrial concerns do not venture to locate in a wilderness—not in the twentieth century. The employees, up and down the line, would rebel at the thought of being put down in a place where there were no schools, no hospitals, no grocery stores, no water supply, and no houses. Though these things would come eventually, there would necessarily be a period of extraordinary privation. It is a question of which comes first, and these days it is the local sector of the economy that tends to be there before the export sector moves in.

This is quite contrary to the spirit of the economic base theory, which appears to give absolute priority both in time and in dignity to export types of business. First comes the goldminer or the logger, and then the general store, the dentist, and the schoolteacher, according to this logic. But today there must first be a housing tract, a shopping center, and elementary schools designed like posh motels and staffed with teachers holding all kinds of advanced degrees—then the factory moves in.

So, when we are talking in incremental terms, it almost seems that the nonexport sector of the economy is what attracts export employment, and not vice versa. An attractive community with a great diversity of housing, shops, offices, and public facilities is a greater magnet to manufacturing or other types of export employment than a deposit of raw materials or the existence of a transportation breaking point.

The implication is that urbanization proceeds by the enlargement of existing cities rather than by the emergence of new cities. Obviously, something must be wrong with this reasoning, because in 1900 there were scores of cities in North America that did not exist a century earlier. On the other hand, few, if any, new cities have appeared from scratch since 1900, so there may be something in the notion that nonexport employment comes first.

To resolve this quandry, we must consider the nature of people who migrate, now and in the nineteenth century. The urban settlers of the nineteenth century did, in fact, accept great privation. They were willing to live in clusters around factories, mines, and wharves, in makeshift buildings and without even rudimentary urban amenities. (Shortly, we shall raise some questions about why they would do this.) We would probably see new cities springing up in this century if people were willing to pioneer in the same way. But the urban pioneer has become an extinct breed.

What all of this means is that a community improves its economic stability by keeping its lawns clipped, by paying policemen enough so they don't steal, by taking not too much and not too little in property taxes, by having and enforcing building codes, by letting people shop or drink on Sundays if that's what they want, and, in general, by making itself a convenient, attractive, and reasonable place to live. A good place to live is a good place to work, and that is our twentieth century location theory, to an appreciable extent.

BOOSTERISM—"THE FASTEST LITTLE TOWN IN THE WEST"

We have said, in effect, that the economics of location do not guarantee that all the businesses which "should" set up shop in City A will actually go there. More and more of our economic activity is "footloose" in this sense. In several later chapters, we shall see why, on the other hand, City A may attract more factories, office buildings, stores, houses, and so on, than it "should" have—that is, why City A can get too large.

Add the fact that the size of a city as well as the blend of its enterprises is more or less under the control of the city itself, or of other government agencies, and we arrive at the problem of deciding how big a particular city really should be. If there is an answer to this question, it is far from simple, but we can say meaningful things about parts of the problem.

In Figure 10, the average benefit and the average cost of being a member of an urban community are related to the population of that

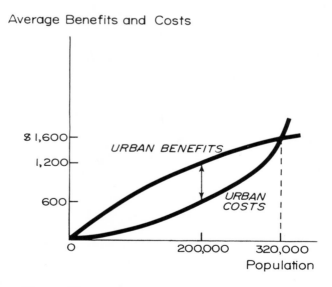

Figure 10. Optimum size for a hypothetical city.

hypothetical city. Because of internal and external economies of scale, and other benefits of urbanization, the line labeled "urban benefits" rises as the population increases, but the rate at which it rises gradually diminishes. Urban costs, however, start very low, rise at an increasing rate, and become greater than urban benefits when the population exceeds 320,000.

Urban costs are hard to measure in any systematic way, particularly if we must convert them all to money equivalents. And it is not at all certain that the average costs associated with urban size come to exceed the benefits at any likely level of poulation. Suppose that we are reasonably sure, for a particular city, that the lines do cross at a population of 320,000, however; we can then say it would be a mistake for the city to encourage expansion beyond that point.

Even if the lines never do cross, there may be a population level for the city at which the difference between average benefit and average cost is a maximum. This is the case in the hypothetical city of Figure 13 when the population is 200,000. Although the average benefit is only $1,200 at that point—less than the $1,600 that might be attained if the city grew to 320,000—the average cost is only $600. The average citizen has a surplus or profit of $600 by virtue of living in the city at that point. The optimum size for a city is the population at which this surplus is a maximum.

This optimum point may exist, and probably is more likely to exist, even though the urban benefit and urban cost lines never cross. There is reason to believe, in addition, that several optimum points of this nature exist along the scale of population growth for a particular city. Merely being aware of this set of possibilities regarding urban benefits and costs, however, does not tell us how big a city should be.

It does mean that we should take an interest in who is promoting the growth of the city, who is opposed to it, and why. The benefits and costs of urban expansion are not distributed in a uniform way over the whole population, but at almost any size level there are some people who stand to benefit by further growth, and these people may be in a position to encourage growth. On the other hand, people who stand to benefit from growth—including, at times, the bulk of the population—may not be aware of the opportunity or the methods to stimulate it.

The difficulty with applying the concept of Figure 10 lies not so much with the measurement of average costs and average benefits as with the fact that there is really no such thing as an average urban citizen, in the sense related to these costs and benefits. Growth affects different people within the urban economy in different ways, so some people will be more aware of the benefits than of the costs of expansion, while others will be stirred to point out the harm that expansion can do. Human nature being what it is, both boosters and anti-growth persons will apply their own views of things to the whole society; and since either point of view can be implemented through group actions—subsidies, advertising, protests, referenda to prohibit growth—the stage is set for conflict.

No one is in charge of seeing the thing whole. Perhaps local government should be looking objectively at the Figure 10 problem, but nonobjective pressures build up on both sides. The problem may, in fact, be objectively insoluble, because no one can say how much benefit to one person outweighs a cost that is borne by someone else. Does a dollar in profit to a downtown merchant count more than a one-minute delay for a thousand commuters, when both are attributable to increased city population? Does the greater land value of a new suburban shopping center outweigh the loss of sales by the older stores downtown? Where different people are involved, there may be no equitable way to subtract urban costs from urban benefits in calculating the optimum population level.

The problem of incidence—of who bears the costs and benefits—can affect an urban community even when that community is entirely passive in its attitude toward growth. These days, many people are reluctant to take jobs in New York City, for example, because housing is expensive, the streets are unsafe, and so on. An employer who needs a particular kind of skilled worker could offer higher wages to compensate for these disadvantages, but a merchant who needs more customers or a real estate investor who wants to see his property increase in value does not have a direct means to provide such compensation. A financial institution may decide to put its national headquarters in a massive new building near the heart of the city, to enjoy the access and the contacts of that location. But pity the man who works for some other company but who must commute through the throngs of people making their way to the new office building. New, potential migrants and firms see the city's promise through almost haphazard filters. No ones moves to City A or decides not to move there because that is "best for the City."

WHERE DO PEOPLE COME FROM?

We have already suggested that the creation and expansion of a city may depend to some extent on the willingness of people to move there or to remain there. Goldminers endured the privation of having no urban services to call upon, not even a supply of housing for purchase or rent. The early settlers in every community established in North America during the nineteenth century simply did without stores, dentists, theaters, hospitals, newspapers, and a long list of things to which many of them had been accustomed in other places, for a time at least. Today, in the absence of a pioneering proclivity, employees stoutly resist transfers to cities where the schools are of less than average quality, where the water tastes odd, where the downtown looks shabby, or where, in other respects, life promises to be less convenient.

The existence of a favorable location or a supply of raw materials in need of processing may thus be a necessary condition for the emergence of export industries and supportive nonexport activities, but it is not a sufficient condition. There must be a supply of people. On the other hand, the people may be there but not the jobs. Alaska possesses vast supplies of raw materials that the world has increasing need for, but migration from other parts of the U.S. to Alaska has been relatively slow—because it's cold up there. Large areas in Appalachia have seen their economic base—mining, primarily—eroded, but the people hang on.

Even if a sufficient *number* of people migrate to a new community, given the size of its economic base and the number of nonexport jobs that would be consistent with that base, the people who come may not have the kind of skills or aptitudes that the employment opportunities of the new city requires. The people who came to the present city of Seattle in 1851 to cut the tall timber were wheat farmers from the treeless midwestern prairie. Many thousands of Negroes came from the depressed sharecropping regions of the Southeast after World War II, seeking industrial employment in Los Angeles. In many ways, the people who come to a community may not match up with the employment opportunities there, in numbers or in categories of skill. The same is true of people who are born in a particular city. One of the things that cities do is to adapt human resources to economic opportunities. This function often seems to be performed inefficiently or even unconsciously, but the fact that there are cities testifies that it does get done somehow.

This cutting and fitting process is represented in Figure 11. To begin with, a basic employment opportunity appears somewhere on the map. It might be, for example, that settlement of a new agricultural hinterland has created the need for a river port to handle, and perhaps process, the produce of the region on its way to the world market. Or a body of iron ore might

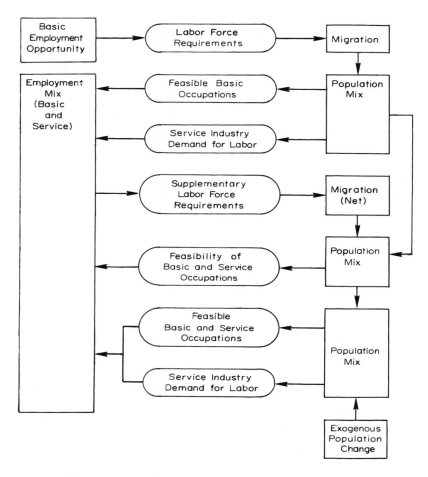

Figure 11.   Urban in-migration for a hypothetical city.

have been discovered, for which there is a market if the ore can be
appropriately processed. There is, in any case, a set of labor force requirements that stems from the size and type of this basic employment opportunity. So many grain merchants, dockworkers, steelmill hands, and so
forth are needed. In some fashion, the word gets out to the world at large,
and the first wave of migration to the city begins.

But who comes, and why? In nineteenth-century North America, there was a large pool of immigrants from an assortment of mainly European countries, whose destination was not Peoria, Illinois, or Wellington, Kansas, but just North America. They included Polish peasants, German intellectuals, British seamen, and Italian fishermen. They did not come because there was a job notice on a factory gate in Cincinatti, but because life was hopeless or beyond endurance in the old country. Thousands of Irish came because it seemed the only way to survive a devastating famine. Jews came to escape extinction in pogroms. Perhaps the majority came because they believed merely that life would be better and opportunities greater, though very few had actual promises of employment before they set sail.

Chinese were transported by the thousands to work on railroads, with no provision as to how they should live once the railroads were built. Africans came in chains, for jobs that other men simply refused to do. The native Indian was debarred from most of the new occupations in a land that had once been his, and his numbers were terribly reduced by massacre and famine. Coherent matching up of new jobs with people who could fill them was the least important factor in nineteenth-century urban population growth.

Following the arrows on Figure 11, early migration creates an initial population mix. There are so many men, so many women, and so many children. So many are between the ages of 20 and 35, so many 35 to 45, and so on. Some speak English, others German, and others Polish, Italian, Greek, Armenian, Lithuanian, or Basque. Some are Lutherans and others are Roman Catholics. Some are illiterate and others have been among the intellectual elite of another nation. Some are carpenters and others have a capacity for entrepreneurship. There may be twenty dentists, or none.

This population mix determines whether the basic industry of the new community is feasible. If the Polish farmer and the German journalist and the others can man the steel mill—and if they are willing to work together and share the community—then the initial economic potential of the community can be realized. Otherwise, it cannot.

The population mix itself gives rise to a schedule of needs for nonexport or service workers. There must be carpenters and masons to build the houses, doctors to look after work injuries and childbirths, clerks to sell yardage to housewives, preachers and newspapermen to keep an eye on the saloon-keepers and the city council.

People in the new community learn new skills, in proportions suited to the specific requirements of the town, or they migrate out. The word goes out for supplementary migration, to fill the gaps and to replace those initial migrants who do not adapt to community needs. The new wave of migrants joins the population mix of the first wave to give the community its socioeconomic cast. An initial equilibrium will be achieved between the list of basic and service jobs in the community, on the one hand, and the descriptive characteristics of the population, on the other. Perhaps there will be exactly as many Norwegian men age 45 to 60 as there are foremen's jobs in the steel mill, and perhaps all those men will occupy all those jobs. But probably not. One of the foremen may be British or Scottish. One of the Norwegian men may be a blacksmith. The diversity of people will be reconciled with the diversity of work through a process of education, adaptation, favoritism, and chance; and in the end, there will not be many more people of working age in the community than there are jobs for them to do. Very importantly, the number of housewives and children in the town will eventually reach approximately normal proportions, as bachelor migrants find brides and other migrants send for families initially left behind.

But that is not the end of it. People get older, learn different skills, have families, move away, and die. These are exogenous changes affecting the population mix. The mix of jobs will change, too, as industrial technology changes and as the service demands of the people in the community change. The processes of in- and out-migration, and of adaptation of individuals to employment opportunities, are continuous.

In the army, human beings are modules, "bodies" available to fill whatever role the situation demands. In urban communities, the personal characteristics of the population are important in two ways. First, they require that some equitable or at least acceptable means exist for deciding who does what job. Second, they imply a particular composition of demands for local, nonexport-type businesses and jobs. Episcopalian communities do not need Greek Orthodox priests. An Italian settlement would be better served by a pasta factory than by a Polish newspaper. A financial district with hundreds of female office employees is a natural environment for some beauty shops and dress boutiques.

Further, the makeup of a city's population affects the processes of government and the quality of its services. Streets in minority neighborhoods are very poorly maintained in many American cities because majority voters are able to secure preferential maintenance for their own areas. Elderly residents may team up in bond elections with single people and childless couples to defeat a proposal for school construction that school-age children badly need. If enough of a town's population feels a repugnance toward "hippies," the local police may show little restraint in harassing long-haired idlers. Big-city bossism and corruption during the nineteenth century often had its roots in a large immigrant population, willing to trade their votes for protection by a political patron. If there is an articulate elite in the city, the chances are good that the city will have an opera house, a museum, some public gardens, and so forth.

It is important, then, just what kind of people decide to come to live in a new, growing, urban community. And it is also important which group comes first. The first arrivals in a new community have opportunities that people who come later will not find. This helps to explain the willingness of nineteenth-century people to pioneer in new settlements, and the reluctance of people to do that now.

One of the principal opportunities inherent in the establishment of a new community is to speculate in land. We shall have much to say about urban land values in later chapters, but it can be said here that many of the westward migrants in nineteenth-century North America were enticed by the thought of buying land cheap and holding it until the growth of urban populations multiplied its value many times. Many family fortunes were established in this way, even though a larger number of people were probably fleeced by land promoters. Lots in Cincinnati that sold for 83.5 cents an acre in 1789 were worth $382 a square foot in 1839.[3] In 1810, a lawyer newly arrived in Cincinnati accepted a copper still in lieu of money from his first client (whom he saved from hanging for horse theft); the copper still was traded for 33 acres on the outskirts of town, land that soon became the heart of the business district.[4] The extraordinary growth of land values in cities has long been a source of wonder and discontent, but it is an unmistakable phenomenon, and it means that reasonably astute—or lucky—early arrivals can prosper while escaping the labor that "economic base" and "nonexport" industry opportunities seem to imply must be done. The best "jobs," after all, are positions of proprietorship.

There are several other opportunities for proprietorship that early arrivals in a community can stake out for themselves and preserve for their families through succeeding generations. Banking is one, not so much because the banker can charge interest to borrowers, but because he can

3. Green, *American Cities in the Growth of a Nation*, p. 49.
4. *Ibid.*, pp. 49–50.

extend credit to new businesses, or withhold it, on the basis of other advantages to himself. That is, he can favor those applicants for financing who want to buy or rent land which the banker, in another role, controls. He can become a partner in new enterprises, or suggest family members or friends for the boards of directors. That is, he could in the frontier community. The banker could play the role of a "gatekeeper." In a similar way, the proprietor of a general store could influence the creation of new businesses, because the merchant could extend credit, which most new arrivals needed, and thus act very much as a bank.

Early arrivals could, of course, constitute themselves as a government and police the activities and the population of the growing city in very direct ways. Unwanted competitors for businesses that the founding families controlled could be, and often enough were, hounded out of town. And tax money could be used to provide public improvements that selectively favored the holders of political power—roads giving access to land such people owned, riverfront wharves, construction contracts awarded to friendly corporations, and so on.

Most of these opportunities have long since been foreclosed by political and tax reforms, which helps to explain why the pioneering spirit seems to have flagged. Land speculation depends, ultimately, upon very rapid actual increases in population if it is to be really rewarding, and with the virtual end of mass immigration from Europe early in the twentieth century, the prospects of a new city emerging almost overnight became remote.

Thus, counting jobs in the export and nonexport sectors tells us rather little about how cities come into being and grow. What matters more, aside from the sheer technology of new basic industry and its locational preferences, is the people who come—their motivations, their cohesion, and their grasp of what a new urban settlement is all about. People who come first can, and probably intend to, lay claims to proprietary and power positions. Later arrivals, if they behave and are otherwise acceptable, can work for wages, but they will have a difficult time getting into business for themselves. The latecomers, unless they bring with them unusual talents or independent wealth, will have to settle for the least desirable jobs and the slenderest prospects for improvement, even in categories of wage labor. In the United States, it has been the Negro who came last to the city. The economic hierarchy of a city is related to its history, though there is evidence of a gradual change in the distribution system for urban opportunities.

MEASURING ECONOMIC BASE

To make practical use of the economic base concept, two things need to be determined for a particular city: the approximate numerical value of the economic base multiplier, and the identity of those firms or activities that make up the economic base. A variety of techniques can be used to do either or both of these things.

First, we must note that any measurement system must relate to categories of available data if the system is to be useful. Table 6 shows the total employment of the United States for 1971, broken down by "industry" according to a classification scheme that has been standardized for

Table 6

United States Labor Force, by Industry, 1971

	Millions of people	Percent non-agricultural
Total population	207.05	
Civilian labor force	84.113	
Employed	79.120	
Unemployed	4.993	
Agriculture	3.387	
Employees on payrolls of non-agricultural establishments	70.699	100.00
Mining	.601	.85
Contract construction	3.259	4.61
Manufacturing	18.610	26.32
Durable goods	10.590	14.98
Nondurable goods	8.020	11.34
Transportation, communication, electric, gas, and sanitary services	4.481	6.34
Wholesale trade	3.855	5.45
Retail trade	11.319	16.01
Finance, insurance, and real estate	3.800	5.37
Services	11.917	16.86
Federal government (civilian)	2.664	3.77
State and local government	10.194	14.12

Source: U.S. Department of Commerce, *Survey of Current Business*, May, 1972, p. S–13.

many statistical purposes. It is actually a summary classification system, because more detailed categories are actually used in the collection of data about the economy. The classifications rest upon a set of detailed definitions so that data gatherers and data users alike may be as clear as possible about what things are included in "contract construction" and in "real estate," for example.

There are several things of general interest in Table 6. For example, agriculture employs only 4.28 percent of the employed civilian labor force—fewer than the number of people unemployed or the number in wholesale trade. But food distribution is classified largely as wholesale and retail trade, and food processing is counted as "nondurable goods manufacturing." The whole category of manufacturing accounts for just over a quarter of total nonagricultural employment and only 23.52 percent of all civilian employment, and it is worth remembering that a large fraction of "manufacturing" employees today hold white-collar jobs. Of every eleven employed people, two work for government—and this excludes people in military service.

These comments are a little beside the point—for the moment, at least. The industrial categories of Table 6 are shown because they are the most familiar and practical categories to use in developing information about a particular city's economic base.

Table 7 shows employment information for a hypothetical city, organized by industrial categories along the lines of Table 6, and arranged to permit the calculation of the economic base multiplier. The first method for making this calculation is called the "whole industry method," which means that all the employment in particular categories is counted as "export." In this example, all manufacturing jobs, all wholesale trade, and all federal government employment is assumed to make up the export base, while every other job category is assumed to be local or nonexport. These export categories add up to 43,000 jobs out of 100,000, giving us a multiplier for this city of 2.33. Since employment information by these industry categories is usually available for each city, from the latest census at least, this method of measuring the base is very simple.

The "value added method," shown next in the table, is the most complex and the most expensive to do, but in some respects it is the "ideal" method. This method requires a survey of all the business firms in the community, asking how much of their value added—the difference between the selling price of their products and the amounts paid to other firms or

Table 7

Alternative Methods of Computing the Economic Base Multiplier for a Hypothetical City

Industry category	Employment (000)	Whole industry method	Value added method		Minimum requirements method	
		Number of export jobs	Percent export	Number	Minimum number	Excess jobs
Construction	5		20	1	5	0
Manufacturing	29	29	90	26	2	27
Transportation	10		50	5	3	7
Wholesale	8	8	75	6	1	7
Retail	12		25	3	12	0
Finance	5		40	2	2	3
Service	13		10	1	10	3
Federal government	6	6	83	5	0	6
Local government	12		0	0	12	0
Total	100	43		49		53
Economic base multiplier (1/% export jobs)		2.33	2.04		1.89	

governments—was generated by sales outside the community. This picks up export activities from industry categories that basically serve the local market but do some business outside the city as well, such as the category for transportation. The result of the survey is a set of percentages that can be applied to the total employment in that industry, giving us the number of export jobs. This method also catches local sales by industries, such as manufacturing, which are primarily exporters. For example, the illustration shows that 90 percent of the value added in manufacturing was sold outside, so that the number of export jobs in that category of industry is 26,000 rather than the 29,000 counted in the whole industry method. Government agencies, too, must be included in such a survey, even though the proportion of "sales" within the city must obviously be based on an alternative concept, such as the population of the city in comparison with the population of the region served by that government agency. Summing up the number of export jobs indicated by the survey gives us a multiplier of 2.04.

A major difficulty with the value added method is that a local supplier, say, of parts, to Firm X is counted as being engaged in a nonexport activity even though all of those parts are ultimately exported by Firm X. This distortion can be removed by careful analysis of the information produced by the survey. The situation that it represents—namely, that a local economy is a web of firms trading with each other as well as with the consuming public and the outside world—suggests an entirely different method of analysis, called input-output studies, which will be described in the next chapter.

The third method of calculating the economic base multiplier, also shown in Table 7, is called the "minimum requirements method." The idea is that every city presumably requires at least a certain percent of its work force in each industry category, just to meet the local needs. If we look at the actual breakdowns of employment for a large number of cities, we will find, for example, that no city has less than 5 percent of its work force engaged in construction, or less than 2 percent in manufacturing. Thus, we write down 5,000 jobs as the minimum local requirement in construction for our hypothetical city of 29,000 workers, leaving zero export jobs in this category, and we write 2,000 local jobs for manufacturing, leaving 27,000 classified as export, and so on through the list. If we find a city among those we are comparing that has no federal government offices at all, we count all 6,000 federal employees in the hypothetical city as part of its economic base. When we add up these excess jobs for a total of 53,000, the indicated economic base multiplier for our hypothetical city works out to 1.89.

The multipliers obtained by these three methods are different. The whole industry method, which is "quick and dirty," gives us the highest multiplier in this illustration. The minimum requirements method, which is harder to apply but only slightly better in concept, gives us the lowest figure. The value added method, which gets very close to actually identifying export jobs if the study is carefully done, produces an intermediate value of the multiplier. Again, these are hypothetical numbers, so the multipliers produced by the three methods do not necessarily have the relationship we found.

Each of the three methods identifies the export industries. Quite obviously, the whole industry method requires us to assume which industry is in the export category and which is not. The other two methods make more qualified statements. For example, the value added method in the illustration says that some construction jobs are paid for by people outside the city, and that 10 percent of the manufacturing output is sold locally. The minimum requirements method implies that manufacturing is 93 percent export ($= 27/29$), while 100 percent of federal government employment is basic. Either of these methods lets the people in the community be aware that a new firm in the service or finance categories may contribute to the economic base, depending on precisely what that firm does.

There is an additional method that is used to identify the sectors of the local economy that contribute to the economic base but that does not provide a meaningful economic base multiplier. This is called the "location quotient," and it is illustrated in Table 8 for the city of Denver, Colorado, in 1970. It does not depend on a survey of local businesses nor upon comparisons with other cities. Instead, it measures the extent to which employment in a given industry category in the city exceeds or falls short of the pro rata share of that city in total national employment. In Table 8, these shares are expressed in terms of dollar earnings rather than numbers of jobs, but the principle applies either way.

First, the total earnings by sector are listed for the city and (not shown) for the nation as a whole. Then the city earnings are calculated as a percent of the national total, for total earnings and for each industry category. In 1970, Denver's total earnings were .6771 percent of all

Table 8

Location Quotient of Earnings for Denver, Colorado, 1970

Industry sector	Total earnings ($ Million)	Denver earnings as percent of U.S.	Location quotient of earnings[a]
Total earnings	4,295.5	.6771	1.0000
Farm	13.3	.0696	.1030
Federal government			
civilian	298.5	1.0447	1.5444
military	114.4	.6748	.9963
State and local government	424.8	.6381	.9419
Manufacturing	808.4	.4591	.6780
Mining	74.3	1.1293	1.6635
Contract construction	322.3	.8344	1.2315
Transportation, communication, public utilities	386.9	.8608	1.2726
Wholesale and retail trade	858.7	.8140	1.2020
Finance, insurance, and real estate	281.3	.8471	1.2500
Services	704.6	.7314	1.0797
Other	8.0	.4363	.6552

Source: U.S. Department of Commerce, *Survey of Current Business*, May 1972, p. 44.
[a] Equals figure in preceding column divided by .6771 (except for rounding errors).

earnings in the United States. Its earnings in federal civilian employment were 1.0447 percent of such earnings for the nation as a whole, and in manufacturing its earnings were .4591 percent of the national total. If Denver had no more and no less than its pro rata shares of federal civilian employment and of manufacturing, the percentages in these categories would both be .6771. Consequently, Denver had 1.5444 times its pro rata share of federal civilian employment and only .6780 of its pro rata share of manufacturing. Clearly, Denver tends to specialize in federal civilian employment and to spend part of what it earns from the rest of the nation this way for manufactures that it must import.

The first and third columns of Table 8 give us a good idea of how important different types of employment are to the economy of Denver. About 65 percent (1/1.5444) of its federal civilian earnings would have been received if Denver had only its pro rata share of that employment, so 35 percent, or about $105 million, is attributable to this export of federal services to other parts of the country.

The greatest degree of specialization in Denver is in the mining category (it is not clear whether this is based on the export of ores or on the earnings of mining enterprises headquartered in Denver). However, only about $30 million in earnings (40 percent of $74.3 million, since 1/1.6635 is 60 percent) is attributable to specialization in mining.

Earnings by industrial classification are available or can be compiled in much greater detail than that shown in Table 8. This means that location quotients reflecting relative degrees of specialization can be computed for many subcategories of employment, and the community can see in this way how its economic fortunes are tied to each of the many kinds of enterprise within it. In Denver, for example, the importance of federal civilian employment and of wholesale and retail trade (where specialization accounts for about $146 million in 1970 earnings), may be interpreted as evidence of relative economic stability, since national activity in these fields tends to fluctuate less than in manufacturing.

The location quotient understates export activities, very severely in many cases. Hence, it does not provide a good estimate of the economic base multiplier. For example, most manufactured goods actually are exported outside the city where they are made, but the location-quotient concept, in effect, sets aside about 25 percent of a city's total employment for "local manufacturing," since manufacturers play that role in the total economy (see Table 6). On this basis, only a small fraction of manufacturing jobs, even in heavily industrialized cities such as Detroit, would qualify as "export" employment.

DISCUSSION QUESTIONS

1. The early economic writers known as Mercantilists believed in maximizing exports and minimizing imports as a national policy. Would this be a wise *urban* policy?

2. What are the basic limiting factors to the ratio of local employment to total community employment?

3. In your community, who engages in recruiting new export-type industries? Of what particular type? With what inducements?

4. Does the economic base multiplier phenomenon create special moral responsibilities for the managers of export-type business firms?

5. Who would benefit most from an expansion of the economic base in your community? In what way? Who might be likely to suffer?

6. The economic base mechanism exists primarily because service industries are attracted to the vicinity of export-type industries. Does this enhance *national* economic welfare?

7. Describe the principal migration waves that contributed to the growth of your community. Who came from where, and why? Is there a noticeable relationship between these migration waves and today's occupational categories?

8. How does national economic growth, other than through population increase, affect the economic base of particular cities? Does this imply that developing nations should have a particular kind of urban policy?

9. Try your hand at designing a questionnaire and survey plan for measuring the economic base of your community. What do you think the major problems would be in securing the cooperation of employers? How would you explain to reluctant respondents the purpose and value of your survey?

10. Find an example of a community whose economic base was exceptionally vulnerable when the oil crisis arose in 1973.

SELECTED REFERENCES

Bose, Nirmal K. "Calcutta: A Premature Metropolis." *Cities*. Scientific American. New York: Alfred A. Knopf, 1966.
A clear and detailed account of the difficulties created when people whose occupations are restricted by ancient religious or cultural traditions live together in an urban metropolis where job opportunities are determined by economics and technology.

Gans, Herbert. *The Urban Villagers*. New York: The Free Press, 1962.
A sociologist's description of life among low-income Italian-Americans in present-day Boston.

Glazer, Nathan, and Daniel P. Moynihan. *Beyond the Melting Pot*. Cambridge, Mass.: MIT Press, 1970.
Two sociologists revisit ethnic communities of New York to update their earlier description of several distinct patterns of social organization and the struggle for economic advancement.

McKelvey, Blake. *The Urbanization of America, 1860–1915*. New Brunswick, N.J.: Rutgers University Press, 1963.
Historical account of several urban phenomena—architecture, transportation, the labor movement, schooling, and the arts—in the U.S., organized topically rather than by city.

Park, R. E., E. W. Burgess, and R. D. McKenzie (eds.). *The City*. Chicago: University of Chicago Press, 1925.
An early statement of principles of urban sociology in the United States.

Pfouts, Ralph W. (ed.). *The Techniques of Urban Economic Analysis*. West Trenton, N.J.: Chandler-Davis, 1960.
An exposition of the economic base multiplier concept and its uses.

Wade, Richard C. *The Urban Frontier*. Cambridge, Mass.: Harvard University Press, 1959.
Colorful histories of the new way cities got started in the American West, with insights concerning the development of public facilities.

5

EVOLUTIONARY
EXPANSION OF
THE BASE

THE BEST-KNOWN CITIES, either in our own nation or elsewhere in
the world, generally seem to fit the description of transportation breaking
points. They tend to be places near the mouth of a river or at the junction
of major interior rivers. Some are waterfront cities at the railhead of land
transportation networks, and others fit the pattern only by being closely
linked with specialized port cities.

There are, of course, many major cities that are not and never have
been ocean or river ports. Las Vegas, Nevada, is an example. Bakersfield,
California, is a landlocked city that nevertheless functions as an industrial
center. For other cities, such as Denver, location along a river does not
reflect historical origin as a port. And the textile mill towns that dotted
New England in the last century depended on their rivers for factory
power, not for transportation.

In any case, port cities are particularly deserving of study because they
are so prominent in the history of urbanization, because a number of them
have grown spectacularly, and because they have been around for a long
time. If we want to know something about the dynamics of an urban

economy, the major port city is a good textbook. The lessons, it turns out, apply to all types of cities.[1]

CINCINNATI

The Mississippi River links the entire central portion of the United States—a rich agricultural area—with world markets through the port of New Orleans. The Ohio River is a branch of the Mississippi River system that flows through the fertile northeastern segment of this great region. The Miami River is a major branch of the Ohio that extends northward, about midway between the Ohio's eastern source and its junction with the Mississippi. Where the Miami and Ohio Rivers meet is the modern city of Cincinnati.

Settlers intending to farm this great region generally found it easiest, in the beginning, to reach it by flatboat, poled upstream from New Orleans. In 1788 a group of these people selected a stretch of land near the junction of the Miami and Ohio Rivers as a place to tie up their boats. They cleared nearby land and began to raise crops. Their marketable surplus had to be transported downstream to New Orleans for transshipment to world markets. And the household goods they purchased with this export had to come back to them by the same route. Thus the boat landing became a funnel through which goods flowed in two directions and in ever-increasing volume. Around it grew a town that was given the name Cincinnati.

This early town was not simply a society of stevedores. Farmers in the region, not wishing to accompany their produce to New Orleans and see what they could get for it there, sold it to merchants in Cincinnati who assumed the risk and did the business of putting this produce on the world market. The merchants also imported household goods on their own account and resold them to farmers in the region. It was difficult to conduct this business in cash, because the United States at this time was a debtor nation, obliged to pay for imports with the little hard money it had. This scarcity of currency was particularly severe along the frontier, and hard money was very difficult to come by. Cincinnati merchants augmented the

1. The following sections draw extensively on Green, *American Cities in the Growth of a Nation*.

effective money supply by granting credit to farmers in the region, making it possible for new settlers to get started and for early settlers to expand their activities.

Among the early residents of Cincinnati was a physican by the name of Drake who qualifies as a prototype of the urban "booster." On his own he published a book about the agricultural opportunities of the region—in glowing but only modestly exaggerated terms—which was widely read by people in the eastern United States and elsewhere who dreamt of becoming prosperous, self-sufficient farmers. The book told them how to fulfill these dreams, and it brought large numbers of new settlers. As they filled up the hinterland of the new city, Cincinnati itself expanded and prospered. Dr. Drake served his community and the region in many other ways, not least by publishing a medical journal on which frontier families came to rely almost exclusively in the absence of opportunities to see a doctor or visit a hospital. Dr. Drake's medical college made a start at providing new doctors for the mushrooming population of the Mid-west.

In the 1820s, river transportation was transformed by the appearance of the steamboat. While steam power was an aid primarily in traveling upstream rather than downstream, the effect of the new technology was to cut substantially the time, risk, and cost of linking the agricultural interior with world markets. The ultimate cost of Midwest produce on the world market was reduced sufficiently to increase the demand for it, and the cost of household supplies and other goods required for the development of the interior fell sufficiently to make settlement even more attractive to pioneers. From both sides the steam boat stimulated the growth of the region and its river ports.

The new technology had an additional impact on Cincinnati. There were mechanics in the city who became adept at repairing steam engines, and from this knowledge soon began to manufacture engines, not only for steamboats but also for distant factories—a sugar mill in New Orleans, for example. A machine tool industry was born. Cincinnati also became a shipbuilding center, the most active in the West.

Coal and iron were available in Cincinnati's hinterland, so the growth of manufacturing was not simply an offshoot of the port activities. But the city very soon began to specialize in a particular form of manufacture—food processing, especially meatpacking, where scale economies made possible by the vastness of the hinterland and the constantly improving access to Eastern and world markets gave rise to large industrial enterprises. Cincinnati secured rail links to the eastern cities to supplement the river and canal routes it first depended on, and the railroads helped protect Cincinnati from demise during the Civil War, a fate which New Orleans, at the mouth of the Mississippi, did not escape.

In the 1830s, Cincinnati instituted compulsory, tax-supported schooling, paved its streets, took municipal control over the water supply, and set up a police force. These things were not done without opposition and delay, and there were other problems, too. Animosity toward German immigrants boiled up into violence, and freed Negroes who had settled in the city before 1829 were driven out by harsh racial laws. Rapidly expanding factories gave rise to an urban proletariat class, and discontent began to emerge when it became clear that most of these wage laborers would remain wage laborers all their lives. (Until this time individual factory workers tended to believe that in due course they would start their own factories and become employers themselves, and this made them tolerant of temporary discouragements and abuses.)

Up to a point, Cincinnati illustrates many important aspects of the relationship between a city and its hinterland and of the internal economic and social dynamics of a modern urban community. The experiences of Detroit were remarkably similar: it was by stages, a port city giving access to the frontier, a repairer of steamships, a builder of engines and wagons, and finally a center of spectacular specialization in automobile manufacture, an industry for which its very origins predisposed it. Chicago is the same story in bigger type: a lake port at the junction of an intensive network of rivers, canals, and later railroads which funneled the vast output of its hinterland through the city; a processor of foodstuffs and other regional exports; an importer and then a manufacturer of goods required for the further development of the region, especially agricultural machinery; a reception center for floods of immigrants making their way toward the frontier; and the inventor of mail-order retail distribution, which made the city of Chicago the department store of the agricultural Midwest.

At the mouth of the Mississippi River, New Orleans could regard the whole center of the continent as its hinterland. But New Orleans did not thrive, as many expected it would, by virtue of its remarkable location. It played but a small role in fostering the development of the hinterland and in making best use of that region's output. For a variety of reasons, New Orleans lost or eschewed the functions of other port cities until it was left with little more than the stevedoring business. In 1850, though New Orleans controlled the export of cotton in a geographical sense and cotton made up 60 percent of the exports of the United States, 40 cents of every cotton dollar went to merchants in New York.[2] Cities like New Orleans are a necessary counterpoint to stories of places like Cincinnati, because the vigor of port cities is not guaranteed by geography. The economics of urbanization are more complex than that.

THE REGIONAL ECONOMIC FIELD

The fact that a city starts as a port does not mean that it continues thereafter to rely for its livelihood on activities directly related to transshipment. Those functions tend to erode. But the hinterland behind the port is likely to foster new activities in the port which, if things go well, ultimately produce an urban community that is very little dependent on the character of its region.

The concept behind this transition is that of the "regional economic field," which is analogous in some respects to the idea of an electromagnetic field. The region, or hinterland, has within it certain resources that can be exploited—fertile farm land, timber, mineral ores, and the like. The cost of extracting these resources and getting them to markets or processors in other parts of the world is less than the prices established in those markets, so that exploitation is a profitable undertaking. The region also has within it, or comes to have, a population which has an effective demand for items of consumption that must be brought in from distant sources. Since resource exploitation and the serving of a dispersed consumer market requires a certain amount of capital equipment, the hinterland also stands in need of initial and continuing investment import for development. That is, farmers need plows, miners need ore-crushing machinery, families need houses and some stores, and so on. The hinterland will require some kind of internal transportation system.

So the newly realized economic value of resources in the region generates impulses for a number of secondary and tertiary activities to be undertaken, some or most of which may be attracted to the port city. This scheme is illustrated in Figure 12.

2. *Ibid.*, p. 73.

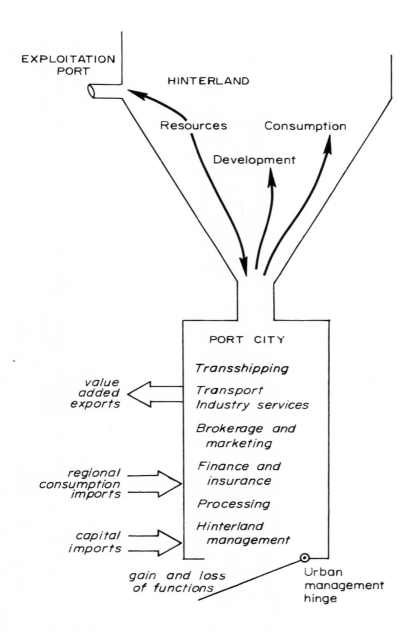

Figure 12. The port city and its hinterland.

The port city is initially an "exploitation port," a place engaged almost exclusively in loading the region's produce—in nearly raw form—for long-distance transportation. It is the mouth of a funnel through which, by a kind of economic gravity, the natural wealth of the hinterland, or things produced by means of that wealth, flow outward. In its earliest days, Seattle was no more than a wharf and a sawmill at the foot of a steep path. Trees cut on the surrounding hills slid down the path by the literal force of gravity.

Virtually all of the (FOB) price received for exports from the exploitation port is regional value-added. The trees, ore, and fertility of the land are there by nature, and the labor force of farmers, miners, and loggers, as well as the people of the port, resides in the region. The region begins with a significant surplus in its "balance of payments," since arrangments have not been made for the import of consumption goods. What becomes of the surplus can be a matter of consequence to the region, as it represents monetization of the natural, physical endowment. It is windfall liquidity that may be "squandered," sequestered, plowed back, or converted into amenity infrastructure. Each of these uses deserves a comment.

"Squandering" implies that money is spent in a foolish way. There is a showplace house in Virginia City, Nevada, which was built and furnished at great expense by one of the successful exploiters of the great silver lode located just across the street. Whether one admires the taste it embodies or not, there is no denying that the house is an example of conspicuous consumption. Other lucky prospectors gambled away their wealth, or had their pockets picked by shady ladies, or were murdered for it. Whether they each got value for money or the money was finally spent in a useful way is a subject for debate. One form of squandering that is nearly incontrovertible is the absorption of new money into transactions balances because of localized inflation. When the price of an egg goes to five dollars and a shovel sells for one hundred, potentially useful liquidity evaporates.

By "sequestering" we mean that the money value of the resources is realized by people outside the region—absentee owners, financiers, or governments. Remittances to people left behind by the early settlers fall in the same category. The recipients may, of course, put some of the funds back to work in the region, but the money will not be conveniently available to meet strictly local demands for credit—to pay workmen to build a wharf, for example, or to purchase sawmill machinery.

"Plowing back" presumes that the region, including the port, has potential that justifies further investment in land, infrastructure (roads, for example), or inventory. It also implies that there is an identity or an affinity between those who initially get the cash in hand and those who perceive investment opportunities.

"Amenity infrastructure" means things like schools, paved streets, a drainage system, a hospital, and even a jail. These things require investment, but they do not expand the export capacity of the region. Hence they are consumer durable goods and, mainly, public rather than private goods. They are not frivolous, because eventually the community would have to provide them, but they are postponable. Unless the townspeople as a collectivity have put the region's resources into public ownership, the town will have to borrow investment funds from private individuals, land-developing organizations, or other levels of government, which means that the route of wealth from its embodiment in natural resources to reincarnation as urban structures may be complex. The more indirect the route, the less likely it is that the new city will reflect the wealth of the region.

For a community to borrow capital funds means that it must have a tax base so that the debt can be serviced and the operating costs of the community can be met. As in the case of getting capital funds, there is the problem of linking the exploitation of the region's resources with the fiscal powers of the urban community. There is no economic principle, and generally speaking no legal principle either, that dictates the share of hinterland wealth that will be received by the urban communities that serve the hinterland. Spending power generated by regional resources may or may not flow through the town, where it may or may not settle down and may or may not be taxable under the customary powers of local government.

The box labeled "port city" in Figure 12 lists several functions that must be performed to link the region's resources to the world market. Transshipping is the function that defines the city in the first place, but other functions may be attracted. Boat and train crews must have at least temporary housing, and ships or locomotives will need to be serviced and repaired. Merchants who buy and then resell the region's produce might find the new port city a convenient place to do business. The same or other merchants may handle the commodities wanted by people living in the hinterland. Merchants will need to finance their trade—that is, they must borrow money to buy crops from the region's farmers, for example, and hope to repay the loan when the goods are sold in distant markets. Part of the risk they bear is insurable, so this function is also attracted to ports.

"Processing" is a large collection of functions—sorting, purifying, storing, packing, fabricating, assembling. Before bauxite becomes quilted aluminum foil on a cardboard roll in an eye-catching box with a serrated metal edge, many physical things happen to it. Between the rough log and a pocketpack of facial tissue lie a series of mechanical operations. Any consecutive set of processing functions may be drawn to the port city. Processing of consumer or capital goods destined for the people in the hinterland—manufacturing their plows or baking their bread—can also be functions of that town.

"Hinterland management" refers to business activities, such as planning logging operations or keeping payroll records for a mine. It also means financial activities, such as the operation of a mining stock exchange, and government activities that relate to the region as a whole, such as the registering of land titles, planning and regulating development, or supplying services such as schooling or medical care for the dispersed population of the hinterland.

The region and the port city itself import consumption goods, consistent with the concepts of the economic base multiplier and comparative advantage. There is also an import of capital for the development of the region—railroads, mining equipment, and so on—and public or private consumer durables such as houses and schools. The physical and financial form that capital imports take, and their scale relative to the size and requirements of the region, depend on the sophistication of the regional economy. Early California goldminers slept in bedrolls on the ground, but later San Francisco townspeople imported whole, prefabricated houses from Boston. Probably some of the long-term financing for the houses was also secured in Boston or New York, but San Francisco very early developed its own capital market.

There is a trap door in the port city box in Figure 12 through which economic functions enter and leave. We have not listed any functions that are agglomeration-oriented rather than hinterland-oriented, but such things become feasible when the new city is a going concern. Manufacturing of items for the world market—like Seattle's airplanes—may be attracted by the local labor force irrespective of material resources in the hinterland. Denver's federal offices serve a region vastly larger than the city's basic raw material hinterland—the mountains it nestles beside. Vancouver, B.C., does not owe its emerging motion picture-making business to the timber and coal that nature put in its hinterland, but rather to the size and character of its urban community. New York City's teeming office buildings deal with the needs and products of the world and not simply in McIntosh apples from upstate. Hartford, Connecticut, does not print its insurance policies on paper made from hinterland timber.

Hinterlands may give birth to cities, but a city may outgrow its dependence on the hinterland and become self-justifying. Beyond that, it may ultimately be the city that gives the resources of the hinterland their value. There are "milksheds" around major urban areas, where dairy cattle are kept to supply the adjacent urban market. The milk is not exported, which makes it different in kind from the timber, ore, and wheat that a port city initially helps to forward to the world market. The urban community may also lay claim to the hinterland as a recreational preserve, running head on into the region's exporting industries.

There is a hinge labeled "urban management" on the trap door in Figure 12. The idea is that if someone were in charge of the city's destiny from the time it began as an exploitation port, deliberate efforts could be made to strengthen, expand, and perpetuate the functions of the city. Communities in the North American West tried very hard in the nineteenth century to bring in railroads as supplementary links to world markets and as more intensive capillaries for the hinterland. They lobbied to be made regional capital cities and tried, by subsidizing operas, building fine hotels, and sprucing up the shopping districts, to become cultural and commercial capitals. They watched jealously the emergence of new exploitation ports.

But sometimes they generously waved new business aside. In the 1870s, Abilene, Kansas, made a present of the cattle transshipment business to Wichita, because the rowdy habits of cattle-drivers and the less endearing attributes of the cattle themselves were not the kind of environment the people of Abilene wanted. Urban management can exclude as well as promote.

CENTRIPETAL AND CENTRIFUGAL FORCES

Efforts by what has been called "urban management" to direct the economic destinies of the city are affected by economic forces that tie the city and its hinterland together. It is convenient to group these under the headings of "centripetal" forces, which pull activities inward, and "centrifugal" forces, which pull activities away from the exploitation port. The result of all these forces is a gradual transition of the local economy from exploitation port—or port of entry for settlers—to "freestanding" urban activities, meaning a situation in which the city is no longer dependent on a base of nearby raw materials. Figure 13 shows this transition.

The centripetal forces are not necessarily felt in the sequence shown. In the order shown, however, this is what the terms used to identify centripetal forces are intended to mean:

Regional processing.— Manufacturing activities involving the region's raw materials exports or its consumption goods imports, pulled to a single point by potential economies of scale.

Regional service center.— The City serves as retail and wholesale center for the region, and is the place to which regional residents must come for personal services, business services, and local government functions. Economies of scale explain this inward force, also.

Regional administrative center.— The development of the hinterland may be directed by people who reside in the city; likewise the marketing of its output and the distribution of its consumption goods.

Nonregional decision center.— The city may become, for reasons unrelated to its hinterland, a headquarters location for firms having interests in other regions.

Interregional transport node.— Transport and communications networks may select the city as a nodal point because of its size and location, making it a "way station" for highway and airline traffic, telephone messages, and so forth.

Agglomeration seekers.— Footloose processing and administrative activities are attracted to a large city because of the variety and quality of supporting and incidental services available there.

Innovation spin-offs.— New products or processes emerge as by-

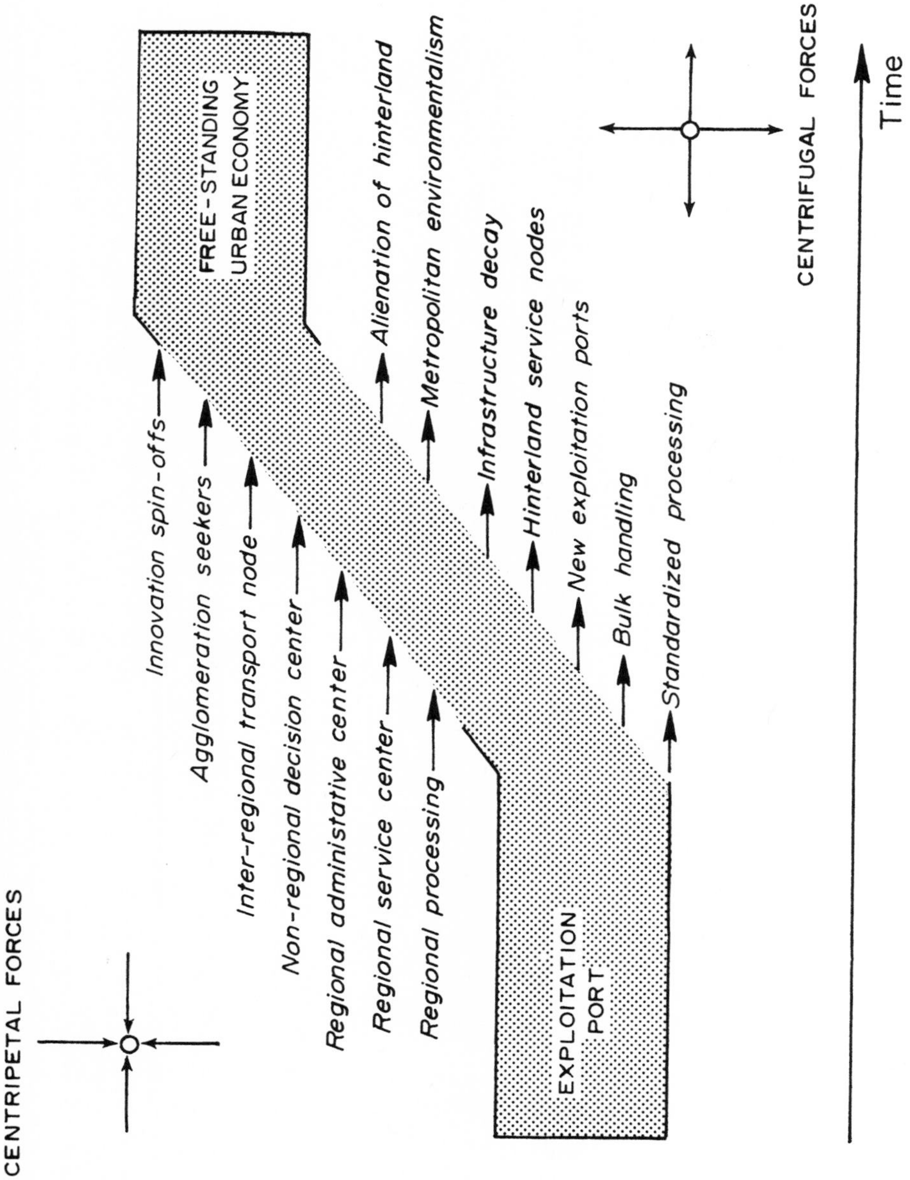

Figure 13. Dynamic forces in the regional economic field.

products of earlier economic activities (to be discussed under the next heading).

These forces overlap, of course, and there is no intention to suggest that they all bring certain quantities of new employment to the city. They are simply parameters the "urban manager" may try to deal with in pursuit of the goals the city identifies for itself.

The other parameters, the centrifugal forces, take economic activity away. There are seven of them:

Standardized processing. — When a local processing activity has established itself in the world market and no longer requires the intense communication exposure and innovative environment of the port city, it can shift to a free-standing industrial location in the environs, for the sake of lower wages, less congestion, cheaper land, ease of expansion, and so on.

Bulk handling. — Scale economies and the ability to forecast heavy demand for output far into the future may lead resources and consumption-goods handlers to create specialized port facilities at some other location. Thus we see large new facilities laid out to handle imported automobiles, exports of wheat, coal, lumber, and other commodities.

New exploitation ports. — Perfection of the hinterland's internal transportation system, growth of the world market, and intraregional political pressures may lead to the emergence of new exploitation ports, which may then acquire other urban attributes.

Hinterland service nodes. — When the hinterland population attains density and stability, retail and personal service facilities will decentralize to some extent.

Infrastructure decay. — The goods handling facilities of the original port city will become obsolete and run down. If they are not replaced, a shift of many port-related activities may follow.

Metropolitan environmentalism. — As the community realizes that its livelihood is being earned in other ways than simply by helping to extract value from hinterland resources, the people in it may decide that early port and processing activities are more of a nuisance than a blessing and may encourge them to migrate to other locations. Obsolescence of the facilities, reluctance of entrepreneurs and the city alike to renew these facilities in the same location, and technological improvements in transportation may combine to get these once-essential activities out of sight without appreciable increases in total transportation costs.

Alienation of hinterland.— This means legal, not sociological, alienation. If hinterland resources come to be owned by people outside the region, the decision to shift management functions relating to hinterland resources may be readily taken. A "foreign" corporation presumably has less compunction about consolidating plants or offices, thus moving jobs away, than a home-based enterprise would have.

Again, these centrifugal forces overlap to a degree, and they have no necessary time sequence. As they come into play, the city is progressively detached from the natural environment that caused it to emerge.

INNOVATION SPIN-OFFS

The brief economic history of Cincinnati at the beginning of this chapter, and the other anecdotes about particular instances of innovation, point to a tendency for urban economies to enlarge their economic bases almost spontaneously. In Cincinnati, as in Detroit and other places, port activities led to the repair of steam engines, which led to the manufacture of engines and machine tools, which led to mechanization of processing activities and a great expansion in the value added by the urban labor force.

Other examples abound, and they add up to evidence that there are specific avenues for innovative expansion. The city of Coventry, England, epitomizes the process.[3] It began as a Benedictine monastery in the Middle Ages, earning reknown as a producer of fine woolen cloth and a center for trade in that cloth. But it was not suitably located for industrialized textile manufacture, so by the early nineteenth century, it relied mainly on two occupations requiring skilled handwork—the weaving of fancy ribbon and watchmaking. Free trade, and the import of cheaper goods from Switzerland and France, had a devastating effect on Coventry's economy, but they did not deprive it of its skilled labor. In the second half of the century, the

3. See R. W. G. Bryant, "The Reconstruction of Coventry," in H. W. Eldredge (ed.), *Taming Megalopolis* (New York: Doubleday, 1967), Vol. II, pp. 765–783.

manufacture of sewing machines and bicycles appeared there. Bicycles have been the precursor of the automobile industry in several places, and so it was in Coventry. By the beginning of the twentieth century, Coventry was the home of Daimler, Singer, Sunbeam, Hillman, Humber, and other automobile firms. The old association with ribbon weaving was revived with the introduction of chemical fibers—rayon and vicose—and the research labs required in those new industries gave the city an entree into the limitless chemical industry. During World War II, automobile plants in Coventry were converted to the production of airplanes. Farm machinery and electrical products are additional spin-offs from the particular kinds of skilled work that have characterized the city since its founding.

The bicycle business explains several things about the prodigious industrialization and urbanization of Japan.[4] With the opening of trade in 1858, the European bicycle became a poular consumer import in Japan. Since it was not feasible to return bicycles to the factories when repairs were necessary, craftsmen in the cities began to acquire the skills necessary to make repairs. Sometimes it was necessary to replace a part and, in the absence of stocks of spare parts or discarded bicycles to cannibalize, repairmen learned how to make the necessary parts. Some came to specialize in particular parts, and eventually there was in a city like Tokyo a manufacturer of every bicycle component. A mercantile firm was then able to assemble completely Japanese-made bicycles from parts made in countless small enterprises, and Japan was soon a major exporter of bicycles. The bicycle skills and the scheme of production were the groundwork for the automobile industry. Indeed, to the present time, this subcontracting system characterizes the Japanese economy.

In Los Angeles, employment in the aircraft industry fell from 210,000 to 60,000 in one year following the end of World War II.[5] Shipyards laid off all but 18,000 of their 90,000 employees. Petroleum ceased to be an export product because of greatly expanded local consumption. The economic base theory foretold dire things for Los Angeles, but in 1950 its total employment was greater than ever before. Many new enterprises were born there, mostly as offshoots of existing industries.

For example, an engineer in one of the aircraft companies went into the business of producing sliding glass doors—a new type of product but

4. The following is based on Jacobs, *The Economy of Cities,* pp. 145–150.
5. *Ibid.*, pp. 151–154.

one related to his skills—and found a large national market for them. Other innovative products that envigorated and enlarged the Los Angeles economy were mechanical saws, bathing suits, shoes, underwear, cameras, hospital equipment, and scientific instruments.[6] Nothing generically new, perhaps, but each a sufficient improvement on older products to win a place in the national and international markets.

One manifestation of the spin-off process, then, is the application of skills necessary for an existing product in the perfection of something else. Another form is mercantile: a man who knows there is a market for widgets—because he is a merchant in touch with industrial and consumer needs in other parts of the world—and who knows how widgets are made and how much they would cost to make locally, goes into the manufacturing business. The transition from the mercantilist period to the industrial age involved such application of merchant's information—and capital—to the establishment of factories. "First you sell it, then you make it," is the slogan of this economic progression. The imagination of merchants is not necessarily limited to trade.

The jobs that an urban economy is capable of doing and the products or services it is capable of selling to the world are not limited to those mechanical activities that convert a regional raw material into a staple commodity for the world market. It has always been true, but it is vastly more significant in this century than before, that traditional forms of economic activity must be supplemented or replaced with things not yet seen. Innovation has become imperative, and while the history of innovation is most encouraging, we can say that the process is neither automatic nor completely spontaneous.

LOCAL INDUSTRY LINKAGES—INPUT-OUTPUT ANALYSIS

Product innovations seem very often to arise out of interindustry linkages. That is, Firm A supplies gizmos to Firm B which uses them in the production of widgets and, in so doing, becomes familiar enough with their specialty to develop a "general theory of gizmos," which suggests new ways in which they can be used. Perhaps by making a small variation they have a new type of product, a gimmick, which they find they can sell to Firm C or to the housewives of the nation. Then they are in the gizmos *and*

6. *Ibid.*, p. 152.

the gimmick business, so the city in which they are located has a larger economic base.

An interesting example is the evolution of the product line of the 3M Company.[7] It began as a very small company supplying sand to foundries, where the sand was used in metal casting. The two owners of the firm decided to try their hand at making sandpaper, not something they had invented, but an additional use for the thing they knew about—sand. They did not know much about making sand stick to paper, but they undertook to learn. They learned so much about adhesives that they were able to produce good masking tape, which is paper coated with a kind of glue—but no sand. Generalizing their knowledge of adhesive tapes, they eventually produced Scotch tape, electrical tape, and magnetic recording tape. Not forgetting sandpaper, they branched out into the building business with roof coatings that look very much like enormously magnified sandpaper—granules adhering to a coated sheet. As their company learned more about the construction business, many other building materials were introduced.

A firm that supplies parts or materials to some other firm has a strong incentive to diversify, and its specialized technical knowledge may suggest innovations that will permit it to diversify. A flow of innovations is of increasing importance in urban-based economic growth, so interindustry linkages among local firms often bear watching.

This brings in by the back door an important refinement of the economic base idea, namely, the concept of input-output analysis. The basic or export firms in a local economy almost always purchase some inputs locally—electric power, components, repair services, telephone service, trucking, and so forth. These supplier firms are really part of the economic base, though they sell their output locally, because they must expand if the export industry itself expands. The expansion of these supplier firms is quite independent of and in addition to the expansion of nonbasic or local service activities which are accounted for by the economic base multiplier.

A numerical illustration will help, though it must be simple because the mathematical principles involved are somewhat difficult. Suppose, as shown in Table 9, that Firm A sells $60 worth of output to consumers, $2 worth to Firm B in the same community, and $3 worth to itself, to be used

7. *Ibid.*, pp. 52–53.

Table 9

Input-Output Linkages
(In dollar's worth of product)

Supplier of input (producer)	Purchaser of output			
	A	B	C[a]	Total
A	3	2	60	65
B	4	2	40	46
C[b]	58	42	0	100

[a] Consumer or export demand.
[b] Local households supplying labor and consuming imported goods.

up (like gasoline used by trucks delivering gasoline) in the process of producing Product A. Firm B sells $40 worth of its product to consumers, $4 worth to Firm A, and $2 worth to itself.

The total output of Firm A, then, is $65 worth of Product A. In producing this, Firm A requires $3 worth of inputs from itself, $4 worth of Product B, and $58 worth of services from local households (labor and capital). Similarly, Firm B's output is worth $46, made up of inputs of $2 from Firm A, $2 from Firm B, and $42 from households.

What will happen to this simple economy if the consumers of A increase their purchases from $60 to $61? Since Firm A uses up 3 units of its own output for each 60 units sold to consumers, it must produce 3/65 of a unit additional for internal consumption in order to get one more unit net for consumers. But to produce 3/65 of a unit of A, an additional $3/65 \times 3/65$ is needed, and so on. In other words, A must expand its output by

$$1 + 3/65 + (3/65)^2 + (3/65)^3,$$

which looks endless but actually is finite, because we can express the relationship between total output, T, and consumption, C, as follows:

$$(60/63)T = C; \quad T = C(63/60); \quad T = C(1.05).$$

So, if $C = 61$, $T = 64.05$, assuming fractional quantities can be used.

If Firm A does not require inputs from any other firms or people, who in turn require inputs of Product A, this is the end of the story. Expansion of Firm A's sales to consumers requires a somewhat larger increase in its total output.

But Firm A, in the example, requires inputs from Firm B. To be exact, each dollar's worth of Product A requires $4/65's worth of Product B, and every $1 increase in the output of B requires an additional $2/46's worth of Product A. So Firm A will have to expand its output, not only by the one unit that consumers are asking for, but also by an additional fraction of a unit that will be used up in the process, plus an amount required by Firm B in the production of extra input for Firm A, plus an additional internal use fraction of that, and so on. Firm B must expand, not only to meet the first-round increase in purchase by Firm A, but also for its own internal use of its own product, B, plus the extra amount necessary to yield that second-round increment, and so on. It takes a good computer to solve even the simplest problem of this sort, but we can eventually calculate the expanded output of both A and B that is required to provide a one-unit increase in the final consumption demand for Product A.

The important lesson is that industry linkages, resulting from input-output relationships, cause indirect demands to arise from any increase in direct, final-user demand. The number of export jobs, to go back to economic base terminology, increases in several interrelated industries whenever the export demand for one of the increases. Not only that, but the various industries involved in such a system will need to expand in different proportions. It makes a difference to the community whether the increased export sales are from Firm A or Firm B. Clearly, if we had an up-to-date input-output simulator system in our city, we would be able to predict in much more interesting and useful detail the consequences of expansion or contraction in one of the basic industries. We could be fairly precise, for example, about power consumption and the number of trucks using a particular bridge. For a number of reasons, however, the application of input-output analysis to metropolitan economies is quite uncommon.

Whether or not we have an input-output table for our city, the principle of interindustry linkages tells us important things about the local economy. Suppose, for example, that in the example above, the city had neither Firm A nor Firm B in its economic base originally, but that Firm A selected the city as a location for its new factory. The question then arises whether Firm B will be attracted to the same city because of a form of agglomeration economy. If agglomeration economies are very strong, then the city will not only get a new industry, but a complex of new industries, several of which may be exporting part of what they make and all of which will be doing some form of business with each other. An early study of the potential effects of a new steel mill employing 11,700 workers, estimated that agglomeration economies would bring another 77,000 jobs in metal-working industries to the area of the new steel mill, followed by 70,000 new nonbasic jobs for a total of 158,700—a very substantial multiplier.[8] Individual firms, then, are not the appropriate units of account for economic base studies, and if our information about the local economy is limited primarily to identification of the export sector, our use of that information should be tempered by recognition of the agglomerative, multiplier, and innovation phenomena associated with interindustry linkages.

Table 10 presents some of the data from a study of interindustry linkages in the Philadelphia area, a study which falls far short of being a complete input-output effort, but which reveals many things about the strengths and weaknesses of the area's economic base. The (a) portion of the table lists the average amount of their inputs that surveyed firms purchased locally, by industry category. The study was limited to manufacturing. Textile firms bought only 23 percent of their largest input item in the area, and apparel manufacturers were least integrated into the local economy, getting only 6 percent of their principal input there. The printing industry, however, purchased 63 percent of its major input locally, and the petroleum industry bought 73 percent.

The (b) portion of the table lists the percent of firms' outputs sold locally, by a more detailed industry breakdown. Thread-making firms sold 44 percent of their output in the Philadelphia area, but wooden-box makers sold 75 percent. Paper-bag makers, however, sold only 5 percent locally. Makers of industrial gasses sold almost all their output within the area. A firm with a high percentage in either portion of this table could be presumed to be drawn to the Philadelphia area because of internal location economies or because of external economies involving other types of inputs, such as labor or services.

The augmented effects of the decision by an export firm to locate in a

8. Walter Isard and Robert E. Kuenne, "The Impact of Steel Upon the Greater New York-Philadelphia Industrial Region," *The Review of Economics and Statistics* (November 1953), pp. 289–301. Cited in William H. Miernyk, *The Elements of Input-Output Analysis* (New York: Random House, 1967), Chapter Three.

Table 10

Indicators of Philadelphia Manufacturing Linkages

(a) Percent of Largest Input Purchased Locally

Industry (selected)	Average percent
Food	42.6
Textiles	23.0
Apparell	6.6
Lumber	54.8
Paper	12.7
Printing	63.6
Petroleum	73.0
Rubber	7.8

(b) Percent of Output Sold Locally, By Value

Industry (selected)	Percent
Thread	44
Cordage	17
Wooden boxes	75
Bags (paper)	5
Engraving	67
Industrial gases	99
Paints	25
Glue	55
Ink	33
Bolts, nuts, etc.	30
Electroplating	81

Source: Gerald J. Karaska, "Manufacturing Linkages in the Philadelphia Economy," in L. S. Bourne, ed., *Internal Structure of the City* (New York: Oxford University Press, 1971), pp. 259 and 262.

community are summarized in Figure 14. Based on its own location determinants, Firm A decides to locate in the community or to expand its activities there. This changes the employment mix of the local economy, at first merely by adding the employees of Firm A but taking into account the indirect requirements of the firm's own production.

There follows a first round of indirect demands for other industries that are of two types: firms linked by input-output technical factors to the new export firm, and nonexport firms that are needed to supply the consumption demands of Firm A's employees. Each of these other firms then faces a location decision, resting essentially on the significance of agglomeration economies. The nonexport industries normally feel a very strong pull toward the location of an export industry such as Firm A, so we might expect them to appear. Technically linked firms—B, C, and so on—may feel various degrees of pull from agglomeration opportunities. Some may decide to locate in the community while others may decide to

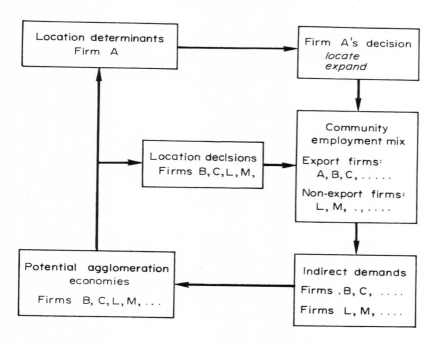

Figure 14.   Combined effects of economic base and input-output multiliers.

maintain the linkage but at a distance. The location decisions made will alter the employment mix of the community further, which will induce second, third, and other rounds of location-expansion decisions by all the linked and nonexport firms, including Firm A itself, until an equilibrium is reached. This scheme should be viewed as a supplement to our previous discussion of the role of local services and migration in shaping the ultimate mix of the local economy.

DISCUSSION QUESTIONS

1. Would a "city state," isolated by transportation or political barriers, be likely to evolve in the manner described in this chapter?

2. Were world population growth and economic development important preconditions to the urban evolution scheme described in this chapter?

3. What should be the operating principles of a "regional development bank" intended to meet the monetary needs of a promising raw-material area? Whose interests should such a bank serve?

4. What is the optimal fiscal system for a developing region and its urban center(s)? Would this be consistent with national fiscal traditions?

5. What are the pros and cons of allowing large resource or transportation firms (for example, mining or railroad companies) to dominate the development pattern of a new resource region and its urban centers?

6. When a mature urban community begins to crowd out regional resource exploitation for the sake of recreation and other amenities, how should the conflict of aims be resolved?

7. Identify the major export-type firms in your community that do not depend directly on regional resources.

8. Identify the major resource-based industries that appear to be migrating away from your community.

9. What is the relationship between input-output linkages among

sectors of a local community on the one hand, and the economic base multiplier on the other?

10. Are local input-output linkages a reflection of external economies? Do they help to define the geographic extent of a metropolitan community?

SELECTED REFERENCES

Friedmann, John, and William Alonso (eds.). *Regional Development and Planning*. Cambridge, Mass.: MIT Press, 1964. Part III, "Theory of Regional Development."
Articles on urban location theory, economic base, and regional economic growth.

Green, Constance M. *American Cities in the Growth of a Nation*. New York: Harper and Row, 1957.
Historical accounts of the establishment and growth of a number of U.S. urban centers, illustrating location economics concepts and the evolution of both basic and service sectors of local economies.

Jacobs, Jane. *The Economy of Cities*. New York: Random House, 1969.
Lively description of the growth of many business enterprises which benefited from urban agglomeration economies, tied together with a set of theoretical perceptions.

Kindleberger, Charles P. *Economic Development*. New York: McGraw-Hill, 1965.
A representative textbook on the principles of economic development, including the concept of the capital-output ratio and the low priority of urban capital formation.

Miernyk, William H. *The Elements of Input-Output Analysis*. New York: Random House, 1967.
A very readable introduction to the concept and mathematics of input-output analysis.

Wade, Richard C. *The Urban Frontier*. Cambridge, Mass. Harvard University Press, 1959.
Colorful histories of the way new cities got started in the American west, with insights concerning the development of public facilities.

6

WHAT GOES WHERE— THE PATTERN OF URBAN LAND USES

IT FOLLOWS from this entire discussion of export and nonexport jobs, and the evolution of the economic base and input-output linkages, that the economic activity of the city is diverse. There are many different occupations, each one requiring space and location for work and for housing. The spatial arrangment of all these users of urban land may be perfectly tidy and discrete, with all the factories nestled together in the southeast quadrant and the grocery stores tucked away in the northwest, for example. Or it may be thoroughly lacking in order, like a child's box of toys. More significantly, it may reflect an order that is not immediately apparent. Whatever the pattern, we next want to show that it has some effect on the quality of work that the city does for the economy as a whole and on the quality of life for the people within it.

GEOGRAPHIC DIRECTION

There are several dimensions to a study of urban spatial arrangement. First, we have to note that these arrangements are relative and not absolute. That is, compass direction is not important; the schematic maps that we can use for this study do not need arrows pointing north. Perhaps we may conclude that factories and houses should be located in opposite directions from the center of town, but we will not produce any strong indication about what should be on the east side and what on the west side. This is not a trivial observation, because it means that an area of indeterminancy exists in trying to decide which land use pattern is best.

Any particular urban area, however, has its own geography. There are hills or mountains, streams and gullies, prevailing winds, districts with poor drainage, subsurface conditions that will support high-rise buildings in one area but not in another, scenic lakes or woodlands, large stretches of flat land, and sometimes significant political boundaries. Pre-urban land ownership lines turn out to be important, too. It is virtually impossible to create a theory of urban land use arrangement that takes all these factors into account. What we can do is to present some theories for land-use arrangements in a "featureless plain," and then treat specific geographic factors as modifications.

DENSITY

One of our dimensions, then, is relative direction. Another is density, the number of occupants or workers per acre, or the ratio of building floor area to land area. It is useful to think of density not as an overall average but as a frequency distribution. For example, a community with 360,000 people and 9,000 acres of land has an average density of 40 people per acre, but this average might derive from very different arrangements:

(a) 120,000 on 1,000 acres (density 120 per acre), plus
     240,000 on 8,000 acres (density 30 per acre)

(b) 240,000 on 3,000 acres (density 80 per acre), plus
     120,000 on 6,000 acres (density 20 per acre)

In fact, any number of alternative arrangements are possible, including, of course, a uniform distribution with everyone at 40 people per acre. The frequency distribution of residential density has an important influence on the spatial pattern of retail and public facilities and on the nature of the transportation system. The frequency distribution of occupational densities—the number of workers per acre—likewise influences the pattern of land uses. Office work often implies rather high densities and factories mean relatively low densities, and this fact may influence their relative locations. In turn, the transportation system of the city, and possibly its amenities, are affected.

LAND-USE CATEGORIES

Our third dimension for the study of urban spatial arrangements is the diversity of land uses, the number of user categories that we consider significant. This can be quite a long list; we can, for example, distinguish convalescent hospitals from geriatric rest homes and see whether they exhibit separate locational tendencies. But for a start, a list of major categories will do. Table 11 shows the results of a study of land use in a

Table 11

Average Distribution of Land by Principal Use Categories,
48 Large U.S. Cities

Use category	Percent of	
	Total land	Developed land
Total Developed	.770	1.000
Residential	.296	.390
Industrial	.086	.109
Commercial	.037	.048
Road and highway	.199	.257
Other public	.153	.197
Total Undeveloped	.230	–
Vacant	.207	–
Underwater	.023	–

Source: John H. Niedercorn and Edward F. R. Hearle, "Recent Land-Use Trends in Forty-eight Large American Cities," *Land Economics* (February 1964). Reprinted in Larry S. Bourne (ed.), *Internal Structure of the City* (New York: Oxford University Press, 1971), p. 122.

Note: Data are based on a survey made in 1963.

number of cities in the United States, using only five categories of developed land and two for undeveloped areas.

Even in this simple breakdown there are several points that the student of urban affairs should note with care. Residential uses take up the largest share of urban land, but less than half. The internal transportation system (not including parking facilities) occupies more than a quarter of all developed land. The public sector is directly responsible for 45 percent of all developed land in this survey (road and highway land plus other public land). Only about 16 percent of the developed land is used for private sector employment-generating activities (industrial plus commercial). Though commercial activities are strategic in the land-use scheme of the whole community, they occupy less than one-twentieth of the land, land that nevertheless becomes very valuable as a result of being useful for such activities.

In the survey, 23 percent of all the land was undeveloped. Some large fraction of the vacant land category is accounted for by the inclusion of as yet unurbanized land on the fringes of a city but within its political boundaries. Vacant land within the built-up city is almost always to be found, however, despite economic pressures for putting it to use. Underwater "land" is included in the survey, partly because it is often subject to being filled, and is thus part of the inventory of potentially usable area.

DENSITY BY LAND USE

The study from which Table 11 is taken also developed information on residential and occupational density, and changes in these densities. These are shown in Table 12, and are interesting benchmarks despite unavoidable limitations in the data. The sample is limited to twelve cities, those with earlier land-use survey information and without major changes in area through annexation. The "early" surveys were made at different points in time for the different cities, on the average about ten years prior.

The residential density works out to about twenty families per acre, assuming 3.5 persons per family, and there is a perceptible downward trend. The decline in industrial density—based on numbers of manufacturing employees—is proportionately greater, while commercial density shows an increase. "Commercial" here does not include many activities associated with office buildings.

Table 12

Average and Incremental Densities for Land-Use Types
in Twelve U.S. Cities

Land use	Residents or employees per acre		
	Time of survey		Incremental[a]
	1963	"Early"	
Residential	67.25	76.75	16.94
Industrial[b]	30.85	36.20	29.41
Commercial[c]	81.82	81.37	21.27

Source: See Table 11.

Note: Data are based on a study made in 1963. The twelve cities, selected on the basis of the existence of land-use studies suitable for comparison and the absence of major annexations between the studies are: Boston, Buffalo, Cincinnati, Cleveland, Detroit, Miami, Minneapolis, New York, Neward, Pittsburgh, Providence, and St. Louis.

[a] Based on twenty-two cities, including the above twelve. The ten additional cities, which had earlier land-use servey information but which experienced significant annexation in the interim are: Chicago, Dallas, Dayton, Long Beach, Los Angeles, Oklahoma City, Portsmouth (Virginia), San Antonio, San Francisco, and Seattle.

[b] Based on manufacturing employment and industrial land area.

[c] Based on employment in wholesaling, retailing and selected services, and commercial land. Finance, insurance, real estate, and professional services are not included.

Differences between cities in the distribution of land to broad land-use categories are reflected in Figure 15. There is enough variation to raise the question of whether any particular set of principles is involved in deciding how urban land is used, though each situation seems to be "explained" by particular circumstances. Detroit, a younger and more automobile-oriented city, has almost twice the proportion of land in use as public rights of way as does Philadelphia, where the narrowness of downtown streets is a clear reminder of colonial times. For all of its well-publicized freeways, Los Angeles uses less land for roads than New York City, but New York's gridiron street plan is recognized as an inefficient way to carry traffic. And the figure for Los Angeles does not include parking lots—which are considerably more abundant there than in New York.

Both Los Angeles and New York take honors in the "institutional and open-space recreation" departments, in contrast to the characteristically manufacturing-oriented cities of Detroit and Pittsburgh, though the reasons are not obvious. The commercial land category in New York is just slightly greater than in Detroit, suggesting the great compactness of those activities in "Fun City."

Residential densities, shown at the bottom of Figure 15, are markedly lower than the averages for twelve cities from the 1963 survey referred to

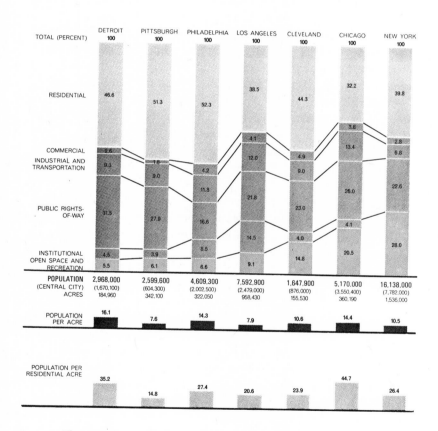

Figure 15. Land use in U.S. metropolitan regions.

Source: Charles Abrams, "The Uses of Land in Cities," *Scientific American* (September 1965), p. 154. *Note*: Population is for 1960, except Chicago (1956) and Detroit (1953).

above (see Table 12), though Cleveland, Pittsburgh, and New York are included in both sets of data. The principal explanation for this is that information in Figure 15 is for metropolitan regions—which can include several counties and even cross state boundaries—while the 1963 survey was directed to the political jurisdiction of particular cities. The suburban areas, with their low densities, bring the metropolitan area averages down.

There is another reason why we might expect different sets of cities to have different residential density averages. A city that has recently grown in population by a substantial amount tends to have a diminishing overall density, if we consider the suburbs as well as the central city. This is because new areas are developed at much lower densities—with fewer housing units per residential acre—than we find in the older city. This is the meaning of "incremental" density in Table 12. For that sample of twelve cities, where the total population divided by the total number of residential acres was 67.25 in 1963, population per acre in land then being added to the residential inventory (in the same political jurisdiction) was only 16.94—one-fourth of the overall density. Using our 3.5 persons-per-family yardstick, this means the new areas had something less than five dwellings per acre, while the average for the city as a whole was about twenty.

Incremental density in industrial employment appears to presage a continuation of slow decline: either more land in use for a stable number of manufacturing workers, or a declining number of workers using the same supply of industrial land. Commercial density increments are very much lower than average density and seem to reflect a contradictory trend. (Additional cities are included in the incremental data.) New commercial land required per employee is nearly four times the average amount so used. Since the information in Table 11 is from a limited data base, extensive factual generalizations from it would not be warranted, but it does illustrate the concepts of average and marginal densities of residence and employment in a realistic context. Indeed, given the rather obvious importance of such indicators of urban land-use trends, it is surprising and disappointing that information about density is not more generally available.

DOES THE LAND-USE PATTERN MATTER?

An entomologist ought to be able to explain why he does not classify a spider as an "insect." Similarly, we are interested in describing and categorizing urban land-use patterns because such patterns are controllable and they affect us in various ways. But the urbanist and the entomologist —and anyone who pretends to scientific objectivity—must keep an open mind and not assume at the outset that the distinctions they are studying will finally turn out to be worthwhile. Maybe a helter-skelter city is really no better or no worse than one where the spatial arrangment of activities follows a clear pattern. Even this would be useful knowledge, although it might seem to repudiate the whole inquiry.

Our problem is to see how far we can go in representing the "good city" on a map. A distinguished architect, Victor Gruen, finds an answer in the Old Testament: "In the beginning God created the heaven and the earth. And the earth was without form," going on to say "from the very beginning of time, we find the urge to separate disparate functions."[1] On the cover of Gruen's book is an urban land-use plan, with a place for everything and everything in its place, in a smooth pentagonal wheel. It is offered as a restoration and a furtherance of Divine intent, for all these years, mankind, "in an unholy conspiracy with the powers of evil" has been "recreating chaos where there was (thanks to the Biblical six days of separating water from land, etc.) order."[2] That seems to make planning of cities a moral necessity; for many of us, a secular basis for guiding the development of a city might be prefereable.

The separation of land uses, which is what city planners do, using the instrument of zoning, is presumably a means to an end rather than an end in itself. That is, by sorting out various land uses within a city, something intrinsically desirable is accomplished. But people desire various things, and urban studies have progressed far enough for us to recognize that no single goal has unquestioned priority. Here is a brief description of several criteria for urban land-use patterns which occur frequently in discussions of the subject:

Efficiency.— Normally this is taken to mean that land uses are so arranged that the aggregate expenditure by the community for internal transportation is minimized. Without attaching some conditions, such as minimum density or a density-transportation cost trade-off, this criterion implies that the best city is one where everyone and everything is crowded

1. Victor Gruen, *The Heart of Our Cities* (New York: Simon and Schuster, 1964), pp. 32-33.
2. *Ibid.*

together in one big room—obviously not an appealing arrangement. The minimum transportation-cost criterion also begs the question of how the savings thus achieved are to be distributed. For example, the crowded cities of Hong Kong and Seoul may be efficient according to this criterion, but we do not know whether the resources saved by this crowding are put to a desirable use.

Fiscal profit. — If the real property tax is the basic revenue source of a community and population-oriented services (education, hospitals, and so on) are its principal expenses, then the local treasury is best off by having as much land as possible occupied by expensive business and industrial buildings and by having as little land as can be managed occupied by lower-income, child-raising families. Since land uses that are less profitable in this sense must be somewhere else, this criterion involves neighboring communities in an indeterminate beggar-my-neighbor struggle, and it invites political fragmentation of metropolitan areas, which may be inefficient in terms of the cost of infrastructure.

Controlling externalities. — Factory noise and shopping center traffic are nuisances and hazards for people in nearby dwellings. On the other hand, factories clustered together can share a rail spur and retail stores clustered together provide greater shopping convenience. Hence segregation of land uses may preserve urban amenities while at the same time helping to reduce transportation costs. There are not many losers in this scheme, but there are some, such as the person who wants to put a store on land he owns in an area designated as residential. There is an unyielding problem in the essential arbitrariness of the land-use zones that are to be enforced, for while all may agree on the principle, there will be much opposition to the particulars.

Residential integration. — Among the external effects of land use which some people think should be reduced by segregating them, are disturbances to life styles and to the tranquility of a residential district that result when different socioeconomic groups and different densities of housing are mixed together. Indeed, private "zoning" through restrictive covenants has been used mainly to achieve this sort of segregation. Recently, this has been seen by many as undemocratic, likely to strengthen class and ethnic antagonisms, and likely also to lock some income, ethnic, and age groups within a deteriorating part of the housing supply. So intermixture of housing types and households is urged by many and endorsed by some legislation.

Stable property values.— The constituency of the real estate industry and the city planning profession has been primarily made up of property owners. "What's good for my property value is good for the community" is the rule that follows from this situation. The property-value argument has been used to buttress the case for segregation of land uses and of residential areas, the idea being that a jumble of stores, houses, offices, and factories encourages people to take their real estate business elsewhere. Since real estate values are in the nature of economic rents and transfer payments, which add up to zero in a welfare economics sense, the logic of the property-value criterion for land-use patterns is obscure at best.

Ethos.— Cities, like nations, have names and seem to have identities transcending the people who make them up. The physical city is often taken to be the embodiment of group characteristics, and most social groups want to create a favorable, or at least unified and forceful, image of their character for the rest of the world to behold. This would make the city a kind of architectural monument, a symbol of collective discipline and taste. It may be admirably functional, but whether it is or not, the city conveys an overall impression on residents and outsiders alike, and some would say that this overall impression should be a factor in controlling the city's form.

Prescriptive order.— If people live in Rome, they are advised to "do as the Romans do," and if they live in a city where cars are very hard to park, they will eventually adjust to the use of public transportation. If very little land is allotted for single-family houses, they will develop the instincts of apartment dwellers. If there are bars, they will play shuffleboard or darts, and if there are no bars, they will stroll in the park—if there is a park. The environment may inculcate values and so, by arranging the spatial form of the city, we may perhaps so alter the behavior of people that it becomes habitual. But, of course, this requires having firm ideas about how people should behave, not an impossible condition to meet. Benevolent moral arrogance is the vanity of any age.

Flexibility. — A city is likely to grow, and much urban planning—both public and business planning—is about what to do when it does grow. This comes down to envisaging both a gradual transformation of all the parts of the city and the movement of its perimeter. But the scale and pace of change cannot usually be anticipated very far into the future, so the flexibility criterion means that a good city is adaptable. It can absorb new elements without becoming grossly unfunctional or unlivable.

This is not an exhaustive list of criteria for urban land use patterns, but if it were, and if we could satisfy ourselves that there was no serious inconsistency among them, then we would be able to select the land-use scheme that is "best" from a set of alternatives. We shall next consider some of these alternatives, their pros and cons; but we shall leave the ultimate judgment to the reader.

CLEAN-SLATE OPTIONS

Almost all cities are "accreted": things have been added or removed without conscious design over many ages. Once in a while an earthquake or a massive bombing raid lets the city start over, and there is a scattering of "new towns" about the world that have been put up more or less whole. But for the most part, the clean-slate approach to the problem of where things should go in cities is an intellectual exercise. As such, it does allow us to make limited experiments with the interactions of various components.

The circular, concentric city comes first. Given a regular surface and bee-line transportation, a circular arrangement minimizes the aggregate mileage in bringing each of the evenly spaced denizens on a round trip to the center. If there are different categories of uses with different transportation characteristics or densities, a map of concentric circles is efficient in the transportation-cost sense. A pioneering work in economic geography, by Johann H. von Thuenen, left no uncertainty about this.[3] His solution to the theoretical and practical problem of what to grow where on an agricultural estate, represented in Figure 16, lends itself to urban land use issues, though with some important qualifications.

The task, in the illustration, is to minimize the total transportation cost involved in getting certain quantities of vegetables (V) and wheat (W) to a central marketplace. Per acre of land, we assume that vegetables bring a

3. Published in German in 1826. For an English translation, see Carla M. Wartenberg, *von Thuenen's Isolated State*, Peter Hall, ed. (Oxford: Pergamon Press, 1966).

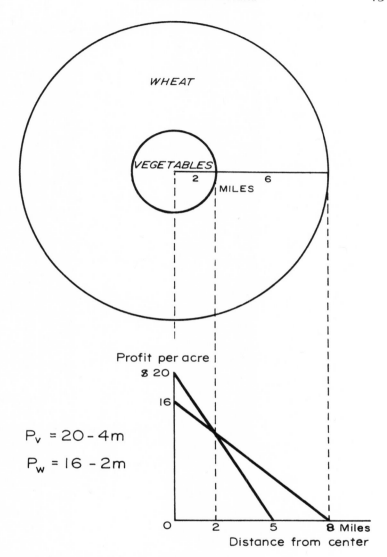

Figure 16. Von Thuenen's concentric circle land use
theory.

profit, after all costs except transportation, of $20, and wheat brings $16 at
the market, but that the cost of transporting vegetables is $4 per mile and
the cost of transporting wheat is $2 per mile. The vegetable grower at the
center thus realizes a profit of $20 while the wheat grower gets $16. One

mile away, the profit after transportation cost is $16 for vegetables and $14 for wheat. Lines V and W in Figure 16 trace the decline of these profit figures from the center to the breakeven margins, five miles for vegetables and eight miles for wheat. To show that minimum total transportation cost is achieved by the arrangment of devoting the inner two-mile circle to vegetables and the remainder of the eight-mile radius circle to wheat, suppose the uses of one acre on each side of the two-mile boundary are interchanged. The cost of transporting wheat is reduced by $2M, where M is the number of miles between the two acres; the cost of getting vegetables to market is raised by $4M. Hence, any such interchange raises aggregate transportation cost by ($4−$2 =) $2M. This result is general for any number of commodities. A system of concentric circles is an efficient land use plan in this von Thuenen situation.

Since von Thuenen owned all the land, the saving in total transport expenditure was realized directly by him, and we can take that as his motive in attempting to rationalize the use of space. It happens, however, that by minimizing total transport costs, he was, at the same time, maximizing the aggregate value of land, if we assume that land value is determined by its capacity to save transportation cost by virtue of being close to the market. This puts the matter in a different light, since it is clear that land from the center to the edge of the two-mile circle is worth more if used for vegetables than if used for wheat. Beyond that wheat pays more. If von Thuenen rented each acre of land to the highest bidder, the bent line from $20 on the profit axis to 8 miles on the distance axis would trace out the profile of land values. This leads to an additional and very significant result. A group of competitive, private landowners would find it in their individual best interests to use land in such a way as to minimize the aggregate transportation costs of the community. They would do this by charging prices or rents and would thus realize as landowners what the consuming public saved by the internal arrangement of land uses. The von Thuenen theory underlies the concept of an "ordered dense cluster," presented in Chapter Two.

To translate the agricultural problem into urban terms we need only assume that some uses of urban land generate more trips, per acre, than other uses do. For example, suppose that each single-family home occupies one acre, that there are twelve apartment units per acre wherever apartments are built, and that each household spends one dollar a year on transportation to and from the center for each mile distant from the center that it resides. Then, moving an acre of apartment dwellers outward in an exchange of land with a single-family household will increase total community transportation costs by $11M, M being the number of miles between the two acres of land. The conclusion is that the apartment dwellers should reside in the inner circle, surrounded by a belt of single-family houses. With similar arguments we can recommend the location or employment and shopping areas in the center, displacing high-density residential areas outward.

A serious problem arises if someone has built a single-family house in the apartment zone and an apartment building in the suburbs. To straighten things out, it might be necessary to demolish the house (with a value of $20,000, say) or the apartment building (worth $120,000, perhaps) or both, in order to save $11M in transportation costs per year. For a large range of the parameters involved, it would be a false economy. These structures constitute "sunk capital," which played no role in von Thuenen's study but which is of great significance in urban centers.

In addition, this suggests that the concentric-circle arrangement has trouble growing. The need for additional apartments may just coincide with the economics of scrapping single-family houses at the edge of this inner ring, but chances are that it will not. The result of discrepancies would be a scattering of apartment buildings throughout the landscape or an irredeemable gray area of old houses just outside the inner circle.

Another practical problem with the concentric-circle concept is that urban transportation systems today involve common-use corridors rather than individual rocket belts. Bee-line transportation from any point directly to the center is unfeasible. In fact, there is a strong technological argument for a transportation system that is a back-and-forth straight line instead of an angular mesh.

This brings us to our second option and Figure 17. The "linear plan" modifies the concentric zones of the von Thuenen scheme into belts that are strung along a straight-line transportation system. The center of town is no longer a point but a line—or at least a succession of points along this line. The business activities—industrial, office, and service, to use convenient labels—are the walls of the transportation corridor. Just beyond is the high-density residential strip, R_H, and in back of that the low-density residential area, R_L.

The growth of the linear city takes the form of grafting module 2, with the same plan of uses, to one edge of module 1, the original city. This

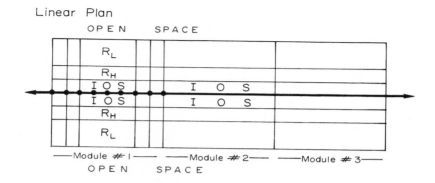

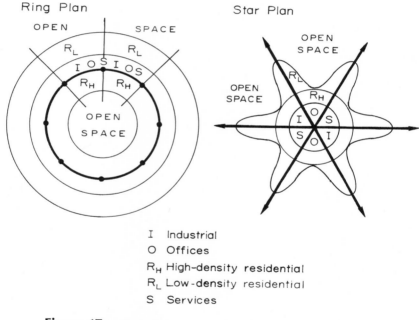

I   Industrial
O   Offices
R_H High-density residential
R_L Low-density residential
S   Services

Figure 17. Variations on concentric circle urban land use scheme.

avoids the bloating of the several zones in a concentric arrangement. It keeps open space within the reach of all the residents of the community via a light network of transportation perpendicular to the spine. It allows the community to use a common corridor transportation system—either rail, bus, or auto, or a combination—to the full. Both capital and operating costs of this linear transportation system seem to make it more efficient than a completely radial system would be, because the marginal costs of the extra distances as the city grows are likely to be less than the average costs, though this depends on where people live relative to where they work and shop.

While the concentric circle pattern suggests growing traffic congestion at its center, the linear scheme is vulnerable to large-scale breakdowns (if a bridge collapses, for example, or a train is wrecked) and would be awkward in the event of an explosive growth in per capita desire for transportation. The linear plan leaves fewer options.

The ring plan is a linear scheme that curves around to form a circle. It has the open space and the linear transportation attractions of the straight-line city, but it provides an optional way to get to wherever you are going. As Columbus explained to Isabella, you can go east by going west, should the need arise. We have shown high-density residential areas occupying the inner portion of the ring, but there is no special virtue in this variation.

The ring presents a problem in accommodating growth. Unless densities rise, open space will be used up. The central area may be entirely filled up but still leave the city without an urban focus. The outer zones may thicken and compel the introduction of radial transportation as a supplement to the belt line. A succession of belts might emerge, but that would bring a problem of tying them together.

Both the ring and the linear arrangement discourage strong urban focus, which is to say that you would have a hard time deciding where to put your department store or your nightclub. Or even your office building, if the presence of other office buildings and complementary business services is important in what you do during the day. This feature appeals to some planning writers who think of it as somehow democratic, or who believe it is most useful to have a succession of specialized centers—one for hospitals, one for movie theaters, one for light manufacturing, one for libraries and museums, and so on. Of course, the people in module 1 might tire of waiting for "dry-cleaning-land" to open up in module 17, and things like that. And the number of reasonable specialties may bear no relation to the eventual length of a linear city.

Urban focus is provided by the star plan, which is a cross between the concentric circle and linear schemes. Instead of bee-line individual transportation, there is a limited number of corridors, for highway or rail

Ideal Maximum Distances to Daily Activities

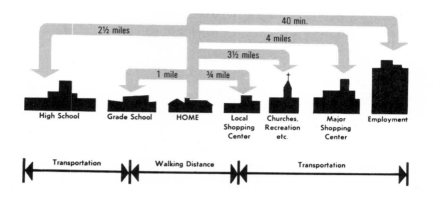

Figure 18. Ideal maximum distances to daily activities.

Source: Urban Land Institute, *The Community Builders Handbook*, Washington, D.C., 1968, p. 33. Reprinted with permission from ULI–the Urban Land Institute, 1200 18th St., NW, Washington, D.C. 20036.

systems or both. Development of the interstitial areas is forestalled, either by land-use regulations or by relative scarcity of an interstitial transportation network. Hence, open space is preserved and is accessible, as in the linear scheme. Transportation advantages of the linear plan may also be realized, as may be any advantages in having specialized subcenters, as these can be strung along one of the transportation spokes (but many users would have to pass through the central intersection).

In the star plan, it would not be unreasonable to show the high-density residential district and the business district as little stars nested within the large stars, but, given the single center, these uses would tend to be concentric rather than linear.

There are no distance scales beside these generalized schemes, and some important details are omitted. Figure 18 makes up for this, in part, with some popular rules of thumb about how far a person's home should be from an elementary school, a supermarket, his job, and so on. These are individualized criteria, but they have implications for any particular land-use scheme. They say that grade schools should be scattered throughout the residential areas (which does not interfere with the generalized schemes presented above) and that a person's house should be no more than four miles from a major shopping center (which might be more difficult to fit in).

The forty-minute limit on the journey to work is a major constraint and can be useful in choosing between alternative land-use schemes. In a perfectly concentric city, suppose that 40 minutes allows a person to cover a radial distance of 10 miles (a radial speed of 15 miles per hour), the maximum radius of the city would be 10 miles, and its area 314 square miles or 200,960 acres. If only 40 percent of the area is residential and the residential density is 28 people per acre, the maximum population is 2,250,752. To exceed this population without violating the 40-minute commuting limit, we would need faster transportation, higher density, more compact nonresidential areas, dispersion of jobs (and the loss of complete centrality), or some combination of these.

OBSERVED PATTERNS

We have now identified some criteria about what goes where in an urban area and looked at some of their implications for idealized urban form. Real-life cities have been much studied, however, and we have ample opportunity to see whether or not they embody some of the abstract concepts.

An early description of typical city patterns, made in 1925, is shown in Figure 19. It is "typical" only in the sense that the sociologist who presented it held it out as the pattern to which cities in general conform, but he did this without providing empirical evidence that it is, in fact, the normal pattern. Indeed, it seems to resemble Chicago in the early 1920s, which is where the article was written.

It is circular (except for a body of water to the right of the heavy black shoreline) and concentric. Residential density declines as one goes farther from the center and income or occupational status rises. Various ethnic enclaves are indicated, bearing suggestive geographic relation to each other ("Deutschland" is just beyond the "ghetto," which meant a Jewish district in those days). "Little Sicily" adjoins the "underworld," and the "Black Belt" stretches from "vice" to "bright light area." While these may be

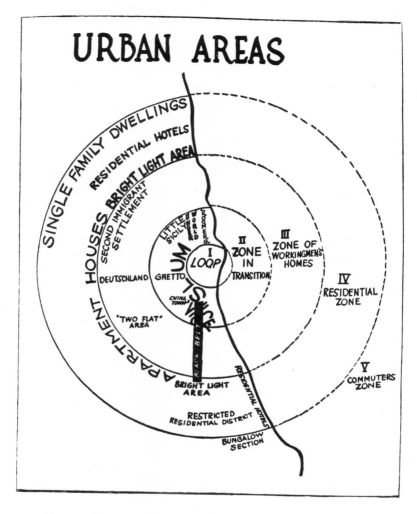

URBAN AREAS

Figure 19. An early sociological view of urban patterns.

Source: Ernest W. Burgess, "The Growth of the City," in
Robert E. Park et al., eds. *The City* (Chicago: University
of Chicago Press, 1925, p. 55.

inaccurate and offensive stereotypes, it is significant that one of the first
urban sociologists considered them essential to his description of how cities
are organized spatially.

Two decades later, another urban sociologist observed persistent socioeconomic enclaves in Boston, not merely ethnic areas but places that had once enjoyed great prestige as fashionable, "elite" districts.[4] His careful documentation supported a thesis that the early character of an urban neighborhood may so clearly stamp it in the public mind that subsequent urban growth, land market forces, and transportation economics notwithstanding, it will retain that early character. Park Avenue in New York and Nob Hill in San Francisco are perhaps more widely known examples of the things the Boston sociologist had in mind.

A combination of socioeconomic continuity and concentric separation is the basis for the "sector theory" of urban residential neighborhoods, enunciated by Homer Hoyt, a prestigious pioneer in urban studies.[5] He undertook to provide a newly created home mortgage insurance agency, the FHA, with guidelines for predicting whether residential property values were likely to fall or rise in particular parts of an urban area. After sifting through large quantities of statistical information—some of which is reflected in Figure 20—he concluded that the high-income area of a community is initially selected on the basis of several factors—the higher ground, an upwind direction, for example—and expands outward in the same direction as the city grows. The original high-income area becomes obsolete and is abandoned to low-income households. Low-income housing appears first in the least desirable sector of the city and also expands outward, but occupies the cast-off districts of the rich as well. Middle-income housing fills the wedges between. Hoyt carefully left room in his argument for factors both natural and human that could distort the pattern. The sector theory has had great appeal to the real estate industry, which is very much in need of intuitively reasonable but not overly complex ways to predict urban land-use changes, at least in broad outline.

When read carefully, Hoyt's theory substantially modifies the concentric circle idea of how cities are shaped. He recognized the important role of the high-speed transportation system that allowed the well-to-do to put a lot of distance between themselves and the unpleasanter portions of the city without much sacrifice of time and convenience in getting to work. The result, illustrated in Figure 21, is a roughly star-shaped urban area, with spokes along the major commuting routes.

Most of Hoyt's background information was pre-automobile. The electric street car was the basic commuter vehicle in American cities from

4. Walter Firey, *Land Use in Central Boston* (Boston: Harvard University Press, 1947).

5. Homer Hoyt, *The Structure and Growth of Residential Neighborhoods in American Cities* (Washington, D.C.: Federal Housing Administration, 1939).

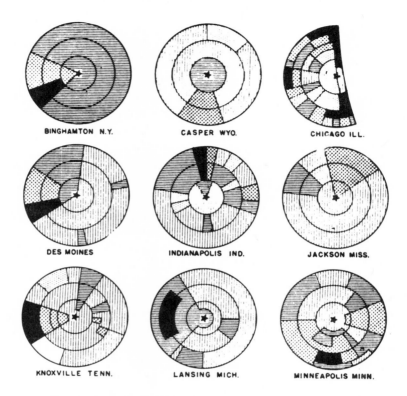

Figure 20. Homer Hoyt's "Sector Theory."

Source: Homer Hoyt, *The Structure and Growth of Residential Neighborhoods in American Cities* (Washington, D.C.: Federal Housing Administration, 1939), p. 115. *Note*: High-income neighborhoods are indicated in black.

1890 to 1935, roughly, and this type of conveyance could not easily serve the interstitial area between the spokes. The automobile, with its cheaper road system and individual vehicles, does permit this area to be filled in, and such seems to have been the trend in more recent years. As Figure 22 shows, however, there remains a strong tendency for urban uses to string out along transportation arteries, sometimes to the point of suggesting a linear urban pattern.

The pattern, in any case, is not very tidy. The arms of the star are

Figure 21. The settled area of the Chicago metropolitan
region, 1936.

Source: Homer Hoyt, *The Structure and Growth of Residential
Neighborhoods in American Cities* (Washington, D.C.:
Federal Housing Administration, 1939), p. 14.

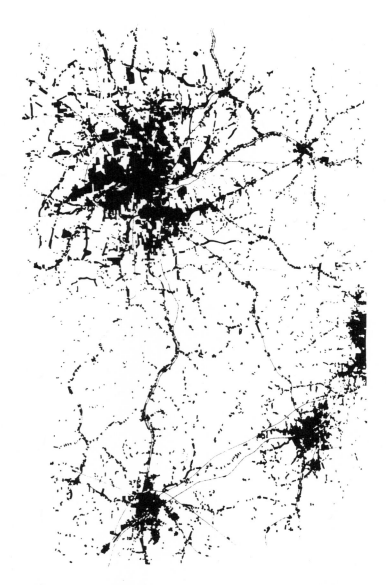

Figure 22. Urban land use in Winston-Salem, North
Carolina, 1958.

Source: F. Stuart Chapin, Jr. and Shirley F. Weiss, *Urban Growth
Dynamics* (New York: John Wiley & Sons, Inc., 1962),
p. 428. *Note*: The community to the south is Lexington,
N.C.; to the southeast is Thomasville, N.C., and part of
High Point, N.C.

frequently interrupted by nonurban space. At intervals, the growth along an arm may branch out in a smaller version of the star, at a nodal point that is larger from its distance from the metropolitan focal point would lead us to expect. Urban growth thus has a tendency to leapfrog to areas not contiguous to the already built-up city, partly because there are nodes of services at those outlying points—schools, stores, police forces, and the like—carried over from the days when these were agricultural market towns. Another reason for the leapfrogging is that intervening land is being held off the urban market, because the owner expects to be favored by increases in its value or because the owner has personal reasons for not giving up his land (a farmer who expects to retire in ten or fifteen years, for example).

Another source of irregularity is the existence of a natural barrier or political boundary. Figure 23, showing the general scheme of land uses in the Philadelphia area, illustrates both points. The Delaware River can be crossed only at certain points, which means that transportation arteries on the eastern side must funnel into those points. The river is also a state boundary, which means that there is a break in business and personal taxation systems and in the provision of infrastructure.

This kind of geographic observation may seem unconvincing; the patterns of development are so splotchy that perhaps no general principles are really at work. The situation calls for statistical analysis rather than staring at maps. This means finding numerical relationships between significant measurable indices, such as distance from the center of town and the number of residents per acre. The Australian economist Colin Clark has been a leader in doing just that, and his findings are so widely accepted as correct that they have nearly become "laws of urban form."[6]

The basic result of Clark's study is the principle of "negative exponential density" in residential land use in cities. Taking information about density-distance relationships from a large number of cities, Clark derived a downward curving line, of the sort shown in Figure 24 at the top. Going outward from the center of the city (any city), density decreases at a decreasing rate, generally in accordance with the equation labeled (a) in the figure. Transforming this into logarithmic terms, equation (b) produces a straight line, the slope of which is the parameter b, called the "density gradient."

6. Colin Clark, "Urban Population Densities," *Journal of the Royal Statistical Society* (1951), pp. 490–496.

Additional investigations of the same kind have shown that this density gradient is smaller (the line is less steep) for large cities than for small cities—see equation (c) and the diagram to the right of it. Since it is also true that cities tend to grow in population at an increasing rate— equations (d) and (e)—causing the density gradient to fall as in equation (f), it follows that the rate of population growth, and density, is greater at the outskirts of the city than it is in the middle, as shown by equation (g) and the last diagram. Indeed, the rate of increase over time in density rises faster and faster as we go outward. This is not very mysterious; if we start with 50,000 in the center and 500 at the edge, adding 500 in each place

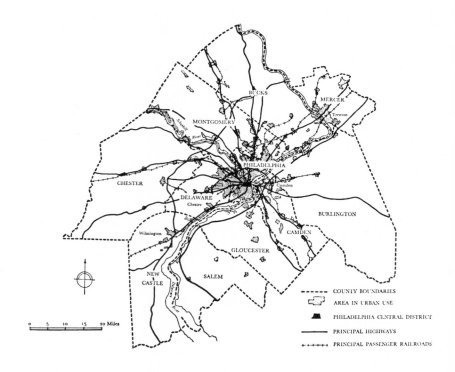

Figure 23.   The Philadelphia metropolitan region, 1950.

Source: Willard B. Hansen, "An Approach to the Analysis of Metropolitan Residential Extention," *Journal of Regional Science* (Summer 1961), reprinted in Alfred N. Page and Warren R. Seyfried (eds.), *Urban Analysis* (Glenview, Ill.: Scott, Foresman, 1970), p. 233.

(a) $d_x = d_0 e^{-bx}$
        d = density
        x = distance from
             center
        b = density gradient

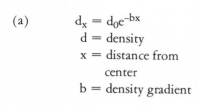

(b) $\log_e d_x = \log_e d_0 - bx$

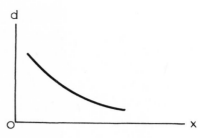

(c) $\log b_j = \log P_0$
                $-c \log P_j$
        P_0 = population of
        smallest city

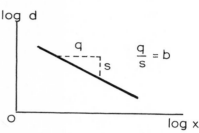

(d) $\log P_{t+1} = k + \log P_t$
            t = time
(e) $P_t = P_0 e^{kt}$
(f) $b_t = b_0 e^{-ckt}$
(g) $(1 + r_x) = (1 + r_0)e^{gx}$
note: c, k and g are constants
      r = rate of population increase

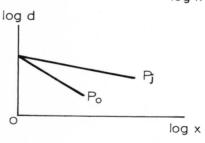

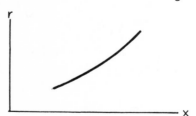

Figure 24. Residential density in relation to distance from the urban center—empirical regularities.

Source: Based on Brian J. L. Berry, "Internal Structure of the City," *Law and Contemporary Problems* (Winter 1965), reprinted in Larry S. Bourne (ed.), *Internal Structure of the City* (New York: Oxford University Press, 1971), pp. 98–99. *Note*: c, k, and g are constants. r = rate of population increase.

145

would mean an increase of 1 percent in the center and 100 percent at the periphery.

Statistical method, then brings order out of chaos. This finding strongly suggests concentric land-use patterns, but it could be made consistent with any of the pure forms illustrated previously. In fact, if we define the "center" of the city to be the point of highest density, then the "negative exponential density gradient" theory becomes at least partly true by definition. In the linear city, for example, the transportation spine could be construed as an elongated "center."

The theory also encounters a problem in geometry. If we define density as the number of persons per acre, rather than per *residential* acre, then density may fall as we go outward even though all the apartment dwellers live in the suburbs and all the single-family homes are in the center—because the area of a circle increases as the square of its radius. Thus, the negative exponential density gradient can leave us unprepared for the highrise buildings on the outskirts of Tokyo, Rome, and other "saucer-shaped" cities, especially after reading that the principle is "universally applicable to cities, regardless of time or place."[7]

In recent years, apartment construction in North American cities has been so scattered as to suggest that something is wrong with the density gradient idea, or, more fundamentally, with the land market. Studies in Toronto (see Figure 25) and elsewhere suggest that apartments are following factories, retail stores, and some office buildings to the suburbs in pleasant disregard for concepts or theories of urban land-use allocation which we have looked at thus far.[8]

The truth of the matter is that when we look at very recent happenings and at urban land uses in greater detail, we learn that much more complex forces are at work. To understand why particular kinds of buildings are located where they are, we need almost to make a thorough study of each individual case.

Take factories.[9] Early manufacturing districts sidled up to the docks and to the railroad yards. For a time they stretched out along trolley lines

7. Brian J. L. Berry, "Internal Structure of the City," *Law and Contemporary Problems* (Winter 1965). Reprinted in *Internal Structure of the City*, ed. by Larry S. Bourne, p. 98.

8. See, for example, W. F. Smith, *The Low-Rise Speculative Apartment* (Berkeley: Center for Real Estate and Urban Economics, University of California, 1964).

9. See Allan R. Pred, "The Intrametropolitan Location of American Manufacturing," *Annals of the Association of American Geographers* (June 1964). Reprinted in *Internal Structure of the City*, ed. by Larry S. Bourne, pp. 380–390.

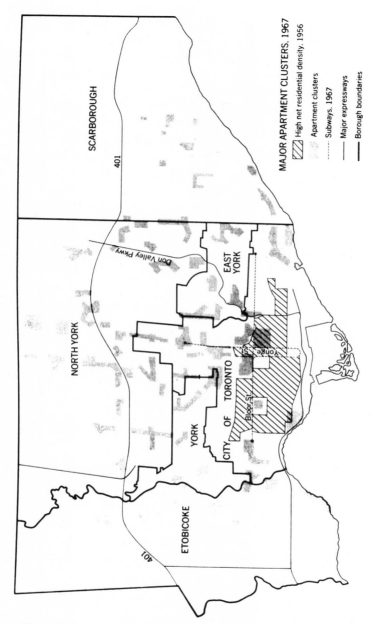

Figure 25. Apartment areas in Toronto.

Source: Larry S. Bourne, "Apartment Location and the Housing Market," in Larry S. Bourne, ed., *Internal Structure
of the City* (New York: Oxford University Press, 1971),
p. 324.

because that was the principal form of transportation for factory workers.[10] When electric power came into use, it was no longer necessary to operate in otherwise inefficient multi-storied buildings huddled around a central steam engine transmitting power by friction belts and pulleys. But one-story factories required more land, which was costly and very difficult to acquire in central areas. So with trucks taking the place of most rail transportation (within the city at least) and with factory workers largely using automobiles to get to work, outlying locations for factories became feasible. Well-designed industrial parks have continued to pull manufacturing toward the outskirts of the city, but normally in specific directions, such as toward airports and along major highway routes.

The automobile was also chiefly responsible for the movement of much retail trade to suburban areas.[11] Before 1920, about 90 percent of department store sales were made in central business districts, but this dropped below 60 percent by 1954 and continues to fall.[12] In 1963 the central business district did only 9.3 percent of the total retail volume of U.S. metropolitan areas with over two million population, and only 24.6 percent of retail volume in metropolitan areas with 250,000 or fewer people.[13] As downtown stores became obsolete and the central business districts became so congested that automobile-driving shoppers were seriously inconvenienced, land developers and retail firms joined forces to recreate a portion of the downtown shopping environment in large, planned, accessible, suburban locations where the low price of land permitted the provision of free parking.

Figure 26 is a very compact summary of the proportions of various types of land uses that we now expect to find in the central business district of the city (CBD), as these proportions vary with the size of the urban area. Department stores, for example, are all in the core in a city of 100,000, but in a city of 10 million they have three-quarters of their facilities in the outlying areas. The relationship is not linear, nor is the rate of the decline alike for any of the types of uses shown. For high-rise residential use, the

10. See James E. Vance, Jr., *Geography and Urban Evolution in the San Francisco Bay Area* (Berkeley: Institute of Governmental Studies, University of California, 1964).

11. See Homer Hoyt, "Characteristics of Shopping Centers," *The Appraisal Journal* (April 1958).

12. *Ibid.*

13. See Urban Land Institute, *The Community Builders Handbook* (Washington, D.C., 1968), p. 276.

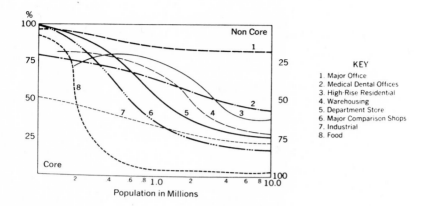

Figure 26.   Proportion of land uses in core and noncore
areas.

Source: Larry Smith, "Space for the CBD's Functions," *Journal
of the American Institute of Planners* (February 1961),
reprinted in Larry S. Bourne (ed.), *Internal Structure of
the City* (New York: Oxford University Press, 1971), p.
358. Reprinted by permission of the *Journal of the
American Institute of Planners.*

curve, drawn from the practical knowledge of a leading urban real estate
consultant, is particularly complex.

The curve for "major office" shows very little decline in the CBD
share of this land use as the population of the city rises. Since the share of
office employment in total jobs generally rises with the size of a city, the
implication is that urban expansion brings with it a need for an absolute
increase in the amount of CBD land use for office buildings. Several
questions arise from this. Will the new office buildings absorb the land
that is being evacuated by industrial, retail, and perhaps even some
residential uses? Where will the additional office workers be found,
and where within the metropolis will they reside? How will they travel
to work?

A recent study of New York City brings these and related problems
into clear focus.[14] Three categories of office work are distinguished. Some

14. This excerpt is a summarization of Emmanuel Tobier's "Economic Development
Strategy for the City: Issues Confronting New York," by L. C. Fitch and A. H. Walsh
(Eds.), pp. 27–85 (1970), published by Sage Publications, Inc.

are related to local population needs—banks, insurance companies, law offices, and so on—and these are appropriately located among residential areas—in shopping centers, for example. People who work in these offices generally live nearby. A second type of office work is done in "back offices" of manufacturing firms, department stores, and other large enterprises. Most of the information flow of concern to these office employees is internal, and there is no strong incentive to separate the office physically from the "main plant." These office workers can be expected to have residential and transportation characteristics like those of the nonoffice employees of the same firm.

The most interesting, and most problematical, part of the office world is that which involves specialized decision centers for national organizations, be they manufacturing, mining, shipping, financial, or whatever. Workers in such offices deal largely with external information and unstandardized problems. Most of their jobs involve extensive contacts with other parts of the business world, so they find it helpful to locate in a cluster of general economic and business information producers and consumers. For reasons that are probably psychological, they perform best when they can communicate face-to-face, and they also seem turned off by vehicular transportation (except elevators) on their way to meetings. They want to be within walking distance of their compatriots in the head-quarters office world. Putting these requirements together with the shift of the economy toward office employment, the consequence is that ever-more, ever-taller office buildings are being jammed together in very limited land area downtown—in a certain few cities.

At the same time, big cities are experiencing a loss of manufacturing employment. Suburban industrial parks attract many firms, as we have noted. Other firms find it beneficial to move to other cities—to the "rest of the world"—where labor costs and land costs, probably taxes, and certainly congestion are less. Such firms produce standardized types of goods, the production and sale of which do not require more than occasional or routine contact with other businesses. Finally, there is a net reduction in manufacturing employment in the national economy, due to automation and the specializing-out of once-factory-related functions such as developmental research.

Now the "sensible" thing would be for headquarters office workers to live in the central city where the office buildings are, while the blue-collar people live in the suburbs where the factories are moving. But in many cities, just the opposite situation can be observed. The various elements of this problem are represented in Figure 27, the background for which is a recent study of New York. Part of the problem is that office work is typically regarded as requiring more skill than manufacturing work does, so "high-skill" and "low-skill" labels are used in the figure.

The central city's housing stock is relatively obsolete. This makes it subject to "filtering down" to people with lower incomes. The availability of such housing, among other factors, encourages low-skill people to migrate to the city where they seek employment. Mainly, they are looking for or directed toward factory work, but this work is migrating to the suburbs. More expensive housing in the suburbs, plus assorted forms of housing discrimination, keeps these new migrants from living close to the factories. To commute to the factories may be more expensive than they can afford—one-third of all the jobs in New York City pay under $90 a week, which is less than welfare.[15] Worse, the new migrants now living in the central city may not hear about suburban manufacturing jobs that are open and which would be worth commuting to.

The high-skill people, for their part, find the suburbs a pleasant refuge from the decay and congestion of the city, and many consider it an escape from unwanted involvements with recent in-migrants and minorities. But for this they must pay in the form of a tedious and expensive commuting trip. Few can get to work without changing their transportation mode at least once. Most push their way into the office buildings through the unsightly rubble of decaying stores and small factories as well as rock-bottom slums—which are just moldering there until the land can be sold for new office buildings.

So the main problems are these: cross-commuting and overloading of transportation channels; and loss of job opportunities by low-skilled workers. The solutions, at least in principle, are not hard to suggest. (1) Move low-skilled people to the suburbs and bring the high-skilled people back to the central city, through a change in the orientation of housing programs. (2) Upgrade low-skilled workers for office jobs. (3) Generate new manufacturing employment for the central city. (4) Improve the spatial functioning of the CBD to make life, and commuting, easier for the office worker.

Given the strong preference for low-density housing among people

15. *Ibid.*

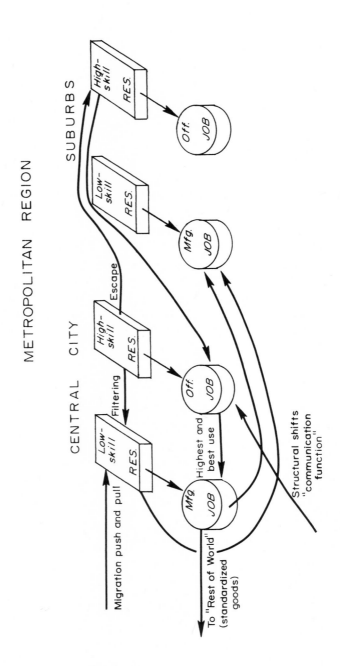

Figure 27. How urban problems arise from the expansion of office employment.

who can afford it, and the sheer dimensions of the problem, Plan (1) might prove to be unworkable. Plan (3) seems to run counter to strong techno-logical and location trends and could produce "make-work" jobs of little social value, but it is not an unreasonable direction to follow. Plan (4), one-sided as it seems, is likeliest to occur for old-fashioned political reasons; it is also relatively cheap, and it does some good and very little harm.

Plan (2), which appears crisp and simple, touches on a basic social instinct. Occupational categories have always helped to define status, and certain kinds of jobs are "good things," as well. On the other hand, perhaps administrative work really is done most effectively by people whose background for generations has been genteel—who knows?

Locational problems—where things go—also beset public agencies in cities. When this concerns infrastructure—streets, sewage facilities, and so forth—the problem is quite involved because private land uses can be expected to shift in accordance with the infrasturcture. Even where it is just a question of locating a specific community service building, the decision process is complex. Hospital service is a mixture of public, private, and institutional activities that serve different needs (such as long-term care, surgery, specialized treatment, teaching, and maternity care)—for different groups of people (particular ethnic groups, low-income people, veterans, children) from different locations (downtown, neighborhoods, suburban) at different levels of quality. A study of hospital location in Chicago (see Figure 28) found something like a concentric spatial ar-rangement of hospital types, plus clear selectivity on the basis of such things as race and income.

Another study, also in Chicago, traced the controversy surrounding the location of a new university campus.[16] A suburban site, which might seem logical in view of where most of the students would be drawn from and which was the consultant's recommendation, was passed over in favor of a very expensive downtown location. It was the suburbanites who supported this choice, not because they felt the univeristy would disrupt their suburbs, but because putting it downtown would be an occasion to clear out some slums. The dwellers in low-income areas who were dis-rupted by the location of the university were essentially apathetic about

16. Roger E. Kasperson, "Toward a Geography of Urban Politics: Chicago, A Case Study," *Economic Geography* (April 1965). Reprinted in *Internal Structure of the City*, ed. by Larry S. Bourne, p. 400ff.

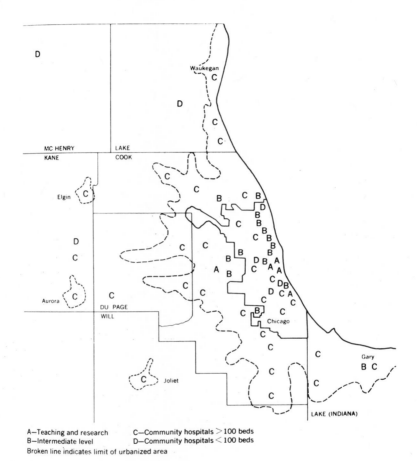

A—Teaching and research   C—Community hospitals > 100 beds
B—Intermediate level   D—Community hospitals < 100 beds
Broken line indicates limit of urbanized area

Figure 28. Spatial distrubution of hospitals in the Chicago area.

Source: Richard L. Morrill and Robert Earickson, "Variations in the Character and Use of Hospital Services," *Health Services Research* (Fall 1968), reprinted in Larry S. Bourne (ed.), *Internal Structure of the City* (New York: Oxford University Press, 1971), p. 395.

civic betterment, being more interested in personal benefits, which the political process could bring them, such as jobs, welfare, and intervention with the police. They were also already in the mayor's political bag, leaving him free to court the conservative (but also "civic-minded") groups living outside the core area.

So it goes. In urban communities a congeries of separate forces is at work deciding what goes where. By business and political means we are apparently becoming more adept at manipulating the detail but less able to give the whole some preferred shape. The form of our city is nearly coherent, perhaps, and it may evolve approximately the way we would like it to evolve. But what can we do if it doesn't? Suppose we would like a linear city and we get a splotchy, bloated star? We cannot go into a department store and pick out the city of our individual choosing. We cannot buy it ready made and whole from a city planner, or a real estate man, or even a government agency. It is about as useless to speculate about ideal urban form as it is to ask a doctor to prescribe a magic potion. Between things as they are and things as we would like them to be lies a process, and the city-forming process is very imperfectly understood.

THE INCREMENTAL APPROACH

The very complexity of the problem—what goes where—is likely to be taken as an argument for "planning," that is, for putting the decision in the hands of presumably well-informed and objective public officials. How could a system of private landowners, each in control of only one small part of the land of the city, possibly produce a scheme of land uses that satisfied any criterion that might be selected—efficiency, stable property values, control of externalities, or whatever? Isn't it possible to put the whole problem into a computer which, with the aid of skillful program design, can print out the answers to "what goes where"?

The answer is no. It is not feasible to make a complete land use plan for a community that clearly maximizes any measure of performance we might select. There are three separate reasons for this, and it is interesting that the theoretically sound and intuitively appealing von Thuenen theory implicitly assumes away all three problems. The difficulties are, first, that there are too many possible combinations; second, that existing, "sunk" capital creates an intractible set of opportunity costs for any proposed alternations in the existing land-use scheme; and, third, that all spatial relationships in urban land use involve externalities.

Figure 29 illustrates the problem of combinations. If we have two lots and two possible users, there are only two ways to match them. Given a "pay-off" matrix such as that shown at the bottom of the figure, we can decide which of these two arrangements is preferred. That is, assume it is worth $2 to have User 1 occupy Lot A, but $1 if he occupies Lot B, and $3 if User 2 has Lot A, but $4 if he has Lot B; then, by matching User 1 with A and User 2 with B, we get a total value of $6. The other way would result in a value of $4. Note that User 2 "produces" more on Lot A than User 1 does, but it is better to let User 1 have Lot A. If we take the pay-off figures to be costs—for transportation, for example—then the minimum value arrangement is preferred. Either way, we have a fairly simple choice, though we might be a little hesitant already to say what the figures in the pay-off matrix mean and where they can be found. Without numbers in a pay-off matrix, we cannot make any land-use scheme at all.

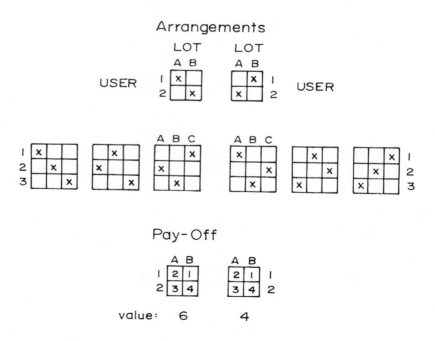

Figure 29.   Combinations of land-use arrangements.

Adding one more lot, C, and one more user, number 3, increases the number of possible arrangements to 6. With the help of an expanded pay-off matrix we can still find the maximum benefit or minimum cost arrangement, however.

The trouble is that the number of significant categories of land use and of available land in a real urban situation is much greater than three, and the number of possible permutations grows very rapidly as the number of categories rises. With two categories we have two choices for locating User 1, followed by only one choice for locating User 2, so $2 \times 1 = 2$. With three categories, $3 \times 2 \times 1 = 6$ permutations. Using the symbol "!" to represent this process, this is what we get:

$$2! = 2$$
$$3! = 6$$
$$4! = 24$$
$$5! = 120$$
$$6! = 720$$
$$7! = 5,040$$
$$8! = 40,320$$
$$9! = 362,880$$
$$10! = 3,628,800$$
$$15! = 1,307,674,368,000$$

Zoning laws in present-day use identify more than fifteen land-use categories, as a rule. In the absence of simplifying (and arbitrary) decision rules, clean-slate land-use allocation thus requires considering in excess of one trillion possibilities about what goes where, assuming the proportions of land to be used in each way are at least pre-established and the pay-off matrix has been filled in. Even in this era of electronic wonders, it is simply not worthwhile to ask a computer to perform such calculations.

How did von Thuenen do it? His pay-off matrix has some very special characteristics that make a mathematically "elegant" optimum solution possible. For three zones and three products, the von Thuenen problem has a pay-off matrix such as the following, reading distance zones from left to right:

10	4	1
8	6	2
5	4	3

The first product outbids the other two for the first zone, the second wins the middle zone, and the third is high bidder for the farthest zone. It is possible to prove that this arrangement maximizes the aggregate pay-off.[17]

For other sets of numbers, such as

$$
\begin{array}{ccc}
10 & 8 & 6 \\
8 & 6 & 4 \\
6 & 4 & 2
\end{array}
$$

there is no unique solution, and for most of the possible sets of relationships within the pay-off matrix there is no mathematical tool for selecting the value-maximizing permutation.[18]

The existence of "sunk capital" means, in effect, that the legendary "city of tomorrow" will be today's city, somewhat the worse for age. Scarcity of capital is a very strong argument against scrapping one of the principal physical assets we possess. Agglomeration economies and other practical considerations limit the opportunity or wisdom of creating entirely new cities for the increase in population. Gradual replacement of the urban capital inventory requires that each new piece be an integral part of an essentially unchanged whole, for when we replace one girder in a bridge at a time, we are precluded from making any major change in the form or the location of the bridge.

The externalities of urban land use mean that for every permutation of land parcels and land users there is a unique pay-off matrix. The transportation-saving effect of having User 1 located on Lot A depends on where all the other users are. This escalates the problem of selecting an optimum overall arrangement because each and every element in the pay-off matrix—assuming we all agreed on a particular way to measure it, such as saving in transportation cost—must be calculated. We can select a formula for performing the calculation and the program a computer to do it, but if we have a 15 × 15 matrix of users and parcels of land to deal with, we need 225 of these calculations for each of 1.3 trillion permutations.

People interact in other ways than by affecting each other's accessibility. They make noise and smoke, rub each other the wrong way, and covet

17. See W. F. Smith, *Filtering and Neighborhood Change* (Berkeley: Center for Real Estate and Urban Economics, University of California, 1964), pp. 67ff.

18. For additional commentary on this type of problem, see Britton Harris, "The City of the Future: The Problem of Optimal Design," *Papers and Proceedings of the Regional Science Association*, 1967. Reprinted in *Internal Structure of the City*, ed. by Larry S. Bourne, pp. 516ff.

each other's share of the housing supply and public facilities. To obtain just one element on one of our too-numerous pay-off matrixes, we must solve deeply philosophical problems about who is entitled to what in the urban environment.

All of this means that comprehensive, once-and-for-all planning of the urban land-use pattern, save on grossly arbitrary principles, is out of reach. It is not an argument against city planning in principle or as practiced, nor is it a call for blind and unchecked forces in the private land market to take full charge. There is an important intermediate possibility, which involves "incremental" planning.[19]

This means setting in motion a land economy or market, the operation of which is subject to rules of the game—zoning, taxes, governmental processes for providing infrastructure—and changing these rules whenever the trend of events suggests that things are working out in an undesirable way. Since we cannot anticipate all the effects of a particular change in the rules—for example, the nature of a housing subsidy—we will need constant feedback about the whole system's response to it and a flexible attitude about changing the rule again and again until it seems to be working out well enough.

This is a "sloppy" and unsystematic approach to the whole mass of urban questions, but it is a feasible one. It invites waste and irreversible mistakes, but it improves the possibility that the mistakes that are made and the wastes that do occur will not be monumental. It says, in effect, that we need to design a system for guiding the development of cities rather than a blueprint for the whole physical creation. The system has two principal parts—the land market and the public sector. Rather than dash off sets of rules for one or both that immediately strike us as being in tune with the best in human nature, it behooves us to see what makes a land market tick and what the central elements in urban policy are. From this knowledge, reasonable first-approximation rules of the game can eventually be drawn.

DISCUSSION QUESTIONS

1.   Can you express in a formula or diagram all the possible density patterns for a population of 360,000 people occupying 9,000 acres?

---

19. See David Braybrooke and Charles E. Lindbolm, *A Strategy of Decision* (New York: The Free Press, 1963).

2. How would you go about measuring the incremental residential density of your community? How do apartment buildings affect the measure?

3. Think of the most attractively laid-out city you know. What makes it appealing? That is, what are your personal criteria for an urban land use scheme?

4. What spatial pattern best reconciles community "progress" with the objective of minimal disturbance to established districts? Would you like to see a shopping center built across the road from you?

5. An eminent architect is supposed to have said that every city needs an earthquake or conflagration once in a while so it can be rebuilt. Could that statement be taken seriously?

6. Under what circumstances does "sunk" urban capital produce significant external costs? What land-use pattern will minimize these costs?

7. Is it true that a person who commutes only occasionally to the city center (say, once a week) creates external benefits for the community by residing on the outskirts?

8. If blue-collar workers live mostly in the central area where offices are, and white-collar people live in the suburbs where factories are, is this a "housing problem," a "transportation problem," a "city planning problem," a "welfare problem," or a "political problem"?

9. What "arbitrary decision rules" usually simplify the land-use allocation conundrum suggested in this chapter (by which clean-slate land-use allocation would require considering more than one trillion possibilities)?

SELECTED REFERENCES

Berry, Brian J. L., and Frank E. Horton. *Geographic Perspective on Urban Systems*. Englewood Cliffs, N.J.: Prentice-Hall, 1970.

An up-to-date and well-illustrated textbook on urban geography, covering patterns of economic activity and land use within urban areas as well as regional and national patterns, with a combination of theory and description.

Bourne, Larry S. (ed.). *Internal Structure of the City*. New York: Oxford University Press, 1971.
A set of readings on the economic geography of particular cities.

Gruen, Victor. *The Heart of Our Cities*. New York: Simon and Schuster, 1964.
A leading architect's interpretation of what is wrong with our cities, how they got that way, and what should be done about them.

Hall, Peter. *The World Cities*. New York: McGraw-Hill, 1966.
A well-illustrated description of seven of the largest metropolitan centers in the world, with emphasis on urban problems and planning approaches.

Hoyt, Homer. *The Structure and Growth of Residential Neighborhoods in American Cities*. Washington, D.C.: Federal Housing Administration, 1939.
The research study commissioned by the newly established FHA in search of principles that govern historic changes in neighborhood housing values.

Scott, Mel. *American City Planning*. Berkeley: Univeristy of California Press, 1969.
A comprehensive and richly detailed history of city planning in the United States—the concepts, legal issues, and administration.

7

THE URBAN LAND
MARKET

WHEN IT COMES to organizing the spatial patterns of urban land use, centralized decision making can be a discouraging, complex job. But even without an effective central authority, people in a community do manage to make decisions—each follows his own ideas of what is best for him and various groups undertake limited collective actions, with all their activities being bounded by physical constraints, such as those of geography and the resources of the area in which they live. This kind of decentralized decision making is often called "the market."

It is the particular nature of a market economy, in urban land and buildings as in other commodities, that decisions about how resources should be used are made for one piece of property at a time and by individuals who can base their decisions on the known pattern of uses of all other pieces of property. The individual decision maker is also free, in a market economy, to ignore the effect of his decision on other people and other properties not directly involved in the transaction. This is represented in Figure 30, where it is contrasted with a system of centralized decision making—nonmarket, "planned" allocation of land within a city to different uses. In the centralized system, all land uses must, in principle, be decided simultaneously, which creates the problem of "combinations" described by Figure 29 in the previous chapter. Also, each use of a given parcel affects the desirability of every other parcel for every use, owing to "externalities." That is, a school or a shopping center influences the

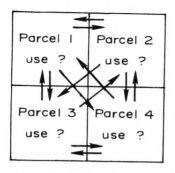

CENTRALIZED PLANNING:

Initially, uses of all parcels are unknown.

Use of each parcel will have some effect on usefulness of each other parcel; initially, these effects are unknown.

All uses must be decided simultaneously.

URBAN LAND MARKET:

Owner of Parcel 1 can select use most beneficial to him, and ignore effects on other parcels.

Usefulness of Parcel 1 is affected by uses of all other Parcels, but these uses and effects are known, or "given."

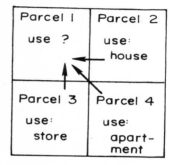

Figure 30. Decisions about land use–centralized planning versus market system.

desirability of nearby housing. The noise of a factory will be most disturbing if the factory is next to a hospital, and so on.

In a market system, the decision maker's problem is quite simple by comparison—how to use his land, capital, or purchasing power to get the best deal for himself, based on known prices and uses for all other properties. Of course, in the market system, there are many decision makers, and each decision that one takes can cause many others to reconsider their own choices about where to live, how much rent to charge, or what kind of building to construct. In our next few chapters, as we describe in outline how individuals make decisions in the real estate market, we shall leave open the question of whether the overall result of numerous independent actions is a reasonable pattern of land uses and an equitable distribution of the housing and other resources the city provides. Later on we shall take a hard look at that basic issue.

Markets in general, and the urban land market in particular, are compatible with centralized decision making to a very considerable degree. Indeed, without standard, enforceable laws regarding contracts, the most familiar forms of market activity would be unfeasible. Without laws establishing rights to land and buildings, an urban land market could not function. Without traffic signals to regulate the pattern of movement, parts of the urban land market—such as the commercial districts—would function very poorly. On the other hand, a rent control law and certain kinds of taxation may cause the land market to behave in an undesirable or an unpredictable way. In any case, it is possible to superimpose centralized decision making on a market process. One way to promote a community land-use pattern that approaches an optimum (assuming we can agree on how to identify an optimum) is to allow the market to operate subject to certain socially imposed controls, and to change those controls whenever it appears that beneficial market adjustments would result. For the market-system decision maker, however, community-provided infrastructure and community regulations in force can be taken as additional "givens," like the pattern of uses on other parcels. They affect the decision that will be made, but they do not complicate the decision process.

URBAN LAND RESOURCES

The urban land market deals in "real estate" resources. We can buy or rent some land or a building in this market; we cannot buy a city plan, despite the fact that we may have very strong preferences about the spatial arrangement of land uses and the nature of the buildings, and the further fact that we end up paying for any overall scheme, whatever it is.

"Real estate" is a fairly archaic term, usually defined as land and buildings, or as rights to use or benefit from land and buildings. Another common translation of the term is "immovable wealth," and, in fact, one basic distinction in law between real property and personal property lies in the fixed location of the former. For things that are movable, possession is normally interpreted as ownership. For immovable wealth, such as land, ownership is proved, not by occupancy, byt by written public records.

"Real property" means land and "improvements"—things such as houses, trees, pavements, and pipes—permanently attached to the land and including such things as built-in cabinets, stoves, wall-to-wall carpeting and venetian blinds that are intended to be permanently attached to the building. "Land" includes, depending on particular laws, air space to some distance above the surface, subsurface minerals, use of adjacent water (as in a river flowing past the property) and access to a public road. It may also include some rights to the adjacent atmosphere, such as to assure continued enjoyment of sunlight or a view.

It is very common to use the word "land" as shorthand for land *and buildings*, and discussions of the "urban land market" should usually be interpreted this way. There is a very practical reason. If a building already exists on a piece of land, we cannot use the land for any other purpose unless we acquire and demolish the building; the price of the land includes the value of the building. It is also the custom in North America to acquire buildings by purchasing the land they lie on, since deeds describe the perimeter of parcels of land and simply include all improvements as part of that land.

The real estate market deals in "land" in this expanded sense. It is a very heterogenous commodity, no two pieces of which are precisely alike. Because of this heterogeneity, there is no observable "price of land" or "price of housing"; these terms are meaningful only as index numbers, and there is no general agreement on how such index numbers should be calculated. The urban land market produces a plethora of individual transaction prices, but it is a very difficult enterprise to judge whether these prices in general are going up or down. "Who gets what" in the urban land market is a more practical thing to be concerned with than what the price of housing or land is, though the allocation of land and buildings is made essentially by means of price.

Real estate "business" also includes activities concerned with the creation of new improvements—houses, shopping centers, streets, sewers, schools, and so on. So another kind of resource administered by the urban land market is "capital," but this term also takes some explanation. Capital is of two kinds: real resources, such as construction labor and building materials, and investment funds. Investment funds are required because payments must be made for the labor and materials as buildings are constructed, and the money thus tied up can be recovered only gradually as income is produced by the durable new inventory. A scarcity of capital for urban development can thus be construed as a shortage of real resources or of investment funds, or both.

Another kind of resource that the urban land market is much concerned with falls under the heading of "transportation." This means both the capital stock of streets, subway trains, and private automobiles, and the resources used in operating them—time as well as fuel and maintenance. Individuals in the urban land markets, such as families in search of housing, take transportation costs into account in making their real estate choices. The overall land-use pattern that emerges from the atomistic decisions of the land market can be judged partly on the degree to which the pattern conserves transportation resources. The land market is thus a "land and transportation market."

MARKET DIMENSIONS

The real estate business is a large assortment of activities. There are several significant types of land use—residential, retail, office use—which are dealt in according to individual sets of rules. There are several functional roles involved in a real estate transaction—the owner, the mortgage lender, the investor, and others. Each participant in the transaction has goals peculiar to the role he is playing and perhaps to himself as an individual. Every person involved is bound by a number of institutional constraints—such as laws, taxation—which also vary significantly by type of property. Figure 31 is a visual representation of the scheme by which land market activities can be broken down, conveniently limited to three dimensions.

Nine use categories are shown, an arbitrary consolidation of the great diversity of urban land uses. The real estate characteristics of these uses differ in significant practical respects, so much so that a thorough understanding of the market for any one of them is the basis of career specialization in the real estate business. Retail stores, for example, are commonly rented under lease terms that allow the landlord to share in the tenant's gross receipts, according to formulas that distinguish categories of the retail business. Lease negotiations thus call for specialized understanding of this slice of the real estate world.

Practical training for a real estate career thus requires vastly more specific information than we can or should attempt to provide in this

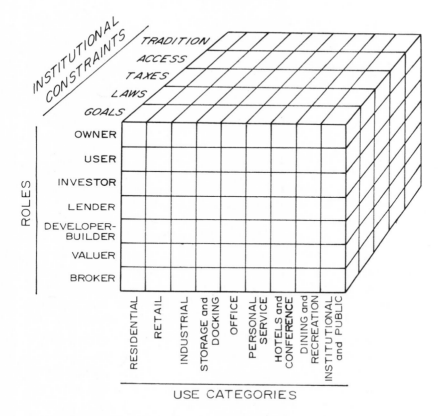

Figure 31. Dimensions of the urban land market.

book. Our object is to explain the basic principles on which real estate decisions are made in an urban land market—to say "why" land use patterns and the prices and condition of the inventory of buildings are as we observe them in our cities. Our examination of the urban land market will take the form of discussing each of the roles identified in Figure 31 by looking at the goals and constraints that relate to that role.

The breakdown of roles requires some interpretation. The *owner* of a piece of urban property is the person who makes the basic decision about how it should be used and when it should be sold. A property manager or a trustee is thus an owner for this purpose. The *user* is the occupant—the tenant in an apartment, a merchant in a retail store, or a business firm in an office building. Obviously, owners may occupy their own premises and thus be users of the property as well; sometimes, as in the case of single-family housing, they are virtually required to become owners in order to be able to use property, because of traditions that have emerged in the urban land market. It is certainly worthwhile to question these traditional restraints, so the separate examination of owner and user roles has some merit.

The *investor* owns financial resources rather than real property, but he proposes to exchange his money for real estate. In effect, we are using the term investor to stand for "buyer." A person who acquires ownership of real estate is perforce an investor, even though the amount of money he himself supplies—the equity investment—is sometimes negligible. He bears the financial risk of the property if he becomes the legal owner.

Real estate transactions typically involve the use of borrowed money, the loan being secured by the property transferred. Hence, the *lender* role often seems crucial to the operation of the real estate market. A mortgage loan desk is a filter through which the details of most transactions in this market are screened. Loans may be placed against real property without a transfer of ownership, when the owner wants to make some building repairs, for example.

The *developer-builder* role is a set of functions involved in the creation of substantially new improvements (buildings). Although the amount of floor space added by new construction in a single year is usually a very small fraction (2 or 3 percent for housing, for example) of what is in the inventory, construction is the basic means by which the inventory and the pattern of land uses change.

The *valuer* role arises from the heterogeneity of the real estate inventory. Since no two pieces of urban property are exactly alike, the concept of a marketplace and a market equilibrium price does not really apply, as we have noted. If two identical loaves of bread in a grocery store have different prices, the careful shopper will buy the cheaper one. But two houses on opposite sides of the street may pose a serious problem for the family in search of a home, because they are unable to say whether the one with the higher asking price is really worth more. They need the help of someone who is skilled in interpreting price differentials for commodities that are imperfect substitutes. The appraiser provides this help, either for the would-be purchaser, the lender, or anyone else who is concerned about it. Local tax collectors who are charged with making levies against property owners in proportion to the value of their holdings must also rely on the techniques that valuers use. The word "valuer" is a compromise between appraiser and assessor.

The real estate *broker* is properly an "agent" who acts for an owner or a prospective purchaser in negotiating and drawing up a real estate transaction. Brokers or agents frequently delegate some of their functions to salespeople, who are the employees of the broker and for whose actions the broker is almost completely responsible. So the word broker here includes the salesforce, if any.

Valuers and brokers perform services for principals in real estate transactions. Many other occupational categories are ancillary to the real estate business but are omitted from our discussion because they are professional fields in themselves. Architects, land planners, city planners, several fields of engineering, lawyers, and tax accountants are included in this list. Market researchers and investment counsellors have joined the list recently, though it may not be correct to refer to them as "professionals" in the sense that law is a profession. The following discussion will frequently touch upon these various ancillary fields, but we will not attempt to define, even in outline, what these specialized service activities do or should do.

Each participant in a market transaction has *goals* which generally relate to the role he is playing and which are defined in quite particular ways. Familiar business objectives, such as increasing profit or investment yield, are not relevant or must be given special interpretation in the real estate business.

There are many institutional constraints in this field that take the form of *laws*. The three main types of laws to be considered are these: (1) Laws about proving ownership. These include definitions of rights to real property and of recognized methods of transferring ownership; and definitions of the legal forms of ownership and business—partnership, corporation, and so on. (2) Lending regulations. These include definitions of the rights of borrowers and lenders; limitations on the activities of financial institutions; and provisions for governmental assistance in real estate finance. (3) Laws governing specific business relations. These include license requirements and limits on advertising; and limitations on land use and construction.

It is necessary to recognize three major forms of *taxation* affecting the real estate market: (1) The real property tax based on value. (2) The tax on income derived from real estate. (3) Taxation of capital gains realized from the sale of real estate assets.

The word *access* in Figure 31 refers to the location of a piece of real estate, taking into consideration three factors: (1) Distance from the urban center and subcenters. (2) The type and quality of services—such as fire protection, schools, and sewage disposal—available to users. (3) Nuisances to which users are exposed, such as odors from a refinery (leaving positive externalities, such as a favored view, to be defined as inherent attributes of the physical property itself or of ownership).

The restraint category labeled *tradition* is very elastic, but it is worth identifying at least these traditions: (1) User parameters, such as the custom that a family requires at least one room per person, or the practice of allowing 250 square feet of floor area per office employee. (2) Trade practices such as customary commission rates, reliance on trade associations for market information and for public relations or lobbying. (3) Labor union practices.

We shall now endeavor to enter at least one useful comment in each compartment of our Figure 31 "filing system" description of the real estate business. Some of the entries will involve us in ad hoc theories, and others will simply have to appeal to more specialized treatises. To simplify a bit, the discussion will refer mainly to a generalized land-use category called an "income property," instead of taking up apartment buildings, retail stores, factories, and office buildings separately.

This entire effort to describe the activities of the urban land market is based primarily on practices common to North America, though many points appear to have wider applicability. What we are describing is also the way things seem to be, not necessarily the way they ought to be.

THE URBAN LANDOWNER

The person who owns real property has the right to control and benefit from its use. He may delegate some of the control to a manager, or control may otherwise be lodged with a trustee. It is easy to confuse the roles of owner and investor, because we normally become owners through acts of investment, but the distinction lies in what is controlled. The owner controls something physical—which we refer to as "land"—while the investor controls money. But when the investor gives up his money in exchange for land, his role changes from that of a money manager to that of a land manager, and his goals or success criteria change.

Goals.— The economically motivated owner of land wants to manage it in such a way that its value is maximized. This involves protecting his ownership (against squatters, for example, or forfeiture for default on a debt or nonpayment of taxes). It also involves selecting the use that maximizes the value of the land, and disposing of it at just the moment when its value to him has reached its peak. Disposition is generally tied in with a decision to make a new investment, and that will be discussed in its turn. The owner's basic objective, then, is to put the property to its most rewarding use.

The term commonly employed is "highest and best use" and it refers to a use of land that maximizes the "residual land value," or *RLV*. This concept is best explained by means of an example, which is presented in Table 13. For a given piece of land, suppose that two types of houses are considered, type *A* with a building cost of $10,000 and type *B* with a cost of $15,000. Together with the lot, *A* would sell for $14,000 and *B* for $20,000.[1] Residual land value is defined as the market value of the developed land less the cost of development. *B* is the highest and best use, because it is the alternative that produces the maximum residual. Alternative *C* is included in the first portion of Table 13 to indicate that the more costly or more valuable property is not necessarily superior from the landowner's point of view.

Note that the ratio of *RLV* to *BC* is an incorrect indicator of preferred land use. For *A*, this ratio is 40 percent, which we might be tempted to think of as a return on investment. For *B*, the ratio is only 33 percent. The investment-return criterion for land use is not relevant, however. Funds for construction are generally borrowed and are tied up for a relatively short period of time. Whatever the source of the construction funds, appropriate interest on those funds is included in the cost of the building. If the landowner decides, on the basis of these ratios, to construct *A*, his net gain is $4,000 instead of the $5,000 he could have realized by

1. Information about probable selling prices may be obtained from a "valuer"—as explained in the following discussion. In any case, these values are determined by the local market as a whole, not merely assumed.

Table 13

Highest and Best Use
(Amounts in 1,000 dollars)

		Alternative buildings			
		A	B[a]	C	
Building cost	(BC)	10	15	20	
Market value	(MV)	14	20	23	
Residual land value	(RLV)	4	5	3	
		A'[a]	B		
Assume A already exists	BC	–	15		
	MV	14	20		
	RLV	14	5		
		A''	B'[a]		
After A' depreciates	BC	–	16		
	MV	7	24		
	RLV	7	8		
		A	B	D'	E[a]
Assume D' will be possible five years from now	BC	10	15	20	–
	MV	14	20	30	–
	RLV	4	5	10	7

[a] Denotes highest and best use.

constructing B. Misunderstanding his role in the land market cost him $1,000. He actually "invests" land rather than dollars.

A more fundamental problem for the owner is that he never really knows all the options he has—the full range of things that the property might be used for and a realistic estimate of the RLV for each.

If we suppose that house A has already been built, the situation is changed. Denoting this existing structure by A' in the second part of Table 13, we find that its RLV is higher than that for B. This happens because the cost required to make A available is zero; the previous investment is "sunk" into the property. So the RLV for A' is the entire market value, and it far exceeds the potential RLV for building B. To demolish *A* now in order to construct *B* would be most foolish, for in addition to spending $15,000 on construction, he would have to give up something worth $14,000, so the loss would be $9,000. An existing building has a very strong hold on the use of land. Though the structure may seem badly obsolete, deteriorated, and out of place, it may be the owner's best option and may be best in a resource-allocation sense as well.

After awhile, *A'* will depreciate further, and the local land economy may raise the market value of *B*. This is shown in the third section of Table 13, with *A"* and *B'* denoting costs and values after some time has elapsed. Now the *RLV* for *A"* has fallen to $7,000 because the relative desirability of the house has suffered, we suppose, and while the cost of *B'* has risen to $16,000, its *MV* has reached $24,000. At this point, *B'* becomes the highest and best use; that is, it pays the owner to demolish *A"*. This process defines the economic life of buildings, though it does not necessarily define the optimum time at which an owner should sell his land. This concept of economic life is relative rather than absolute, since it is not governed solely or even principally by the physical state of the original structure. The structure's economic life continues through changing uses, too, in the sense that differs from that used in connection with producers' durable goods such as machinery.

In the last section of Table 13, we go back to alternatives *A* and *B*, neither being built, and consider, in addition, house *D'* costing $20,000 to build and having a market value of $30,000. We assume, however, that because of zoning laws or gradual changing of the demand situation, this more profitable improvement cannot be put on the market until five years have elapsed. Our best choice, then, is to hold the land vacant, calling this alternative *E*, for five years. By attaching a value of $7,000 (discounting the *RLV* of *D'* at 7.5 percent, for example) to *E*, we imply that waiting five years to build *E* is better than constructing either *A* or *B* now. The "highest and best use" in this case is the absence of use. To be more realistic, we might consider putting the land to temporary use, such as the erection of billboards, but the complication would not be all that instructive. In a sense, all urban land uses are temporary, and we have to consider that the whole chain of prospective uses for a given piece of land is reflected in the market value, or the price that any informed purchaser of the land would offer.[2]

2. See W. F. Smith, *Aspects of Housing Demand* (Berkeley: Center for Real Estate and Urban Economics, University of California, 1966), Chapter Four.

Laws.— The physical dimensions of what an urban landowner owns are defined by written public records. The records must contain accurate maps and surveying descriptions sufficient to resolve differences about where property lines lie, and they must also preserve evidence of changes in ownership and of claims against property that fall short of ownership.[3] Recognizable changes in ownership can come about through voluntary sale (private deed), public acquisition (condemnation, expropriation, compulsory purchase), squatting (adverse possession, effective if it meets particular legal tests), inheritance by bequest or by statute, geological forces (such as the shifting of a stream's course), default on a mortgage or nonpayment of taxes (foreclosure), voluntary gifts to a public agency (dedication), grants by government to private parties, and other events. In the absence of heirs, property of a decedent reverts to the state (escheat).

Property may be owned by a single individual, by several individuals having defined shares, by married couples, by partnerships or corporations formed for the purpose of ownership or for the conduct of some other business requiring the use of real estate, and by various types of public agencies (such as a city or a port authority). A mortgage lender or a trustee is considered to be the legal owner in some cases but with many ownership rights left to the borrower or beneficiary. Some categories of individuals and businesses (felons or noncitizens, for example) may be denied the right to own real property. Ownership may be limited to the lifetime of an individual or may be deferred until some future event occurs (for example, a son's ownership may begin when his widowed mother dies).

An owner may offer his property as security for a debt, and if such a loan is made, the public record will be amended to reflect a lien. (The record should be corrected when the loan has been paid.) Liens may also come into existence because of liabilities the owner has incurred in other ways (such as by failing to pay a plumber or a merchant), sometimes without the owner being aware of the fact. Failure to discharge such debts will lead to a legal process of liquidation, with at least partial loss of ownership, but the owner generally is allowed time to recover it by making good the indebtedness.

3. For fuller discussion of all points relating to urban land law, see Robert Kratovil, *Real Estate Law* (Englewood Cliffs, N.J.: Prentice-Hall, 1974).

The owner's right to determine the use of property is circumscribed by regulatory powers of government, or "police powers." Zoning laws, for example, specify which uses are permitted and how much of the ground area may be covered. Other statutes restrict occupancy (the number of persons in a dwelling), use (such as conducting business of some sort in one's home), the presence of mechanical equipment and cleanliness (fire codes apply here), the keeping of animals, and so on. These restrictions and changes in them affect the value of an owner's property, often quite significantly, but losses in value caused by exercises of the police power are generally not compensable. Private ownership must be surrendered to public agencies if the property is deemed necessary for some public use (a school or a redevelopment project, for example), but only upon "just compensation" being given to the owner.

Ownership rights may also be restricted by conditions in the deed by which the properties were acquired (restrictive covenants); one such condition, for example, might bar the removal of trees. And owners may give others the right to cross over their properties (easements). Legal owners of real property are liable in the case of criminal acts committed there (prostitution, for example) and for civil damages when innocent visitors are injured. The condition of the property (for example, piles of rubble in which rats breed) may be deemed a public nuisance, for which the owner is also liable.

Taxes.– Real property taxes in North America are annual charges equal to perhaps two percent, on the average, of market value, and 15 to 25 percent of gross rents. There are two basic elements: special assessments to pay for improvements, such as sewers or sidewalks, which benefit particular properties; and taxes for the support of general government. Without public expenditures of either type, the usefulness of urban real estate is very much diminished, but the quid pro quo is not necessarily precise or equitable. Since the level of public expenditure is beyond the control of an individual property owner, it is normally to his advantage to minimize the amount of tax he has to pay, other things being equal. Even though an increase in taxes may be shifted to tenants, this is usually difficult or time-consuming. Thus, owners may be reluctant to repair or remodel their buildings if this will result in reassessment. A level of taxation that requires the owner to pay more in a given year than he receives from the property's use is a strong inducement to change the use to something more intensive.

Income produced by investment real estate is taxable as personal income, or as business income which, when distributed after taxes, may be taxed again. The owner is allowed, however, to charge against gross income an amount for capital consumption or "depreciation" that is generally much in excess of the property's loss in economic value during the tax year. This allowance, in addition to clear-cut business expenditures for interest and property taxes, reduces taxable income below the level of cash "throw-off" from the property and softens the impact of the tax rate schedule that applies.[4] Capital gains taxes, when applied to urban real estate, are said to serve the purpose of recapturing increases in land value caused by the growth of the community, which growth the individual property owners did nothing to bring about. The tax is calculated as a fraction of the difference between what the owner paid for the property and what he received for it on sale (after adjustments for such things as excess depreciation allowances). It is, once again, a factor in the real estate investor's decision when he tries to anticipate the whole sequence of events consequent upon a specific real estate investment. The owner, as such, is affected by capital gains taxation primarily by unanticipated changes in such tax provisions since he acquired the property. A person who expected to have $100,000 on the sale of his property may find himself "locked in," unable to bear this cost of an otherwise desirable transaction. One option the owner has is to refinance his property—to borrow as much of the $100,000, for example, as he can find someone willing to take a mortgage for. If he desires to change the use of the property—demolishing an old building and build something new, he may find himself liable for capital gains taxation, depending on the legal form of the ownership. High capital gains tax rates encourage circumvention of the normal market process by encouraging owners to lease instead of selling or to make unrecorded sales.

Access.— The location of a property relative to the center of town and subcenters, the types of services available for users of the property, and any nuisances that interfere with its use are factors that affect the owner but which, generally speaking, he cannot control. Part of the value of his property is determined by its relative location, which also influences the

4. This subject is treated more fully in Chapter Eight, in the discussion of the real estate investor's role.

"highest and best use" that may be made of it. The important concept of
"site rent" is illustrated in Figure 32. Suppose that the owner's property is
at distance OA from the center and that the outer edge of the city is at B,
twice as far away. A person living at B spends a certain amount per year on
transportation, say, \$200 (= BD). If he lived at A instead, he could save
\$100 (= CF), and so would be willing to pay the owner at A this amount.
The site rent at distance OA, then, is \$100. By the same reasoning, the site
rent at various locations diminishes from \$200 at the center to zero at

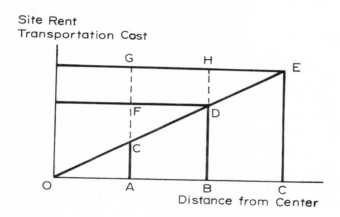

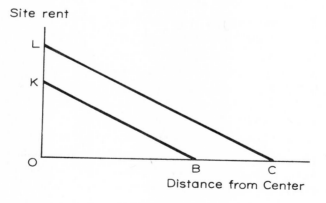

Figure 32. Site rent and transportation cost.

distance *AB*, and this is represented by line *KB* in the lower portion of the figure.

Suppose, now, that the population of the city grows, spreading to *OC* distance from the center. The maximum transportation cost is now $300 (= *CE*) per year, and in an economic sense the person who lives at *B* now "saves" $100 a year by virtue of his location. The owner at *B* is now able, in any case, to ask a site rent of $100 for the location, and the owner at *A* is able to raise his demand for site rent to $200 (= *CG*). Line *LC* in the lower diagram shows that the whole structure of site rents shifts up as a result of the increase in population. Recalling the discussion of von Thuenen's competitive land value scheme in the previous chapter, it follows that population growth may not only shift the site rents up for given uses, but sometimes introduce more intensive uses for a given property. The owner, then, has a powerful interest in the growth of his community through the expansion of the economic base, for it brings increases of a windfall nature to the value of his property.

As a manger of part of the urban landscape, the property owner should keep abreast of plans in nearby zoning, because these things constantly shuffle the options that go into his highest and best use calculations. But to have anything other than a passive role with regard to these factors and to the health of the economic base, he must normally engage in group action—that is, he must be involved in the civics of the community.

Traditions. — Local civic action, in fact, was for a very long time nearly the exclusive preserve of urban property owners in North America. For generations, only "freeholders" could vote. It was not until 1972 that tenants were allowed to vote on money matters in municipal elections in British Columbia. This does not mean that local government effectively serves, or served, the interests of property owners, because it is, after all, a political process, where the output often seems quite unrelated to the input. It is enmeshed in constitutional and legal arcana. It deals with the collective interests of people whose motives are individual.

Land ownership is also influenced by traditions regarding separate titles for land and buildings. Commercial property in North America often enough involves a ground lease, but the normal arrangement and the expectation for other categories of property is that the owner of the building owns the ground as well. The provision of insurance for titles is

an accepted buiness practice in the United States, while the function is
performed by public agencies in parts of Canada.

Relationships between landlord and tenant are defined by statutes,
but tradition really governs. Whether there will be a lease, whether it will
be recorded, what its length will be, and what clauses will be included—all
are questions usually resolved in favor of custom. A lease can provide
security as well as income for the owner, and it is common for landlords to
select tenants on the basis of credit records. But a very long lease, or a
master lease given to an operator who intends to make subleasing arrangements, creates valuable property rights for the tenant. Under these
circumstances, the tenant becomes part owner, in both a practical and a
legal sense. Month-to-month tenancies give the landlord the right to
change his tenants and raise rents, but custom usually forbids the owner
from doing these things except in extreme cases. Thus, long-term tenants
may be found to pay rents well below the market value of what they
occupy, less than new tenants in the same building, and even less than the
out-of-pocket costs they occasion for the owner—all in the absence of a
binding lease. Residential landlords not uncommonly subsidize long-term
tenants, especially if there are no mortgage payments to be made. That is,
landlords may be prone to let historic costs and out-of-pocket costs
influence the rents they ask, even from new tenants. Charging "what the
traffic will bear" is a business precept that is often ignored in real estate.

THE VALUER

A family shopping for a house can usually form a rough opinion
about what a particular dwelling is worth. A real estate agent generally
suggests an asking price when undertaking to sell someone's property.
Builders, developers, architects, and others closely involved in construction
are good judges of what things cost and probably of what they will sell for.
The "owner" in the preceding section needs an idea about market value in
order to decide about his property's best use. A retail merchant forms a
pretty good idea of the value of nearby properties. Most of the principals
involved in a real estate transaction know the rudiments of valuation, yet a
large proportion of these transactions are carried out with the assistance of
a valuation specialist.

There are several kinds of valuation problems. Estimating construction or reconstruction costs from architectural plans is one activity.

Another is market analysis to determine whether a proposed shopping center, for example, is feasible. Investment analysis is a method of determining an investor's rate of return from the purchase of income property. Engineering studies to determine the practicality and cost of excavating, for instance, fall into another category. Our discussion will be limited to "appraisal" in the generally accepted sense of impartially estimating what a piece of real property will bring on the market, and to assessment for property tax purposes where it differs from appraisal. (Assessment for income, gift, estate, and capital gains tax purposes generally conforms to standard appraisal practice.)

An appraiser's estimate of value tells the seller of property that he cannot expect to get much more than, for example, $80,000. It tells the prospective buyer that he is not likely to find a similar property for much less than $80,000, and it tells the mortgage lender that a loan of $60,000 secured by a first mortgage on this property could probably be recovered in full in the event of default and foreclosure. The appraiser's fee or salary may be paid by any one of these parties, but if he follows the prescribed rules of the game, his estimate of value is likely to be accepted by all three, since separate estimates by other appraisers—who also adhere to the rules—will be very close. The appraiser thus helps people make up their minds about a real estate transaction. Real estate resources are more "mobile" as a result.

The appraiser's contribution may be largely psychological, like the bridegroom's best friend who reassures him on the eve of the wedding that he is "doing the right thing." Or it may be seen as a communication function, a digesting of arcane, copious, and inaccessible market information. Given the nature of real estate, people in the market need both. Sometimes appraisals are perfunctory, as when a lender agrees in advance to make a loan equal to 80 percent of whatever the buyer offers for the property, for example.

One of the most important kinds of appraisal work is in connection with condemnation or expropriation—the taking of private property by a public agency. Determining "just compensation" to the owner requires value estimates that will stand up in court, because the owner can contest the amount offered him. It is therefore up to the courts to decide, in effect, what method appraisers can use, because a valuation based on an unrecognized method will not be sustained. Similarly, where disputes arise concerning property taxes, community property settlements, the proper conduct of a regulated mortgage lending business, or other matters where there is a question about the value of real estate, the appraiser may find himself explaining his method to the court. So the practicing appraiser is much influenced in his choice of methods by the existence of a judicial tradition.

Goals.– We can say that the appraiser's goal is to arrive at an estimate of value by following a prescribed method. The customary method in North America is to make three conceptually different estimates of value and to take a weighted average.[5] A greatly simplified version of these three approaches is presented in Table 14. (Appendix A describes the "income approach" more fully.) The market-comparison approach involves selecting a sufficient number of properties that are reasonably similar to the property being appraised, and which have recently changed hands. The selling prices of each of these comparison properties are adjusted to compensate for their differences from the property being appraised. For example, *A*'s location is better, so $1,000 is deducted from its selling price. *C*'s condition is worse, so $1,000 is added to its selling price. Traditions governing this adjustment process are relatively weak, but if the appraiser has information about a large number of real estate sales, he can usually find cases that justify the specific adjustment he makes. The adjusted selling prices of the comparison properties are averaged together, often with subjective weights.

The cost method requires an estimate of the value of the land occupied by the property being appraised, a figure that is determined by going through the market-comparison approach once again, this time for recent sales of undeveloped land. To this is added the estimated cost of constructing the existing building, given its dimensions and materials and today's prices for materials and labor. Appraisers generally rely on published indexes of construction costs for typical buildings instead of pricing all the components of the building themselves. Then an allowance for depreciation (and obsolescence) of the building as it stands is subtracted. This deduction can be calculated by means of a formula–a straight-line write-off, based on the fraction of such a building's economic life that has expired–or by estimating the cost of restoring the building to a new condition, or in other ways. The result, in the example, is a value estimate of $27,000.

5. One widely used textbook that describes these methods in detail is Alfred A. Ring, *The Valuation of Real Estate* (Englewood Cliffs, N.J.: Prentice-Hall, 1970).

Table 14

Standard Appraisal Method, Much Simplified

Market-comparison approach

	A	Properties similar to subject B	C
Price	$24,000	$28,000	$18,000
Location	−1,000	−2,000	+2,000
Condition	+1,000	−3,000	+1,000
Adjusted price	$24,000	$23,000	$21,000
Estimated value of subject; $23,000			

Cost-of-Replacement Approach	
Cost to acquire similar land	$ 4,000
Building cost new, 1,500 sq. ft. @ $20	30,000
Less accrued depreciation	7,000
Estimated value	$27,000

Income Approach[a]	
Adjusted gross annual income	$ 4,000
Adjusted operating costs	2,000
Projected net income	$ 2,000
Multiplier (or capitalization factor)	10
Estimated value	$20,000

Summary	
Market comparison estimate	$23,000
Cost estimate	27,000
Income estimate	20,000
Opinion of Value of Subject Property	$23,500

[a] The income approach is closely related to real estate investment analysis; modern computer techniques enable the income property analyst to provide far more detailed and useful information than this simple illustration suggests. See Appendix.

The income approach involves projecting the rental income and the operating expenses from the property, usually by taking recent accounting data for the property and adjusting it to reflect normal market practice (such as the level of repairs) and changes likely to occur in the near future (higher property taxes, for example). The adjusted net income is capitalized, often simply by applying a multiplier derived from recent sales experiences of similar rental property (see note to Table 14). Multipliers for *gross* income are very widely used. The income approach in the illustration produces a value estimate of $20,000. The separate estimates are reworked, weighted, or just turned over in the appraiser's mind to produce a final opinion of value such as $23,500. The appraiser may reason, for example, that the cost approach is too high because the market for such properties is overbuilt, and the income approach is unreliable because properties of the type he is appraising (single-family houses, for example) are not generally rented. Too wide a spread between his separate estimates, however, calls for reexamination of his data.

These three approaches to valuation came together into a prescribed routine by a process of evolution. There are theoretical and even semantic problems in each, and there is no theory, beyond the "buckshot" principle, to justify using three. In recent years, the standard method has come under sharp attack.[6] One recurring theme in this attack is that the appraiser's basic job is to predict selling prices, and that this is a problem very much within the purview of statistical theory. Computer routines to perform multiple regression analysis, in particular, have been shown to perform at least as well as appraisers in predicting selling prices.

For example, if we have information about many houses that have recently been sold in our city, including the price (P) that was paid for each, the age (A) and number of bedrooms (B) in each, the computer will tell us how much each year of age and each bedroom adds to or subtracts from the probable selling price. It will give us an equation such as: $P = -200A \times 7,000B$. We can use this to predict the selling price of a house that the owner wants to sell. If his house is twenty years old and has three bedrooms: $P = -200(20) \times 7,000(3) = \$17,000$. The result is an estimate; how far off it might be depends mainly on the quality of data used to develop the equation and on the complexity we permit the equation to assume. The computer will provide information about the reliability of our equation.[7]

It is clear that statistical methods will ultimately alter appraisal

6. See, for example, Richard U. Ratcliff, *Modern Real Estate Valuation* (Madison, Wis.: Democrat Press, 1965); and Paul P. Wendt, "Recent Developments in Appraisal Theory," *The Appraisal Journal* (October 1969).

7. See Gene Dilmore, *The New Approach to Real Estate Appraising* (Englewood Cliffs, N.J.: Prentice-Hall, 1971), pp. 145–179.

practices, but there is resistance to drastic change by appraisal organizations.

The goals of a property tax assessor in estimating value differ from the goals of the general appraiser in two important ways. One is that the estimated value of a property must be broken down into the value of land and the value of buildings. Laws require this, though it is not clear why, but there is no method that appraisers as a group accept as valid for making such a separation. In fact, recalling that "land" generally is understood in real estate discussions to include improvements because the improvements are irretrievably sunk investments, many feel that a separation of land from improvement value is specious.

The other difference is that assessors are concerned with relative rather than absolute value. As long as people pay taxes that are a uniform percentage of the value of their property, the assessor is free from public criticism, whether the values he has in his books are fully equivalent to market value or not. His job is equitable valuation, not the prediction of selling prices. The laws he works under, however, often require him to keep his assessed values equal to a prescribed fraction (such as 25 percent) of market value, in effect forcing him to make correct estimates of absolute real estate values. But the same laws often provide leeway in the method of determining "market value" for property tax purposes. For example, an assessor may be required only to give "consideration" to all significant property characteristics in estimating value, leaving him free to decide the monetary effect of each characteristic.

Laws. –   Real estate appraisers are not required to hold licenses in the United States or Canada, except in the state of Nebraska, though the institution of such a system is frequently proposed. Paradoxically, laws require in many cases that appraisals be obtained—for mortgage loans, in public property acquisition, and in various disputes involving real estate. This gives rise to courtroom efforts by contending attorneys to discredit witnesses who claim to be appraisers. For this and other reasons, appraisers value membership in trade associations—appraisal societies—that limit their membership to experienced or "qualified" people.

Appraisers estimate values of ownership interests, rather than physical property, so it is necessary for appraisers to understand the laws that define various interests in real property.

Taxes.— Property taxes are an item of operating expense in the appraiser's income approach. Other than that, taxation does not show up in standard appraisal format. In recent years, it has become manifest that the market value of income property is affected by tax laws such as those relating to depreciation. But appraisal practice has resisted incorporating such factors, one line of reasoning being that the tax consequences of ownership are characteristics of the person who owns rather than of his property (see Appendix A).

Access.— It is a familiar dictum of appraisers that the three factors that determine real estate value are "location, location, and location." Yet location studies are not part of the standard appraisal method. The market approach is supposed to confine its sample of properties to those that are reasonably close together, and a further adjustment on account of "location" is common. In some fashion, the appraiser must make his mechanical three approaches to value consistent with: (a) forecasts of changing economic, social, and business characteristics of the neighborhood (for example, Hoyt's sector theory); (b) the special nature of public services (such as schools) in the area; and (c) the changing relative accessibility of the area to the rest of the urban area as suburbs spread farther, new shopping centers are built, and new transportation infrastructure is created across the city and its environs.

It might seem that appraisers would be in the forefront of research into the dynamics of urban land-use patterns. Apart from absorbing Hoyt's sector theory, however, there is virtually no interest in such research evident in appraisal trade-association publications. Urban land-use "models" have been developed, or are in the process of development, primarily by scholars in the fields of transportation and city planning.

The appraiser's report normally includes an opinion concerning the highest and best use of the property. In principle, this means that the appraiser has estimated the residual land value for every feasible use of the property. In fact, if it seems likely that there is some use superior to the present use, a very different technique of analysis is called for, such as a development feasibility study (see Chapter Ten).

Traditions.— Most of what appraisers do is governed by tradition, which we have discussed. There are important questions as to whether some of these traditions should be discarded and whether real estate appraisal "as we have known it" will be with us ten or fifteen years hence because of such developments as multiple regression analysis.

A few miscellaneous customs, in addition to those already mentioned, are worth noting here. One is that appraisers often serve an apprenticeship, of sorts, in the field of real estate sales, or that they combine appraisal work with that of being an agent. One reason for the closeness of appraisers and brokers is that the sales information which appraisers need comes from completed transactions in which brokers have participated. Another is that appraisers often find it best to hold a real estate broker's license in case they should appear to be performing a broker's duties in some instance; having the license, there is then no need to avoid making active use of it. Another reason is that brokers and salesmen frequently study appraisal as a means of doing a better selling job and may become proficient enough to do appraising per se.

Appraisers often prefer to express an opinion of a property's value "free and clear," disregarding the existence of a mortgage or other liens. That is, they normally value the property, not the equity.

Mortgage lenders, and mortgage insurance agencies like the FHA, employ a large fraction of all practicing appraisers. Since the loan is critical to most real estate transactions, and since mortgage appraisals will be made in any case, it is natural that many buyers and sellers rely on those appraisals instead of hiring their own appraisers. An FHA appraisal virtually dictates the price of the house.

Mortgage appraisals are primarily "in-house" documents—studies done by and for the lending institution, though they might actually be used by other parties in a transaction. It is likely that such appraisals emphasize the "approach" that seems most logically related to the circumstances, with less attention to the other two approaches. For existing, single-family dwellings, the prices of similar, recently sold homes is the preferred indicator. For a tract of homes under construction or just completed, the cost approach is relatively easy, since the developer will make his land, labor, and materials cost information available to the lender, and competition will generally keep the selling price of the completed homes fairly close to their total actual cost (allowing some normal profit to the developer). Income property calls for careful analysis of investment appeal—that is, use of the income approach—because the mortgage lender is, for practical purposes, in partnership with the owner of such property.

DISCUSSION QUESTIONS

1. In a market system, the owner of a parcel of urban land *may*, in principle, ignore the "external costs" (disadvantageous results to other people) of his choice of land use. Do you think the logic of the market system *requires* that external effects be ignored?

2. Several economists have concluded that the heterogeneity, durability, and interdependence of real estate as a commodity rule out the possibility of equilibrium in the urban land market. Do you agree? If it is true, what are the practical implications?

3. "Since 'real property' means merely the exclusive right to *use* land or buildings, it is not conceivable to have a society in which private real property does not exist." Do you agree? If it is true, does that mean there is no way to dispense with the urban land market?

4. Suppose the owner of land parcel A had no way to borrow the cost of constructing an improvement. How would this affect the "highest and best use" of parcel A? Of parcel B across the street?

5. One of the situations shown in Table 13 says the highest and best use involves demolishing an existing (and still usable) building. Could there be a situation in which the best thing to do would be to physically damage an existing improvement without demolishing it altogether?

6. Despite the fact that population growth is likely to raise property values, property owners in some communities have been known to oppose growth. Would that have to be illogical or mistaken on their part?

7. Do the appraiser's "three approaches" provide all the information a landowner needs to determine his highest and best use?

8. If appraisal enters at least indirectly into almost every real estate transaction, and all appraisers use pretty much the same methods, are estimates of market value just self-fulfilling prophecies? Or do appraisers merely "read" basic economic information that their judgments do not affect?

SELECTED REFERENCES

Barlowe, Raleigh. *Land Resource Economics*. Englewood Cliffs, N.J.: Prentice-Hall, 1958.
A textbook intended primarily for students of agricultural economics but examining urban land-use questions with the same microeconomic concepts.

Kratovil, Robert. *Real Estate Law*. 6th ed. Englewood Cliffs, N.J.: Prentice-Hall, 1974.
A textbook for real estate practitioners, covering property rights, transfers, liens, landlord-tenant relations, and related topics.

Ratcliff, Richard U. *Urban Land Economics*. New York: McGraw-Hill, 1949.
A textbook on the economics of land use, development, and redevelopment in the United States, including the forces which contribute to the location and growth of particular cities and the essential criteria for government involvement in land-use control and housing construction.

Ring, Alfred A. *The Valuation of Real Estate*. Englewood Cliffs, N.J.: Prentice-Hall, 1970.
An introductory textbook on appraising organized around the standard "three approaches."

Turvey, Ralph. *The Economics of Real Property*. London: George Allen and Unwin, 1957.
Theoretical examination of the "highest and best use" concept, employing conventional microeconomic analysis.

8

LENDERS AND
INVESTORS

LONG-TERM LOANS used in purchasing real estate are commonly secured by mortgages. That is, default on the loan gives the lender the right to recover the indebtedness through a forced sale of the property if the mortgage lien has been recorded against the property. Mortgage financing is a critical requirement for most real estate development and acquisition, and in the aggregate accounts for a significant fraction of all financial activity in the nation. Mortgage transactions, however, bypass the organized "money market" almost completely, even though there is no separate financial center for the mortgage business. Instead, it is a highly dispersed field of activity; a large part of real estate business "know how" is information about possible sources of mortgage loan funds.

LENDERS

Goals.— Three basic classes of mortgage lenders must be distinguished. *Originators* advance money (often borrowed from commercial banks) to developers or purchasers of real estate but soon sell the mortgage paper thus created to a long-term investor. The originator may earn either a "finders fee" or a profit in this way. The originator may be a subsidiary or affiliate of a real estate development company, such as a house-building concern, for which quick handling of buyers' mortgage loan applications is an important aid in selling; in that case, the originator's goal or pay-off is hard to distinguish from that of the developer. Even after placing new mortgage loans with long-term investors, the originator may continue to "service" them—collect and account for monthly payments, look after delinquencies, and so forth—for a stipulated, often customary fee (such as one-half of one percent of the principal).

Long-term *holders* of mortgage investments who want to liquidate a particular loan or group of loans can endeavor to find another mortgage lender who is willing to buy. There is a limited opportunity to sell loans to *traders*, a category of lenders consisting primarily of governmental organizations concerned with housing (the Federal National Mortgage Association, nominally a private corporation, the Government National Mortgage Association in the U.S., and the Central Mortgage and Housing Corporation in Canada, for example). Traders provide liquidity for mortgage loans by standing ready to buy them; in principle, the trading function would require that loans purchased from one long-term investor be quickly resold to another, but in fact, the principal mortgage trading agencies have accumulated such large inventories that they themselves are a major type of long-term lender. Private individuals or strictly private businesses can and do trade in mortgages, earning profit from differential prices rather than earning interest on long-term loans, but this kind of market facility is not uniformly available.

Our principle concern is with the *holders*, or long-term investors. The prototype mortgage lender is a savings bank, with long-term deposits that must be invested safely. Real estate mortgages are an attractive use of such money because they are long-term contracts at fixed rates of earnings, with the principal secured by liens against an immovable asset that generally increases in value over time. Commercial banks make mortgage loans, but generally as a function of their savings departments, thus separating their long-term business from the short-term business on both the deposit and the investment sides. Life insurance firms have policy reserve funds to invest, and building societies, savings and loan associations, or other variants of credit cooperatives have long-term savings funds to put to work. Real estate mortgages meet their investment needs, too. A significant proportion of all mortgage loan investments are made by private individuals, usually by taking a mortgage note in lieu of cash payments for property which they previously owned. Recently, groups of individuals have been formed into mortgage investment trusts to make high-yielding debt investments directly rather than through traditional financial institutions.

Each mortgage lender has some goals or criteria peculiar to himself or itself, but virtually all relate to combinations of these factors:

1. Type and location of property (homes, apartments, land, shopping centers

2. Property risk, largely a function of its newness or degree of absorption by the land market.

3. Transaction size—for example, one two-million-dollar shopping center loan versus 100 single-family home loans at $20,000 each.

4. Credit worthiness of the borrower (for example, the monthly income of the home buyer) and the transferability of the obligation.

5. The upper limit of the ratio of the loan amount to the value of the property used as security.

6. The ratio of aggregate mortgage loan investment to total assets of the lender.

7. Willingness to make short-term mortgage loans for construction.

8. Willingness to accept other than first mortgages as security.

9. Expectation about how long the individual mortgage investment will be held.

10. The term of the loan and amortization plan—whether loans are fully amortized, level payment contracts, interest only until maturity loans, and so forth.

11. The desired rate of interest, of loan processing or other fees ("points") and of penalties for prepayment by the borrower.

12. The range of trade-off between various pairs of items 1 through 11—for example, whether a larger loan ratio, together with a higher interest rate, is acceptable, or whether the borrower's substandard personal credit can be compensated by a relatively short loan term.

It would be excusable to jump immediately to our section on "tradition," because, with the exception of item 11, the price of money to the borrower, it is primarily tradition and the laws confirming tradition that define the goals of particular mortgage lenders for this whole list of items. Competition in the general money market makes itself felt in the mortgage interest rate, and individual lenders may experience financial pressure to accept riskier loans, but otherwise neither the marketplace nor refined investment analysis appears to have much influence on the behavior of mortgage lenders. They have a "style" but not a strategy.

For example, a loan-to-value ratio of two-thirds (for first mortgages) was a deeply rooted tradition until it was edged upward by government loan insurance programs. A family actually paying $250 a month in rent will be turned down for a mortgage loan requiring payments of $225 if the lender's rule of thumb says that their $800 monthly income does not justify spending more than $200 for housing. Some life insurance companies commit the maximum allowable portion of their assets to mortgage loans while other companies make almost no such investments. Financial institutions avoid making loans in areas of minority occupancy or racial change despite abundant evidence of at least acceptable investment opportunity there. Loans with interest rates that are variable according to changes in the general conditions of the money market have been very difficult to introduce in the United States.

In general, we can say that there is very little "trading-off" (item 12 above) in the dealings of a particular lender and not much more when a prospective borrower shops among different lenders. The principal reason is the great heterogeneity of the real estate commodity (and personal credit) that is used as security. Information necessary to estimate appropriate trade-offs is in very short supply, and lenders find it safer to stick to familiar patterns.

The basic goal of a mortgage lender, in principle, is to realize the highest possible rate of earnings on his entire portfolio of assets. Such is the force of traditional and legal constraints, however, that the lender is more likely to think in terms of a target rate of earnings rather than a maximum. He may make loans at 8 percent when he could be making them at 11, and feel he has done his job, if the cost of money to him is 5 percent. But if the cost of money—the rate he must pay to depositors or policyholders—goes up to 6.5 percent, he has few options for preserving the necessary spread, and he has probably accumulated little in the "good" times to tide him over the more difficult ones. Recurrent liquidity crunches which mortgage lenders experience are largely attributable to inflexibility lenders as a group have imposed upon themselves. Their lending and borrowing cycles do not coincide, and they have few options to bridge the gaps that inevitably appear.

Laws.– The right of a mortgage lender to secure the repayment of a defaulted loan by taking over the property or having it sold is created, defined, and circumscribed by a large body of law, the exact nature of which varies among jurisdictions. Generally, the defaulting borrower does not forfeit whatever equity he may have, though in times past he did. For example, if the outstanding debt is $12,000 and the sale of the property brings $15,000, the lender is entitled to no more than $12,000 plus interest and costs. If the sale brings only $10,000, the borrower remains liable in principle for the remaining $2,000 plus.

Generally, a mortgage lien that is recorded prior to an additional lien on the same property is satisfied first in a foreclosure action, with the residue, if any, going toward the junior (usually the second or third) mortgage. Thus, the risk for a junior-mortgage holder is much greater than that of the first- or senior-mortgage holder, especially if the market value of the property is likely to fluctuate substantially.

The defaulting borrower normally has some period of time during which he may redeem the property by making good the default, and he may do this even after the property has been sold to another party.

Residential mortgage loans may be insured by a government agency in Canada and the United States, and by some private agencies. This means that the outstanding balance of the loan, above the amount realized through foreclosure sale, will be substantially repaid from an insurance fund. Loans must meet a number of criteria as to type of property, price, borrower's credit, and so forth to be eligible for this type of insurance protection. Mortgage insurance was introduced mainly as a program of government to broaden homeownership opportunities by encouraging lenders to make greater amounts of such loans on terms that larger numbers of households could meet. It may or may not have the effect of subsidizing mortgage lenders (a complex theoretical as well as statistical issue), but it does influence the behavior of these lenders in a significant way.[1]

Institutional mortgage lenders—banks, savings and loan associations, life insurance companies, credit unions, trust companies, and others—are regulated in considerable detail by governmental agencies, primarily at the state or provincial level. Savings and loan associations, for example, must invest almost exclusively in residential mortgages, of which only a small fraction may be on other than single-family homes, while commercial banks may hold only government bonds if they choose. The quality of

---

1. Various forms of government assistance to housing are described and discussed in Chapter Eleven.

mortgage appraisals is subject to audit, and upper limits on loan-to-value ratios are enforced. Delinquent real estate loans must be reported. Usury laws constrain loan terms. Liquid reserves are required according to fixed sets of rules. Interest rates paid to savings depositors have legal ceilings, and so on. The scope and strength of such regulations is such that government is very clearly a partner in the real estate mortgage loan business, though without benefit of a comprehensive, consistent objective.

Taxes.– Mortgage lenders receive interest income, plus windfall gains or losses through foreclosure and the purchase or sale of mortgages from other lenders, and some fees. As they are not owners of real estate, for tax purposes, the special real estate provisions of personal, corporate, capital gain, and estate or inheritance taxes have no special relevance except as they affect the value of the mortgaged property and the financial position of the borrower. Individuals, partners, and some forms of trusts making mortgage loan investments may escape the level of taxation that applies to corporations.

Property taxes are the responsibility of the owner of the property, who is the mortgage borrower. Because such taxes take so large a share of the income of the property (or of the homeowner), however, and because nonpayment of property taxes jeopardizes the owner's title, institutional mortgage lenders usually want to be assured that the tax is paid as it comes due. Thus, lenders often require homeowners to include amounts for taxes (and insurance) along with remittances on the mortgage debt, and the lender administers a trust fund for the payment of taxes.

Access.– For reasons that are partly legal, partly traditional, and largely practical, mortgage lenders usually confine their loans to certain geographic areas—even to a single neighborhood in a particular city, but quite often to the confines of a single state. Large life insurance companies dealing with mortgage correspondents or through their own branch offices are sometimes an exception to this. Savings and loan associations and similar organizations that are in the nature of credit cooperatives make loans only to members—that is, to depositors, though this can be a nominal arrangement—and so limit their lending radius. Amalgamations of mortgage-lending organizations, the trading of mortgages, and other devices can extend the radius. The basic reason for the limitation, in any case, is the heterogeneity of real estate. A banker in Salem, Oregon, knows the economy of that town better than he knows the risk of a real estate loan in Wellington, Kansas. Local specialization is one way to deal with the great heterogeneity of real estate, in mortgage lending as in other aspects.

Local financing institutions are likely to be as well informed about land-use trends and real estate development opportunities as any person or group in the community. Because of the high leverage of real estate loans and the fact that developers are able to minimize personal risk in many ways, the local mortgage lender is often the principal risk-bearer in developments (saddled with the losses of an unsuccessful project but not participating in the profits of a successful one). These factors, taken together, mean that it is the mortgage lender, primarily, who makes market analyses and feasibility studies which it might seem the developer ought to be responsible for. We shall nevertheless defer the description of how these studies are made until Chapter Ten.

Traditions. — We have already said that tradition plays a very large role in deciding how a mortgage lender responds to a loan applicant. Mortgage "risk analysis" can nevertheless appear very systematic; in fact, the method of such analysis is a tradition in itself.[2] The lender's decision problem is two-fold: whether to lend at all, and how much. The two questions are interlocked, for the loan applicant may be deemed unable to afford the property. The property is appraised and the maximum first mortgage loan is determined by taking a prescribed fraction, such as 75 percent, of the appraised value. If the property has certain characteristics deemed unfavorable, such as location in a neighborhood of changing land use, the loan application may be rejected without further ado. If the property is acceptable security to this lender, the borrower's income, obligations, and credit history will be examined. Again, certain facts such as the probable instability of income (from employment or from the property itself) or previous bankruptcies, salary attachments, or financial difficulties will call a halt to the process. If all goes well, it is time to see if the borrower's expected income will be sufficient to make the payments required under acceptable loan conditions (the term of the loan may be shortened for older properties, for example, requiring rapid amortization).

2. For a more detailed discussion, see Sherman J. Maisel, *Financing Real Estate* (New York: McGraw-Hill, 1965), Chapter Eight.

The appraisal and risk-rating schemes developed by the FHA have had a great influence on the mortgage lender's decision-making process. The FHA system is essentially a sizable check list of things that must be considered separately (such as the make-up of the city's economic base) and assigned scores that are then weighted and combined into an overall score, which must be at least equaled if a particular loan application is to be accepted. The whole system of "things to consider" and weights or scores to be assigned, however, is subjective or intuitive at root. The system seems never to have been subjected to statistical or logical evaluation.

Tradition often permits lenders to require additional security, such as liens against personal property or the rental income of the mortgaged property.

THE INVESTOR

The real estate investor is an investor who decides to put some of his money into real estate. This deceptively simple statement masks several useful and interesting facts. First of all, the basic precepts of investment in general apply to real estate; the object is to trade money or credit for some other form of asset that promises the highest return subject to conditions that the investor wishes to impose (concerning risk or liquidity, for example). It may be true for some individuals that real estate is the only form of investment available to them, but alternatives are usually present—buying government or business securities, speculating in commodities, financing a small business, purchasing life insurance, or just putting money in a bank. The ebb and flow of money in the real estate market is part of an overall flow of money among the several sectors of the economy, the aggregate of which may rise or fall as a result of government's monetary policy. Real estate investment cannot be isolated from other forms of investment, either in concept or in practice.

Second, investments may be made in the form of equity or debt, purchasing either the right to receive profits (along with liability for losses) or the right to receive a fixed percentage return on money loaned plus eventual repayment of the principal. It is customary to interpret "investment" in real estate to mean equity finance or ownership, since most of the lending is done by financial institutions—banks, insurance companies, savings and loan associations, trust companies, credit unions, and the like.

This is not to say that an individual or group of individuals is precluded from making a mortgage loan secured by real estate, but the distinction is common enough to warrant our using it here. This section, then, assumes that an investor is a purchaser of real estate rather than a lender.

Third, as an object of investment, real estate has at least five distinguishing characteristics.

1. The opportunity for *leverage* is very great; a large fraction of the purchase price can usually be borrowed, so that the financial results of equity investment are magnified. Indeed, it is possible to acquire real estate with zero equity, which makes it hard to apply standard investment criteria such as the yield or rate of return.

2. Real estate tends to *rise in value* and to display marked stability in value, as compared with common stocks, for example, because the basic commodity, land, is essentially fixed in supply and has few meaningful substitutes in the eyes of users.

3. Real estate investment is characteristically *illiquid*. Once property is purchased, it is difficult to sell, in comparison with securities, for example, because each property is unique and because the market institutions for conducting transfers of real estate ownership are not highly developed.

4. Real estate investment is subject to special income and capital gain tax provisions. For example, deductions are permitted for depreciation, though the property normally increases in value with the passage of time, and these allowances may be partly recaptured at the time of sale. Tax provisions are significant enough to obscure the "fundamental" investment performance of real estate and complex enough to make the careful investor seek professional advice or avoid real estate altogether.

5. Real estate investment may be carried out in a number of legal forms, some of them peculiar to this kind of investment and each having distinctive tax implications—estate and gift taxes as well as income and capital gain taxation.

Goals.— There are two major types of real estate investment that can be distinguished by their characteristic objectives. One is "appreciation"—holding property because of an anticipated increase in value, which in turn may be "active" or "passive." Active holding occurs when the investor initiates a change in land use, and we will consider this in a later chapter as "development." Passive holding does not contemplate a change in the use of the property during the holding period; since this type of value increase depends primarily on location factors, we shall discuss it below under the "Access" heading.

The second type of investment is best referred to as "income" holding, meaning that the investor expects periodic (but not necessarily constant) amounts of spendable cash income from the property. Income properties frequently appreciate in value as well, principally because of rising levels of rental income. Thus, the investor's return is a combination of net cash flow in an annual stream during the holding period, plus a lump sum to be received at the end of that period—called a "reversion." The reversion includes the increase in equity due to amortization of loans used to finance the purchase, which implies that the net cash flow in a particular year is less than "economic" income by the amount paid on the principal of the mortgage loans. The investor may just wait for the reversionary sum to be received when the property is later sold, or he may realize it earlier by refinancing the property (increasing the mortgage). It is increasingly customary and realistic to estimate both cash flow and reversion net of income and capital gain taxes.

Table 15 illustrates the manner in which yield is calculated from projected income, expense, and selling-price data for a real estate investment, which is assumed to be held for a period of ten years. The word "projected" is important, because real estate investment must be made on the basis of anticipated yield; the final results may turn out to be quite different, and it is actually very difficult to find out what yields have actually been realized by other prior investors. In the example, gross rental income from the property is the same in each year, as are operating expenses and, hence, net cash income ($86,000). The amount paid for interest decreases, however, as the principal amount of the mortgage is progressively reduced. Tax depreciation, an expense for tax purposes but not an out-of-pocket cost, decreases because of the depreciation method selected in the example. Net taxable income thus increases sharply over the ten-year holding period, so the income tax liability goes up as well, and it is largely this factor that encourges the investor to limit the length of the holding period. Net cash flow after taxes diminishes during the holding period (only the first and last years are shown).

The reversion is equal to the projected selling price less the mortgage

Table 15

Calculation of Real Estate Investment Return

	First year	Tenth year
Current income		
Gross income	$156,750	$156,750
Less operating expenses	70,750	70,750
Net cash income	$ 86,000	$ 86,000
Less interest	35,832	21,053
Less tax depreciation	45,500	28,665
Net taxable income	$ 4,668	$ 36,282
Cash flow after taxes		
Net cash income	$ 86,000	$ 86,000
Less mortgage payment	54,483	54,483
Less taxes (50% of net taxable income)	2,334	18,141
Net cash flow	$29,183	$ 13,376
Cash received at sale (reversion)		
Selling price (assuming 2% depreciation)		$800,000
Less repayment of outstanding mortgage		418,627
Less capital gains tax (25% of $225,874)		56,468
Final cash receipt		$324,905

Calculation of rate of return $280,000 = \dfrac{29,183}{(1+r)^1} + \ldots + \dfrac{13,376}{(1+r)^{10}} + \dfrac{324,905}{(1+r)^{10}}$

Source: Sherman J. Maisel; *Financing Real Estate* (New York: McGraw-Hill, 1965), p. 364. Assumptions: Value at time of acquisition, $1,000,000. Mortgage (20 years @ 5.5%), $660,000. Equity (cash), $280,000. Tax rates are illustrative. Tax depreciation allowances diminish over time. Market depreciation (@ 2%) is not necessarily a forecast; it may be an intentional error on the side of conservatism.

balance at the end of the holding period, further reduced by the capital gain tax. The capital gain is equal to the selling price ($800,000) increased by the accumulated amount of tax depreciation taken (the sum of $45,000 + . . . + $28,665 = $365,874) less the acquisition cost of the property ($280,000 × $660,000 = $940,000). At the time of sale there may be other forms of taxation (recapture of "excess" depreciation) and selling expenses, in practice, that are omitted from this example.

The yield or rate of return (often called the "internal rate of return") is that discount rate, r, that makes the present value of the cash flow and reversion receipts equal to the equity at the time of purchase, employing the formula illustrated in the table. This is a pure rate of return on the investment over and above the rate for return of the equity. It is a complex calculation, most efficiently done by means of a computer program (for further discussion, see Appendix A). Supposing that this projected yield is found to be 8 percent, the investor now has a means of comparing it with yields anticipated from other investment opportunities in order to select the one that is best. The best investment is not necessarily the one with the highest yield, however, because there may be more risk connected with one type than another, and the investor's individual attitude toward risk must then be taken into account. There is also the problem of finding a reinvestment opportunity for the funds eventually recovered from this real estate investment; a relatively high yield may return the investor's principal at a time when it is difficult to make another attractive investment.

The investor's goal may be simplified down to that of finding the investment opportunity with the highest yield perhaps, but the method of predicting the yield for any one investment requires the investor to make several decisions. Figure 33 identifies the major points at which the investor's strategy with respect to a single property he is looking at will influence the yield on that property. The yield is sensitive to leverage; for example, he may be able to borrow 60 percent of the purchase price at an interest rate of 8 percent, or 75 percent of the price at a rate of 9 percent. Although it is generally true that an investor benefits by borrowing as much as he can, as long as the interest rate is less than the property's free and clear yield, this rule is clouded by the tax deductibility of mortgage interest and hence is tied in with the investor's tax bracket rate. The investor also has options concerning the method of taking tax depreciation deductions, as well as in setting up the legal form of his ownership —forming a separate corporation, for example. He must initially assume what the holding period will be, but at various times while he owns the property, his holding-period decision may be revised. These various decisions interact, so possible combinations must be considered.

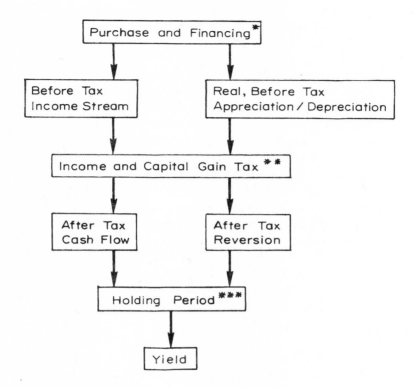

Figure 33. Factors affecting real estate investment yield.
* Leverage decision.
** Decisions regarding tax depreciation method and legal form of ownership.
*** Anticipated or actual length of time before the investment is liquidated.

For example, a ten-year holding period, with accelerated depreciation and 60 percent leverage may produce a yield of 8 percent after taxes, while a seven-year holding period, straight-line depreciation, and a 75 percent mortgage may provide a 9 percent rate of return.

The cash flow in a particular year may be negative, requiring additional out-of-pocket investment by the owner; rapid amortization of the loan can cause this to occur, for instance. During the period of ownership,

it may be profitable to make additional capital investments for modernization or enlargement, though the criterion for profitability may be
elusive. That is, we can estimate the effect of additional investments on the
original yield forecast, or simply consider the investor as an owner at that
point, endeavoring to increase the money value of his equity interest.

In the illustration in Table 15, the value of the property, $1,000,000,
exceeds the cash equity plus mortgage by $60,000. There are various ways
in which such differentials can arise—a favorable purchase price, for example. Also, as the mortgage loan is amortized, the investor's equity
increases. Thus, in these two respects the equity during the holding period
exceeds the amount of cash initially put up by the investor. In the extreme
case, the investor may put up no cash at all, and yet, with the passage of
time, he will have a paper equity that can be realized through sale of the
property. Whether such "ex post" equity qualifies a purchaser to be
classified as an "investor" is mainly a semantic problem. It can be a tax
problem, however, if owners of real estate are classified as "dealers"—people
who buy and sell real estate at a profit—because they may then have to pay
ordinary income tax rather than a lower schedule of capital gain tax on
their earnings.

Laws.—   The investor depends on the system of title registration
and real estate transfers to accomplish his objective of becoming the owner
of income property. The legal form of ownership selected—individual,
partnership, corporation, etc.—is influenced by the amount of equity
money required and by laws concerning taxes and liability. Many real
estate properties are small enough that a single individual can provide all
the equity money needed. With leverage, a person may acquire property
valued at $250,000 by investing as little as $25,000 of his own money. But
larger projects generally require the pooling of investment funds by a
group of individuals. A corporation can be formed to hold the title, with
individual investors holding shares of stock and subject to limited liability.
But the corporation is taxed on its earnings, which are taxed again when
distributed, and it also is denied some advantages that noncorporate
investors may have in accounting for depreciation and capital gains.
Special forms of partnerships are available that provide limited liability
without double taxation; these are called syndicates and trusts, differing
with respect to some aspects of taxation and to the transferability of

participants' shares.[3] Control over the formation of these groups may be exercised by governments under laws dealing with securities.

Real estate investors generally employ leverage and so benefit from the existence of mortgage-lending institutions, which in turn benefit from various forms of governmental supervision and assistance. Leverage opportunities for residential investment properties are particularly aided by governmental programs of mortgage insurance and mortgage trading that are intended to improve the supply of housing.

Taxes. — Much has already been said about the significant role of income and capital gain taxes in real estate investment, and greater detail would be tangential to the purpose of this book. Professional advice on tax matters is something that every prospective real estate investor should seek. On a different plane, it should be observed that markedly favorable tax treatment of real estate investment very often amounts to a subsidy, the purpose of which is to stimulate urban development and thus improve housing conditions, the urban environment, or construction employment, or all three. But governmental enthusiasm for such stimulus, and for this taxation method to achieve it, waxes and wanes. It is not clear whether the benefit of the tax concession for real estate is enjoyed by the users of real estate or is captured by investors or landowners. Thus, tax rules relating to real estate are subject to recurring major changes.

Access. — With some oversimplifying, we can say that income-oriented real estate investors give particular attention to tax factors while appreciation-oriented investors think hardest about factors of location or accessibility. For the income investor, the land use has already been determined and will change only gradually. The appreciation investor expects the land use to change relatively soon and in a major way. This latter point of view is represented in Figure 34, which employs the von Thuenen concept of land value as related to land-use patterns.

Initially, there are high-density uses that produce a land value slope, H, and low-density uses having a much less steep land-value function, L. They divide the use of the land at distance OA from the center, producing

3. See Alan R. Cerf, *Real Estate and the Federal Income Tax* (Englewood Cliffs, N.J.: Prentice-Hall, 1965), Chapter Eleven.

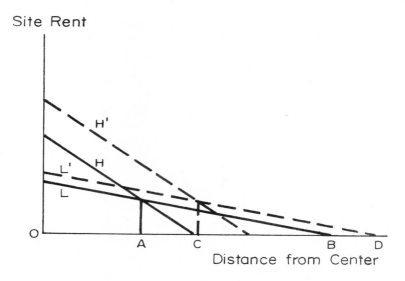

Figure 34.   Factors leading to property appreciation.

a two-stage profile of land values. If we now have an increase in the demand for both types of land, shifting H upward to H' and L upward to L', three important things happen. All land in use, from O to B, increases in value. Land in the belt described by AC changes in use from low density to high density, with very high proportionate increases in the vicinity of A. Land in the ring between B and D enters into urban use for the first time, with a proportionate increase in value that could even be infinite.

Appreciation within the circle OA generally does not provide the most attractive opportunity for investors who want to benefit by a rise in value. Because it is central, the present landowners tend to ask prices for it based on the expectation of continuously growing future site rents. Because it is already developed, the improvements and nearby infrastructure are probably obsolescent, so that deterioration and congestion cause users to trade higher transportation costs for greater amenities by looking outside the central city for new housing, stores, or factory locations. In the ring CB, which is also already built up, the tax cost of relatively new infrastructure absorbs or anticipates some of the increase in values, and for institutional reasons most of the property is owned by users (homeowners).

Speculative or appreciation opportunities are thus greatest in the areas of land-use change, *AC* and *BD*. The practical issue for the real estate investor is whether he can purchase land in these areas at prices that do not fully reflect the improved opportunities for use. Why should the owner of such land sell it for less?

The answer is that owners may not have the *information* that investors have. It is not certain which direction urban expansion will take in a particular community, even though there may be no question about the scale of expansion. Investors may have a better understanding of where new roads or bridges are to be built or of how to persuade local officials to provide this infrastructure. Investors may be able to influence rezoning decisions or at least get earlier indications of zoning changes. Of course, the investor's superior information may relate simply to the economic base; he may know that a new factory is coming before other people in the community hear about it.

The investor may affect the pattern of land use changes by *preempting* opportunities. For example, if there will clearly be an opportunity to develop a shopping center on one of the four corners of a suburban highway intersection, none of the four present landowners is certain that his piece of ground will be selected, so he cannot ask a shopping-center price for the land. An investor who is able to persuade a shopping-center developer to commit himself to one of these sites is in a good speculative position. This type of investor is active rather than passive and might be termed a developer. In his investment role he reduces uncertainty about a change in use and so raises the value of something he controls.

There is another category of real estate speculation, which we can call "bandwagon" trading, and it is characteristic of districts relatively remote from existing urban centers where some form of real estate development (as for recreation or second homes) is a plausible expectation but not an immediate likelihood. It rests very much on psychological impulses; Buyer A gets a block of virtually unused land and sells portions of it to B, C, and D by describing the future user demand for the land in very optimistic terms. B resells his little parcel to E at a fine mark-up, using the same rosy forecast of increasing value. C and D point to the quick profit made by B as evidence that values are indeed rising, and they sell off to F and G, who can't wait to get in on a good thing. The first, unwarranted prediction that values will rise becomes a self-fulfilling prophesy. There are several regrettable consequences of speculative bubbles like this in real estate, which we shall consider further in other sections.

Traditions. — Most real estate investors appear to use much simpler measures of success than the "internal rate of return" concept described above. For example, cash returns in the first year divided by initial cash equity provides a crude rate of return. Another measure is the reciprocal of this, which indicates the number of years it will take to recover the initial cash outlay. It is possible to justify these simplifications in part on both theoretical and practical grounds, but the real reason for their use is that investors are unfamiliar with the more sophisticated system of measuring return. Even the simple concepts are so difficult to assimilate that many people and institutions for whom real estate investment would be appropriate and profitable avoid the real estate field entirely.

This is related to another characteristic of real estate investment, namely, that the use of consultants or expert advisors is quite limited. Most investments in smaller income property are undertaken with no more information or analysis than is supplied by the real estate agent, though some agents undoubtedly are very skilled in this field. The agent is rewarded by commission, however, rather than being paid for financial advice. He would thus find it advantageous to manipulate the investment analysis so as to encourage the investor to make the purchase.

Investment in real estate is very closely related to the valuation of property, the success depending on the price paid, and appraisals for income property usually take a form very similar to an investment analysis. It is customary, to a degree, to expect appraisers to perform the functions of an investment counsellor, though a very significant distinction between valuation and investment analysis is overlooked when this occurs. Very simply put, the investor's problem is to determine the rate of return, r, given the income from property, I, and its price, P; if the income stream is continuous, $r = I/P$. The appraiser seeks to determine value, V, based on a projection of income and a discount rate, d, supposedly given by the marketplace; again, assuming continuous income, $V = I/d$. If $d = r$, then $V = P$, implying that the investor is typical of the market and that the asking price for a property reflects all future increases in income or value that anyone anticipates in connection with this property. Under such circumstances, real estate investment differs but little from buying a bond.

There is no necessary relationship between d and r, however. The investor may well anticipate a different level of I than the market does in general, because of better information, special tax advantages, or other factors. Denoting this as I', we get $r = I'/P = I'/V \neq d$. The investor may have a different discount rate, d', than the market does because of unusual attitudes toward the risk associated with the particular property, for example, and this would mean that the value, V', which the investor attaches to the property is $I' / d' = V' \neq P$.

That is, the investor's particular evaluation of the property bears no necessary relationship to its market value or price. Consequently, an appraisal in the normal sense of the term—a prediction of the price that will be paid in the market—does not tell the investor what the property is worth to himself, nor does it tell him what it will yield. It does tell him the minimum price he should expect to pay (and if this exceeds V', he should not purchase the property). It also provides an estimate of P, which he needs to forecast his investment yield, r. The real estate investor should be very careful, then, in using an appraisal in conjunction with an investment decision. In practice, it seems that the conceptual issues are often misunderstood by both investors and appraisers; each wants to know what the property is "worth," but this means different things to different people. The investor wants to derive the yield rate, while the appraiser makes an assumption about the discount rate.

Real estate investors, as such, have no widely known trade associations in the sense of organizations that conduct analytical research, public relations, or lobbying activities. Several trade journals are published that contain information and advertising useful to investors and owners of income property.[4] Statistical information about investment returns in real estate is virtually nonexistent, being transmitted by word of mouth, if at all.[5]

DISCUSSION QUESTIONS

1. In North America, the mortgage lending process tends to be very "impersonal" in comparison with the way real estate credit is extended in other parts of the world. That is, a borrower is

4. For example, *The National Real Estate Investor*, published by Communication Channels, Inc., New York City.

5. A very interesting recent report on investors in apartment properties is *Study on Tax Considerations in Multi-Family Housing Investments* (Washington, D.C.: U.S. Department of Housing and Urban Development, 1972). Though probably the most comprehensive effort yet made to gather information about real estate investment results for public discussion, this report is based entirely on interviews with a nonrandom sample of 137 people.

nothing more than a set of verified credit statistics to the lender;
his needs, social position, or past history as a customer of the
same lending institution carry little or no weight per se. Is this an
unfortunate aspect of our business traditions?

2.   During the 1930s, large numbers of residential mortgages were
foreclosed when homeowners lost their jobs, but foreclosure sales
in the depressed real estate market of the times meant heavy losses
for the lenders, too, Does this mean that a mortgage does not
provide much real security for a loan?

3.   What do you think is the main argument for "variable interest
rate" mortgages, in which the interest rate is not fixed for the term
of the loan but can be raised or lowered as money market conditions change? What is the principal objection?

4.   "All real estate investment is speculation." Do you agree? Is
"speculation," under some particular definition, clearly undesirable?

5.   Suppose you had $10,000 to invest and a real estate broker asked
you to consider buying a small apartment house he had listed for
sale. What would you want to know about it to decide whether or
not it would be a good investment for you?

SELECTED REFERENCES

Cerf, Alan R. *Real Estate and the Federal Income Tax.* Englewood Cliffs,
N.J.: Prentice-Hall, 1965.
Illustrations of tax computation in a wide variety of real estate
situations, based on laws and regulations in force at the time of
publication.

Kinnard, William N., Jr. *Income Property Valuation.* Lexington, Mass.:
Heath Lexington Books, 1971.
An appraisal textbook concentrating on methods of capitalizing
projected income.

Maisel, Sherman, J. *Financing Real Estate.* New York: McGraw-Hill, 1965.
A textbook covering the roles and operations of major types of

mortgage lending institutions, as well as the elements of real estate investment analysis.

Roulac, Stephen E. *Case Studies in Property Development*. Menlo Park, Calif.: Property Press, 1973.
Summaries of numerous actual real estate investment and development situations, emphasizing problems in organizing investor groups.

U.S. Department of Housing and Urban Development. *Study on Tax Considerations in Multi-Family Housing Investments*. Washington, D.C.: U.S. Government Printing Office, 1972.
The report of a survey of apartment investors in the United States, reflecting the range of investment objectives, rates of return achieved, and the influence of income tax factors on investment behavior.

9

MARKET SEARCH

SINCE WE ARE discussing investment real estate, users are tenants—families renting places to live and businesses renting places to work. As noted above, leases represent one category of property rights, and the leaseholder may look upon the property somewhat as the landlord or owner does. But essentially, for the user, real property is either a consumption good or a business input, not an asset.

THE USER

Goals. – The real estate user's goals are most in need of clear definition at the time when he is searching the market. Generally, the situation is that the choice is far wider than the user can actually make himself aware of. To get the most in terms of location or amenity for his rent dollar, the tenant should not only identify every property on the user market that could reasonably be adapted to his needs, but he ought to continue to do so even after settling down. The costs of real estate market information are high, or the supply of it is imperfect, so users frequently settle for something less than perfection. The range of choice is further limited by the rate of turnover of suitable types of property and by the user's commitment to his present location. A family may allow a month in a new community to find and move into an apartment, for example, and so limit themselves to places that happen to come on the market in the early part of that month. A business firm, knowing its lease is to expire and will not be renewed, has lead time to look around but a fixed time at which it must be out of the present premises. Better places that are expected to be vacated shortly thereafter must be dismissed, and so must suitable places that are vacant and for rent but that cannot be held until the present lease expires. The user's objective, then, quite apart from knowing what he wants in terms of location, lease arrangements, amenities, space, and so on, is to make an efficient search.

To treat urban land users' goals in more detail, we must give up the convenience of lumping various land-use categories together as "investment real estate." Each type of land use has its own requirements, a full knowledge of which becomes the real estate businessman's major stock in trade. A very general comment or two on the principal categories may be of interest here and would hopefully stimulate further inquiry by the reader.

Residential tenants consider the privacy and status that a particular building or unit will provide them, quite apart from whether the internal space construction and state of repair suit them. Convenient location is growing less important because mobility (usually through automobile ownership) is increasing, but the quality of nearby shops and schools are likely to be considered by the homeseeker. Since moving from place to place is a costly chore for households, a stable tenancy seems to be preferred.

Retail stores fall easily into two categories—those depending primarily on traffic generated by a cluster of retail facilities, and those that do not benefit particularly from having other retail stores as neighbors. Even free-standing shops, however, are attracted to centers of gravity or convenient crossroads in residential areas.

Industrial firms tend to avoid areas of nonindustrial traffic congestion, preferring locations where long-distance transportation equipment can reach the factory directly and to which factory employees have ready access. Areas where there are likely to be community complaints about noise or pollutants are avoided. Storage and docking activities have less concern for worker access or community complaints but must be even more directly tied in with long-distance transportation.

Office space users in the market consider the kinds of face-to-face contact that their work requires and the prestige that particular buildings will give to their firms. There is a wide spectrum of interest in both of these attributes, however.

Personal service firms—such as laundromats, shoe repair shops, and beauty shops—like free-standing retail stores, are drawn to residential focal points, though some categories rely on traffic generated by a cluster of stores or by common parking arrangements.

Hotels and conference activities make highly specialized and often large-scale uses of real estate, which may involve layers of ownership and tenancy; they are thus conducive to joint-venture types of operation. For practical purposes, the developer is the user; locational demands cannot be generalized.

Dining and recreation establishments have weak centrality. They gravitate toward specialized districts but there are many exceptions, and the ability of the operator is usually far more important than the real estate in determining the success of the enterprise.

Laws.— With or without a recorded lease, the relationship between a landlord and a tenant is governed by statutes and their interpretation. Thus, the lease may indicate that Mr. and Mrs. Kravitz are entitled to occupy apartment 504, but it is the law which spells out what they may or may not do there and which creates their right to exclude other people— even the landlord in many cases—from that place during the period of the lease. Landlord-tenant law appears to be in a state of flux at the present time, and is moving primarily in the direction of strengthening the tenant's position. Tenant unions are becoming recognized intermediaries, and mediation services are offered by some cities as a public service to disputing landlords and tenants, both primarily in the residential real estate field. The most important aspect of landlord-tenant law, of course, is that the tenant's rights expire with the passage of time.

A person need not have a license to rent real estate (though he may need a business license to use it). He must be legally capable of making a contract, however, and this creates difficulties when a group of people want to share a rental, whether an apartment or a business property. Someone must be responsible, not only to the landlord but also to other parties—for example, to someone injured while visiting a rented place of business.

Rent control laws, which take many forms and which appear and disappear, create substantial property rights for tenants, the general effect of which is to diminish the tenant's mobility.

Taxes.— The usual presumption is that property taxes are borne by the tenant, either explicitly under the terms of a lease, or through the operation of the market.[1] If taxes go up, rents go up sooner or later. Since a large component of local property taxation is in the general nature of a "user charge"—for the use of streets, schools, fire protection, and so on—the incidence of the tax does not raise a large problem. There is an element of perversity, however, in heavy taxes on close-in property based on the value of centrally located land, when those taxes are used to provide transportation systems for people who live or work farther out; the nonusers are taxed for the benefit of the users. More generally, property users are able to select their locations so as to minimize the tax burden; in a metropolis with a number of separate political jurisdictions, this "voting with their feet" by users can materially affect the spatial land-use pattern.

The entire rent a business tenant pays is normally considered a deductible expense as far as income taxes are concerned. This makes the use of real estate something of a bargain for taxpayers in high brackets. A firm that occupies elegant offices for $10,000 a year would save only $2,500 a year by moving down to something that rents for only $5,000 if the marginal tax rate that applies were 50 percent.

Access.— It is the user of real estate who is most clearly aware of the close relationship between urban land-use and transportation. He has to decide what trade-off he should make between the price he pays for occupancy and the transportation cost he involves himself in by selecting a location. The less expensive the land he occupies, the farther it will be, generally, from centers of employment, shopping, and recreation. The location premium is established by the needs and relative location of other people in the community, however, If he has no particular need to get into the central business district (CBD) each day, he would nevertheless be asked to pay a rent for a downtown apartment that was based in part on the locational advantage to a person who was obliged to make such trips. On the other hand, though he may work in the CBD, he may consider that a lot of driving time and gasoline spent commuting will be an inexpensive way to enable his family to enjoy living in a pleasant but remote suburb. Wherever he decides to locate his residence or his business, he will incur some transportation cost and pay some site rent, and it is up to him to find the mix that suits him best. Business firms, of course, need accessibility

1. For a discussion of the incidence of property taxes on housing, see Walter A. Morton, *Housing Taxation* (Madison: University of Wisconsin Press, 1955), Chapter Six.

more than householders do, but their needs differ. Furniture stores, for example, need quite a bit of display space, which would be very expensive in the center of town. Fortunately, furniture shoppers are willing to make special trips to off-center locations, so these merchants can occupy somewhat cheaper land.

The location of urban land is not the only factor, however, which affects a user's selection. Since he is neither an investor nor a developer who would be interested in constructing his own building, he is looking for land with buildings already in existence, the size or condition of which must be taken into account in searching the market. Thus he must optimize in several dimensions—advantages expected to be derived from location, the site rent or location premiums asked by the market for the alternative sites, the suitablility of the building for his intended use, and the opportunities for bargaining. Figure 35, illustrating the way a selection might be made, simplifies some of these dimensions.

In the figure, the site rent (SR) line is the owner's opportunity cost or asking price for use of the land at various distances from the center, while the location value line (LV) represents the advantage of access to the center that this particular user would enjoy. Beyond distance OA, inaccessibility makes the location value less than the asking rent, so the user's options are

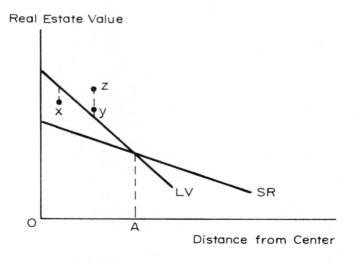

Figure 35. User's selection of real estate.

confined within the distance OA (or within some ring of this circular area). Supposing that three buildings are available within this area, and assuming that the site rent which the user would actually pay is determined by LV, the question is whether the net intrinsic advantage of an available building offsets a feasible but less desirable location. The vertical distance from the LV line to x, for example, indicates that this building's condition or its rental terms would detract from the user's normal expectations of business; for y and z the business would be aided (or the household's comfort enhanced) by the structure and the rental terms. The good points of building y, however, are not sufficient to overcome the locational advantage of x, even when x's nonlocational bad points are thrown into the scale. Building z is the reasonable choice; its real estate value, a composite of location and nonlocation factors, appears greatest to the prospective user.

Traditions.–   The amount of housing space that is adequate for a family, the minimum condition and facilities of that housing, the amount of office space required per clerical employee, and even the size and condition of retail facilities, dining and recreation facilities per customer, or per dollar of sales are fixed primarily by custom. The number of floors a building may have without being equipped with an elevator, whether there is a usable cellar, a central heating or air conditioning system–and, of course, many architectural details–reflect customs that are sometimes endorsed by statutes or deflected by salesmanship. Architects, engineers, and social scientists will probably rationalize these concepts as time goes by–the astronaut's capsules being portents–but this is likely to modify the use and development of urban space only very gradually. The infrastructure of the community–the streets and utility system in particular–are more subject to rationalization than is private enclosed space. For example, overhead utility lines were necessitated by a change in infrastructure technology, but now seem likely to be forced underground by community concern for appearance.

It is generally customary to give tenants the option of renewing a lease, though perhaps under terms more in line with market conditions at the moment. Lease breaking is sanctioned more often than common lease terms would suggest. Commercial tenants increasingly see the percentage lease as a customary arrangement, though it is a relatively new concept. Whether a prosepctive user in the market for real estate employs an agent to negotiate the lease or to locate suitable properties, or an appraiser to say whether the rent is reasonable, are things determined partly by consideration of expense and partly by tradition.

THE HOMEOWNER

Approximately 60 percent of the households in North America are homeowners. This ratio is reasonably stable, allowing for the fact that the age structure of the population, which influences the choice between single-family housing and apartments, has been disturbed by the low birthrates of the 1930s and the post-World War II baby boom. Young households, consisting of unmarried people or newly married couples who have not started raising children, do not feel the need for the privacy and low density that the single-family house provides, or if they do, they may not be able to finance the purchase of a home. Old people, past the child-rearing stage, may find a single-family home too expensive or too much trouble to maintain. Families in large, densely settled communities have limited opportunities to enjoy single-family housing, and highly mobile people may opt for rental housing. For the mass of child-raising, lower-middle-income or better families, however, homeownership is the characteristic way of meeting housing needs. Single-family housing is the largest private use of urban land, and areas of such housing are focal points for public services such as schools and retail facilities like shopping centers and doctors' offices.

Home ownership means that the user of real estate is also the investor and the owner. For better or worse, the family that wants to live in a single-family house is generally obliged by the nature of the housing inventory and the customs of the market to assume the roles of investor and property manager. A variety of inducements to homeownership are provided by governments in Canada and the United States, and where housing policies are defined on a national level, they generally include some kind of suggestion that homeownership serves a national and community purpose.

The question whether it costs more to own than to rent a dwelling is worth exploring, though it cannot be resolved in general and is often not a real option since single-family houses for rent are scarce, and child-raising families are excluded from apartments more often than not. Table 16 is a schematic summary of the costs and benefits for owners and renters. All the costs shown for the renter are money costs included in his rent. Costs of the

Table 16

Comparison of Home Ownership and Renting

	Owner	Renter
Costs[a]		
Property tax	M+	M
Insurance and repairs	M−	M
Interest on debt	M	M
Interest on equity	I	M
Management	I	M
Income tax on gross rental value	−	M
Benefits		
Shelter	+	+
Mobility	−	+
Security	+	−
Appreciation	±	−
Status	+	−
Services	−	+

[a] M = money cost; I = imputed cost.

homeowner include some money items and some that are imputed—which he should realize he is paying but which are not out-of-pocket. Interest on the homeowner's equity is one imputed cost, and the amount of the interest is properly the opportunity cost of the money invested by the owner rather than the amount he could earn in a savings deposit, for example. The family that goes without vacations, medication care, a new car, or other consumption items in order to get the down payment for a house together has a high opportunity cost. The homeowner's labor in keeping the house and yard in shape is also an imputed cost. Money costs for repairs may be less for the owner than the renter, assuming the same kind of dwelling for each, because the owner is likely to be more careful in his use of the property. Tenant and owner pay interest on the mortgage debt.

Property taxes for the owner are shown in Table 16 with a plus sign attached. This is a consequence of the owner's reduced mobility. As the years go by and he continues to occupy the house, its relative location is changing because of population growth in the community. For this and other reasons, the land value rises, as well as the property tax rate, perhaps, and so his tax burden increases. Elderly people are often forced to give up their homes because the land value and the taxes have increased while their incomes have declined. Renters are able to adjust their location and thus the "site rent" they pay as the community structure changes.

Homeowners are not required to declare as income the rental value of the house they occupy, and this is a form of subsidy. In the United States, but not in Canada, homeowners can report as expenses the interest and property taxes they pay, just as the owner of a rental property can, but the landlord must report the income.

Transportation plus site rent is a cost associated with the use of housing, but it is not shown in Table 16 because it would be offset by "accessibility" as a benefit. There is no clear presumption that owners get more benefit from accessibility than renters, or vice-versa.

Benefits are treated as plus or minus entries. Shelter, of course, is something both the owner and the renter get for their money. The owner has less mobility but more security than the renter. Appreciation of residential real estate is a loss for the renter, because his rent money buys progressively less—depending on what the source of appreciation is. For the owner, appreciation is a plus or minus item; you may buy a house for $15,000 and sell it ten years later for $30,000, but by that time it will probably cost you $30,000 to get a similar house. Home ownership is a good investment primarily because it is a hedge against inflation—a way of avoiding loss rather than a road to riches. It does involve a family in a contractual savings program quite often, because mortgage lenders want the mortgage amortized, but the net value of this discipline to the homeowner depends on his other needs for cash—to send a child to school, for instance.

Home ownership provides status in several ways. A person's credit rating is measurably better if he owns a home—mortgaged or not. He has a more effective voice in civic affairs. He is looked upon as stable and responsible by police and business associates. And, of course, there is simply the tradition that home ownership is expected of a capable household head.

When a tenant wants to go away on a trip, he lets the manager or landlord know, so someone will keep an eye on things. The homeowner is usually hard-pressed to make other arrangments. Tenants are more likely to have other facilities they can share—a swimming pool, laundry machines, and so forth—at less expense than the homeowner would have to bear for exclusive use.

A household head becomes a homeowner essentially by passing the personal credit test of a mortgage lender. The prosepctive buyer must have funds from some source to bridge the gap between the mortgage loan and the purchase price of the house. This gap can be narrowed by proposing to buy a less expensive house, by waiting a few years longer to increase the family savings balance, or by securing additional loans. This last may run him afoul of the second-lender criterion, which is that his obligations in connection with the house should not take more than a fixed percentage of his income, often 25 percent, and often figured on income after other fixed obligations such as insurance or installment payments are deducted. Last but not least, he must appear to the lender, on paper, as a person of good financial habits and a steady income.

Government assistance to home ownership (apart from the tax benefit) is mostly in the form of long-term, high-ratio mortgage loans, given directly by government agencies or by financial institutions relying on government mortgage insurance programs. The longer the terms of the mortgage, the more home a given monthly housing budget will buy, up to a point. The higher the ratio of the loan to the purchase price, the sooner the young family can accumulate the necessary down payment.

The average homeowner moves about every seven years. From the time a home is first purchased, the family usually increases in size so that more space is needed, and its income rises as the house they live in gets older and obsolescent. There are also job changes significant enough to require selling the house and moving to another place. Increasingly, family dissolution brings about the sale of homes, often accompanied by mortgage default and foreclosure. The homeowner's cost of moving is substantial because real estate commissions may have to be paid, mortgage prepayment penalties may be imposed, and interest and taxes accumulate on the house that is up for sale but no longer occupied.

The homeowning neighborhood tends to generate social pressure for good maintenance of individual houses. This means labor and expense for the family, but it produces external benefits relating to the attractiveness and value of the environment generally. While the system operates, the homeowning family shares in its benefits. The same family is something of a constraint on the behavior of the homeowning family, because the nieghborhood takes on certain interpersonal characteristics of a village.

THE BROKER

The real estate broker, or agent, is directly and physically involved in matching properties with users or investors. He is paid a percentage of the sales price when the transaction is completed, and this compensation is the focal point of laws and customs that govern his behavior. Paid real estate agents must ordinarily hold licenses, so that an unlicensed person who helps to arrange a real estate transaction—even between personal acquaintances—and accepts compensation for doing so, is subject to prosecution. Attorneys, trustees, and individuals holding powers of attorney for either party are commonly made exempt from this restriction on real estate agency.

Goals.— In the majority of cases, the broker is an agent of the seller, so that his responsibility and objective is to get the property sold for the highest price in the shortest time—a contradiction that is resolved by putting a time limit on the contract between the seller and the agent, such as ninety days. The contract is called a "listing agreement," because by it the broker adds this property to the list of real estate he is offering to the market. The listing agreement specifies an asking price, and the agent is entitled to his commission if he finds a qualified purchaser willing to pay that price within the listing period.

This asking price is normally construed by all parties as an upper limit, and the buyer offers something less. For example, if a house is listed for $25,000 and there is an offer of $21,000, the broker is not entitled to his commission unless the seller accepts in writing the offer of $21,000. Frequently the seller will respond to the first offer by lowering the asking price—to $24,000, for example. Eventually, buyer and seller may agree upon a price of $23,000, and when they do, the agent is legally entitled to his commission. By custom, however, the agent then helps to complete the complex paperwork that is required before title to the property can be transferred. This paperwork may be concerned with paying off an existing mortgage loan on the property, creating a new loan, obtaining evidence of title and perhaps title insurance, resolving questions about accrued or prepaid property taxes and insurance, registering the change of title, and other steps the particular transaction may call for. Many of these functions may be performed by an escrow agent—not paid by commission—but it is the broker who puts the necessary documents and money into the escrow agent's hands.

The listing agreement has some of the elements of an option. The seller whose property is listed at $25,000 cannot refuse an offer of that amount during the listing period without possibly incurring a liability to the agent and to the person who makes the offer. A person who makes an offer of $21,000 cannot easily rescind it, though he may immediately decide to back away from the deal. In practice, offers to sell property and offers to purchase it are frequently qualified by various conditions that protect the parties or give them some opportunities for escape. For example, the buyer might offer $23,000, conditional upon receipt of an appraisal of $23,000 or better and upon the buyer's ability to secure a mortgage loan of $19,000. The seller might specify that the purchaser be "acceptable" to the seller on personal grounds (a clause that has been used to discriminate on the basis of race).

Brokers really have three goals—to get listings, to find buyers for listed properties, and to protect their good name. A property listed by one agent may be sold by another agent, providing there is an agreement about the splitting of commissions. A good job in explaining the process of negotiation and sale to the seller—including a reasonable forecast of the cash proceeds of the sale—and accurate handling of the necessary paperwork will build the broker's reputation as a good person to list with. The broker's good name among purchasers depends particularly on his candor in finding the property that best meets the buyer's needs and in giving practical assistance with applications for mortgage financing. Of course, getting the property sold within the shortest time helps both the agent and the seller. The agent must be wary throughout of things that would jeopardize his license, such as charges of misrepresentation or mishandling of deposit money.

Real estate agency is a highly competitive, personal-service business. Entry into the business requires a license—which can usually be obtained after a brief period of study in preparation for standardized examinations—and almost no capital except money to live on while chasing the first sale. The customary commission rate (6 percent in the United States and Canada on houses, for example) and the high price of real estate mean that a person can earn a living with one or two sales a month. Many agents and salesmen sell real estate as a supplementary source of income–housewives, retired military people, and professional athletes in the off-season, for example. Many try real estate and give it up when the rate of sales proves disappointing. Ease of entry and the high earnings of successful agents result in a tendency for this business to be overpopulated.

Laws. –   This overpopulation endangers the ethical standards of real estate agency. Selling real estate is sufficiently complex that buyers and sellers usually have to take much of what the agent says on faith, and the buyer also entrusts the agent with deposit money. The seller cannot know if the agent's game is to buy the property himself at the listing price and immediately resell it to someone who has already offered more.

The licensing requirements for real estate agency are supposed to protect buyers and sellers from dishonest practices that would be not only possible but likely without a licensing system. The license is usually easy enough to obtain, but it subjects the holder to a set of regulations and a system of hearing complaints. Revoking or suspending a license is the public administrator's tool for keeping the agency business honest.

Regulations that are enforced by this means range from the precise (for example, not engaging in the business while the license is suspended) to the obscure (for example, "misrepresenting" a house as being in "good condition" when it turns out to be in violation of the building code). One of the most serious areas of ambiguity concerns the agent's responsibility to the buyer in the usual case when the agent is working for the seller. The seller's bargaining position is harmed if the agent tells the buyer about material defects in the property, but failure to disclose a material defect may violate other principles of law.

Taxes. –   A real estate agent's income is derived from services and, hence, is taxed as ordinary income. The fact that he is in the real estate business makes it difficult for him to secure capital-gain tax treatment for investment properties he may come to own.

Brokers dealing with income property must become very familiar with tax laws affecting real estate, because purchasers are concerned with after-tax earnings the property will produce. For several years, many brokers in the United States and Canada were selling "tax shelter" rather than real estate per se. High depreciation allowances attributable to a building could offset the owner's income from other sources. Trades or exchanges of properties are ways of deferring capital gain tax liability. In these and many other ways, tax aspects have become very significant in real estate transactions, so that the broker who hopes to handle income property must be prepared to offer tax advice, hazardous though that might be.

Access. – Brokers tend to specialize geographically. The smaller the radius over which a broker travels to list and sell property, and the more intimately knowledgeable he is about properties and trends in his area, the better the job he can do for all concerned. There is also specialization by type of property–commercial, industrial, and residential–though large, multi-departmental real estate firms are to be found in many cities. Rarely does a real estate firm do business in more than one urban area. Knowledge of local land-use laws, local market conditions, local sources of finance, and dependence on local trade associations are factors that keep the agent from going beyond his own "turf."

The broker sells "location" as well as physical land and buildings (and tax shelter), so he must know what that means to the people who show up as prospective buyers. This means knowing how far the property is from downtown, from shopping centers, from schools, from parks, and from other destinations the buyer might frequently have. It means being able to describe the immediate neighborhood in terms the buyer cares about–the pedestrian volume if it is a retail property, or the noise level if it is an apartment building, and so on. It means keeping up with plans to change the zoning or widen the roads in the area, for example. It means knowing what people want and expect with respect to "location," so that the agent's knowledge of one community is not easily transferrable to another.

Real estate brokerage is essentially a business of communication. The broker's ability to reach prosepctive buyers is limited by the communications media at his disposal. People passing his office window may notice pictures of listed properties and drop in to talk about them. Classified newspaper ads reach a wide local audience but are so terse that they are really just invitations to make personal contact with the agent. Signs posted on property are effective, because real estate investors do look around through areas they are interested in, and because the chance to see the property before contacting the agent screens out people who are looking for something else. Inevitably, an agent spends a lot of time giving information to people who will buy something else, so that his efforts confer a "communication externality" upon people in the community generally.

Ideal matching of owners or users and properties requires, in principle, that every property on the market be considered by every prospective purchaser or user. With many agents in a given community, this is not likely to occur, because each one has a small fraction of all the listings and he will try to sell the prospect something on that list, though there may be something far more suitable in some other agent's list. "Multiple listing" arrangements deal constructively with this problem; groups of brokers in a community agree to pool their listings—distributing copies to every member—and to share the commission in a specific way. Multiple listing arrangements are limited primarily to the single-family dwelling market, however. People wanting to invest in income property must solve the communication problem by making inquiries with a number of agents or by hiring their own agent to make the necessary search.

Traditions.—   What has been said earlier with respect to advice on tax matters can be extended to investment counselling generally. Real estate agents find themselves dealing with the general investment problems of their clients (both sellers and buyers), though obviously they are trying to promote one particular kind of investment—real estate—and probably one specific property. The real estate agent doesn't sell securities or life insurance, and the stock brokers or insurance agents don't sell real estate, as a matter of custom. This is the *modus vivendi* and not necessarily an ideal arrangement. If the investor is capable of relating a real estate offer and a stock market situation in his own mind, or has a competent investment advisor to do that for him, he may do the best thing with his money. Otherwise he is fair game; if he only talks to stockbrokers, he'll never know what he is missing in real estate—and vice versa.

Real estate agents deal in leases as well as in ownership interests. An important exception is that rental housing is not generally leased through agents in North America. New housing is normally sold without the use of a broker, though limited selling services may be contracted for by the builder. A large minority of real estate transactions are conducted without the help of agents, but usually when the parties have some experience in the real estate business and generally with assistance from an attorney.

Trade associations play a large role in the business life of a real estate agent. The local association—the "board"—is a meeting place for the exchange of ideas and information and is the administrative home of the multiple listing service. The boards keep in close touch with local government in matters of zoning, public improvements, property taxes, abatement of nuisances, and many other matters in which agents collectively tend to assume the role of guardians of the interests of property owners. State, provincial, and national associations of boards propose, oppose, and conduct research and public relations activities relating to real estate legislation—or, even more broadly, to community issues such as revenue sharing or school bussing. Membership on the board is not automatically accorded to holders of real estate licenses and, in fact, a large minority are not members. The trade association tries, by limiting membership, by educational programs, and by conducting public relations activities, to improve the "image" of member brokers, which may help them to get business from property owners and buyers who are wary of getting involved with an agent.

Licensing laws and regulations are administered at the state and provincial level by agencies of government which, on close inspection, turn out to be controlled by the real estate licensees themselves—primarily, indeed, by the boards. This is not surreptitious; it is written into the law. In California, for example, seven of the nine members of the state Real Estate Commission, including its chairman, must be active brokers. Naturally enough, nominations for membership on the commission come primarily from the boards through their state association. It is a case of an industry regulating itself through statute (as well as informally through a trade association), presumably in the public interest. In fact, it is in the interest of real estate agents to keep the conduct of the real estate business honest; the honest agent would lose business to the dishonest man, and the public would soon quit entrusting business to either of them. That, indeed, was the situation that led to the adoption of licensing laws, at the suggestion of the scrupulous agents who wanted protection from the other kind. The system of regulation that results, however, tends to assume that what the competent and honest real estate agent does is, in itself, good for the community. That there may be too many agents, that their methods of matching users and properties may be inefficient, that their rigidly traditional commission rates might be higher than necessary or too inflexible, or that real estate brokerage would best be merged in with some other activity such as mortgage lending are issues that the existing system of regulation has no interest in exploring.

DISCUSSION QUESTIONS

1. Take a look around a retail district in your city. Is there a shop that would do better in some other part of town? Does the district lack a type of store or service that would probably be able to pay rent in this district?

2. Would it be a good idea if all commercial leases (for stores and offices) had the same term and expired on the same day?

3. Do you think that commercial tenants should have a legal right to renew their leases, providing they are willing and able to pay the generally prevailing level of rents in their districts?

4. See if you can identify a commercial building in your town that was originally designed for a different type of land use. Do you think buildings should be designed so as to be adaptable for a variety of uses?

5. There appears to be a trend toward relatively formal associations of commercial tenants, renter households, and homeowning households in their respective neighborhoods or districts. Do these associations serve the interests of the community as a whole as well as the interests of their members?

6. Do the generalized "pros and cons" of home ownership in Table 16 apply to condominium housing? To mobile homes?

7. If home ownership is less expensive than renting in the long run, as is often asserted, why do most forms of government housing aid for low-income families provide rental units?

8. In your community are there neighborhood place-names which most people understand? What is the origin of the boundaries of an identifiable residential neighborhood? Are they likely to shift as time goes by?

9. Make a list of all the questions you think a real estate broker (or salesman) should be able to answer about a house he has listed for sale. Be as specific as possible. Is there other important information that the prospective buyer should be able to obtain by himself?

10. Customary commission rates on residential sales have gradually increased over the past two decades. Does this imply that there are not enough real estate brokers or salesmen?

SELECTED REFERENCES

Beyer, Glenn H. *Housing and Society*. New York: Macmillan, 1965.
A compendium of statistical information about housing and residential construction in the United States and description of various principal types of housing.

The National Commission on Urban Problems. *Building the American City*. 91st United States Congress, First Session.
A summary volume which reports the findings of a major congressional investigation of housing and urban problems in the United States; critical attention is directed particularly to local land-use regulations and property taxation.

The President's Committee on Urban Housing. *A Decent Home*. Washington, D.C.: U.S. Government Printing Office, 1968.
Factual information about the housebuilding industry in the United States, quantitative and qualitative needs for housing construction, the supply of land, building materials, labor and finance for the housing sector, and a critical examination of federal housing programs.

Ratcliff, Richard U. *Urban Land Economics*. New York: McGraw-Hill, 1949.
A textbook on the economics of land use, development and redevelopment in the United States, including the forces which contribute to the location and growth of particular cities, and the essential criteria for government involvement in land use control and housing construction.

Unger, Maurice A. *Real Estate*. 5th Edition. Cincinnati: South-Western Publishing Company, 1974.
A textbook primarily intended for active or aspiring real estate brokers and salespersons.

10

REAL ESTATE DEVELOPMENT

REAL ESTATE DEVELOPMENT is a special kind of manufacturing. Inputs are purchased at their market prices—land, labor, materials, and working capital. These inputs are put together to form a product that is sold in the marketplace. The difference between the costs of the inputs and the selling price of the product is the developer's profit. Of course, what he sells is an investment good, and it will be sold on the basis of investment yield (though home buying may be considered an exception to this). The developer may, in fact, produce the apartment building, shopping center, office building, or even the single-family house for his own investment or use. But the development process is finite, and investment returns cannot begin until that process is complete.

When the apartment building, shopping center, hotel, or whatever is ready for use, it has a value, and that value, less the money costs of the resources embodied in the product, is the measure of the developer's success. He may make a profit of $50,000 by producing a property that has a long-term investment yield of 10 percent, for example, or a profit of $20,000 on something with a yield of 18 percent. What the developer himself "invests" is primarily his time and knowledge, and if the same effort is required to realize either $50,000 or $20,000, the developer will presumably do the thing that brings him the greater dollar profit. Why investors pay what they do for particular types of property is not the

228

developer's concern. Real estate development and real estate investing are different things.

There is a tendency for real estate development organizations to specialize by type of property—residential, commercial, offices, or industrial property. The apparent reasons for this will grow clearer as we proceed, but one of them must be mentioned at the outset. Real estate development is closely intertwined with building or construction activities. House builders develop houses, and they would not know how to erect a thirty-five story office building, as a rule. A construction firm that has mastered the art of putting up office buildings does not necessarily know how to put together a shopping center development, though they might bid successfully for construction work on it. All real estate developments involve builders, but not all developments are instigated by builders. Developing and building are not synonymous.

The developer is an entrepreneur. He buys things, including the services of a construction firm, which he hopes to sell at a profit. His entrepreneurial profit is not a wage for doing carpentry or mixing concrete or supervising the people who do things like that. On the other hand, there is no rule that says a developer cannot hammer nails or that a carpenter may not perform the function of a developer as well as sawing lumber and hammering nails into it.

Real estate developers are not very visible as a group. They are not listed as such in the telephone directory or reported on in the census of occupations. What they earn is a total mystery as far as national income statistics is concerned. Very often the person or firm who instigates real estate developments wears another, more visible hat—as builder, contractor, broker, architect, investment syndicate organizer, or landowner. This obscurity is unfortunate, because it leaves government agencies concerned with the condition of urban real estate very much in the dark as to who is knocking this real estate together and why.

Partly in the hope of dispelling common misconceptions, we shall present some prototype development situations in which the role and the objectives of the developer are emphasized.

RESIDENTIAL TRACT DEVELOPMENT

One point is that anyone can be a developer or call himself one. Suppose that "we" decide to develop a small tract of houses. What steps must we follow and how much profit will we make? A brief outline of our financial story appears in Table 17, which assumes that four houses will be built, each to sell for $25,000. A one-year development period is fairly typical, though we might have been thinking about these particular houses or this land for several years, and we might be putting to work knowledge gained over a long period. The steps are as follows.

    1. Acquire the land, at the assumed price of $20,000. We can finance this by giving the seller an IOU (a purchase-money mortgage), by getting a new mortgage, or by putting up our own cash—or by some combination. There is no rule that says we cannot borrow the cash we need from a friend, relative, or silent partner who may or may not want to hold a mortgage but who probably will expect interest.

    2. Secure necessary government approvals. This will probably involve filing a map showing the proposed lot lines and documents indicating that title to the land we propse to sell to home buyers is reasonably clear, that water and utilities will be available, that there is access to principal highways, that acceptable sewage disposal facilities will be installed, that construction and maintenance of streets is assured, and that other things

Table 17

Residential Tract Development

Object: Produce four new houses to sell for $25,000; complete development and sale within twelve months.	
Costs	
land	$ 20,000
materials	21,000
direct labor	13,000
subcontracts (plumbing, electric, etc.)	30,000
interest and miscellaneous	4,000
Total	$ 88,000
Selling Price	
4 houses @ $25,000 each	$100,000
Profit[a]	$ 12,000

[a] Includes imputed wages of management by the developer and interest on his out-of-pocket cash investment.

are as required. The government offices are no rubber stamps; our plans may be picked apart and substantially amended before approval is given.

3. Line up construction financing. We will call on several potential mortgage lenders to see if they would be interested in putting up the larger part of our development costs and to arrange for commitments for permanent mortgage loans for our prospective customers. It will be a great help in selling the houses if we can say that such and such a bank has already agreed to lend, say, $20,000 to any qualified home buyer. Even better, if we can secure the approval of a government mortgage insurance agency such as the FHA or CMHC, a lower interest rate and a longer-term loan for perhaps $23,000 may be arranged, although this will involve us in a cumbersome bureaucratic process. For all this we will need precise building plans and other architectural work, which we may arrange to pay for "later."

4. Arrange with a contractor or a group of contractors to do the physical work of preparing the land, putting in at least rough roads, constructing the housing, and arranging for utilities to be hooked up. In Table 17, $13,000 is shown for "direct labor," the workmen we ourselves employ or those who work for a general contractor. This usually means most of the excavation and foundation work and carpentry. The rest of the labor cost is shown as subcontracts.

5. Buy the building materials, which small developers usually do from local suppliers of just about everything. Some materials and equipment (stoves, water heaters, etc.) may be bought on trade credit—the interest cost of which is buried in the price—while proceeds from the construction loan may be used to pay for the rest as well as paying for labor as it is performed. Interest accumulates after these loan funds are disbursed. Care will have to be exercised that money is not paid out for material not received or labor not done.

6. Start selling. It will be helpful if we finish one of the houses early as a model for house-hunting families to walk through. We can put an advertisement in the Sunday newspaper and take the real estate editor to lunch, in hopes of favorable mention in his column. We may make a deal with a local broker to handle the paperwork of the sales, but we must be careful, because the regular 6 percent commission would be a large share of our hoped-for profit.

If the normal incidence of strikes, bad weather, vandalism, and excess competition do not unreasonably hold back construction and sales, we have $12,000 to spend at the end of the year. We also get back the cash we put in for land and other things; imputed interest on that cash is part of our $12,000. Whether we "made money" or not depends on what we think our time and our cleverness is worth.

Throughout the development process we shall be borrowing money and paying bills. Matching up these money flows effectively minimizes the amount of cash we shall have to lay out, which affects the imputed interest cost and also the maximum size of the project we can handle. After all, would it take that much more development time or know-how to turn out a tract of eight houses for a "profit" of $24,000 (or better, if we get quantity discounts on materials, for example)? Even more critically, if we fail to keep the cash flow situation in bounds during our development process, we might suddenly find ourselves insolvent—bills due but no cash in the till. That will be the end of our venture, and the $12,000 profit will probably end up in someone else's pocket.

The developer's profit depends primarily on the skill with which he acquires land and his success in marketing what he builds. These two interact, since the location of his tract helps determine how readily he can attract buyers. This interaction is suggested by Figure 36, in which the LL curve is the set of combinations of land prices (governed by accessibility) and absorption periods that are available to the tract developer. More accessible land costs more, but it will help sell the houses faster. Since the house buyer will pay the accessibility value of the land, it might seem that the developer ought to use that land which will result in the minimum absorption period, but, in practice, this is not necessarily his best option.

The reason is that the developer's land profit (the change in residual land value) is his protection against unanticipated increases in costs. Such increases might come about because of building code requirements that were overlooked initially, difficulties encountered by or with the contractor (strikes, for example), poor cost estimating, poor marketing strategy or timing, or many other "mistakes" and "accidents" that do crop up in real estate development. If he gives away too much of this protective margin by buying the most accessible land he can find, he incurs serious risk of financial loss. On the other hand, very cheap land that is poorly located will extend the expected absorption period and raise the developer's interest costs. A profit curve—as visualized by the developer at the time he is shopping for land—is shown in Figure 36, with a peak at point B where the land price is OF.

Land within the absorption range OA or beyond the period OC

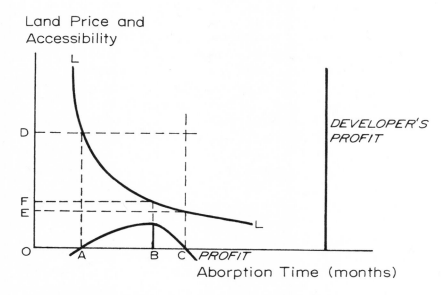

Figure 36.   Land purchase by residential tract developer.

would appear unprofitable to this developer. Between *A* and *B* the risk of abnormal cost increases during development outweighs the interest cost of absorption, while the opposite situation prevails between *B* and *C*. A land price greater than *OD* is too high, in any case, and one less than *OE* is too low.

   Most of the cost of absorption comes from interest (and taxes) on completed buildings and on tying up of the developer's liquid cash that he would like to put to work again as soon as possible. This cost can be substantially reduced by acquiring very inexpensive land, at price *OE* or less, and holding it until absorption conditions improve—as the population of the city expands or new highways are put in, for example. There is a limit to this private "land banking," though, because interest and taxes on land held for a very long time can drain the developer's liquid cash and dilute his credit.

   The other large element in the developer's profit equation is market-ability—which means building the kinds of houses people want to buy. Tract developers rarely employ market analysis to determine what they should build. Probably the typical situation is one in which the individual

developer limits himself to a type of dwelling he knows best, say houses in
the $35,000 to $40,000 price range, and he identifies land that would be
considered suitable by purchasers of such housing. A common measure of
suitability is the asking price of the land plus land-improvement costs,
because there is a rule-of-thumb relationship between the price of a
completed dwelling (including land) and the developed value of that land.
For example, if the developed value of land is $5,000 per lot, we often find
houses built on such land selling for four or five times that amount,
$20,000 to $25,000. A land value of $10,000 anticipates a home-buyer
market in the $40,000 to $50,000 range, where this rule of thumb applies.
The developer brings his idea to the local bank (or other lender), where the
real market analysis will be done, even if it is only an application of this
rule of thumb in conjunction with the sector theory of urban expansion.

Of course, developers and lenders keep an eye on rates of absorption
that other developers are experiencing. If $35,000 houses are going like
hotcakes, then there will be a go-ahead for more of the same as long as the
developer is competent and his land is reasonably suited to the market. If
there are many $25,000 houses standing around unsold, then developers
who concentrate on that part of the market will be advised to hold off
for awhile.

The market for new houses usually is most active in the upper-middle
price ranges. This disturbs many observers who think that the house-
building industry is neglecting the lower-income market and that something should be done—by public construction or by subsidy—to change
this. In fact, lower-priced housing is supplied mainly from the inventory of
existing buildings rather than from new construction.

The main points of the issue are illustrated in Figure 37. We start, in
diagram (a), with a frequency distrubution of potential-buyer households
by income and with a distribution of the inventory (the housing supply)
by price and rent level. The two curves coincide by definition at the outset,
because $10,000 houses are occupied by $10,000-house families, $15,000
houses by $15,000-house families, and so on. In (b), the demand curve
shifts upward as population grows, and it shifts to the right as incomes
rise. The initial supply distribution, (c), shifts to the left in diagram (d) as
the inventory of houses ages and they become less valuable in a physical
sense. Putting these new demand and supply curves together, in (e), there
is a surplus of houses in the lower price and income ranges and a deficit in

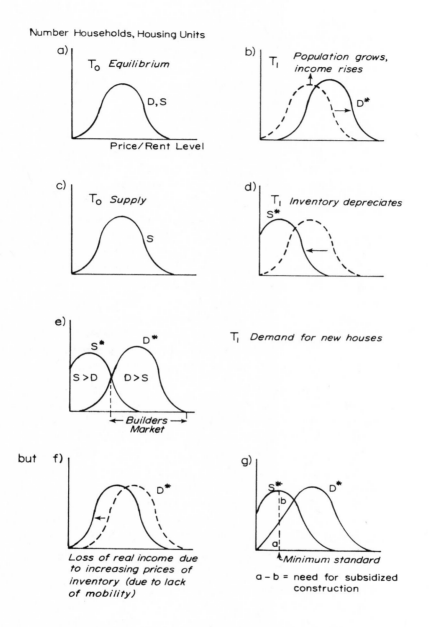

Figure 37. Price level of new housing.

the upper ranges. Builders of new houses cannot compete with the excess low-priced, older inventory, but they find a large market at the upper-middle income and price level.

There is a problem in this view of the market since, as diagram (f) indicates, rising prices of existing houses reduce the purchasing power of families in the housing market, shifting the D curve back to the left. Existing houses rise in value as they get older, partly because families with rising incomes remain in the same dwellings. A neighborhood where incomes averaged $5,000 initially becomes, over time, one where average income is $10,000, though the houses are older and obsolescent. A family in search of housing looks for a neighborhood where income levels are generally similar to its own, and the price it pays for housing is governed more by its income than by the physical condition of what it buys or the original construction cost of the house. The result is to pare down the apparent surplus of low-priced inventory but without changing the principle that the new-house market generally starts at or above the community's average income level.

Diagram (g) applies this concept to the question of the need for subsidized housing in the case that some of the existing inventory of dwellings is so old and dilapidated that it is below a socially identified minimum standard. Families in the "a" area thus require some surplus of acceptable housing, measured by the "b" area, so it is only the difference "a − b" that measures the need for subsidizing housing construction to eliminate the occupancy of substandard dwellings. Houses in the "b" area, however, may be unavailable to people living in substandard housing, by reason of location, discrimination, or other imperfection in the distribution of housing.

It is not price alone that sells houses or determines the absorption rate. In recent decades tract developers have found that good land planning is an important marketing tool, because home buyers are concerned with the attractiveness of the neighborhood in which their families will be living. The most obvious aspect of modern land-planning practice is curvilinear internal streets, as illustrated in Figure 38, with frequent cul-de-sacs. This pattern discourages through traffic (which the old-fashioned gridiron plan actually invited), leaving the residential streets free of noise, congestion, and hazard. These curving internal streets cost less per mile to build because the expected usage is less. Utility lines that are not rigidly rectangular may also be a source of economy. A less-obvious virtue of recent land planning is that it may permit house lots as well as streets to be laid out in better conformity with the topography—curving gently up-hill rather than running straight up a slope. Costly and unsightly retaining walls are less necessary, more of the natural land contours and vegetation can be preserved, and often a larger number of lots can be achieved per acre.

Land planning is probably the most significant "technological" advance in house building in recent decades, because in a market sense it provides "more house for the money." Obviously, though, a very small tract does not provide much scope for isolating the land plan of a neighborhood from its surroundings. Hence, there is evidence of a scale economy in recent house building, relating to the amenities of the neighborhood rather than to the physical construction of individual houses.

The house-building process itself is often regarded as archaic and in need of modernization, so that the cost of housing can be reduced. Research and experimentation, such as the United States government's "Operation Breakthrough," have been directed toward finding ways to increase the use of labor-saving machinery and industrial management techniques in house building. Mobile, modular, or other types of "factory-built" housing have been the focus of attention, but major opportunities for cost reduction in housing have not yet been identified.

Outright scale economies in the traditional house-building process appear confined to a rather modest level of output, between 500 and 800 houses per year.[1]

Builders producing much below that level are not able to schedule work carefully to avoid paying for slack time and cannot obtain quantity discounts on materials. On the other hand, the supervisory capacity of the one-man house-building firm is strained beyond that level, and the organizational structure necessary in larger firms generally does not pay for itself through further production economies. Just as fundamentally, large-scale output involves substantial market risks. The larger the share of the yearly local new-house market that a particular builder gears up for, the more likely he is to be disappointed. Just as we take small steps in a dark room, the house builder tries to finish things off in fairly small packages because his knowledge of the market's depth is usually very limited.

1. John P. Herzog, *The Dynamics of Large-Scale Housebuilding* (Berkeley: Center for Real Estate and Urban Economics, University of California, 1963), p. 27. An earlier but still basic work on the subject is Sherman J. Maisel, *Housebuilding in Transition* (Berkeley: University of California Press, 1953).

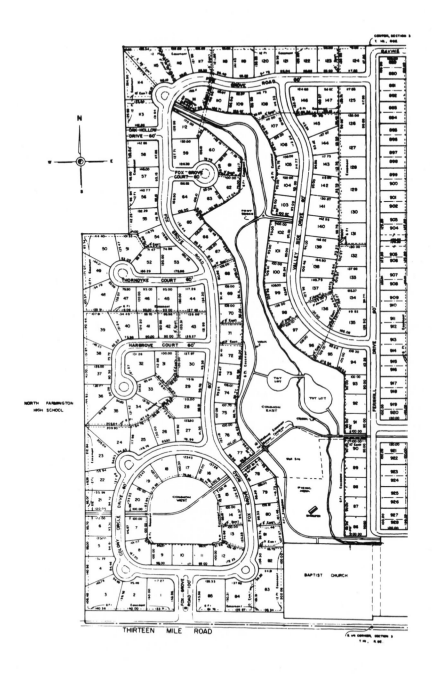

A SMALL APARTMENT BUILDING

Next we can try our hand at developing a twenty-unit apartment building. Referring to the numerical presentation in Table 18, these are the steps we might expect to follow.

1. Locate land that is suitably priced, that is zoned for apartments or could be rezoned, that seems to be favorably located to attract and keep the kind of tenants we envisage, and that is large enough, given the various local regulations, to accomodate the kind of building we expect to build. We will probably have a land budget in mind of, say, $2,000 per unit, or $40,000. The land we find will probably have an old single-family house on it, or perhaps two old houses on adjacent lots, and the price, of course, includes the houses which must be demolished. We can acquire the land for cash, if we have it, but a large mortgage can normally be arranged.

2. Get plans drawn and approved and secure the necessary permits. In the table, our estimated construction cost is $240,000, or $12,000 per unit.

3. Arrange for a construction loan and also, perhaps, for a permanent loan to replace the construction and land mortgages when the building is completed. Table 18 assumes we can borrow 90 percent of the construction cost.

4. Pull together enough cash resources to provide whatever initial equity is required and to deal with probable negative cash flow periods during construction. This cash may come from mortgages on things we previously developed and still hold, from personal assets or personal borrowings, from silent partners, or from full-fledged partners. We could even incorporate and sell shares. Assuming we have obtained the land without committing cash, our equity requirement is $24,000, but precisely when this amount must be paid out will depend on the arrangments we make with the lender, the contractor, and the various suppliers.

5. Make our arrangements with a contractor or builder and get the

---

Figure 38.   Land planning in a residential tract.

    Source: Urban Land Institute, *Community Builders Handbook* (Washington, D.C., 1968), p. 106. The plan is from the Thompson-Brown Company, developers, for a development in Farmington Township, Michigan. Copyright by ULI—the Urban Land Institute, 1200 18th St., NW, Washington, D.C. 20036.

Table 18

Apartment Building Development

Description: a 20-unit building to rent at $175 per unit per month.	
Costs	
Land @ $2,000 per unit	
(financed by mortgage)	$ 40,000
Construction @ $12,000 per unit	
(90% construction loan)	240,000
Developed cost	$280,000
Market Value	
20 units @ $175 per month	
Annual gross income	$ 42,000
Gross rent multiplier	
(Local market factor)	8
Value	$336,000
Developer's Profit	$ 56,000

construction underway. It will probably take one year, more or less, from the acquisition of land to completion, depending very much on the contractor's other obligations and problems that arise concerning building inspections by the city or the lender. Quite apart from curiosity, we will want to keep an eye on the construction process to prevent errors or avoidable waste and delays, so a knowledge of construction fundamentals will be necessary. The builder will also confront us with many choices for building hardware, wiring details, decorative features, and so on—which were not anticipated in our original plans.

6. Look for prospective investors who might buy the property upon completion (or perhaps during construction). Projecting rents at $175 per month for each of 20 units, a gross of $42,000 per year, and applying a multiplier of 8 (which we find by talking to local brokers and appraisers or to the mortgage lender), the market price of the completed property will be $336,000. If we sell out at this price, our profit of $56,000 may be deemed a capital gain or ordinary income, depending largely on whether the development of real estate is a regular source of livelihood for us.

7. When the building is completed, assuming we have not yet sold it, we must try to get it rented as quickly as possible. Of course, rental income will be helpful in meeting our cash obligations for the mortgage and taxes. But having 75 or 80 percent of the building occupied will also make it easier to refinance the property–paying off the land mortgage and the construction loan. If we can get a permanent loan for 83 percent of the market value, or $280,000, we get back all the cash that we tied up in the development; the $56,000 equity is our paper profit. We may decide to retain ownership of the new apartment building for awhile, at least, especially if there are tax advantages. We can borrow against the equity to finance another development or to buy groceries.

Whether we sell to an investor right away or retain owernship, the new apartments begin to produce a stream of benefits for its owner. These annual benefits include spendable cash flow (which will be tax free if the depreciation allowance gives us zero taxable income for the first few years), amortization which increases our equity, and appreciation in the value of the property by virtue of local land market trends. For example, in the early years we might have $5,000 spendable cash flow, $5,000 amortization, and $7,000 appreciation.

In the United States, an owner may enjoy tax shelter for other income as well, if the property's taxable income is negative. If an investor purchases the development with a cash equity of $100,000, these figures add up to a return in the first year of 12 percent, but there is a problem of adding apples and oranges; only the spendable cash is hard money, and part of it may be taxable.

The numbers in Table 18 are, in effect, a summary of a "feasibility study." If things go as planned, we will not lose money, since the expected market value of the property–the capitalized value of the stream of future benefits–is greater than the sum of our costs for land, labor, materials, and borrowed money. The profit on the development is often referred to as an "increment in land value," because with a brand new $240,000 building, the property has a value of $336,000, leaving $96,000 for land that we got for $40,000. This term, however, obscures the role of the developer by suggesting that the original landowner sold out too low. In reality, not "anyone" can or will develop real estate; special knowledge and analytical skills are required, and people who possess these expect to be paid for their contribution to the development process. We lack meaningful information about how much developers generally earn, so it would be hard to argue that they get too much or too little. Some part of the land value increment, however, is attributable to the developer's personal input.

A feasibility study does not demonstrate that the developer has hit upon the ideal way to use either his time and abilities or the land he has acquired. It is not a "highest and best use" study that defines the optimum use of the land (from the market point of view). If several feasibility studies are made for the land in question, covering all reasonable alternatives for its use, then among these studies we would find one with the highest "residual land value"–the difference between the market value upon completion and the cost of construction–and that would be our highest and best use.

A geometric approach to this task is shown in Figure 39, which asks the question: How large a building, measured by money outlay on construction, should a developer construct on a given piece of land? Two types of buildings are considered: A, which might be an office building, and B,

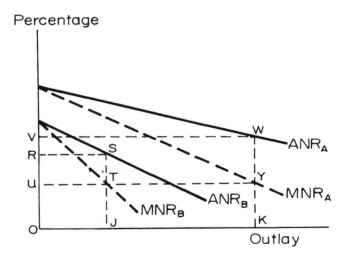

Figure 39. Marginal analysis of lot development intensity.

Source: Ralph Turvey, *The Economics of Real Property* (London: George Allen & Unwin, Ltd., 1957), p. 53. ANR = average net returns, for buildings A and B. MNR = marginal net returns, for buildings A and B.

an apartment building. For either type there is a range of possible outlays (which we can think of as representing the number of stories the building can have). The cost of investment funds for the construction is assumed to be OU, on the vertical axis, measured in percentages. The average annual net returns, per dollar of outlay also expressed in percentage terms, decline as the size of the projected building increases because of scale diseconomies in construction costs (need for more elevators or heavier supporting walls, for example) or because the market demand for space is price-elastic (the more we put on the market the less we must ask for it). Because ANR falls, total net revenue per dollar of outlay falls at a faster rate, giving us the MNR lines in the figure. An additional dollar of outlay produces a return just equal to the interest cost of money, OU, when building A is size OK and building B is size OJ. This marginal method maximizes the value of the rectangles $UVWY$ for building A and $URST$ for building B, which measures the total annual net income to the property over and above the income required to pay for construction funds invested. Clearly the developer maximizes these areas with outlays of OK for building A or OJ for building B; presumably he would prefer to construct building A, and he now has a guide as to how large that building should be.

But what does he maximize by this procedure? It is the profit to the developer who got the land at a price of zero, and it is the maximum (annual) amount any other developer could afford to pay for the land. It is, in fact, the residual land value. By choosing building type A and outlay level OK, the developer is maximizing the residual value of the land and the increment in land value. The developer thus tends to put land to its "highest and best use," in the market economy sense of the term.

In most urban situations, the developer is constrained by zoning and building regulations. Since he supplies only a small share of the market, ANR tends to be rather flat and MNR nearly parallel to it. Hence, the problem is usually to select the optimum building type, A rather than B, for example, and construct the most intensive building of that type that local regulations permit. The usefulness of this marginal concept is limited to cases where the new building might actually tend to saturate the market, as in a major office-building project. But the marginal concept does confirm the more general criterion of developer optimization based on maximizing the land-value increment. This often boils down to a careful selection of the site and the timing, with particular effort toward paying the minimum necessary price for land.

How would a developer, such as ourselves, determine that there was a market for twenty new units to rent at $175 per month? Formal market analysis is very rare; a realistic description of the thought process, somewhat simplified, might be as follows: (1) The developer finds an area in which some new apartment construction has occurred and notes the unit-size categories (one-bedroom, two-bedroom) and rent levels that seem to rent up the fastest. (2) The developer investigates the area to see how much further construction of this type is in the advanced stages of planning. (3) If the signs are reasonable, he acquires a parcel or two of land in this area and takes his proposal to a prosepctive source of construction financing—a local bank, for example—where information about citywide housing demand, vacancy rates, recent building permits, and other pertinent things are generally held, at least in someone's head.

That is, the developer relies on the lending agency for market information and judgment. The points of greatest uncertainty, as a rule, have to do with location. Does a high vacancy rate on the other side of town matter, for instance? Is it important for a new apartment building to be within walking distance of downtown or of a public transportation station? Recent suburban apartment construction has raised doubts about locational principles that were once very firmly held. Another judgmental problem concerns the interaction of the existing housing inventory (or office buildings, stores, and other structures) with new construction. High vacancy rates in slum areas, for example, do not necessarily mean that the demand for well-constructed, new apartment units is weak.

A SHOPPING CENTER

With growing confidence we might next tackle a shopping center project. The success criterion, creating maximum incremental (residual) land value, is the same as for residential developments, as indeed for all real estate development. Nevertheless, in the case of shopping centers there are a few specific points to be considered, and there is, in addition, the clearest concept for measuring the market demand we have for any type of real estate. Market analysis and feasibility studies for shopping centers were developed into logical and very practical form in the great wave of suburban shopping center construction that occurred after the Second World War. Table 19 describes the general format of such studies.

To start with, marketing people know how far people are willing to

Table 19

Shopping Center Market Analysis and Feasibility Study

	Department store	Apparel stores	Total
Per capita retail sales	$180	$70	
Total trade are potential (projected)	$36 mil.	$14 mil.	
Less downtown sales	25%	40%	
Suburban potential	$27 mil.	$8.4 mil.	
Less competition	$ 8 mil.	$1.1 mil.	
Center potential	$19 mil.	$7.3 mil.	
Normal sales per sq. ft.	$55	$60	
Warranted space	345,000 sq. ft.	122,000 sq. ft.	
Planned space	250,000 sq. ft.	50,000 sq. ft.	300,000 sq. ft.[a]
Net rent per sq. ft.[b]	$2	$5	
Total net rent	$500,000	$250,000	$750,000
Capitalized (× 8.2)	$4.1 mil.	$2.05 mil.	$6,150,000
Construction cost @ $20 per sq. ft.[a]	$5.0 mil.	$1.00 mil.	$6,000,000
Residual land value	−$.9 mil.	$1.05 mil.	$150,000

[a] Three or more times this amount of space must also be allowed for parking, malls, and so forth. Construction cost per square foot of sales area includes allowance for creating these other areas.

[b] Includes percentage on sales above a minimum.

travel to get to particular kinds of stores. One rule of thumb is five miles for comparison shopping, which would apply to wearing apparel and department store type merchandise. Having a prospective site to analyze, a piece of land large enough to hold a set of complementary stores plus parking and accessible from major roads, we can draw a circle of a five-mile radius around our site to describe the trade area for our center. The trade area must exclude the downtown, though, and otherwise conform to natural boundaries such as rivers, so it will be only roughly circular. We then project the population of this area as it will be when our center is completed and has gained local consumer acceptance. One way to do this is to estimate the "holding capacity" of the area when it is fully built up at its typical present density (quarter-acre house lots, for example). Assume this projected population as 200,000.

Marketing people can also tell us how much is usually spent per capita in retail stores of different types. This is partly a function of family income, so we must survey that, apply sales distribution percentages, and arrive at such figures as $180 per person department store sales and $70 per person apparel store sales. In reality, we would estimate such sales figures for all the categories of stores that are likely to be included in our shopping center, but only these two categories are shown in Table 19.

We next subtract the estimated retail sales by people in our trade area that they will make downtown—again guided by widely available market studies. From this suburban potential we further subtract an allowance for the sales local competitors can expect to get. These figures come from on-the-spot surveys of existing stores and information concerning stores that are likely to be built, relying on the concept that sales by retail stores are generally proportional to their floor area. Potential sales at the center then work out to be $19 million in the department store and $7.3 million in the apparel stores.

The normal sales volume per square foot of store is another figure that is relatively constant and well known for each store type. Dividing such numbers into the center potential sales figures gives us the maximum amounts of space that would be warranted for stores at our center. With an eye toward conservatism—we will be talking to mortgage lenders about financing our development and to store operators about signing leases there—we compose a space plan that is well within the warranted figures and which adds up to a "balance" of store types within the center. For the two categories in our illustration, 300,000 square feet of store area is thus planned.

We must project the rents the shopping center enterprise will collect from its tenants, most of whom will pay a minimum guaranteed rent plus a percentage on sales volume. We suppose that these work out to forecasts of $2 and $5 per square foot for the department store and the apparel stores, respectively, and that these rents are net after operating expenses (but not interest, amortization, or depreciation). The forecast of annual net rental income to the center is $750,000. We capitalize this by applying a gross income multiplier of 8.2; in reality, a more complex capitalization calculation would probably be made for this type of development. The capital value of our proposed shopping center is $6,150,000.

Putting construction cost estimates on the basis of retail store area, we develop information about how much it is going to cost to build the center, except for the land. The figure in the illustration is $20 per square foot, but the reader might see how sensitive the financial results of our development are to slight variations in this cost figure. It works out to $6 million, however, taking the numbers as they stand. The residual land value, our feasibility or success criterion, is $150,000. If we don't have to pay more than this amount for the land, the project is feasible. Our profit depends on how much less than $150,000 we can get the land for—assuming all our sales and cost projections prove to be realistic.

Although we are ultimately interested in the total column of the table, something very important about shopping center development and operation is revealed by the detail for store types which we carry through in the table. The residual land value for the department store is negative because of the low rental figure per square foot. (This is something of an exaggeration in order to emphasize the different rules of various stores in a center.) Should we raise the department store rent? Or, perhaps, decide not to have a department store in our center?

In fact, the department store is our "traffic generator." Without it, we would not get anything like the projected sales volumes in the apparel stores, which are in the nature of satellites to the department store in the eyes of shoppers. Thus, the rent that apparel stores (and other store types, to varying degrees) pay in the shopping center may contain a kind of subsidy to the department store or other traffic generator. Our residual land value, and our profit, will get much larger than $150,000 if we add more stores of this satellite nature to the center, once we have the department store there. There is some optimum complex of traffic generator and satellite stores that most completely exploits the retail potential of a site, and this complex is what the developer tries to visualize in this analysis. Thanks to well-developed market research methods and relatively predictable shopping behavior patterns among the population, the shopping center development process generally appears far more rational than other types of real estate development, so that the chances of approximating the optimum pattern are good.

Financing of the shopping center development is an expanded version of apartment or tract financing. The land may be obtained for a note that the seller holds or may be separately mortgaged. Construction financing is sought from lending institutions. Some cash equity will be needed. Upon completion, the land and construction mortgages are paid off and a permanent mortgage is placed on the property. The completed shopping center may be sold to an investor organization on the basis of its cash flow, equity build-up through amortization and appreciation (and possible tax shelter for the investor's other income). If it is sold, the developer realizes his "land value increment" profit, perhaps in cash, though he may take a second mortgage for part. If the developer retains the property and refinances it for its cost, his profit is a paper equity, but he can borrow against that if he needs funds for his next real estate venture.

Shopping center developers often employ consultants to make market analyses and feasibility studies and to negotiate with mortgage lenders, department store chain organizations, architects, and construction companies. It is likely, then, that the developer is the owner of a favorably located land, or an "active-appreciation" type land investor who acquired it because he believed it had potential that the land market generally was not aware of. An investor of this type is likely to measure his success in terms of land profit rather than "yield," since his opportunities for leverage are great.

DEVELOPING A NEW TOWN

Having gotten this far in the real estate game without losing money, we might as well do the world a favor and put together an entire city. Since we are people of taste as well as expertise, we will, of course, avoid all the mistakes that plague old-fashioned, haphazard cities, even as we make a convenient bundle. This simultaneous achievement is our due as activists in the "new real estate."

One convenient aspect of making a whole new town is that we can get the necessary land very cheap. Tundra, jungle, or prairie might be suitable for the purpose, so long as the economics of location are not wholly disregarded, because we will need some kind of economic base. Profits from the development, which might have gone to real estate speculators in the ordinary process of suburban sprawl, can be captured and used for the benefit of people who are going to live and work in our new city.

Another advantage we should be aware of from our tract and shopping center development experience, is that the order, attractiveness, and functional efficiency of large-scale land use planning is a powerful marketing tool. People and businesses looking for a place to settle down do give favorable consideration to developments where compatible activities are grouped together, incompatible things separated but easily reached, natural amenities have been preserved or enhanced, and where a full complement of public services has been provided for in an economical way. We can also create subtle architectural uniformity—not oppressive, but enough to give the town an "image" that residents will want to have rub off on them.

At the same time, we shall be siphoning off population and other land-use increments that threaten existing large cities. We cannot profit directly from this externality of our development, but we may be able to use it as an argument for some kind of governmental subsidy. For example, we may need to have the power to condemn land in the area we want for our city or some of its services (such as a reservoir or a large park). Mortgage insurance for our construction borrowings would be helpful, or we may want to borrow extensively from public agencies at modest rates of interest.[2]

Our first back-of-the-envelope financial analysis will probably be encouraging. Keeping our plans and figures modest, we might estimate total construction cost to be $10 million and the market value on completion to be $15 million, for a tidy $5 million profit. Since most of the construction and land costs can be borrowed, the leveraged rate of return could look very impressive if this were our success criterion.

The problem, however, is time. Figure 40 shows the financial experience of our enterprise over a span of eighteen years. The top diagram presents the picture of accumulated outlays and revenues as time passes, and the lower diagram portrays yearly outlays and receipts. It will take many years while we have the land under control to make consistent, attractive plans for the physical and financial aspects of the entire community, to secure the approval and cooperation of hosts of separate agencies in several levels of government and of utility companies on such things as density, new highways, commercial zoning, hospitals, the school program, solid

2. For critical and descriptive studies of new town developments in the United States, see Edward P. Eichler and Marshall Kaplan, *The Community Builders* (Berkeley: The University of California Press, 1967); and Philip David, *Urban Land Development* (Homewood, Ill.: Irwin, 1970), Part VI.

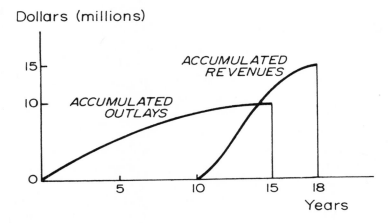

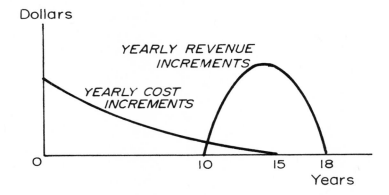

Figure 40.   The cash flow problem in new town development.

waste disposal, homeowner mortgages, water supply, and so on—all in complete detail. We shall go into brush clearing and dirt hauling on a massive scale. We will have to create and run a construction camp, with medical facilities and probably a police force to take care of the crews of workers. Our negotiations for materials and construction contracts will be prolonged and complex, dealing in very large sums so that even the smallest points will seem worth bickering over. We will probably have a complex partnership of some sort to provide the necessary equity, and the partners will need constant wooing, replacement, or weeding out. An office force of considerable skill and versatility will have to be pulled together from someplace, for what everyone will know is not a permanent job.

So we assume in the diagram that ten years go by before we can start selling off or renting portions of our development, by which time most of our ultimate construction investment, including interest on construction funds, has been committed. Actual construction continues, we suppose, until year 15, but absorption requires another three years. About year 14, our accumulated revenues surpass accumulated outlays. Accumulated revenues exceed accumulated costs by $5 million. But did we really make money?

The lower diagram helps answer that question. The area under the revenue curve is greater than the area under the cost curve, by this same $5 million. We do not begin to receive this, however, until approximately year 14, when accumulated revenues permit us to pay the principal and interest on all our borrowings. What this prospect of gain is worth to us at the beginning of our enterprise depends on the rate at which we discount it for time, and possibly for risk. If absorption is slow or discount rate is high, then our money returns may seem meager, either in present dollar value or as a rate of return on equity capital that we will have to advance. If our equity is substantial, the yield on it after all is said and done may not compare favorably with alternative real estate or other type investments that involve less delay. It is also likely to be a particularly illiquid investment on our part.

Another problem is that in years 1 through 10 our cash flow will be negative. Money will have to be borrowed continuously to pay for further construction and to pay interest on previous borrowings. Mortgage investors are likely to be very skeptical about a situation that takes so long to prove itself, and we must either pay a premium rate of interest to get the money or put it up ourselves as additional equity.

It would help very much if we could stage the development—complete one section of it first and put it on the market—because this would reduce the period of negative cash flow. But this runs into the problem of balance; customers will be reluctant to come to a place without a reasonable complement of stores and public facilities. We can stage the residential and employment sections (industrial or office areas), but the basic work on public infrastructure—streets, water supply, electricity—will probably have to be nearly complete before we can put any portion of the development on the market. We may be able to provide just one neighborhood elementary school for a starter, but if the whole community will require only one high school, that may have to be completed during the initial stage. The full range of retail and service facilities envisaged for the town will be unavailable, of course, until the whole project is complete and marketed.

A new town, in the proper sense of the term, is self-contained with respect to employment. Otherwise, residents have to commute to some other city to work, and the community we are building becomes just a large suburb. Basic industry employers, however, and business firms generally are increasingly conscious of agglomeration economies that exist in the major metropolitan areas. Firms that do not value these agglomeration economies may not make up the kind of economic base that we—or the mortgage lenders our residents will be dealing with—will consider ideal. The result of all this is that serious doubts arise concerning the rate of absorption—that is, of employment and population growth—for a new town development, in the absence of strong governmental pressures to direct expanding firms away from existing urban areas. And our success rides on this will-o'-the-wisp absorption rate.

New town developers are also obliged to plan the entire fiscal system of the community, anticipating the size of the tax base, the salaries of teachers, the capital and operating costs of parks and sewage treatment plants, the means available to raise capital for public investment, and even the probable attitude of the eventual local government toward land-use controls and public expenditures requiring debt or subsidy. In this respect, they must do, or attempt, fiscal planning that existing cities rarely, if ever, succeed at. Real estate developers naturally acquire great familiarity with local government and its fiscal problems, but they are not necessarily competent to design and deliver a set of public facilities that will prove to be both sufficient and solvent.

Perhaps, then, we shall decide to back off from the new town undertaking, worthy and promising though it might seem at first blush. What has happened to many recent development enterprises that were billed as new towns or new communities indicates that the game may not be worth the candle.

ADVANTAGES AND RISKS OF LARGE-SCALE DEVELOPMENT

The discussion of new town development points us toward a more general issue—does it pay to "think big" in the real estate development business? Suppose we have a chance to acquire a very large piece of farm land close to a major city with a growing population—how ambitious should we be in trying to meet the future real estate needs of the community?

Accepting profit as our criterion, our first thought will be to find out what kind of land use produces the highest residual land value. It turns out that downtown office buildings win on that score, with land values in excess of one million dollars per acre.[3] We can keep this office building figure in mind for the long run, but it would be better to turn our attention to something else.

The next best thing would be a regional shopping center, requiring about thirty acres and generating a land value in the range of $500,000 to $750,000 per acre. But it takes a population of 150,000 or more to support such a center, and the annual growth of the community may be so spread out along its fringe that many years must go by before there is sufficient trade area population for a center on our land.[4] A four-acre neighborhood shopping center might give us a land value of about $60,000 per acre, and it would require a population of 10,000 or so within one mile.

Retail uses are thus attractive in terms of profitable development potential but are dependent on residential growth. They also require relatively small amounts of land. With ample land at our disposal, why not build ourselves a trade area? An attractive new residential area could bend the direction of population growth toward our area, and we could capture an important external benefit of residential development by putting a shopping center at a focal point within our housing area.

For a regional shopping center trade area, something like 50,000 new houses are required, which means about 20,000 acres. If this is not too large an undertaking for us, we can ultimately produce land values of perhaps $10,000 per gross acre in housing, plus $750,000 per acre for thirty acres in the shopping center. We can probably develop some apartment buildings near the shopping center, for a value of $75,000 per acre or better.

The absorption rate problem is against us, however. There will be competitive developments in other parts of the urban fringe, and the annual rate of new housing absorption in the whole community may be

3. For an interesting summary of this kind of information, see Larry Smith, "Space for the CBD's Functions," in *Internal Structure of the City*, ed. by Larry S. Bourne, pp. 353–360.
4. For population requirements of shopping center trade areas, see Urban Land Institute, *Community Builders Handbook*, p. 267.

something like 15,000 units. We would be lucky to get 20 percent of the whole growth market, and constructing 3,000 new houses a year would tax our real estate expertise. While we were trying to do our best in the housing market, someone else might preempt the shopping center opportunity. Holding onto 20,000 or so acres of land for fifteen to twenty years could be very hard to finance.

So we might settle for a more modest scheme. Just a year or two of house building might give us the trade area population to support a neighborhood shopping center. With a planning horizon like that we could not only realize many of the principal amenity advantages of large-scale tract development, but we could bring in at the same time the supermarket, drugstore, and stationery shop, some small offices for doctors and dentists, a branch bank, and other services as a further help in marketing the homes. A few apartments might fit into the scheme which, along with the shopping center, we might want to retain as income property for the long run. The short absorption period would help us find financing for construction.

OVERLOADING THE INFRASTRUCTURE

The smaller development also exempts us from concerns that become major problems for the new town developer or for the real estate organization attempting to manage a 10,000 to 20,000 acre suburban development complex. We do not have to worry about sewage plants, hospitals, and public improvement bond issues. We don't have to prove to our financial backers that the tax base will support the schools that children from our development will attend.[5] The matter may arise in zoning discussions, but, here again, the limited-scale development has the advantage.

In short, it will be easier for us to market our houses and cheaper for us to put the development together if we tie into existing public services as well as into the general retail, service, and employment fabric of the community. People will come to buy homes from us partly because there are good department stores and office jobs downtown, available by freeway directly adjoining our development, because there is a medical complex in the city, a high school and elementary schools nearby, a sewage and waste

5. There is an increasing tendency, however, for local governments to require such evidence in connection with even modest-size development proposals.

disposal system, a good water supply, parks, museums, and so on. But we will not have to see to it that any of this is provided or that the facilities which exist are expanded to take care of the new population we house.

Except for the completely new community, of which examples are scarce, real estate development is an exercise in overloading the urban infrastructure. Every shopping center, office building, apartment building, housing tract, and industrial park dumps more cars on the neighboring roads and into the central business district. New family housing means more children signing up for free, compulsory, primary and secondary school education and, increasingly, for junior college. Every kind of development adds to the flow of sewage into the mains, encumbers the logistics of solid waste disposal, and removes open space. Redevelopment of land already in use generally intensifies this overloading effect.

Such things are external costs to the community, though not necessarily money costs, resulting from real estate development. It is not the developer's want of social responsibility that leads him to overload the urban infrastructure, but simply the existence of the option. The "nice guy" who tries to protect the rest of the community by providing new schools and parks in his housing tract sufficient to the needs of his own customers will have to ask a higher price for his houses, and his customers won't get appreciably more. The overcrowding caused by just one small real estate development is negligible. A school, like an elevator, can always hold just one more person.

Indeed, it is the user of real estate—the developer's customer—who does the overloading, and there is a practical economic reason for his doing so. Suppose, for example, that there are 30 children in a schoolroom, sharing 1,200 square feet of space and 480 minutes per day of a teacher's time. If a thirty-first child enters the class, he will have the use of 38.7 square feet of space and 15.5 minutes of teacher time. Each of the original children will give up 1.3 square feet and one-half minute. Leaving aside the nature of the tax system, the cost of the new child's education is borne in the first instance by the children already there. Why should the parents of the additional child take it upon themselves to build 40 square feet of school and hire 1/31 of a teacher when their child can get 38.7 square feet and 15.5 minutes per day of teacher time free?

The costs involved are "external"—they don't have to be borne by the person who causes them. The same thing occurs when a person stands in line for a bus or a supermarket checkstand; regardless of his relative position, he slows up the bus trip or the shopping task for everyone else just by being there, and he does not compensate the people who are thus inconvenienced. Each additional car on a commuter route slows down every one of the other commuters. Each additional citizen makes it more difficult for others to get their ideas across to local government and for local police to keep track of what is going on. Always it is the others who pay.

Of course, the other side of the coin is external benefit. A school with a large enrollment can have more specialized facilities. A supermarket or department store with many customers can provide a greater variety of goods from which all will benefit. A large volume of commuter traffic may justify an expressway or a rapid transit system. The greater the population of the community, the more diverse and stable its economic base and the more interesting its array of consumer facilities.

The difficulty is twofold. One part is that the external costs may cancel out the external benefits at some level of urban size; we shall return to this "optimum city size" question in Chapter Fourteen. The other part is that we have a "system" problem, which is symbolized in Figure 41. Starting with a city that has an acceptable pattern of land uses and internal activities, assume that growth occurs that doubles the size of the city in a certain period of time. Eventually the stock of houses, stores, offices, and infrastructure of all types must be expanded, roughly in proportion to

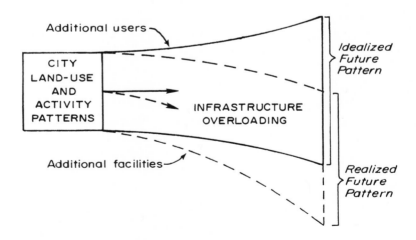

Figure 41.   Urban expansion system.

population growth. The solid lines indicate that there is an expanded counterpart of our original, "acceptable," internal pattern for each size level through which the city will grow. We could assure that this pattern would emerge by laying out the city on a double scale in the first place—deciding where the roads and the schools would be and applying both minimum and maximum land-use controls throughout the entire area. People or businesses would not overload the infrastructure because expanded infrastructure would be there before the additional people arrived.

What takes place in reality, more often than not, is that new populations and businesses crowd in upon the existing infrastructure. They buy or rent land and buildings from people in the real estate business who know that infrastructure cost externalities can be translated into increments in residual land values. New houses, stores, offices, and factories are developed where streets, water and sewage systems, schools, and complementary private land uses already exist, because these developments are easier to finance and to market than similar new buildings in self-contained and immediately self-financing districts somewhere else.

The community must respond to the overloading of its infrastructure, and the tax base to pay for new infrastructure does generally expand with the city's population and business. Piecemeal expansion of the infrastructure may, however, produce an evolution of the city's land use and activity patterns away from the pattern we might have preferred if all the growth had been anticipated and provided for in advance. The dashed lines in Figure 41 suggest that the sequence of step-by-step responses to bits of infrastructure crowding ultimately results in a city that no one really had in mind or would have designed at the outset.

For example, in Figure 42, tract builders may cluster their five- or ten-house developments along Route 1, an old highway leading out of town. Eventually, traffic builds up to the point that Route 1 must be made over into a larger, modern, and much more expensive channel for commuter automobiles. The opportunity to put in Route 2, leading away from town in a new direction, has then disappeared. The primary school near Route 1 may be replaced with a larger structure or an additional school will be built quite close by. The improved highway and the additional school facilities along Route 1 will attract still more intensive housing and retail developments which, in another view of things, might have become a distinct and more agreeable subcommunity somewhere else in the suburban fringe. Eventual replacement of septic tanks or gravely overloaded

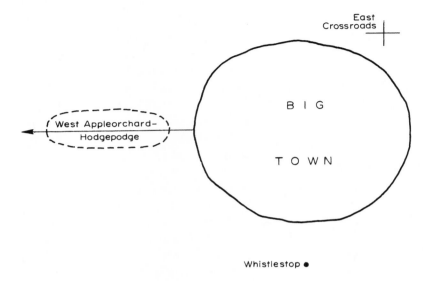

Figure 42.   Overloading the infrastructure.

Note: Any similarity to actual place names is purely coinci-
dental.

sewer lines will be costly, or even unfeasible, because of the intensive use of
the land around the Route 1 spine.

The intuitive reaction to this problem would probably be that more
"planning" is necessary. Indeed, the scenario we have described is the basic
concern of the modern city planning profession. Trying to prevent West
Appleorchard from becoming West Hodgepodge is the conscientious city
planner's abiding concern. His limitations are severe, however. He cannot
require developers or their customers to start afresh over in East Crossroads. He cannot build Route 2 in that direction or transfer building funds
from the West Hodgepodge school district. Once the population along
Route 1 has reached a certain point, he cannot withhold commercial
zoning completely, though he knows that a shopping center there will
help to lock in the growth pattern. Indeed, the assessor sees the price of
land going up around Route 1 and raises property taxes so much that
undeveloped land has to be put on the market, and the planner can't
stop that.

The fundamental barrier to more consciously planned development, though, is the difficulty of forecasting. In fact, neither the city planner nor the tract developer nor the banker nor anyone else in town knows for sure that alternative suburban places, East Crossroads and New Whistlestop, will become self-sustaining suburban communities in the reasonably near future. They will not even start growing unless some roads and schools are put there, and such investments would appear risky, unnecessary, and perhaps legally unfeasible. The taxpayers in Bigtown won't feel like paying for infrastructure in the now unpopulated reaches of suburbia. More school kids? Well, there's room in West Appleorchard.

Someday things might get so bad in Bigtown or West Hodgepodge that a few families may flee to East Crossroads, where they may have to pay penalty taxes for getting their children into a distant school and where they shall have to endure commuting over little farm roads. A tax base will emerge, which will begin to justify a school and some better roads, and a new growth nucleus will appear on the urban landscape.

Is it unfortunate that urban expansion occurs largely in this way? Our local government and real estate business institutions are geared to the overloading-patching up syndrome, and it is consistent with our limited skills at forecasting aggregate urban growth. Although it does seem, in some respects, to be a parody on the concept of rationally managing our urban environment, it does function, and there does not seem to be any full-fledged alternative. Clearly, though, it may be worthwhile to think about system alternatives.

DISCUSSION QUESTIONS

1. Identify a housing tract, an office building, or some other real estate under construction in your community. Who is developing it?

2. Is some portion of the real estate inventory in your community "overbuilt"? If so, why did this happen?

3. Do you have any evidence to believe that "land speculation" in your community has caused housing developers to construct the wrong quantity or types of houses?

4. Could you identify the sections in the outskirts of your city that are likely to be developed within the next five years? Between five and ten years from now?

5. When someone says that new houses are "too expensive," do you think they mean that smaller and cheaper dwellings are what are needed?

6. Some large supermarket and department store organizations prefer not to operate in planned shopping centers; could there be any practical reasons for that decision?

7. Find out what the steps are in developing industrial real estate.

8. On the basis of the descriptions in this chapter, would you reasonably expect to find developers specializing in particular types of real estate—homes, apartments, or office buildings—instead of being general-purpose developers? Can you find any contrary examples?

9. If your employer told you that you were being transferred to a "new town," what reservations, if any, would you have about accepting the transfer? What advantages, if any, would you fore-see?

10. See if you can find a current real estate development enterprise in your community that is *not* "overloading the infrastructure" in some way. Do you think public officials and neighboring land-owners are aware of the kind of overloading that occurs in most cases?

SELECTED REFERENCES

Community Builders Handbook. Washington, D.C.: Urban Land Institute, 1968.
    A practical guide for real estate developers; each principal type of land use—housing tracts, shopping centers, office buildings, marinas, and so forth—is described in terms of significant design and feasibility criteria.

David, Philip. *Urban Land Development*. Homewood, Ill.: Irwin, 1970.

A case study textbook written for use at the Harvard Business School, with detailed descriptions of many real-life real estate development and investment undertakings, including a shopping center, a new town, and several housing projects.

Eichler, Edward P., and Marshall Kaplan. *The Community Builders*. Berkeley: University of California Press, 1967.
A compact summary of a major research project which examined the problems and potential of numerous "new town" undertakings in the United States prior to enactment of laws providing government assistance; the book is critical of the new town concept.

Maisel, Sherman J. *Housebuilding in Transition*. Berkeley. University of California Press, 1953.
The report of a careful, detailed study of house construction costs for housebuilding firms of different sizes, measured by the average number of homes completed per year; economies of scale are identified.

National Association of Home Builders. *Land Development Manual*. Washington, D.C.: The National Association of Home Builders, 1969. Practical information for builders concerning soil quality, land preparation, site planning, installation of utilities, and related topics.

President's Committee on Urban Housing. *A Decent Home*. Washington, D.C.: U.S. Government Printing Office, 1968.
Factual information about the housebuilding industry in the United States, quantitative and qualitative needs for housing construction, the supply of land, building materials, labor and finance for the housing sector, and a critical examination of federal housing programs.

Smith, W. F. *Housing: The Social and Economic Elements*. Berkeley: University of California Press, 1970.
A primarily theoretical analysis of the housing sector of the national economy, emphasizing market forces, decision systems, and resource constraints which explain the condition of the housing inventory.

11

CUMULATIVE EFFECTS
OF INDIVIDUAL
LAND-USE DECISIONS

IN THE PRECEDING CHAPTERS, we have examined the decision-making problems of real estate owners, users, developers, and lenders and have discussed the ways in which real estate agents and appraisers influence these decisions. From these descriptions the reader may get some ideas, or at least some questions, that will help him find a rewarding career in real estate. Urban land economics, however, is a subject that goes beyond the management of one's personal or business affairs to consider how the decisions of numerous individuals in many roles affect the overall development of an urban community. How do they add up?

In his classic treatise *The Wealth of Nations*, Adam Smith argued that the production and consumption of commodities can be regulated effectively by the "market." If the supply of one thing is small, relative to the demand, its price will rise above cost and the resulting opportunity for profit will encourage producers to expand the supply. If demand falls, producers will lose money unless they turn out less of the commodity. Each consumer and each producer will respond to the price established in the marketplace and the cumulative effect of all their responses will be the allocation of scarce resources to those kinds and quantities of goods that most completely meet the needs of the whole group of consumers.

To a considerable extent, these same basic "supply and demand" principles apply to the market for real estate–land and buildings. An increase in the population of a city tends to push up the price of houses, and higher prices encourage developers to increase the supply of houses. The demand for all types of real estate is "price elastic" to some degree–that is, if its price falls, people will tend to purchase a greater quantity. Real estate demand also has "income elasticity," which means that if the income of a user of real estate goes up, that user is likely to increase his consumption of real estate (but not necessarily by the same proportion).

MARKET EFFECTS OF DURABILITY

Real estate has certain characteristics that limit the usefulness of ordinary supply and demand concepts and which, therefore, raise particular questions about the ability of the urban real estate market to regulate the use and development of land. Principal among these characteristics is the durability of land and buildings. Land does not wear out physically (so far as its urban usefulness is concerned), and buildings can last for centuries. Land does not have to be produced, and, indeed, it is very difficult to produce at all in the usual sense. Buildings that already exist dominate the supply picture most of the time, and in most communities such buildings have no "cost of production."

One important function of the real estate market arising out of this durability is deciding which family or business firm is to use which house, office building, store space, and so on. This would not be a problem if all the users were alike and all land and buildings were alike, but, as a matter of fact, both users of urban real estate and the land and buildings available to those users are very heterogeneous. Families differ in age, income, size, and housing preferences. Business users of real estate have different location preferences and rent-paying abilities, as well as individual space requirements and different needs for special facilities. Each piece of land is in a unique location, and the various buildings in the inventory differ in age, style, and condition.

The real estate market must match up users with elements of supply without the benefit of normal concepts of "cost." The basic principle is the same as in an auction–each lot, house, or office space goes to the highest bidder. That bidder withdraws from the auction with the real estate he now

controls, but comes back sooner or later to see what that real estate will
bring on the market and to see whether something better or more suitable
is available. Families and businesses change with respect to their real estate
needs as time goes by, and buildings grow old and obsolete while the
relative location of each parcel of land is altered by the changing form of the
community. So the auction is continuous, with only a small fraction of the
users and the properties on the market at any one time.

Prices arising in this auction have no necessary relation to the historic
cost of the properties being traded, either in the sense of the amount
originally paid to develop land or construct a building or in the sense of the
money price at which the current owner acquired the property. To illustrate: suppose two nearly identical ten-unit apartment buildings, constructed in 1934, stand side by side. The owner of one developed it himself
at a total cost of $27,000 and has now paid off the mortgage; property taxes
amount to $40 per month per unit, and other operating costs (manage-
ment, repairs, utilities, insurance) bring monthly unit costs to $70. The
other apartment building was purchased last year for $30,000 cash and a
$90,000 mortgage which requires monthly principal and interest payments
of $80 per unit; property taxes and other current costs are the same as for
the first building. The minimum market rent for any unit in either building
could be as low as $30, and there is no upper limit in the short run. Rent
below $70 a month will eventually cause the properties to be taken over by
the assessor unless assessments fall to reflect the condition of market
demand. Rents below $150 per month will bring about foreclosure of the
mortgage on the second property; neither of these involuntary transfers of
ownership will change the market rent. A rent level of $150 per month will
mean zero return on equity to the owner of the second property but a 35
percent return or better for the owner of the first. Of two things we can be
fairly certain: the market rent will be about the same in both buildings
(though rents actually charged may be different), and the hardship or
windfall benefit arising for either owner will not play a part in deciding
what that market rent level will be.

Carrying the example a bit further, suppose that the owner of the
second property bought it last year because the rent level then prevailing,
say $190 per month, promised a good return. Today, however, a new and
much more attractively designed sixty-unit building is opening up across
the street, with rents at $195. Unless demand for apartments is growing
vigorously in his area, last year's prudent real estate investor is in for hard

times because he will probably have to cut his rents back or put up with high vacancy levels, or both, and his leveraged equity is in danger. Unanticipated competition is not the only hazard for such investors; improved infrastructure or public services in another part of town might pull his tenants away, or some new facility nearby that his tenants dislike (a halfway house for former drug addicts, perhaps) might push tenants out of the area.

There is one sense in which "cost" is related to the auction price of real estate, and that is the cost of constructing an equally suitable new building within the locational radius of the property in question. If total development costs for an apartment building competitive with the two 1934 models discussed above required monthly rents per unit of $210 (after adjusting for quality and location differences), market rents for the two older buildings would not go very much higher than this figure. If they did, developers would be likely to get busy, just as profit-motivated producers respond in Adam Smith's scheme, to increase the supply. Real estate developers, however, are probably less dependable in this respect than entrepreneurs in other lines of production, because they can only respond if there is mortgage money, if there is land on the market already supplied with infrastructure, if local government agencies do not impose excessive restrictions, and a few other "if's," including the existence of people willing and able to function as developers. Should any part of this picture react sluggishly to market rent levels above development costs, market rents will be uninhibited by competitive new development costs as well as by historic costs or acquisition prices of existing buildings.

This large degree of freedom from cost of production means that the difference between the market rent of any two houses has no necessary relationship to their physical or qualitative difference. For example, the rent for house A (or its sales price equivalent) might be $200 and that for house B $175, though B is only half the size of A, three times as old, and in very poor condition. Under different market conditions, the rent for house C, just a few years older than A, in almost equally good condition, and even having 10 percent more floor space than A, might be $140. There need be no "physical" factor to explain the difference, such as "location" in any of its various senses. All that is needed to cause such rent differentials is a spread in the purchasing power or differences in housing tastes among the families of the community. Once the better dwelling is acquired by those who can and will pay most for housing quality, the next best house will go to the next most affluent family in town at whatever that family can afford to pay. The same principle applies to office space, stores, factories, and other categories of private land use.

Buildings are not completely durable; unless there is some effort and expense to maintain them, they will decline in quality. This is the source of a further distinctive property of the real estate market, for the owner of a building can select the maintenance level that best suits his objectives. The owner of building A, for example, may be getting $200 in rent and spending $30 a month to keep it in good shape, leaving a net of $170. Suppose he finds that cutting maintenance back to $10 a month will cost only $10 a month in lower rent, higher vacancy, or reduced long-run capital value; under those circumstances his net per month will be $180, and it will pay him to let the property run down. Eventually, this situation does develop for most buildings, just as there comes a time in the life of an automobile when it is not worth fixing up every little thing that goes wrong. For urban real estate, the "optimum" maintenance level, as viewed by the owner, can vary substantially with shifts in the market; how often a house is painted or an office lobby spruced up does not depend primarily on the materials originally used or the recommendations of an architect, builder, or engineer. In this respect, too, the market is quite free to ignore what has gone before.

The durability of real estate influences decisions about current development in two important ways. One, which might be called the "forward bias" of real estate development, is the tendency of today's landowners, developers, investors, and their mortgage lenders and appraisers to plan for land uses that promise to be most attractive to the market ten or twenty years from now, rather than trying to meet the desires of users in the market today. A family with imaginative plans for a new type of house and income enough to pay for it over twenty years or so is likely to be turned down by mortgage lenders, because they want to have loan collateral that can be readily sold should the need arise. Bankers thus prefer that their mortgage borrowers live in houses that look pretty standard, and the people who build houses cannot overlook that preference. Income property investors tend to exert a similar drag on building innovation. The result is that land is developed and buildings are built with an eye to what the market is expected to want several years hence.

The other main effect of durability on development can be called the "darned sock syndrome," because it harkens back to a philosophical conundrum about a sock that was darned each time a hole appeared so that eventually it had all been mended. The question is: Is it still the same sock? Perhaps there is no answer, but for a similar problem in urban real estate there must be an answer. Each part of the city—streets, buildings, utility systems, and so on—fits together with the other pieces, like all the individual girders in a steel bridge. Since the whole structure is durable and only a few parts need to be rebuilt at any one time, the opportunity does not arise to change the design of the whole city, or of the bridge, even though every part is replaced in some finite period of time, such as a century. The original form tends to recreate itself.

Actually, cities are more flexible in this respect than steel bridges. Large chunks of infrastructure reflecting new technology and new needs, like freeways and sports complexes, can push aside sections of old streets, dwellings, and shops if the community is willing to bear the cost. If investors are willing to bear costs privately, block upon block of city land can be cleared and reshaped, as Rockefeller Center was in New York City. Most importantly, new buildings are not always limited in height or design to match their surroundings and gradual intrusions of new land uses appear in most city districts. This all means that cities have something of a patchwork quality, without any assurance that the patches will ultimately merge into recognizable design. But at least there is a chance to try out something new. The opportunity is limited, of course. One investor, one developer, or one householder on his own generally finds it foolish not to conform his land use to neighboring patterns of use. On a street of $30,000 homes, a $75,000 dwelling will usually sell below cost; and on the street where expensive shops cluster, the owner who rents to "Second-Hand Rose" is probably short-changing himself.

The durability of real estate, then, creates special market conditions in which supply and demand do not adjust as well to each other as economics books might suggest happens in markets for other goods.

LOCAL GOVERNMENT RESPONSE

Basically, people in a community have a stake in the effective operation of the local real estate market, and they can use community means to help that market work. Without exception, city dwellers are in the real estate market as buyers or sellers or both. They want the supply of particular types of buildings or land uses to increase or decrease in reasonable harmony with changes in that type of demand. They want some rough equity, at least, in the quality of housing or location that every person's dollar buys.

One thing local governments can do rather successfully in this direction is to ward off windfall losses of property values. Land-use controls such as zoning and building controls, and scrutiny of proposals for new private developments or infrastructure, can serve to soften the impact of competition and obsolescence upon existing urban land wealth. On the other hand, if market rents seem to be climbing above equivalent new construction costs, new developments may be approved more quickly and with less asked from the developer. This may be a little like pushing on a string, however; city governments cannot compel developers to increase supply.

Windfall gains, like the rising value of the apartment building constructed in 1934 for $27,000, in the earlier illustration, are probably inevitable as cities expand and construction costs rise. If local government can so affect the local land market that such increases in property value become somewhat predictable, then expected appreciation will tend to bring down the required rate of cash return to investors and hence permit lower rents. In this indirect way, tenants can share in land value appreciation.

So what local government can contribute to the performance of the real estate market is stability of expectations about land-use changes. It costs very little in hard cash to exercise land-use controls for this purpose, but it does require good collective judgment and information. There is some point beyond which a community cannot seek to stabilize local property values by exercising its police powers, and that is to shut out change or growth completely. Exclusionary zoning or limits on new private developments and public infrastructure that diminish mobility and competition in a city's region raise doubts concerning the right of communities to self-government. The police power is not a community's absolute and irrevocable privilege, but a right to be used responsibly. Changes in land value, in land use, and in urban amenities are inevitable; the best a city can do by collective action is to reduce uncertainty about such changes.

FEDERAL RESPONSE TO REAL ESTATE MARKET CONDITIONS

In the United States, the federal government does not plan urban land uses. It cannot adjust the supply of real estate to the level of demand through land-use controls and infrastructure decisions as local governments can. The national government does have vast power to affect the outcome and operation of local land markets in other ways, however.

One of these is subsidy. The structure of local market rents for housing generally puts minimum adequate housing out of reach for some families, and public concern requires a remedy. One approach is to pay some part of the development cost of new housing for the families in question, such as land acquired by urban renewal and made available below market price, or income tax concessions to developers. In United States public housing projects, debt service costs are wholly or partially borne by the federal treasury while local governments exempt these projects from property taxes.

Another subsidy approach is to increase the purchasing power of low-income families, as in one recent federal program in the United States that pays mortgage interest costs above one percent for qualified families. The welfare allowance system in its several forms in the United States contributes money for household necessities, including housing.

Either approach has drawbacks. New construction for low-income families often costs more than suitable existing housing could be purchased for on local markets, and provision of land is difficult. Housing allowances, on the other hand, may simply drive up the market price of substandard and standard dwellings alike, producing little or no improvement in overall housing standards. Obviously, some combination of augmenting purchasing power and stimulating an increase in the supply of standard housing seems to be what is required, but this kind of tandem program has proved hard to design.

There is another variant, which is to combine housing allowances that can be spent on existing standard housing with a program to stimulate increases in the supply of standard housing through rehabilitation of substandard dwellings or through tax or other incentives to encourage new construction of housing for some higher-income group in the expectation that families across the income spectrum will move up to better housing, opening up some minimum standard dwellings toward the bottom of the inventory for the families in need. This type of program has political disadvantages because it seems to subsidize the well-to-do rather than the families who need hlep.

The national government is able to prod local governments to make basic improvements to their infrastructure, by constructing sewage treatment plants, for example, or by acquiring open space. These efforts tend to enhance the purchasing power of the buyers of local real estate services by upgrading the amenities they can use in conjunction with the real estate they buy or rent.

National governments have assumed substantial responsibility for managing flows of investment capital among various sectors of the economy, from housing construction to business plant and equipment investment, for example. Periods of "tight money" are critical stages in the separation of local market rent levels from the cost of new development, so monetary and fiscal planning at the national level can contribute in an important way to keeping local land markets within realistic bounds. Unfortunately, there are influential schools of thought on national economic policy which hold periodic local real estate stringency to be an acceptable price for achieving other national economic goals such as employment stabilization or improvement in the balance of payments.

In the United States and several other countries, national governments have done much in recent decades to improve some of the basic financial institutions through which real estate business is done. Mortgage insurance and secondary mortgage markets organized under the aegis of government have given real estate markets much better access to long-term capital.

Neither local nor national governments intervene directly in local real estate markets to establish rents and prices or to decide who uses what part of the real estate inventory, except in those times and places when rent control becomes imperative. The usual posture of government is to keep a fairly watchful eye on what is happening in these local markets for land and buildings and to offset in some manner the more serious of the apparent failings of that market.

DISCUSSION QUESTIONS

1. "The real estate market rations the inventory of land and buildings more efficiently than it governs the development of new land and improvements." Do you agree?

2. In this chapter's example of apartment buildings constructed in 1934 but acquired at widely differing prices by their respective

owners, the statement is made that "market rent will be the same in both buildings." Why is this true—or is it?

3. To what extent do the characteristics of real estate discussed in this chapter support the contention that investment in real estate is particularly risky?

4. Is it the inherent nature of the real estate commodity that prevents supply from adapting smoothly to demand, or the archaic organization of the real estate business in all its branches?

5. "City planners should not try to disregard the law of supply and demand." How would you respond to this statement if you were a member of your community's planning commission?

6. Do you think a government-run "trade-in" program for housing—allowing all owners to sell when they choose at a fixed price, and the houses thus acquired to be resold—would be an effective solution to the low-income housing problem? Would it be financially realistic?

SELECTED REFERENCES

Aaron, Henry J. *Shelter and Subsidies.* Washington, D.C.: The Brookings Institution, 1972.
An economist examines the extent and incidence of subsidy contained in all major federal housing programs— mortgage insurance, public housing, below-market interest rates—and in personal income tax regulations which allow deductions for depreciation, interest, and property tax.

Downs, Anthony. *Federal Housing Subsidies: How Are They Working?* Lexington, Mass.: Lexington Books, 1973.
The chairman of a research firm and frequent consultant-advisor on federal housing policy identifies alternative strategies for government housing assistance and examines the effectiveness of each major federal program.

Grigsby, William G. *Housing Markets and Public Policy.* Philadelphia: University of Pennsylvania Press, 1963.
A largely theoretical analysis of a metropolitan housing market,

focusing on the "filtering" issue—whether construction of new housing for higher-income families provides adequate older housing for low-income families.

Scott, Mel. *American City Planning*. Berkeley and Los Angeles: University of California Press, 1969.
A comprehensive and richly detailed history of city planning in the United States—the concepts, legal issues, and administration.

12

FINANCING URBAN
DEVELOPMENT

REAL ESTATE DEVELOPMENT, which is generally taken to mean private construction activities and the creation of urban infrastructure by local government, both require economic resources for which there are competing demands in the national economy. A tract of houses or a shopping center requires labor, materials, and land which could be used for something else—producing automobiles, growing lettuce, or maintaining part of an army, for example. There has to be some process of deciding what proportion of the nation's economic capacity for producing goods and services shall go toward building up the physical plant of cities. We turn next to a look at how macroeconomic processes—the allocation of resources among broad sectors of the economy—affect the physical urban environment.

The investment character of urban development is important in this context. Houses, streets, stores, schools, and other urban physical structures are capital goods that require the use of savings. Savings are scarce in most economies, and they are looked upon by economists as the basic "growth" resource, the factor that allows a country to accumulate a stock of labor-saving and cost-reducing machinery so that it can expand its output of consumption goods and sell more in world markets. Savings used for urban development do not augment productive capacity in this sense, and so there is a general feeling among economists that urban development occurs at the expense of economic growth. Urban scholars do not always share this feeling, however.[1]

This dependence on savings means that urban development is closely bound up with the financial system of the nation—the set of organizations, laws, and attitudes that brings together spending power not used for consumption and that decides what use to make of this spending power. Individual savers or investors can choose among uses of their money, but their choices are influenced by the structure of the financial system, by tax laws, by monetary policy, by programs of subsidy, and by many other factors. For example, in the United States, the interest on local government bonds—the usual means of financing urban infrastructure—is exempt from federal income taxation, which gives this kind of investment a favored position in the capital markets. On the other hand, real estate equities are traded in the securities exchanges only to a very limited extent; homeowners do not incorporate and sell common stock in order to raise the equity required of them. In short, urban development finance is in a separate corner of the national money market.

PATHS TO URBAN CAPITAL FORMATION

The issue about the proper share of urban development in total economic activity is clearest if we think first in terms of a "developing" country, a nation in which economic growth is a high-priority goal. Figure 43 may be helpful in understanding the kind of decisions that are called for in that situation. We have, first, a set of resources at the outset of our planning period—labor, raw materials, some capital equipment including railroads, docks and power plants as well as some factories and machinery, and land in the sense of physical space. These resources must be allocated among consumption, exports, and savings. Exports return in the form of imports of consumption goods or investment goods, and the savings are used to make investments. A developing nation has difficulty in reducing consumption so as to increase the supply of savings because incomes are low, and it must therefore make very careful decisions about how the available savings are to be used. The basic choice, so far as we are concerned, is between investments in urban development and in "industry," recog-

1. See, for example, William L. C. Wheaton, "Sinkong" in *Third Internation Symposium on Regional Development* (Tokyo: Japan Center for Area Development Research, 1969).

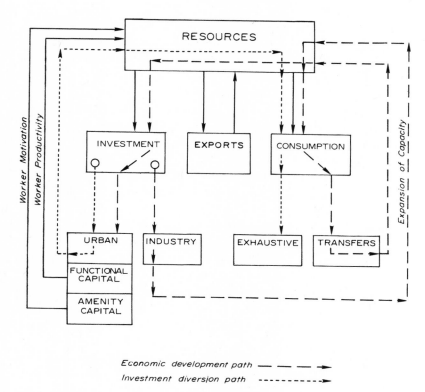

Economic development path — — — —▶
Investment diversion path   ----------▶

Figure 43.   Urban investment in economic growth–
alternative paths.

nizing that power plants, railroads, and the like are necessary for the
expansion of manufacturing activities, and recognizing also that agriculture, mining, logging, and other extractive activities qualify as "industry."

Modern development economists tend to recommend that most
investment go to industry. This is not because they consider the improvement of urban living conditions unimportant as a goal, but rather
because they believe it is a goal that can be postponed and that will be easier
to reach later when the basic productive capacity of the nation–its per
capita GNP–has been substantially enlarged.

This concept is labeled "economic development path" in Figure 43.
Industry investments expand capacity and increase incomes. Some of the

increased income is spent for the use of urban capital goods—houses, stores, and streets. This urban capital has not been expanded, so the increased spending takes the form of an "income transfer." This means that house rents and land prices in cities go up, for example. The people who receive these transfer payments, or other people who want to take advantage of rising prices, supposedly begin to increase the supply of houses, stores, movie theaters, and so on. This adds to the supply of capital resources that the economy possesses, which allows people in the long run to make "exhaustive" use of more buildings and facilities than before. The word "exhaustive" refers to the fact that physical resources are used up and disappear, something that does not happen when transfer payments are made.

The "investment diversion path" starts out by allocating savings directly for urban development—new houses, schools, water supply systems, etc. This investment may be "functional" in a narrow sense if it makes the labor force more productive.[2] That is, clean water or warmer housing may reduce time lost through illness. Less crowding at home may improve the worker's morale on the job, and, in the long run, better schools might allow him to adapt more readily to complex new kinds of work. Urban conditions that are simply more enjoyable—a house and garden for his family, clean streets and a well-kept park, the use of modern, attractive, and well-stocked stores—represent "amenity capital." If the worker has to pay more to enjoy these things, he may be motivated to work harder or longer to get the money for them. In either case, through increased productivity or greater motivation, urban investment may have the effect of expanding the labor resources of the nation. The construction of urban capital itself, however, directly adds to the nation's stock of physical resources.

The decision question is really whether anything serious is lost by the delay in urban development under the "economic development scheme." Of course, the urban population has to put up with inconveniences in housing, utilities, transportation, congestion, pollution, and so on, but if savings are well invested in promising new industries, then the day will come when there will be a much greater amount of resources available for correcting these problems, or so it is argued. Better living conditions in the

2. See Leland S. Burns *et al.*, *Housing: Symbol and Shelter*, International Housing Productivity Study (Los Angeles: Graduate School of Business, University of California, 1970).

future city may offset urban sacrifices today, for the same population group if not for precisely the same individuals.

Suppose, however, that the delay makes it more difficult or even impossible to build the future city, for some reason. In that case, single-minded emphasis on industrial expansion would turn out to have been a mistake. It would mean that the costs of the increased output had been understated, like selling five-cent apples for four cents. There is no way of making it up "on the turnover." To make this decision in economic strategy, we need to know much about the way urban development actually occurs, and more particularly how it can get locked into unwanted and destructive patterns.

The problem of economic strategy relating to urban development exists in all economies, whether they are classified as "developing" or "advanced." Table 20 presents some relevant information for two of the most completely developed economies in the world, the United States and Canada. It is not possible from readily available national income data to say precisely how much of the GNP of either nation goes into "urban development," as opposed to the expansion of business productive capacity (consider power and water facilities, for example), but several interesting points emerge from numbers that do come readily to hand.

Canada's per capita GNP in 1970 was about 83 percent of that in the United States. Total private investment, on a per capita basis, was higher in Canada. (Canadian and U.S. dollars exchanged at close to par in 1970.) Per person, Canada invested less than the U.S. in machinery (87 percent of the U.S. figure) but substantially more in all construction–$270 would have given Canada proportionate construction investment, but the actual figure is $411. Given the fact that Canada is engaged in reaching out to tap extensive new natural resources, much of this construction investment may be developmental. But a large part of it undoubtedly accompanied the expansion of the housing inventory–for streets, schools, water and sewer systems, and so forth.

Canada's problem, then, if the income gap between the two countries is to be closed, is to expand its productive capacity, but the rapid growth of population that may be required to make the best use of its natural resources diverts investment potential into urban development. (It may be noted that U.S. housing investment in 1970 was very much below levels prevailing a few years prior; 1971 housing output in the U.S. was about two million units, so Canada's apparent edge in housing investment must

Table 20

Capital Formation in the United States and Canada, 1970

	United States		Canada	
	Total[a]	Per capita	Total[a]	Per capita
Gross National Product	$974.1	$4,796	$85.4	$3,991
Private investment[b]	135.3	666	15.0	701
Machinery	65.4	322	6.0	280
Construction	66.1	325	8.8	411
Housing	30.4	150	3.6	168
Disposable personal income	687.8	3,387	54.0	2,523
Personal consumption expenditures	615.8	3,032	50.0	2,336
Personal saving	54.1	266	3.1	145
Housing starts (000 units)	1,469	.007	190.5	.009
Population (million persons)	203.1		21.4	
Housing construction as percent of GNP	3.1		4.2	
All construction as percent of GNP	6.8		10.3	
Private investment as percent of GNP	13.9		17.6	

Sources: U. S. Department of Commerce, *Survey of Current Business*, May 1972; statistics for Canada, *National Income and Expenditure Accounts*, First Quarter, 1972.

Note: Terms used are comparable but not identical for the United States and Canada.

[a] Billions of U.S. and Canadian dollars, respectively.

[b] Gross private domestic investment in the U.S.; gross fixed business capital formation in Canada.

be qualified.) Despite much lower personal savings per capita (55 percent of the U.S. level), Canada clearly has total investment resources that compare very favorably; its critical problem is allocation. It is possible to make a flat statement, however, that neither in the United States nor in Canada does any agency of government or business have the responsibility or power to decide how aggregate new investment shall be allocated among sectors—to say, for example, that construction shall be 10 percent of GNP and housing shall be half of that. Allocation happens by an essentially self-operating process, influenced by government and business to be sure, but not in a deterministic nor fully conscious way.

HOUSING IN AFRICA

The root of the problem is that we do not know how much urban development is enough. Where clear policies are in effect, as in numbers of developing nations, they are generally swayed by economic advisors who have little familiarity with, and possibly not much occasion to reflect about, urban problems. Otherwise, traditional business and governmental factors are so arranged as to impede—or in some cases to accelerate—urban development, with or without explicit arguments for doing so.

The problem of providing housing for the urban population of Africa is a dramatic illustration of the universal "growth vs. urban development" dilemma; a brief description of it will tell us how to evaluate urban development efforts in any land.[3] In the early 1960s, the entire African continent (except the Union of South Africa, which is excluded throughout this description) had a population of about 275 million, growing at an annual rate of about 2.2 percent. The growth rate during the decade of the forties had been only 1.6 percent. About 8 percent of the total population was in urban places of 20,000 or more, which means there were some 22 million people living in cities, a large proportion of whom had come but recently. Urban population was rising at about 7 percent per year. The existing urban housing supply, and public infrastructure related to housing, is in generally poor shape as well as being overcrowded.

The need for housing (as distinguished from effective market demand) was calculated by planners on the assumption that there are five persons in the average household and that there should be at least 100 square feet of housing space per person. That is, for every million of urban population there should be 200,000 houses of about 500 square feet each. The land requirement was assumed to be something less than double the housing space requirement. If overcrowding were to be eliminated in

3. The following is based on D. A. Turin, "Housing in Africa: Some Problems and Major Policy Issues," in *The Economic Problems of Housing*, ed. by A. A. Nevitt (London: Macmillan, 1967).

twenty years and the growth of urban population accommodated, it would be necessary to build about 9,000 houses each year per million urban inhabitants. The removal of grossly substandard houses would add from 2,000 to 5,000 to this number for an annual target of 11,000 to 14,000 dwellings per million inhabitants. Very few "advanced" nations construct housing at a rate of 10,000 per million inhabitants per year.

Without an extraordinary diversion of resources, it seems inevitable that urban housing conditions in Africa will worsen year by year. But the economic resources of the continent are slender and such diversion is unlikely. Per capita GNP is about $100 (with wide geographic variations), and only about 16 percent of GNP, or about $5 billion, goes into capital formation of all types. Housing and related urban facilities account for about 16 percent of this investment, or about 2.7 percent of GNP—less than $3 per capita. Housing construction costs run about $2 per square foot, so that the minimum size new house costs about $1,000.

Housing costs are relatively high for a number of reasons. About half of all building materials have to be imported, including everything made of steel, all electric fixtures, half of the ceramics and paints, and about a third of the wood and cement. Most of the imports are from non-African countries, meaning that hard currency is required. The need for imports contains some anomolies. For one thing, Africa has to export hardwood to earn foreign exchange with which to import softwoods used in housing construction. Another striking fact is that an investment of about $2 billion would, it was estimated, make Africa self-sufficient in cement, paint, and other construction materials; for lack of such investment, about the same amount of money is spent each year on hard-currency imports, adding up to $20 billion in a decade. Opportunities to borrow or otherwise obtain this $2 billion for development of the construction industry are very limited, however. International agencies and aid-giving developed nations rely on the advice of development economists in deciding where to place available capital funds, and the advice is almost unanimously favorable to investment in export-producing industries rather than those that make living conditions better or even those that tend to reduce imports. Imports can be held in check, at least theoretically, by various regulatory devices not requiring large capital outlays. So, if there were a fund of $2 billion available to African nations, many "better" ways of using it than in residential construction could be found, according to the conventional wisdom. Meanwhile, urban housing conditions worsen and the import drain goes on.

Housebuilding requires many labor skills that are in very short supply in Africa despite extensive underemployment among the general population. In particular, very few site supervisors or clerks are to be found and virtually no architects or planners. Construction firms created and run by Africans are practically nonexistent. The reasons are partly educational and partly a legacy of limited entrepreneurial interest or opportunity. Of all the children of primary school age, only 18 percent actually go to school; only 1.5 percent of the children of secondary school age get to those schools.

Institutions for housing finance are largely governmental and many are carryovers from colonial periods. Funds are scarce but interest rates tend to be low or even nominal while amortization periods are generous. Home-building associations of a cooperative nature receive deposits from low-income people, in the main, and make the preponderance of their housing loans to upper-middle income families. Thus, it is mostly the labor and material cost rather than the interest rate that tends to pinch off housing demand. The minimum house costs from five to ten times the annual income of unskilled workers. Efforts to design a cheaper house run into problems of maintenance and replacement, since it would suffer more rapid deterioration and obsolescence.

So there is a growing deficiency in Africa's urban housing supply. Some avenues of improvement are open—essentially diverting investment capital and foreign exchange into this sector—but little is likely to be done along these lines. One recurrent response from ecnomic planners it to say that urban population growth should be discouraged, chiefly by letting conditions of city life deteriorate to the point that would-be migrants turn back. But to that, the United Nations official who made this study of African housing replies: "It is open to question whether the continent with the lowest rate of urbanization of all should aim at further limiting the growth of its urban centres, which are by and large the main poles of progress."[4]

URBAN CAPITAL ACCOUNTING

The previous example and the earlier part of this chapter contain an implicit assumption that urban capital formation is subject to real resource constraints. That is, labor, materials, and capital equipment used for

4. *Ibid.*, p. 214.

housing or other forms of urban development must be diverted from other sectors of the economy. Scarcity of these physical inputs or a great need for them elsewhere in the economy means that housing, schools, streets, and so on cannot be provided. There may be another, nonphysical constraint on urban capital formation, however, arising from the structure of financial institutions. That is, there may not be enough money.

Money is not a real resource but rather a social convention. So dependent, though, are market economies on money that production and distribution can stagnate if monetary systems are injured or if they are inappropriate. After World War II, German currency lost value so rapidly that producers of commodities and services were reluctant to accept money in exchange. The terrible inefficiencies of barter brought business very nearly to a standstill, and inflation deprived almost everyone of his savings. After currency reform in 1949, the German monetary unit once again had stable value, people began to produce things for sale, banks had usable money to lend, and the "economic miracle" began. Communist armies in Hungary at the end of the war destroyed the business economy of that nation by printing enormous quantities of paper money. Since J. M. Keynes' landmark book was published in the 1930s, economists, businessmen, and government leaders have generally acknowledged that problems in controlling money supply can prevent physical resources from being fully employed.[5]

So it is not facetious to draw a distinction between a scarcity of real resources and a scarcity of money. We know that in some circumstances physical deprivations can be attributed to purely monetary phenomena, so that people go without food or live in crowded and decaying buildings while fertile land is uncultivated, machinery rusts, and skilled workers are idle in the streets. To a degree, the physical growth or improvement of cities may be held in check by monetary factors that are peculiar to it, with the result that cities look more like sore spots in the economy than focal points of general economic progress.

A simple accounting scheme for the money flows that are necessary for urban capital formation will help to convey the idea. In Figure 44, the sequence of annual events within the housing sector of a hypothetical

5. J. M. Keynes, *The General Theory of Employment, Interest and Money* (New York: Harcourt, Brace and Companh, 1935).

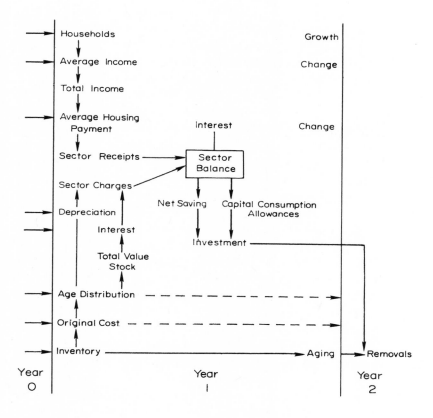

Figure 44. Housing sector accounting model.

Source: From W. F. Smith, "Economics of Housing Policy in Developing Nations," paper presented to the Conference on The City as a Center of Change in Asia, The University of Hong Kong, 1969.

Assumptions made for hypothetical community:

Number of households 100
Average annual income $1,000
Average housing payment (7% of income) ... $70
Original cost of each house $1,000
Annual depreciation cost (100 yrs. S/L) $10
Average depreciated house value........... $500
Average interest cost (@12%)............. $60

community is portrayed. There are 100 households, each with an income of $1,000, of which $70 is spent on housing. Total receipts of the housing sector, then, are $7,000. The inventory consists of 100 houses, each costing $1,000 to build originally and ranging in age from 0 to 99 years. That is, one new house is built each year and the house that becomes 100 years old is destroyed or abandoned. Houses depreciate at the straight-line rate of 1 percent of their original value each year, so that $10 per house and $1,000 in total is charged against the sector. The average age of the inventory is 50 years, and the average house has a value of $500, so that the inventory's undepreciated value is $50,000. With an interest rate (debt and equity combined) of 12 percent, the inventory incurs interest charges of $6,000 per year.

If nothing happens to the size, income, or spending habits of the population, or to the rate of interest and the cost of construction, the housing sector of this community is in equilibrium. Each year the depreciation fund is just sufficient to build a new house of the standard type, maintaining the average age and value of the inventory in use. The average household gets the use of a $500 house for one year for a price of $70.

Turning to Table 21, we can trace the changes in the quality and the price of housing in this community that are brought about by an increase in population at the rate of two new households per year. We assume that these new households are just as productive as the people already in town, so that their annual income is the same $1,000. They are able to afford the same $70 a year—$60 for interest and $10 for depreciation—as the original population, and we might assume that they will therefore be able to purchase or rent the same $500 house. But because of one vital but meaningful assumption we have made, things will actually work out quite differently. Housing standards will sink, inflation peculiar to this sector will occur, and the physical condition of the city will change for the worse, probably permanently.

The upper half of Table 21 is based upon the additional assumption that the community continues to replace houses as they reach the age of 100. In the first year, before any new households arrive, there is just one new house to be built, for replacement, and there is just enough in the depreciation fund that year to put up the standard $1,000 house. In the second year, however, three new houses are to be built—one for replacement and two for expansion—but the sector receipts, less interest due,

Table 21

Impact of Urban Growth on Condition of the Housing Inventory

Year:	1	2	3	4	5	6	7	8	9	10
Two additional households per year										
Number of households	100	102	104	106	108	110	112	114	116	118
Average $ income	1,000	1,000	1,000	1,000	1,000	1,000	1,000	1,000	1,000	1,000
Average $ housing payment	70	70	70	70	70	70	70	70	70	70
Average $ housing value	500	490	482	475	470	466	462	459	457	456
No. houses over 100 yrs.	0	0	0	0	0	0	0	0	0	0
No. houses to be built	1	3	3	3	3	3	3	3	3	3
Average $ value of new house	1,000	333	380	421	457	489	518	543	565	585
Growth without replacement										
Number of households	100	102	104	106	108	110	112	114	116	118
Average $ income	1,000	1,000	1,000	1,000	1,000	1,000	1,000	1,000	1,000	1,000
Average $ housing payment	70	70	70	70	70	70	70	70	70	70
Average $ housing value	500	490	482	475	470	466	462	459	457	456
No. houses over 100 yrs.	0	1	2	3	4	5	6	7	8	9
No. houses to be built	1	2	2	2	2	2	2	2	2	2
Average $ value of new house	1,000	500	570	631	686	734	777	814	848	878

allow only one-third of the normal construction budget per house. Three new houses are built at a cost of $333 each, substantially inferior to the dwellings this community has been used to building. The average house value is reduced to $490. In successive years, the newcomers contribute more and more to the depreciation fund (and, of course, the average outlay for interest falls), so that the quality of new construction gradually rises. By year 10, however, new housing is being constructed at less than 60 percent of the preexpansion quality standard, and the average family is getting about 9 percent less housing for the same money. The inventory includes a larger and larger proportion of "substandard" new houses. This deterioration of the inventory occurs despite the fact that the purchasing power of the newcomers is equal to that of the original inhabitants.

In the lower half of the table, we assume that when growth begins, the policy of scrapping 100-year-old houses is given up; thus, only two new houses are required in years 1 through 10. The quality of new houses is substantially better than in the previous case, though still below the original standard. Since 100-year-old houses continue in use after their entire original value has been lost through depreciation, however, the average housing value declines just as rapidly as in the previous case. The community's new housing is somewhat better, but an increasing part of the inventory consists of superannuated dwellings. These very old dwellings are likely to be clustered together in the same part of town, so that the city has a growing district of irreversible decay.

How realistic is this hypothetical situation? There are several ways in which a market economy might be expected to respond to the shortage of development funds that produces the gloomy result of the example. One is that development capital may be attracted from beyond the boundaries of this community. There could be a surplus of depreciation reserves in the areas from which the newcomers migrated. But geographic mobility of urban development funds requires special types of financial institutions, completely satisfactory examples of which are lacking. Capital mobility would not help in the case of net population growth in the nation as a whole unless savings were diverted from other sectors of the economy, through interest rate competition, for example. Interest rates for housing, however, tend to be held down by custom in most places, and it also seems that interest-elasticity of demand is greater for housing and related urban facilities than it is for industrial investment, so that interest rates would rise for everyone but the absolute share of housing in total savings would not increase very much.

Entrepreneurs might respond to the rising "profitability" of this community's housing sector by producing *more* houses, while what is needed is *better* houses. More housing units would simply dilute the market value of all the dwellings in the inventory. An entrepreneur who somehow manages to put a $1,000 new house on the market in year 10 will either realize an inflationary windfall in selling it or allow the buyer to realize the windfall by reselling it. The decline in the value of the community's housing dollar will not be arrested, and families who might have been housed in cheaper new dwellings will just have to double up somewhere else. So, entrepreneurship is not the entire answer to the problem.

URBAN DEVELOPMENT AND INFLATION

The example seems to suggest that funds for urban development could be provided, where necessary, simply by creating more money. If the hypothetical community went to the bank in year 2 and found $3,000 in the vault marked "depreciation reserve," the physical integrity of the housing stock would be assured—regardless of where the extra $2,000 came from. Modern monetary systems have means of creating spending power, which they use, and so it is really a question of the rate at which the money supply should be increased and the reasons that are considered adequate for doing so. Should the money supply be enlarged for the purpose of letting communities avoid physical decay?

Increasing the money supply may stimulate the output of goods and services, in the now-familiar Keynesian perspective, if labor, raw materials, and other physical resources were not fully utilized to begin with. With more goods and services in the marketplace, monetary expansion may not bring about increases in the level of prices, but if even some real resources are scarce, there is likely to be a degree of price inflation. Inflationary policies are generally avoided by political and economic leaders for three reasons: the balance of payments will suffer if export prices rise, people on fixed incomes will lose purchasing power, and consumers generally interpret the rising "cost of living" as a threat to their standard of living or at least their aspirations. A family that is looking forward to buying a new $30,000 house next year is understandably dismayed when the price of the house goes up to $35,000. So ideas about creating more money or credit are not to be put forth carelessly.

The hypothetical community in our preceding illustration should suggest, though, that the very absence of new money for urban development can bring about a special kind of price inflation. Though families continued to pay $70 per year for housing, the real value of the average dwelling fell continuously while the community was growing. Getting less for the same money is not very different from paying more for the same physical quantity, as the recent history of the five-cent candy bar illustrates.

Another hypothetical example, in Table 22, puts the matter in more explicit terms. Here we hypothesize an urbanized nation with an initial population (L) which we shall say is 100. The nation's total money income (Y) is $100 and its physical output (Q) is 100 units. There is also something called "environmental output" (E), of which we assume 100 units are available each year. This represents use of the housing inventory, the streets and schools, the water supply, the parks and trees and air—things already there to be used on a pro-rata basis by the population, but the usefulness of which is not measured in Q and which escapes the price system (in our example).

Next, we have five economic indicators: the conventional price index, represented as total money income divided by total units of market goods and services; the index of market output or conventional GNP per capita (Q/L), which is the living standard expressed as the sum of market output and environmental output divided by population; environmental output per capita (E/L); and a "true" price index that includes environmental output as well as market output, in relation to total money income.

The nation now increases in population and productivity, the latter thanks to savings invested in factories, machines, and requisite infrastructure such as power plants and railroads. No savings are diverted to expand or protect environmental resources, however, in line B of the table. We assume that population has doubled and that GNP output (Q) goes up even more because of this single-minded growth policy. The external signs are good: the conventional price index stays at 1.00; GNP per capita rises by 25 percent. Taking the nonmarket environment into account, however, the accomplishment is dubious. The living standard has fallen and the "true" price index is up 43 percent.

What has happened in the example, basically, is that we have diluted

Table 22

Growth, Environment, and the Price Level

	L	Y	Q	E	Y/Q	Q/L	(Q+E)/L	E/L	Y/(Q+E) × 2
A. Initial state	100	100	100	100	1.00	1.00	2.00	1.00	1.00
B. Growth with neglect of environment	200	250	250	100	1.00	1.25	1.75	.50	1.43
C. Growth with monetized environment	200	350	250	200	1.40	1.25	2.25	1.00	1.56
D. Above (C) plus incomes policy	200	250	250	200	1.00	1.25	2.25	1.00	1.11

L = population
Y = total money income
Q = physical units of market goods and services
E = physical units of nonmarket environment
Y/Q = conventional price index, relevant for balance of payments

Q/L = GNP per capita, in conventional terms
(Q+E)/L = living standard
E/L = environmental output per capita
Y/(Q+E) × 2 = "true" price index

the environment by failing to respond to the increase in its use. The failure to respond may be due to a scarcity of physical resources, but it can be caused—as our previous example showed—by an inelastic supply of money or credit. Which is more likely? If the money necessary to restore the nonmarket environment is provided, does it have to be at the expense of growth in the usual sense?

This is a factual question, for which only the circumstances of a particular time and place can provide the answers. A country engaged in all-out war just lets its housing inventory slide, because any new construction would be at the expense of factory output or military manpower. A country recovering from an economic depression may find environmental investments a preferable way to prime the economic pump and get people back to all other kinds of work as well. A nation enjoying stable expansion at close to full employment levels has to consider whether environmental deterioration is not too high a price for that growth. A developing country usually has surpluses of the kinds of resources that urban environmental development requires: substantial underemployment, particularly among recent rural-urban migrants, is characteristic of such economies; land in the vicinity of cities is physically available, though not served by infrastructure; and traditional construction materials are in elastic supply.

Line C in Table 22 assumes that the real resources to restore the environment are not lacking, and that an increase in the money supply will be basically all that is needed to maintain environmental standards. That is, the value of the environment will be partly monetized; spending power will be increased so that people can produce and pay for environmental output—the payment being in the form of user charges or taxes. People who work at widening the streets will be paid by people who enjoy the reduced congestion and, in this sense, street widening will be incorporated into the market economy. People who breathe cleaner air will pay the people who make it clean.

Total money supply, in line C, is $350, reflecting the increased output of environmental services as well as the productivity and growth—based on the increase in GNP. The living standard rises, but so does the conventional price level. The "true" price index rises even more, to 1.56, because we are now paying people to keep things from getting worse, a cost of growth.

The increase in the conventional price index (Y/Q) to 1.40 may threaten our exports or cause unwanted redistribution of incomes. Of course, it is possible, in principle, to push down the unit prices of market goods (Q) enough to allow people to pay what is required for their share of the environment and thus keep total income from growing faster than market output. We call this an "income policy," and if it works, we shall have a combination of good things—improved living standard, stable prices in the conventional sense, and no deterioration in environmental amenities. There will continue to be inflation in the "true" price index, but this will not hurt our balance-of-payments situation.

What this abstract illustration implies is that our monetary institutions are not well adapted to the needs of the urban environment. When a city's population grows, concomitant with industrial development, there is a need for more housing which calls for new financial resources. But financial resources are not created for this purpose, even though physical resources for the job may be quite adequate. More housing requires extension of the urban infrastructure by means of public investment in roads, water systems, and the like, but financial return from such investment is not anticipated. The urban environment becomes overburdened, but this real cost is not reflected in GNP data or in the financial results for investment in new factories.

URBAN DEVELOPMENT SUBSIDIES

In due course, the decline in urban living standards becomes a social issue. Congestion, pollution, and substandard housing conditions become manifest and seem to conflict with economic indicators of rising GNP. The situation could have been forestalled if urban development were fully integrated with financial systems and national income accounts to begin with, but the normal response to the problem is not to bring about that integration but, rather, to treat the ultimate symptoms by means of subsidies.

A subsidy is a transfer of spending power rather than an investment. If a government agency uses tax revenue or borrowed money to make a loan of one million dollars to a new factory, the expectation is that the factory's output will bring in funds to repay that loan at interest. But a grant of money to a community for new roads or to a family for housing is not premised on financial return. This creates very difficult problems in deciding how much money should be given away in total and just what things it should be given for. The investment process is selective and self-limiting; the business of giving money away is not so tractable—everyone wants his share. The investment concept justifies creation of new monetary resources, but grants do not.

The most common form of housing subsidy is public construction and management of dwellings that are made available to occupants for less than full financial cost.[6] For very practical reasons, the housing is usually of minimum standard type, and the selected occupants are families with low incomes. The larger effect of the subsidy is to make financial resources available to the housing sector with administrative rather than market restrictions on their use. Families who are the recipients of a "gift" cannot object if they get multi-family rather than single-family dwellings or if they would rather live in some other part of town.

Another public device is to socialize housing credit, setting up a public agency to channel savings into housing development where it seems that the private money market is not doing the job. This usually involves the public agency in making policy decisions about the type and location of new housing to be built—its price categories, its density, whether it is to be sold or rented—without market information relating to what people want. Private mortgage lenders and housing developers are involved, but they are subject to administrative decisions about what to finance or build because they are using public funds. This cumbersome system tries to deal with a monetary problem by administering construction activities.

Urban planning in the broad sense—providing as well as designing infrastructure such as streets, utility systems, schools, and parks—is seldom accompanied by financial analysis which demonstrates that capital sums laid out will generate a stream of payments sufficient to recover those sums, and this is a great handicap to planners who conscientiously desire to protect or enhance the urban environment. They ask for capital grants to redevelop slums or build a park, a transit system, or a sewage treatment plant in the belief that the community needs those things. They generally shy away from trying to show that the community can afford those things even though it may be true.

A community's physical plant must ultimately be self-financing. Now

6. Public housing in the United States, which accounts for 2 percent of the nation's housing investment, is an example. Interest and principal payments on bonds sold to construct that housing are provided by the federal government, while local governments exempt this housing from property taxes.

that most of us live in cities and most of the national income is generated in cities, there is really nowhere else to look for the money to build what is necessary and desirable there and for which the physical resources are generally at hand. The physical environment of the city is not a charitable cause but a commodity that only happens to fit poorly into existing market institutions. Ultimately, the financial concepts relating to urban development must be redefined in such a way that purely monetary restraints do not cause the urban environment to deteriorate, to "self-destruct."

These days one can see in the large cities of India thousands upon thousands of unemployed men moving aimlessly through the streets. Land is available in large tracts of some cities, at least, already laid out for housing developments. Brick and cement plants, the source of the principal house-building materials, operate well below capacity for want of market demand. There is a desperate shortage of housing, causing countless families to sleep in flimsy shacks not served by water or sewage disposal facilities, joined to the city only by muddy trails. All that it would take to use the resources to meet the need is money—pieces of paper. Appeals for subsidy fall on deaf ears in this desperately poor nation.

Winston Churchill is said to have remarked, because of his experience with the economy of Britain during World War II, that anything that is physically possible is financially possible. A shortage of gold, of foreign exchange, or of domestic savings deposits does not mean that people cannot use their labor, raw materials, and factories to make the things they want to use. But it takes an essentially monetary innovation to put those resources together. It should be financially possible to let the cities, which support us and in which we must live, grow and remain livable, because it is physically possible and because we waste physical resources by allowing our urban environment to decline. Urban development is not necessarily at the expense of other kinds of economic development.

FLUCTUATIONS IN URBAN CAPITAL FORMATION

We are making the point that monetary expansion for the purpose of maintaining the urban physical plant is worth considering. Historically, urban capital formation, particularly housing, has tended to be something of a residual use for investment funds which become available through the ordinary economic process of saving. That is, housing construction acts as something of an economic balance wheel, rising to take up the slack in employment when business investment falls off and dropping back again when these other uses of savings are on the rise.

The clearest examples of this, for the United States, are the three recent war periods, 1941–1945, 1951, and 1966. Of course, at these times there was a sharp rise in government spending, but this was accompanied by industrial expansion. Investment in housing declined sharply in all three cases. It could hardly be said that there was a decline in housing demand at these times; the readily acceptable explanation is that funds available for capital formation in the nation as a whole were allocated away from the housing sector and into the industry-cum-government sector.

Figure 45a identifies, in very simple form, the sources and uses of investment funds (to be distinguished from physical resources at the disposal of the nation at large in any one period of time. The primary source of such funds is savings—from households, businesses, or government—money received but not spent for the consumption of goods or services. Since J. M. Keynes, monetary expansion must also be taken into account as a possible source of investment funds.[7]

The "funds available" block in Figure 45a represents the nation's capital market, which in reality is made up of many different types of institutions and individuals scattered across the land. The funds are certainly not all heaped up on a table somewhere for parceling out, but the end result of all the decisions made in this "market" is a specific allocation to various investment undertakings.

Urban capital formation is divided into two sections in the figure: expansion of the plant to accommodate increases in urban population, and replacement of the existing plant with something better. These are distinguished because they apparently behave differently with respect to fluctuations in the level of investment in "business plant and equipment." In Figure 45b, the total available capital funds, CF, is allocated by the interest rate among business investment, OF, urban expansion, OG, and urban replacement, CG.

In the upswing of the business cycle, plant and equipment investment expands to OF' at the expense of urban capital formation, which falls to OC'. The main mechanism for bringing this about is the rate of interest—that is, the price of investment funds. We assume, for simplicity, that total funds remain the same—that is, $CF = C'F'$. This price rises as business expansion

---

7. Any modern textbooks on the principles of economics describes the manner in which monetary expansion occurs.

a)

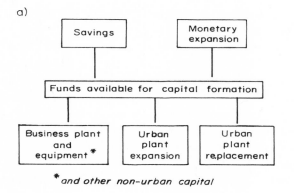

* and other non-urban capital

b)

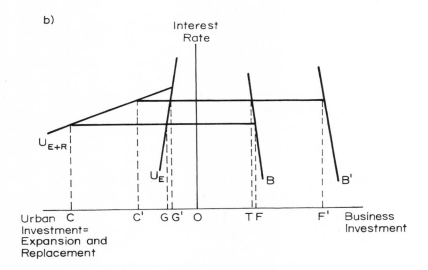

Figure 45. Allocation of national investment funds.

gets underway, but plant and equipment investment is less interest-elastic than urban investment. Interest is a relatively small element in the cost of manufactured goods and is passed on to consumers, absorbed by higher profits from greater use of industrial capacity, or offset by the greater technical efficiency of new machinery. Interest is a large part of the user cost of urban capital, however, and there is virtually no means of offsetting it. The level of urban investment simply has to be cut back from *OC* to *OC'*. Which component of urban investment—growth or replacement—is more interest-elastic and hence more likely to bear the burden of this shift in the allocation of investment funds?

This is an empirical question that has not been resolved. From an intuitive standpoint, however, it is reasonable to suppose that the demand for *more* housing, when population grows, is less elastic than the demand for *better* housing. It is easier to postpone improvement in the urban capital stock than it is to delay adding more houses, streets, water mains, schools, and so on for additional people who need these things. A growing population tends to pay the higher price for housing—the interest component of that price, in particular—when the alternative is to have people standing in the street. So it seems likely that it is primarily urban plant replacement activities that fluctuate inversely to changes in nonurban investment. Figure 45b shows a reduction in urban replacement, from CG to $C'G'$, proportionally greater than the cutback in urban expansion from OG to OG'.

Suppose interest rates rise because total capital funds available shrink, from CF to $C'T$; such a period of "tight money" could result from an increase in government borrowing for space or military programs, for example. Business investment is reduced only slightly in the diagram, from OF to OT, and the reduction in urban expansion projects is also relatively modest, from OG to OG'. These reflect the assumption of relatively inelastic demands. Interest-elastic demand for urban replacement, however, will cause that activity to fall off sharply, again by CG to $C'G'$. Conversely, when there is an abundance of capital funds for investment, or when business investment slackens, the assumptions in Figure 45b would produce a dramatic burst of urban replacement activity.

The "monetary expansion" block in Figure 45a allows total investment to exceed total savings.[8] This is not inflationary, in the traditional sense, if the economy's output grows as a result of the new capital plant. More money is offset by more goods and services. The output of the urban plant, however, is not measured completely or realistically by the price system, which means that monetary expansion for the sake of urban capital formation often appears unwarranted.

REPLACING URBAN CAPITAL

A simple way of separating "growth capital" from "replacement capital" is to subtract from total investment the amount required because

8. Keynesian economists may want to think of this as "ex-ante" savings.

of an expansion in the population. Thus, if 1,500,000 houses are constructed in a particular year while the number of families rises by 1,000,000, we can say that half a million dwellings become available to replace less desirable existing units. If the money amount of this total house-building effort was $30 billion, then the replacement investment was on the order of one-third, or $10 billion.

Figure 46 is based on this concept applied to housing construction in the United States from 1889 through 1969. The excess of "starts" (housing units constructed) over the net increase in number of households fluctuates in a manner suggestive of other well-known macroeconomic variables—unemployment and government spending (especially military) in particular. At approximately twenty-year intervals, the "excess" becomes negative, meaning that new households had to squeeze into the inventory by "conversion"—dividing one existing dwelling unit into two or more —or filled up houses that were overbuilt in the preceding boom. Clearly, household formation does not set a rigid floor on the level of housing construction. It has generally taken an economic catastrophe, however, to cut housing output below the "growth" level.

Replacement—capital formation in excess of growth requirements —has at least three components or three degrees: attrition losses, as from fire or flood, must be replaced; some rate of investment is required beyond this to keep the average quality (or the average age) of the inventory from getting worse; any remaining investment has the effect of upgrading the inventory. Since per capita real incomes are generally expected to increase over time, the third of these replacement concepts might be further divided into investment that raises the inventory quality in proportion to the rise in average real income, and a final component of "pure" improvement.

In any case, replacement investment is what we must have if living standards are not to fall, and this is as true of urban capital goods as it is of machines and factories. Taking housing as an index, however, it seems that we cannot hope for very much improvement. Figure 47 shows the trend of the "value replacement rate" of the U.S. housing inventory for an eighty-year period.[9] The rate rarely exceeds 2 percent and appears to be centered at something less than 1 percent. Taking the average inventory value and the average amount of replacement investment during this

9. "Value replacement rate" is defined here as the current dollar housing investment in excess of growth requirements, as a fraction of the capital value of the inventory at the time of investment.

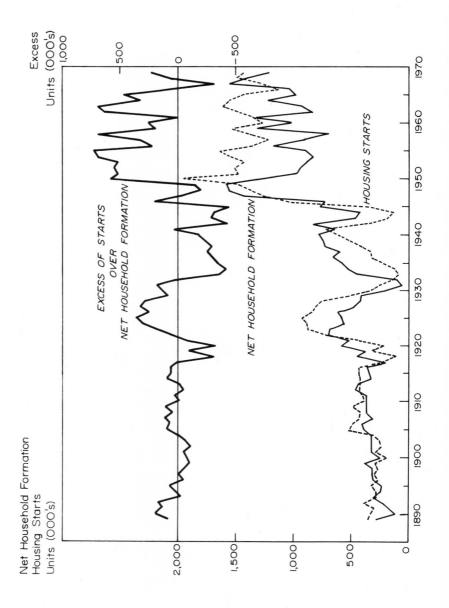

Figure 46. U.S. housing starts and household formation.

period, the rate is one-third of 1 percent, which implies a replacement cycle for U.S. dwellings of 300 years.

Three hundred years may be an acceptable service life for a dam, or a castle, or a bridge. But the typical house in this country does not strike even its fondest admirers as being good for that period of time. The rate at which an item of consumer durable goods loses value is necessarily a subjective thing, since there is no concrete measure of its productivity in widgets per hour or in down-time per week. Pitted roads are inconvenient and slummy houses are demoralizing, but we don't have money measures of inconvenience or degradation. So it is not possible to say flatly that a three-century replacement cycle for U.S. housing is too long to prevent a decline in the nation's housing standards. But it is not a rate we can be cheerful about, either.

Corresponding information for other types of urban investment is lacking, and there are problems of "nonlinearity" in the requirements for urban infrastructure. Does the need for streets increase more than pro-portionately to the growth of the population of a city, for example? Or should a growing city stop expanding its parks and provide a museum instead? The number of dollars invested would not indicate whether they were invested wisely, and there are many categories of local infrastructure to look at. We can only observe that it is very easy to let the urban infrastructure get overloaded, let alone make investments to raise its average quality; people do not pay less in taxes when the roads or school-rooms they use become more crowded.

To replace the inventory of urban capital means to discard a portion of it, to tear down or at least abandon some old buildings, to remove old paving, to demolish an old school building or a hospital. It involves absorbing a capital loss, and it is pertinent that "urban renewal" in the U.S. and Canada has been understood mainly as a scheme whereby the federal government absorbed the capital losses of run-down houses that were still capable of being rented or sold but which it was decided to demolish. The market's nongovernmental approach to these capital losses is to inflict them willy-nilly on people who own things that are rendered obsolete and valueless by something new.[10]

Women's fashions have always been the most terrifying example of this competitive process, with U.S. automobiles not far behind. Annual

10. Joseph Schumpeter called this road to economic progress "creative destruction."

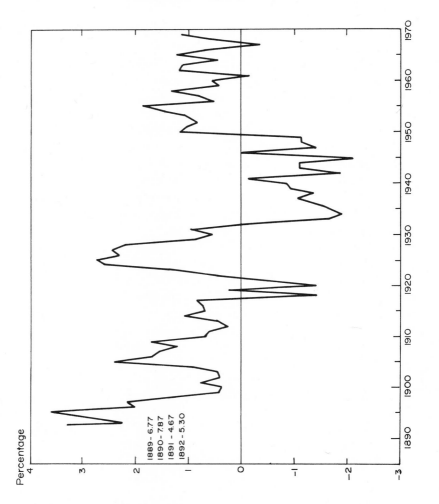

Figure 47. Value replacement rate–U.S. housing inventory.

design changes wipe out billions of dollars in the value of last year's still usable products. Housing is less influenced by sheer fashion, though in a rental market, people will migrate fairly rapidly out of the old stuff and into the new without caring too much that the old landlord's investment is diminished as a result.

This says that some degree of overbuilding is essential to the replacement process—a fact that U.S. and Canadian urban renewal programs overlooked to their grave discomfort. And the further inference is that the replacement rate for urban capital may be low because there are institutional barriers to this beggar-my-neighbor process.

Financial institutions and governmental agencies involved with housing, for example, are most vigorous and critical when housing output seems to be in excess of "demand" (growth). Mortgage lenders may be concerned, quite naturally, about the impact of overbuilding on the value of mortgages they hold on previously constructed houses. Government agencies are concerned about the solvency of the lending institutions.

A governmental housing agency would have to think long and hard about tearing down some old public housing to provide something up-to-date, because the additional investment will not bring in any additional revenue. By the same logic, municipal schools, hospitals, and similar facilities (including jails) rarely seem worth replacing because the city is already deriving about all the revenue available. The effect of replacement may be approximated by constructing expansion facilities at ever-higher levels of cost or quality so that the average condition of the inventory is upgraded. Unless there is growth, however, this route to replacement is not open.

There is, then, no automatic tendency to replace or to upgrade the urban capital plant. If anything, there is a tendency to minimize the rate of replacement. The financial logic is that providing the urban community with an improved physical environment does not significantly increase its money income, so the capacity to pay for these things is in doubt. An alternative financial concept is urgently needed if urban physical development and capital formation are to come under control.

DISCUSSION QUESTIONS

1. If you were an economic consultant to a developing nation, how would you go about estimating the proportion of investible funds to be devoted to urban capital formation?

2. Does urban capital formation increase the productivity of the national economy? In what sense, if any, are urban centers "the main poles of progress" (p. 281)?

3. Do you agree that environmental deterioration is a kind of "disguised inflation"? Would it be easier to deal with if we did not have to worry about the balance of payments and international currency exchange rates?

4. What conditions must exist if additional transfer expenditures for the use of urban capital goods are to provide effective stimulus for the expansion of the inventory of urban capital goods?

5. Why is the problem illustrated in Table 21 beyond the capacity of an individual entrepreneur to remedy?

6. Do you agree with the statement (p. 292) that "investment justifies the creation of new monetary resources, but grants do not"?

7. Is the differential interest-elasticity explanation of contracyclical fluctuations in urban capital investment convincing or realistic? Is there a more likely explanation?

8. In what institutions and by what mechanics are "replacement" or "depreciation" reserves for urban capital accumulated?

SELECTED REFERENCES

Burns, Leland S., *et al. Housing: Symbol and Shelter.* International Housing Productivity Study. Los Angeles: Graduate School of Business Administration, University of California, 1970.
A report on case studies of housing improvement programs in a number of communities around the world; the object of the studies was to measure the social benefits from public investment in new housing.

Grebler, Leo, D. M. Blank, and L. Winnick. *Capital Formation in Residential Real Estate.* Princeton, N.J.: Princeton University Press, 1956.
A scholarly study of long-term trends in housing construction in the United States and in the stock of housing units.

Kindleberger, Charles P. *Economic Development.* New York: McGraw-Hill, 1965.
A representative textbook on the principles of economic develop-

ment, including the concept of the capital-output ratio and the low priority of urban capital formation.

Nevitt, A. A. (ed.). *The Economic Problems of Housing*. London: Macmillan, 1967.

Papers and summary of discussion presented in an international conference of housing experts, covering rent control, postwar reconstruction, and the role of housing in the economies of developing nations.

Samuelson, Paul A. *Economics*. New York: McGraw-Hill, 1967.

An introductory economics textbook by a Nobel prizewinning scholar; differing theories of the process of economic development are described.

Wendt, Paul F. *Housing Policy: The Search for Solutions*. Berkeley: University of California Press, 1962.

Description of government programs for housing in the United States, Great Britain, West Germany, and Sweden, primarily during the immediate postwar period.

13

URBAN PUBLIC FINANCE

AN URBAN COMMUNITY is a microcosm of the "mixed economy" which economic textbooks describe. That is, decisions about the use of resources are made by the marketplace and by collective institutions (government) in some interactive way. The development and management of the urban physical plant is a joint public-private enterprise. The interaction occurs in three principal areas:

1. Private development and use of land is constrained by the availability of publicly provided infrastructure—if there are no streets, there can be no new buildings.

2. Users of real estate constitute a community with specific demands for public services (as distinct from infrastructure)—they want laws to regulate the community and policemen to enforce these laws, they want to hire schoolteachers, sanitation workers, and so on; a demand for land is, at the same time, a demand for government.

3. By custom, most local public revenue is provided by an ad valorem tax on private real estate, which influences land-use decisions and acts as a constraint on the scope of collective activities.

JOINT GOODS AND MERIT GOODS

There is a demand for government—for public infrastructure and public services—because there are several things people want that cannot feasibly be provided through the marketplace. We cannot buy the streets we need to use in individual packets along with our gasoline, and it does

304

not work out if we try to provide ourselves with individual police forces or fire protection. It is feasible but inefficient for people in a community to obtain water or dispose of wastes by uncoordinated efforts. It is possible for people to secure private open space–back yards–but a large public park is something that many people want as well. Thus, people in a community pool their demands for certain types of goods and services.

This was not always the case. Cities that grew up in Europe and North America during the industrial age learned about "joint goods" by trial and error. Street vendors in early London set up stalls in the streets because that gave them maximum exposure to people passing by, but finally people couldn't get by the vendors' stalls. Streets had to be cleared and maintained as "public rights of way" which no individual could claim a specific piece of as his share. Rich people who surrounded their property with lights to discourage thieves found that the light inevitably also protected their neighbors and passers-by, who escaped paying the cost of the lights. Public lighting and a public police force, the cost of which was borne by and the benefits received by the community as a whole, finally emerged as the most practical solution. Private, competitive fire-fighting companies in early American communities would not attack a blaze in a nonsubscriber's house, with the result that small fires often spread into urban conflagrations.

Public schooling emerged only after much longer struggles, because education is not necessarily a "public good" in the sense that street lighting is. It is feasible to charge fees to the people who receive the benefits (the parents of the school children), and the scale economies fall short of creating a school monopoly situation in communities of more than very modest size. Private market-supplied schooling is feasible. In a sense, it is the businesses and property owners in the community who benefit from the existence of a school, because children finishing school will be literate employees and will both understand and respect "private property signs." Still, schooling improves a child's earning potential, so it is reasonable to consider that he is the principal beneficiary.

The real case for free, compulsory education as a function of local government is equity. Children whose parents could not afford private tuition would suffer for a time because of that poverty and would transmit their disadvantage to their own children. Resources would be wasted by the community at large, of course, but this loss would have a serious and essentially unfair incidence. Public education is thus described as a "merit good"—something provided by the public for the benefit of individuals.[1] Merit goods require income redistribution, in effect, while joint-demand goods do not. Local government is involved in the provision of both. Some of its activities are a combination of the two; schools are used and paid for by (almost) all, but some pay more and others pay less than a pro-rata share of the cost.

Either category may require infrastructure or public services, or both, which means that the city must invest in capital goods and maintain a labor force. This two-dimensional distinction can be illustrated as follows:

PUBLIC EXPENDITURE CATEGORY

	Infrastructure (Capital Investment)	Services (Payments to Persons)
Joint Goods	streets water system	police sanitary workers
Merit Goods	hospitals schools museum	welfare teachers jailers

All local government expenditures can be made to fit within this classification system, though sometimes a conceptual problem is involved. For example, we show payments to jailers as a "merit" good, because, in fact, only a few people in the community receive the services of jailers—at least directly (and those people would prefer not to be so favored). But some school children would rather not be in school, either. The receipt of merit goods is not necessarily by choice, and we can broaden the term to include "demerits" as well, if we like.

The purpose of the classification device is to show that certain local government functions involve income transfers—for which the property tax system of the community is generally inappropriate—and that current expenditures as well as capital investments by communities depend very much on revenue derived from real estate taxes. These current expenditures are far more volatile than the carrying cost for infrastructure investment.

1. For an excellent discussion of the public goods vs. merit goods distinction, see Julius Margolis, "The Demand for Urban Public Services," in *Issues in Urban Economics*, Harvey S. Perloff and Lowdon Wingo, Jr., eds. (Baltimore: Johns Hopkins Press, 1968), pp. 527ff.

REVENUE AND EXPENDITURE MAGNITUDES

Table 23 summarizes local government revenue and expenditure experience in the United States for 1966. It is interesting that the dollar amount of local government revenue from local sources works out to $196, or about $600 per household, $400 of which comes from property taxes (from commercial, industrial, and other property, as well as residential), because problems arise from the feeling that these absolute amounts are too high. But the percentage distributions in the table are more informative.

Table 23

Local Government Revenues and Expenditures, United States, 1966

(a) Local Government Revenue in the United States, Within and Outside Major Metropolitan Areas, 1966			
	All local governments	Within 39 largest SMSA's*	Outside 39 largest SMSA's*
Total amounts (in millions)	$56,125	$27,893	$28,232
Per capita	286.56	350.77	242.67
Percent distribution, by sources (total)	100.0	100.0	100.0
From local government sources	68.3	72.1	64.7
Taxes	48.7	52.7	44.8
Property taxes	42.5	44.0	41.0
Nonproperty taxes	6.3	8.8	3.8
Benefited user charges and assessments	15.0	14.4	15.5
Water supply revenue	3.8	3.7	3.9
All other	11.2	10.7	
Miscellaneous local nontax revenue	4.6	4.9	4.3
Intergovernmental revenue	31.7	27.9	35.3
From state governments	29.2	25.3	33.0
From federal government (direct)	2.5	2.6	2.3

Table 23 (continued)

(b) Estimated Revenue Relationships of Local Government Expenditures for Various Functions, 1966

	Percent of all local government expenditure, net of intergovernmental revenue and user charges		Percent contribution of various sources to financing for particular functions		
	38 largest SMSA's (col. a)	United States (col. b)	State and federal aid (col. c)	Local benefited user charges (col. d)	Local "general" resources (col. e)
Total	100.0	100.0			
Education	38.3	43.5	43.5	6.4	50.1
Police protection and correction	11.6	9.0	3.4	...	96.6
Interest on general debt	6.6	5.9	2.0	...	98.0
General control and financial administration	6.3	6.4	2.8	...	97.2

Health and hospitals	5.9	5.3	11.6	36.1	52.3
Fire protection	5.6	4.5	2.0	...	98.0
Streets and highways	5.3	7.0	43.9	6.7	49.4
Parks and recreation	4.4	3.3	2.0	14.7	83.2
Sewerage	2.9	2.7	6.8	45.8	47.4
Public welfare	2.8	2.3	81.2	...	18.8
Refuse collection and street cleaning	2.7	2.1	2.0	25.2	72.7
General public buildings	2.0	2.2	2.0	...	98.0
Water supply	1.9	2.0	...	77.9	22.1
Libraries	1.4	1.3	12.0	...	88.0
Housing and urban renewal	.5	.4	50.1	42.3	7.6
Airports, terminals, parking	.2	.2	9.6	83.2	7.2
All other	1.5	1.8	n.a.	n.a.	n.a.

Source: *Building the American City*, Report of the National Commission on Urban Problems to the Congress and to the President of the United States, House Document No. 91–34 (Washington: U.S. Government Printing Office, n.d.), Tables 2 and 3, pp. 409–410.

n.a. –not available.

Note: Because of rounding, detail may not add to totals.

*SMSA is a census term, Standard Metropolitan Statistical Area.

Cities receive financial assistance from other levels of government, mostly on a formula basis for specific functions—such as welfare—adding up to nearly a third of all city revenue. This assistance is concentrated in those functions that represent merit goods—schools, hospitals, and welfare, in particular. Aid for streets and highways is an anomoly, but it is explained by the traditional linking of such funds to the gasoline tax which is administered by other levels of government.

The formulas employed in determining the amount of aid for these merit-goods functions generally require the local government to bear a portion of the cost, even though the standards of expenditure may be established by another level of government. An urban community is not free to decide how much income it will transfer in the process of running its school system, for example.

Cities are left largely to their own devices in the financing of "joint goods"—police forces, general government, fire protection, parks, and sanitary services. Infrastructure costs, such as interest on the general debt, are also borne almost entirely by the local government, though "education" and "hospital" categories of expense presumably include some capital costs.

Water supply is an interesting expenditure category because it is nearly a pure joint good and it is mostly sold to users. Together with the category, "airports, terminals, parking," water is provided by public enterprises in the narrow sense—self-sustaining businesses that are owned by government only because that is functionally convenient. These things fall into the "natural monopoly" or "public utility" category of things that people need and for which economies of scale are very great. Both of these categories imply substantial infrastructure investment not reflected in "interest on general debt."

For some types of joint goods, then, it is feasible to charge consumers on the basis of the quantity used—water or parking space, for example. For other joint goods—such as police and fire protection—this is not feasible and general taxation is required.

THE PROPERTY TAX

From Table 23, again, property taxes provide 87 percent of all local government tax revenues. Larger metropolitan areas are slightly less dependent on this tax (the ratio is 83 percent) because they have developed other kinds of tax resources, primarily income and sales taxes. This means, of course, that the ratio for other local governments taken together is even higher—92 percent. A city's fiscal problem is first and foremost a property tax problem.

The concept of the property tax levy is simple. Certain properties are exempt, such as churches, public property, and some others. For the rest, the assessor determines the value of each piece of property, which is in effect an estimate of what it would sell for. Then he adds up all the values of taxable property and divides that sum into the amount of revenue required; the result is the tax rate. Say the aggregate value of properties on his list is $100 million and the revenue needed is $2 million; every property owner gets a bill for 2 percent of the value of his property. Differential rates for different categories of property are generally precluded by law. This tax is a lien against the property; if it is not paid, the property may be sold at auction to satisfy the debt. If the owner tries to sell the property without paying the tax that is due, it will be deducted from the proceeds of the sale. It is not possible to move one's property to a city where the tax rate is lower, of course, so the imposition of the tax does not diminish the supply of private real estate, at least in the short run.

The property tax is reasonably well suited for financing joint goods—things like streets, water supply, police, and to some extent, schools, that everyone will use or benefit from.[2] If it is feasible to levy user charges for such things, by installing water meters, for example, then most public finance experts believe it is preferable to do so. The reason is that people who benefit from joint goods do not necessarily want to pay for them. If water is not metered, then the marginal cost of water to the individual consumer is zero, and he may use it extravagantly and impose a burden upon general taxpayers. If he can use the city streets and avoid paying for them by residing just outside the city's taxing jurisdiction, so much the better. But user charges are not feasible as a means of rationing the use of many joint goods, and so general revenue from the property tax is relied upon.

The property tax tends to make urban infrastructure investments self-financing, and this is something very much in its favor. If a new development of houses and stores calls for a public outlay of, say, $5 million for streets, utilities, and schools, requiring perhaps $400 thousand in annual

2. A person may benefit from a public facility without actually using it, as in the case of a park which is there in case he one day decides to visit it. The fact that he has the option of using it is, in itself, a benefit he may be willing to pay for.

carrying charges, and the development will add at least $400 thousand (plus amounts necessary for teachers' salaries and other current expenditures) to the annual revenue of the city, then there is no financial barrier to approval by the city of the new development. The capital funds can be borrowed, presumably, in some money market, on the strength of the increased public revenue that will be generated.

Without this self-financing feature–which in fact does not obtain in many parts of the world–infrastructure investment needed to facilitate private additions to the supply of houses, shops, and other consumer capital is likely to be very uncertain. The capital market is not ready to supply money as a gift, and governments at any level are remarkably reluctant to do so. The city may, of course, be able to demonstrate that income taxes, business taxes, or sales taxes will increase sufficiently because of the new development to repay the capital cost of infrastructure at interest, but the property tax is a more nearly automatic device. It simply adds a surcharge for public services on the prices people pay for the use of housing, stores, and other private real estate.

The property tax at best, however, is not quite the same thing as a user charge, because the basis for the tax–property value–does not measure benefits derived by taxpayers from public services. The discrepancy is clearest in the case of a "site value" tax levied on land alone, a system advocated by many serious students of local government finance.[3] Although it may be argued whether the value of land can, in principle, be separated from the value of developed property in a particular case, it is intuitively clear that site value and the tax that is proportional to it are decreasing functions of distance from the center, or centers, of an urban community, as shown in Figure 48a. This is, indeed, the same thing as location or site rent discussed in Chapter Seven, to which is applied a constant tax rate.

Under this scheme, people who live closer to the center of town pay more tax per capita than people who live farther away. Those who live farther away make greater use of the transportation and utility systems of the community, however, as shown in Figure 48b. If streets and water

3. This is the famous "Henry George" issue; George's 1879 book, *Progress and Poverty*, convinced many that buildings should be exempt from property taxation. For a present-day commentary, see Dick Netzer, "The Budget: Trends and Prospects," *Agenda for a City* (Washington, D.C.: The Brookings Institution, 1966), pp. 679ff.

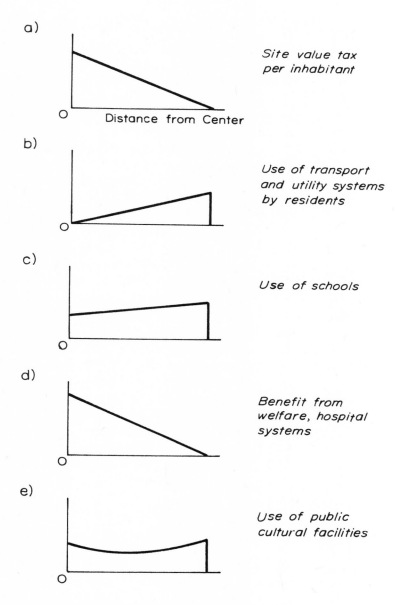

a)

Site value tax
per inhabitant

Distance from Center

b)

Use of transport
and utility systems
by residents

c)

Use of schools

d)

Benefit from
welfare, hospital
systems

e)

Use of public
cultural facilities

Figure 48. Locational incidence of site value tax and
various public expenditures.

mains are paid for entirely out of revenue derived from site rent taxes, then the people close in are subsidizing the people farther out. Benefits from the school system are shown in Figure 48c as gently rising functions of distance, on the assumption that schools farther out are newer and therefore better, though clearly this need not always be the case. In Figure 48d, the use of hospital and welfare services is shown as a decreasing function of distance from the center, because it is generally true that the lower-income people who receive these benefits live closer in; this would contradict the intention of providing subsidized services, however.[4] This kind of property tax cannot redistribute income effectively. In the last part of the figure, the use of cultural facilities, such as an opera house or a museum, is shown as a U-shaped function of distance; people who live downtown might find it easy to avail themselves of these opportunities, while people in the affluent suburbs constitute the basic "demand." Figure 48e might also be said to represent the benefit derived from police protection.

Site value taxation would, according to its advocates, encourage better construction and maintenance (because buildings per se would not be taxed), discourage the speculative holding of land, and capture some of the increment in land value due to urban growth for public use. We shall return to the matter of recapturing land increment at a later point. It is clear, however, that a site value tax is quite different from a user charge. In principle, site value taxation would encourage a dispersal of urban population toward the periphery of the city, as indeed the common form of the existing property tax tends to do for the same reason.

The general real property tax, on buildings as well as land, is commonly regarded as "regressive." In New York City, for example, it has been estimated that the real estate tax on housing takes 8.4 percent of the income of households with less than $2,000 annual income, 5.2 percent of income in the $2,000–$3,000 class, 3.8 percent in the $3,000–$4,000 class, and so on, diminishing to about 2 percent for incomes of $7,500 or more.[5] Low-income families, to repeat a point made above, tend to live on high-valued, central land while offsetting commuting costs by higher-income households which escape the property tax. It is also true that higher-income people spend relatively less for housing and have more of

4. It may not help matters very much that welfare recipients living in the center of town enjoy superior accessibility in return for their site rent, but the point should not be overlooked.

5. Netzer, "The Budget: Trends and Prospects," p. 681.

their wealth in forms other than real estate. The days when a man's real estate was a good measure of his income have long since passed.

Regressivity makes the property tax quite unsuitable as a means of financing merit goods—which are in effect means of redistributing income. It doesn't make much sense to require the poor to pay the cost of their own welfare checks, for example, unless we quite cynically believe that this will sweep the problem under the carpet. So it remains a vast anomaly of urban governments in North America that so much of what they are charged with doing is in the nature of redistribution while their nearly exclusive source of revenue is a regressive tax.

Regressivity is enhanced where the opportunity for "flight" exists, that is, where the metropolitan community is composed of several tax jurisdictions that compete with each other for residents. A person who has his residence in Marin County, just north of the Golden Gate Bridge, cannot be required to contribute to the welfare costs of San Francisco through his property tax. Some suburban communities, by preventing the construction of lower-priced housing or apartments, exempt themselves from the task of supporting schools, hospitals, welfare payments, and many other "merit" goods (including jails) intended for the poorer people of the metropolitan community. Real estate cannot be moved from one tax jurisdiction to another, but people who use real estate can, by and large, move themselves. This tends to limit the extent of income-transferring functions performed by city governments, though by tradition the city is responsible for such things as education, health care, and welfare.

Indeed, the property tax that is the necessary and perhaps "natural" source of revenue for joint-demand infrastructure, often carries such a transfer burden that infrastructure investments may be discouraged. When a family is already paying $50 to $100 a month in property taxes, it is likely to oppose increases even for things that provide a *quid pro quo*, like street paving or a better-looking city hall.

THE MIX OF PUBLIC GOODS

A community consists of people who share certain needs that cannot be satisfied on an individual basis—needs for streets, schools, police protection, utilities, and other "joint goods." But the individuals who share these needs do not necessarily regard it as inevitable that they should be the ones to pay. In its public behavior as well as its private activities, an urban community is prone to overload the communal infrastrucutre—that is, the environment—by shifting resource costs to other people in other communities. A set of towns around a lake or bay, pumping sewage into each other's back yards, so to speak, is the classic example. Air pollution is another source of "spillover effects," as wind currents carry soot, smell, and heat far beyond the boundaries of even the largest city. People would have to have more conscience than they do to voluntarily spend the money it would take to stop up chimneys and treat sewage solely for the benefit of people on some other part of the landscape.

And if just one small community made the effort, it would probably go to waste. Pollution of a lake or bay won't abate unless most of the contributing communities make simultaneous efforts and investments to prevent it, and there is always the uncomfortable fact that the more communities that do act to check pollution, the less other communities will feel constrained to do likewise. It always pays an individual not to go along, to let the other people clean up after him.

In Figure 49 we symbolize the kinds of choices an urban community faces with respect to urban public goods. Should the streets be paved? Should there be sidewalks? Should there be an art museum? A clinic for expectant mothers? A zoo? A sewage treatment plant? Special schools for retarded children? For each of these and the countless other expenditure or consumption options the people in a community have for collective action, there is the additional question of how much should be spent, plus administrative or distributional questions about specific locations, fees to be charged, or other means of deciding which people will benefit.

Available income is divided first between "urban" goods and services and "other," with "urban" expenditures being those for the use of private real estate and for all local public purposes. It is the latter, of course, in which we are interested at the moment, so the purpose of this part of Figure 49 is simply to remind us that the total amount of money that people spend on urban public goods and services has alternative uses, and that the public slice of the pie is variable.

The two major categories of public expenditures are "joint" and "merit," following our earlier classification. The letters in the small boxes that follow in the diagram refer to the whole list or menu of expenditure options we want to classify. Examples of public goods represented by these

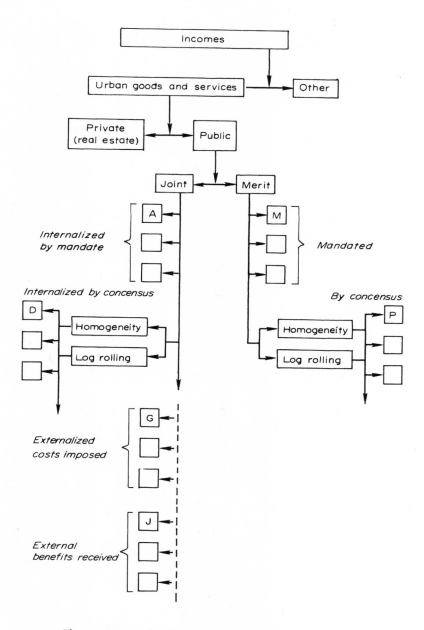

Figure 49. Selecting the mix of urban public goods.

letters are: A, police protection; D, a park; G, sewage treatment; J, a regional airport; M, welfare services; and P, an opera house. These are only examples. They are relatively easy to classify by this scheme—in contrast, for example, to the important expenditure category of schools, which might justifiably be listed in all the sections of this chart.

Some public expenses, on both joint-demand and merit goods, are mandated by other levels of government or fixed by tradition as a function of urban governments. Self-policing is a function that comes close to defining a city as a political entity. Welfare has been a traditional responsibility of local government for centuries, since people without means first went "on the parish."

The word "internalized" in the diagram means that people who receive the benefits pay the costs. Obviously the distinction would not apply to merit goods. Joint-demand goods, like the use of streets and the enjoyment of police protection or a park, are paid for by beneficiaries, either because they are obliged to—that is, mandated—or because they have agreed to do so through their governmental system. One thing that needs to be said about taxes is that payment is not optional, and if a city has decided to build and maintain a park, the individual taxpayer has no choice about contributing to the cause. But many things, like parks, a sewage-treatment plant, or an extra-high-quality school system, can at some point be decided upon, yes or no, by the citizenry—or at least "for" them by those in authority. So the community as a whole has some decisions to make about the specific types and aggregate amounts of costs it will bear. A choice to bear a cost is what the diagram means by internalizing a community function.

The community has two basic ways to arrive democratically at a decision to internalize the cost of a joint consumption activity. A majority of voters will support an expenditure proposal if it will provide something they share a homogeneous desire for. For example, few would oppose having some form of public fire protection. The other way to get a yes vote on an expenditure is by exchanging favors—"logrolling." A bond issue for a senior center *and* school improvements has a better chance politically than one for either alone. Instincts in support of special types of merit goods can be mobilized in the same two ways.

The broken line at the bottom left in the figure means that public expenditure very often falls short of the costs that the people in a community impose on the rest of the world. Our example, G, is a sewage-treatment plant—one that is *not* built, the community decision being to save money by dumping the effluent in the river and letting the folks downstream worry about it. When things get bad enough, the entire set of communities may internalize the cost through environmental investments (as discussed in Chapter Twelve), following the logic of homogeneity—that each and every community would benefit.

Last, external benefits may be received by the community. People in Hooterville can fly in and out of the municipal airport of nearby Macropolis, or have a picnic in the park there, often without paying the full costs of same. One of the best reasons for not building a swimming pool in your backyard is that the neighbor may let you use his pool, and contiguous urban communities follow the same principle to some extent. It is hard, in practice, to deny nonresidents access to a city-subsidized transit system, the library, the park, the museums, and so on. Because the marginal costs of additional service are low, large cities are often willing to contract with smaller places for services such as fire protection and schools. The effect may or may not be a clear subsidy to the smaller community, but it saves that community the expense of being self-sufficient.

We have been a little vague about the dimensions of the community—whether we are talking about a whole city or a school district, and so forth. Indeed, the mesh of local governmental jurisdictions is a fairly complex mat of interests. People who want an expenditure pattern other than that obtaining where they now live can try to establish a separate, coexisting regime by forming a mosquito-abatement district, for example, superimposed on other, wider-spreading urban obligations. They can try to move to a community where the expenditure pattern conforms closest to their own sense of what is right and necessary or, of course, they can go fight city hall. It is coincident views about public expenditure patterns that define "community," and not the other way around.

BENEFIT-COST ANALYSIS

The list of community expenditure options is really endless. Someone in the community can always come up with a new project which he believes the community should undertake, an appeal for more money for old projects or for quite a different way of carrying them on. Suppose, for example, that it has been proposed to acquire land for a very large park or "open space" that would be protected from development. Is there some way to analyze a public undertaking, which is often in the nature of a capital investment, to see whether it would be worth what it would cost?

Table 24 is a summary of a study made in connection with just such a problem. It reflects a technique and illustrates a number of serious conceptual problems. The present value of total benefits is put at something over $1.5 billion, of which only $15 million—really a nominal amount—is attributed to the free use of the park by citizens. A significant amount of rental income from franchise operations—food stands and boating, for example—is predicted. More than three-fourths of the total estimated benefit, however, comes from savings in costs of utilities and public service

Table 24

Benefit-Cost Analysis, an Illustration
Present Value of Cumulative Benefits and Costs
of Creating a Large Park and Open Space
(In $ millions)

Benefits	
Lease income	$ 354
Recreation user benefits	15
Utilities	
Gas	145
Electricity	213
Water	416
Telephone	65
Governmental services	
General government	121
Public works	112
Public safety	86
Total benefits	$1,527
Costs	
Acquisition	$2,123
Administration and maintenance	28
Total costs	$2,153
B/C ratio: 1,527/2,153 = .71	

Source: Based on a study done primarily by Development Research Associates, for "People for Open Space," a San Francisco area citizens' group.

to the developed portion of the community brought about by greater density there. That is, with a large amount of land set aside for open space, the community would have to shift to a land-use pattern of smaller house lots and more apartment units per acre as population growth continued. Fewer miles of water mains and of police-car patrolling would be required. These potential savings were estimated from observations of utility and government costs in communities with various densities. One might suppose that the psychological objection that people apparently have to higher density would be taken into account, but it was not. Nor was it considered that people who have given up their private backyards for the sake of a large, common "backyard" would have to spend time and money making use of the park.

The cost shown is almost entirely for the purchase of the land. This could be based on an appraisal-type estimate of what the park authority would have to pay to private landowners—that is, the money cost. Purchase of land, however, involves a transfer payment since the economic resources of the community are not affected by a change in ownership. What matters in terms of resources is the alternative use of the land, or more precisely the impact on the net economic product of the entire community of setting this land aside. Farm or dairy products, for example, might have to be brought from a greater distance after nearby agricultural land was taken over for a park.

There is demonstrably no direct link between the "marginal social value" of urban or urbanizable land and the price for which it can be acquired. For example, the whole tract might be owned by a philanthropist who will sell it for one dollar. Or it might be owned by several speculative developers who trade land between themselves and create evidence of a high market value. The price paid is a significant element in the public decision, but it is not an intelligible indicator of resource cost. A corresponding statement can be made with respect to increases in land value that are frequently counted among the benefits of other public projects such as urban renewal. Individuals spend money; communities spend resources.

In any case, the open-space project of the illustration has a benefit-cost ratio of 0.71. This would seem to indicate that the project is not feasible or desirable, but in fact it is only a preliminary point. The great and diffuse benefit of "having" open space—considered too intangible to be measured —is perhaps sufficient to close the gap, and the body politic will be asked to decide if it is. Thus, the technique measures measurable things and leaves it up to the community to speculate whether immeasurable costs and benefits offset the net measurable cost or net measurable benefit. Since no one can offer a complete list of immeasurable things to be considered in a particular case, the benefit-cost approach to public decision making is, at best, an aid to public discussion and not a substitute for it.

The benefit-cost approach is a partial substitute for the marketplace, however. Producers and consumers in the marketplace do decide what to make and what to use, based on private benefits and private costs. Public benefit-cost analysis differs from marketplace decision-making in three basic ways.

1. Benefit-cost analysis *internalizes* things—like the saving in utility costs due to higher density development—which would be external to private decisions.

2. Benefit-cost analysis recognizes, though it may not measure, *intangibles*, for which there is no counterpart in private production but which are akin to consumer "utility." Thus, benefit-cost analysis envisages the community primarily as a consumer.

3. Benefit-cost analysis makes *interpersonal* comparisons that do not arise in the microeconomic world of the consuming firm and the consuming household. Costs that are borne by one group of people are often set against benefits that may be received by some other group or arbitrary schemes of compensation to the "losers"—like people evicted by urban renewal—may be set up.

Given all this, the benefit-cost ratio, as illustrated in the case of the regional park, is still not a decision-making device because there are presumably many other potential activities for the same local government having at least acceptable ratios. Does a community do everything for which the benefits promise to exceed the costs? If investment is involved and total investment funds are limited, presumably some projects will have to be selected and others passed up, but the ratio of total benefits and costs is not necessarily the ideal indicator of public priorities.[6] Some economists would prefer a marginal benefit-marginal cost concept and others would calculate an investment rate of return for each proposed project to select the one with the highest "yield."

6. See Ronald W. Eash, "Economic Techniques for Evaluating Mutually Exclusive Alternatives," *Chicago Area Transportation Study* (C.A.T.S.) *Research News* (July 1971), pp. 1ff.

At the present time, there is no standard format for urban benefit-cost studies and not much conviction about their usefulness. The difficulty in applying the concept to urban problems may be an indication that urban life defies efficiency criteria—a point we shall deal with in the remaining chapters.

RECAPTURING LAND VALUE INCREMENTS

Whether we attribue it to transportation savings, inherent urban productivity advantages, or some other factor, the land in cities seems to rise almost continuously in value. Windfall fortunes are created; it may take a clever man to know which land is going to rise in value and to acquire that land at a low price, but the value of the land does not rise primarily because of his own efforts. Consequently, urban land seems to be a very good object for taxation, redistributing "unearned income," and financing necessary public activities at the same time.

Indeed, the late nineteenth-century American reformer, Henry George, believed that no other tax would be necessary at any level of government if urban land value increments could be recaptured.[7] In particular, he felt that there would be no need to tax buildings, and his site rent tax would be an effective deterrent against holding land out of use until increasing scarcity made it still more valuable. Further, it has been held that a tax on land cannot be shifted by the owner to the user. The land increment tax has considerable appeal on several grounds.

There is not much doubt that land can be taxed. In feudal times, the holders of land had to turn over a (usually large) fraction of their crops to the local nobleman, and in modern times, a significant fraction of the rental value of urban property is taxed away—about 20 percent in North America. Capital gain and estate or inheritance taxes also apply generally to land.

Henry George apparently never advocated socializing urban land, though that it what his criticisms of the urban land market might seem to imply. He may have been aware that public ownership simply transfers the onus of collecting rents from private owners to a public body; such complaints arose recently in Hong Kong when the government—which actually does own most of the city's land—announced stiff increases in land

7. Henry George, *Progress and Poverty* (New York: Doubleday, 1926).

rents, for example. Public ownership may easily lead to erosion of revenues that the use of land produces, allowing people to use it free or at nominal prices, and to purely administrative systems of deciding who should have the use of each piece of ground. Putting the legal title to urban land in the name of the government does not socialize "property" in any case; new rights are created in the nature of leasehold interests that can be traded for windfall private gains. This is the effect of quasi-socialization of housing through rent control, for example. Privileged tenants are in a position to take under-the-table payments in return for "subletting."

Urban land prices have escalated in some instances—notably in several Asian cities during the past decade—to the point that serious practical problems have arisen. Construction programs to relieve severe housing shortages have been blocked by land costs exceeding available budgets. Of course, income has been redistributed as well by this inflation, toward the lucky few who control land. So, "ceiling prices" for land are sometimes proposed, meaning that sales proceeds beyond a certain limit should be substantially confiscated. The effect, however, tends to be that land transactions go underground, not that the availability of land to users is improved.

Urban land prices serve to ration that land among competing users. If there were more substitutes for land, the absolute level of those prices would be less likely to rise and the issue of recapturing land value increments would not emerge. But substitutes—larger buildings on existing sites and the development of new land around the city—may be infeasible for technical reasons (for example, earthquake hazards) or institutional reasons (such as hesitancy to extend the urban infrastructure). Recapture of the increment in land values will not make the community, as a whole, better off, but improvements in the effective supply of urban land would. People would get more transportation or more floor space for their real estate budgets instead of just the right to crowd together on land that is artificially scarce.

So it seems like a poor policy to make the provision of merit goods and joint goods by urban government depend on the exploitation of a monopoly, for that would be a disincentive for improving the supply of urban space. Increase in urban land value is not the unencumbered pot of gold or social windfall that Henry George and his followers have taken it to be, but rather a symptom of the productivity of the urban economy on the one hand and of the imperfect organization of the urban land market on the other. Productivity is subject to general income taxes, to user charges and excises payable out of income derived from any resource, including land. But the idea that urban land, in and of itself, is uniquely productive is spurious.

The idea of "land banking" by a municipality—reserving fringe land for future development through advance public acquisition—is somewhat problematical as a response to private land increment windfalls. On the one hand, the local land-banking authority may use its powers to maintain a scarcity of developed land and thus preserve the flow of land taxes into the local treasury. But the authority might instead feed land into new development at such a rate that values and taxes for existing developed land do not rise. The latter approach implies that the land banker would not make much profit for the community, because potential land increment would be transferred to the land users of the community as lower land prices.

So a municipal land bank may be either a high-profit, restrictive approach to development land supply or a no-profit, collective prepurchase of fringe area land. The no-profit concept, however, requires that development be fostered through the provision of infrastructure as well as of low-priced land. If a public agency controls the suburban land market, it may be able to administrer the development of that land so as to reduce the absorption period for new developments and to achieve land-planning amenities. This can be done in cooperation with a consortium of experienced private developers, in a public-private joint venture that makes use of private developers' experience with the market. It seems likely that suburban development will move in this direction, though the hazard exists that ill-defined public goals may delay or distort development responses to urban land needs.

Many of the potential benefits of land banking can be achieved through the sale of development rights, where appropriate public powers exist. This requires, in effect, that all fringe land be zoned at first for nonurban uses and that developers must buy a change in zoning. This gives local government the opportunity to feed land into the market as it is deemed necessary and to select those development schemes that create the fewest external costs. Of course, it is also a way of capturing land value increments, but that implies a policy of preserving the scarcity of land.

DISCUSSION QUESTIONS

1. In your own mind, how do you divide responsibility for the production of goods and services between the public and private sector?

2. Having answered Question 1, which of the public sector's economic functions do you think properly belong at the local government level? Why?

3. Now, having identified the desirable economic functions of local government, what is the most appropriate way to finance each one?

4. Does competition (for residents, employment, and so on) among separate cities in the same metropolitan area seriously restrict the choice of taxation systems which local governments have? Is this competition "socially useful"?

5. Make a list of the "merit goods" you receive. Do you really deserve them all? Are there others you should be receiving (does "the world owe you a living")?

6. What "joint goods" do you help pay for that are not really worth their cost to you?

7. Would it be better to have a panel of "experts" determine the mix of urban public goods, instead of the logrolling or consensus system?

8. What is your definition of the "land increment problem"? What is your prescription for it?

9. Outline a cost-benefit study for a child-care center program for your neighborhood or city. Whom do you consider competent to put money values on the intangibles involved?

SELECTED REFERENCES

Fitch, L., and A. H. Walsh (eds.). *Agenda for a City*. Beverly Hills, Calif.: Sage Publications, 1970.

Research papers based on careful studies of New York City, covering such topics as the relationship between transportation systems and types of employment, and the origins of the city's financial difficulties.

George, Henry. *Progress and Poverty*. New York: Doubleday, 1926.
The major work of America's most famous urban reformer, first published in 1879, which argues for a restructuring of the property tax system.

Moynihan, D. P. (ed.). *Toward a National Urban Policy*. New York: Basic Books, 1970.
Essays on a variety of urban issues loosely related to the role of the federal government.

Netzer, Dick. *Economics of the Property Tax*. Washington, D.C.: The Brookings Institution, 1966.
Economic analysis of the ad valorem tax on land and buildings; primarily theoretical but with reference to the practical operation of the system in the U.S.

Perloff, H. S., and L. Wingo, Jr. (eds.). *Issues in Urban Economics*. Baltimore: Johns Hopkins Press, 1968.
A book of readings on most aspects of urban economics—housing, land use, taxation, employment, and public services.

14

URBAN DYSFUNCTION

IN AN EARLIER CHAPTER, we described at length the economic advantages of urbanization. Passing mention was made of some *dis*economies of urbanization, or more specifically, of urban scale—the size of a particular city. These diseconomies are varied; some are technologically inherent, others are due to habits or institutions of the people who live in cities, and some are more difficult to offset than others.

AVERAGE TRANSPORTATION COSTS

It is easiest to start with the technological diseconomies of urban growth. Figure 50 is concerned with the large category of urban costs that fall under the heading of "transportation." This includes the costs of automobiles and gasoline, travel time converted into some money measure, public transit vehicles, roads, parking facilities, and utility infrastructure —watermains, sewers, power and phone lines. It also includes public or governmental costs that are transportation-related, such as mileage costs for police and firemen, and social or external costs, such as gasoline smog, noise, road hazards, and psychological discomforts caused by traffic congestion. All of these are a function of the average distance over which an urban resident travels.

This average distance tends to increase with the population scale of the community, but not necessarily. There is an interesting benchmark case of growth by "replication," which means that a city doubles in size by splitting into two contiguous but interacting cities of the same size. In that portion of Figure 50 labeled "replication," the average resident in the

328

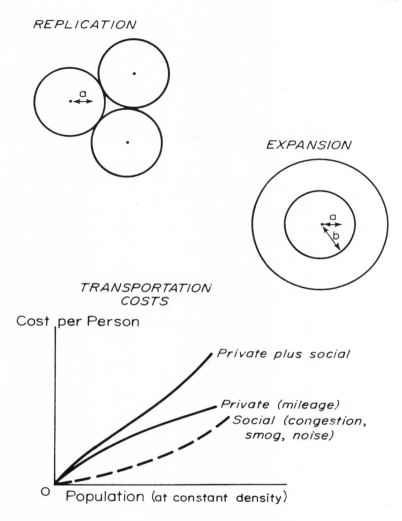

Figure 50.   Transportation costs and urban growth.

original city lives at distance *a* from the center. The city can double, triple, or quadruple without changing this average distance, if the successive modules are completely self-contained. Of course, this means that the several agglomeration economies that a city is thought to provide cannot be enjoyed.

In the city that grows by expansion, the distance between the center and the place of residence of the average inhabitant increases, from *a* to *b* in the center portion of the figure. In the graph below, this rising average distance is shown by the line labeled "private (mileage)" cost, which increases at a decreasing rate in the expanding, monocentric, circular city. It is important to note that we assume for the moment a constant density—the number of inhabitants per square mile. We are also making an implicit assumption about the nature of the transportation system.

In deference to modern times, we add a dashed line at the bottom of the graph to represent "social" or external costs associated with transportation, and with the automobile in particular, things such as congestion, smog, and noise that individual users of transportation devices inflict upon other users and on the general public. This line rises at an increasing rate on the principle that the capacity of the environment to absorb pollutants of these kinds is inelastic. If each of ten drivers honks his horn once, each person hears ten honks; if there are twenty drivers, each person hears double the number of noises, though spatial dispersion may reduce their intensity. If there are only a few cars, their exhaust may be blown away quickly, but if there are many, the quality of the air deteriorates.

It is almost obvious that the more cars there are heading for the center of town, the more difficult it will be for everyone to get there, but this does not deter the individual from joining the crowd, since most of the resource cost he creates is "external." An analog of this condition, in Table 25, shows that individuals find it worthwhile to contribute to congestion beyond the efficient service capacity of the infrastructure. The example is that of a boat taking on passengers who want to cross the river to earn money there by picking apples. The more passengers the boat takes on, the slower the journey, and each passenger sets some value on his time.

If there are eight passengers, the journey is eleven minutes, so that the profit from the journey to each passenger is one cent. This makes it a worthwhile venture from the standpoint of the last passenger to come on board; a ninth passenger would still break even. But with eight passengers, the total net benefit resulting from the use of the boat is only eight cents. This is less than half the total net benefit realized if only four or five passengers got on the boat. The point is that individuals externalize costs which they create—that is, other people bear them—so that the socially optimum capacity of the infrastructure or environment is exceeded. It pays each individual to waste community resources, though the same individuals constitute the community that suffers.

Table 25

Social Versus Private Optima in the Use of Infrastructure

Number of passengers	Journey time in minutes	Net benefit per passengers	Total net benefit
1	4	8¢	8¢
2	5	7	14
3	6	6	18
4	7	5	20
5	8	4	20
6	9	3	18
7	10	2	14
8	11	1	8
9	12	0	0

Assumptions: Passenger embark on a boat that will take them
across a river where they can pick apples.
Each person can pick 12¢ worth of apples.
Each passenger adds one minute to the travel time.
Each passenger values his time in the boat at 1¢.

Source: Gabriel J. Roth, "Road Pricing as an Aid to Urban Transport Planning," (Symposium on) *Systems Analysis for Social Problems*, edited by Alfred Blumstein et al. (Washington: Washington Operations Research Council, 1970), pp. 197–209.

This is why the people in an urban community find it desirable to regulate the use of infrastructure in various ways. Tolls and admission fees limit the use made of bridges and museums. Burning of rubbish is restricted to days when weather conditions minimize external costs. Parking meters prevent individuals from tying up curb space that shoppers need for quick errands.

Zoning regulations limit the use of privately owned land in such a way that external benefits are created and external costs are avoided. Retail nodes pull similar stores together to make comparison shopping easier for the customer and more profitable for the merchant. Excluding factories from residential areas makes the neighborhood quieter, and excluding apartments from single-family-house areas reduces the number of cars that will be in the streets when children are walking to school.

All of these regulations, known collectively as exercises of the "police power," are created and administered on an ad hoc and nearly intuitive basis. There are engineering data about bridge capacity, and there have been studies about the effect of zoning or land-use planning on the quality of neighborhood life. But we never know precisely what money value to place on time lost or nuisances experienced in a particular situation. So there tends to be a feedback process of trying out a regulatory device (like exempting cars with two or more passengers from bridge tolls) and giving it up if it doesn't seem to be an improvement. Even zoning, which should in principle be comprehensive and inflexible, tends to be administered piecemeal.

New technology, like systems for the collection and disposal of sewage and the substitution of electric and gas heat for soot-producing home stoves, comes along occasionally to push down the social cost line of Figure 50. This gives urban expansion a new lease on life. The largest technological issue relating to urban size is probably intracity transportation, however, and it is not yet clear whether the technology offered as a solution to several urban ills will really be an improvement.

The choice is between a mass transportation system, such as a subway or bus, and the private automobile system which, rather recently, has come to prevail in many cities. More precisely, the question is how much of the transportation job should be taken over by a rail system and how much left to the automobile and the bus. Intuition probably says that a rail system is cheaper, because it carries a larger number of people over a very thin strip of land and does not require vast areas to be tied up for parking. It also produces less air pollution, perhaps less noise, and it may be safer. A major drawback, however, is that the use of urban rail transit is highly peaked during the morning and evening rush hours (see Figure 51); trips for shopping and recreation at other times of the day tend to be made by car. If you see a woman standing at a bus stop in the rain, her arms burdened with soggy packages and her hands tethering an unhappy infant or two, she is probably there because she does not have the use of a car that day, not because she is an admirer of mass transit.

If the transit system is to carry the full peak load without discomfort, then it must be very massive in terms of rolling stock and labor force, most of which will be idle during most of the day. A rail system is also very capital-intensive and "lumpy" as an investment; a city either has a subway system or it doesn't, and to install one these days may mean an investment of more than one billion dollars. Urban streets, on the other hand, can be extended in very small pieces. Subjectively, there are people who actually enjoy driving to and from work because it is the only time they have entirely free from bosses, telephones, and domestic hassles. The family car, moreover, is a household necessity which cannot be charged up entirely to the expense of commuting. Most of the family's automobile costs would continue if we left it in the garage in the morning and took a bus.

OPTIMUM URBAN SCALE

In any case, average transportation costs rise as the city's population goes up, so long as density remains constant. But it is possible to trade off density and transportation costs so that a large city usually has areas of

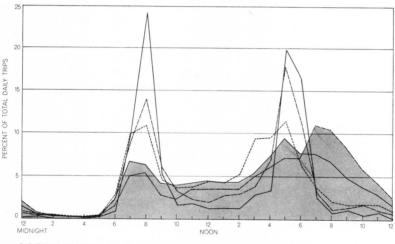

——— SUBURBAN-RAILROAD PASSENGER

—— — SUBWAY-ELEVATED PASSENGER

---- MOTOR-BUS PASSENGER

——— AUTOMOBILE DRIVER

—— — AUTOMOBILE PASSENGER

"PEAK" PROBLEM is more acute for public-transit systems (*colored curves*) than for private automobiles (*black curves*). For many transit companies 80 percent of the volume of travel is concentrated in 20 hours of the week. Such sharp peaks lead to high operating costs, since the capacity for meeting peak loads without breakdown is far in excess of the average capacity of the system. The source of this difficulty is the fact that mass transit is increasingly confined to serving commuter journeys. The concentration of journeys in narrower bands of time has accompanied the movement toward fewer workdays in the week and less work in shifts. Data for chart were drawn from Chicago Area Transportation Study.

Figure 51. The peak load problem in urban transportation.

Source: John Dyckman, "Transportation in Cities," *Scientific American* (September 1965), p. 165. *Note:* Information plotted is from a study of Chicago. Shaded areas are for automobile use.

much higher density than we find anywhere within a smaller city. Figure 52a represents this trade-off; the city's growth in population tends to push up the cost of space (in mileage, location rent, or other forms of cost) so that people tend to use less space. This means rising density, which in Figure 52b is shown directly related to "crowding and pollution."

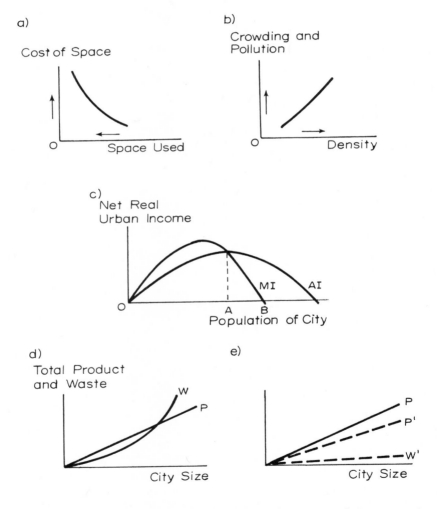

Figure 52. Optimum urban scale and the internalizing of externalities.

The relationship between density and crowding is not really a matter of definition. People can live several hundred to the acre and never feel the worse for it if they occupy well-soundproofed tower apartment buildings with locked underground garages from which they can take off directly into the metropolitan milieu like a missile leaving a silo. Or they may enjoy rubbing shoulders. So, if crowding is an external cost of urban growth, it is so partly for psychological reasons.

"Pollution" is likewise partly subjective. An urban community produces physical waste products essentially in proportion to its population, given the income, consumption habits, and technology (see Figure 53). Some of these wastes are discharged into the atmosphere, so that the quality of the atmosphere deteriorates as urban density rises. But some people think factory smoke smells like money, and they like it; people with asthma may die from it. The largest volume of waste is sewage, which may seem very inoffensive once it is dumped in some other community's water supply. Solid waste may turn into valuable landfill for a luxury marina, converting a swampy bird refuge into a profitable, taxpaying eyesore. Pollution, somewhat like beauty, is in the eye of the beholder. Most people these days would rather behold less of it, and that is subjective. Subjective or not, the extent to which pollution is a problem is related to density.

Figure 52c supposes that we can identify average real income (AI) of urban residents, that is, money income minus money costs for such things as transportation and further adjusted for psychological discomforts arising from pollution, congestion, and so on. The shape of the curve shown presumes that these costs and discomforts eventually overtake agglomeration economies of all types as the population of the city, and its density, rises. Given these conditions, there is some population level, OA, for the city which permits average net real income of the residents to be maximized. There is another population frontier, OB, beyond which the expansion of this particular city would be detrimental to the society at large—to the nation. (Figure 10, Chapter Four, introduced this subject.) It is an interesting puzzle to decide which is the "optimum scale" for this city.

But there is a more meaningful side to the problem, which Figures 52d and 52e illustrate. In Figure 52d the gross product, (P), of the city rises with city size, but the waste, (W), that occurs due to scale diseconomies—higher transportation costs, crowding, and pollution—of resources exceeds the useful product so that the net real income of the community is zero. This occurs at the population level in Figure 52c for which AI is zero. In a restricted sense, this is an economic maximum population level.

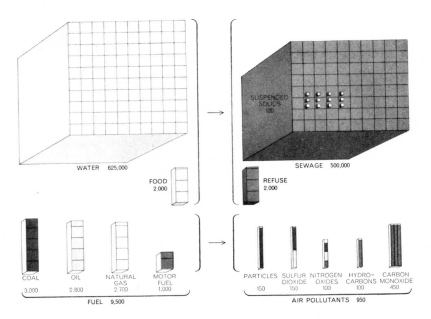

Figure 53.   Urban pollutants.

Source: Abel Wolman, "The Metabolism of Cities," *Scientific American* (September 1965), p. 180.

People are not helpless in the face of urban scale diseconomies, however. If the smell and danger from garbage become excessive, they can bury it. They can put antismog devices on their cars or factory chimneys. They can sort out land uses, decentralize employment centers so commuters don't all run together in the middle of town, buffer transportation noises, have parades to break down civic anomie, and do many other things to counter the more or less technological minuses of living together. This means expending some resources to offset the kinds of waste we are talking about. In Figure 52e, the usable product, P', is less than the gross product, because the city is internalizing its external costs, but the level of waste, W', does not rise at a faster rate. The city does not self-destruct, and there may be no economic upper limit to its population.

Is this too hopeful, merely a pollyannish dismissal of real urban problems? Doesn't the cost of controlling or offsetting waste mount up so that usable product will actually turn downward when population reaches a certain level? Is it technically feasible to offset all of the forms of waste associated with urban expansion?

These are partly technological questions. In the early days of flying, it was considered impossible to get above a certain altitude because ice would form on the wings. When it accumulated so as to offset the lift, the plane would crash. Some aviators refused to buy this irrefutable principle of physics, however; they crawled out on the wing and chopped off the ice. Eventually a way was found to use a little of the plane's energy output to keep the wing tips warm. People who work in a dynamo do not shut the place down and go home when the sun sets, because they can use a little of the output to keep the place lit.

It is not so much a question of whether the technology exists to offset urban wastes by means of a sewage treatment plant or smog control devices, as it is of whether these are too costly and whether they will actually be put to use. Perhaps resource cost is a constraint, but that is not what most people seem to mean when they complain about the costs of combating urban pollution. They want someone else to pay. They want the costs to remain external. In fact, we do not have social, political fiscal, or financial institutions adapted to the job of completely internalizing the external costs of urban growth. Why should I ride the bus to work if that only leaves more room on the road for someone else to drive? Why should City A do a favor for City B by treating its sewage before dumping it into the river they share? Where will the money come from for a park?

IRREVERSIBLE DECAY

Externalities provide a clue to the source of still another type of urban problem—spreading seas of decaying structures. Our basic concept concerning the economic life of a building is that the residual land value (RLV) in some new use increases over time and eventually becomes greater than the present value of income expected from the existing building (PV). This present value decreases over time because the structure, and possibly the neighborhood infrastructure as well, becomes deteriorated and obsolescent. This is illustrated in Figure 54a, in which OA is the economic life of the building. At the end of that time it will pay to demolish the old house, for example, and construct something else, like an apartment building. (See the discussion of "highest and best use" in Chapter Seven.)

This ought to lead to an orderly process of replacing obsolete buildings and reusing land. The building is presumably fully amortized in OA years. In fact, several problems arise that put off the demolition of old buildings and the reuse of land. One of these is that urban density has tended to fall.[1] When the old house was first built, the expectation might have been that the succeeding land use would be a ten-story apartment building. But as time went by, people got used to living in automobile suburbs and generally lost their inclination to live in old-fashioned apartment blocks. Now only some old houses will be torn down to make way for apartment buildings, and most of these will be three or four stories in height instead of ten. Some apartment buildings and offices are being built on new suburban land, and most new retail store construction is taking place on such land. The opportunities for profitable redevelopment of the site have slackened off since the old building was put up. This is shown as a downward shift of RLV to RLV' in the figure, and an extension of the economic life to OB years—despite the fact that the initial development is fully amortized in OA years.

Now there occurs something else to discourage a change in the use of the land, an idea known as the Prisoner's Dilemma. The origin of the idea is a "game-theory" problem in which two men are arrested on suspicion of committing a crime, separately questioned, and given the chance to get a light sentence by confessing and implicating the other person. Under some circumstances, it will be each man's better option to confess even though both might be innocent.[2]

This hypothetical puzzle has important applications to urban real estate problems. The man who owns an old building in a slum may not find it worthwhile to demolish and replace it because the surrounding slums deprive him of access to the higher-rent market his new building would require. If there are only two landowners in this kind of situation, their options might be expressed as follows, in terms of yield on their combined financial holdings:

1. Note that this is not in conflict with the idea above that density is higher in larger cities.

2. The case, and the following real estate application, are discussed by Otto A. Davis and Andrew B. Whinston in "The Economics of Urban Renewal," reprinted in *Urban Renewal: The Record and the Controversy*, James Wilson, ed. (Cambridge: MIT Press, 1966), pp. 54ff.

		OWNER II	
		Invest	Not Invest
	Invest	7,7	3, 10
OWNER I			
	Not Invest	10,3	4, 4

This means that if both owners replace or fix up the old buildings, each earns 7 percent; if neither invests further in these buildings, their earnings are each 4 percent. But if only Owner I replaces his old building

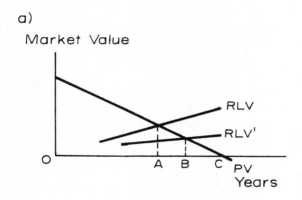

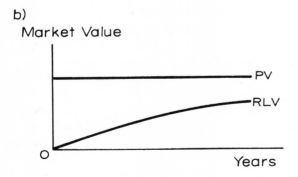

Figure 54.   Effect of urban externalities on the economic life of buildings.

with a better one, all he gets is 3 percent, while the effect of his better-looking building enables Owner II across the street to raise his rents and get an income of 10 percent. It works the other way around if Owner II invests and Owner I does not. The upshot is that both owners will probably decide to neglect their properties even though they would both be better off if the two properties were redeveloped or improved. (The reader can decide whether the community would be better off.)

If the two owners would get together, or if one would buy out the other, the dilemma would disappear. Federal urban renewal schemes in the post-World War II period have, in effect, promoted this kind of coalition—but they have generally managed to lose money rather than make the profit that the Prisoner's Dilemma implies can be obtained. In fact, it is very difficult for public or private agencies to acquire land on sufficient scale to overcome the external costs of nearby blight. Building on new land in the suburbs is much less complex.

In any event, the Prisoner's Dilemma and the historic trend to lower urban density combine, in Figure 54b, to suppress RLV, the opportunity for recycling of previously developed land.

The present value function in Figure 54b is shown as a horizontal line. The market price or rent of a building does not decline regularly with the age of a building, even if the price or rent is corrected for changes in the general price level. Buildings continue in use without replacement, not because the users' incomes are inadequate, but because capital funds for replacement are difficult to mobilize, a point made in Chapter Twelve. This may come about partly because financial institutions internalize some of the external costs of obsolescence: new replacement housing would cause the market value of existing houses to fall, so financial institutions are the principal investors in the existing inventory.

So we show the PV line resisting the economic effects of deterioration and obsolescence. RLV may never catch up with it, even past the point OC in Figure 54b when, in some sense, the value of the original structure may become negative. Used or not used, decaying buildings just lie there, as the people who live in cities are abundantly aware.

EXTERNALITIES OF PERSONAL BEHAVIOR

We can show by "metabolic" studies and by microeconomic analysis that certain urban problems *ought* to exist; density makes the streets noisy and refuse accumulates, sewage is spilled untreated into rivers, and districts of housing deteriorate into slums. But when surveys are made of what people in a city *think of* as urban problems, the results do not always conform to our observation of physical phenomena. A recent survey in Boston, for example, asked people to name the biggest problem facing the city. Physical things such as housing, transportation, and pollution got fewer than one vote in five—and many of those votes came from wealthy people of more than average education who presumably escaped the direct impact of the problem they named as most important. Though there were many people below the official "poverty level" in the sample, fewer than one person in ten said that jobs were the biggest problem. What people complained about most was other people. "The issue which concerned more respondents than any other was variously stated—crime, violence, rebellious youth, racial tension, public immorality, delinquency. However stated, the common theme seemed to be a concern for improper behavior in public places."[3]

We could consider this to be a reflection of the time and the place. Surveys in Tokyo find people most concerned with housing and air pollution; street crime is almost nonexistent, and "racial tension" would be meaningless in Japan's nearly homogenous society. North American cities are highly heterogeneous, not only in the sense of ethnic and religious differences, but in terms of "life style" as well. People in their teens and early twenties are no longer cowering recruits into a clan, but almost an automous republic within the urban community, with novel standards of dress, diet, fraternity, and work.

Different types of people rub each other the wrong way, creating external costs that are subjective but entirely real. Perhaps it is immoral or regrettable that some people feel uncomfortable when a minority family moves in next door, but the discomfort is real. Babies that cry in church or kids who have tantrums in a department store make innocent adults squirm. The thought of someone drinking in a public place on the Lord's Day is very offensive to many. Sloppy, psychedelic paint jobs on rattletrap cars make a "social statement" that most people would rather not be exposed to. There are even people who take offense at the sight of a pretty girl in Hot Pants—and feel compelled to scold other people for looking.

3. James Q. Wilson, "The Urban Unease," *The Public Interest* (Summer 1969), pp. 25–39; quotation from p. 26.

If people in a community all had the same moral values, spoke the same language, came from the same racial stock, wore the same clothes, and aspired to the same things in life, they would be less likely to take offense at each other's presence or behavior when clustered together in the city. But a city that thrives is likely to attract people of many different natures and leanings who will find each other mutually hard to take.

Quite apart from population heterogeneity, urbanization itself may be the source of external costs arising from personal behavior. City life does not come by instinct. Children have to be trained not to run into the street, or into the neighbor's garden. Motorists who pay no heed to cars lined up behind them can jam up an intersection while trying to make a turn. People watering lawns have to avoid dousing passers-by. A bus or taxi queue doesn't work unless almost everybody plays the game. Urban anonymity is a vast encouragement to theft and to straying from traditional morality.

People in cities have to open their eyes to some things, close them to others, and reconcile themselves to a set of rules that may or may not seem to make perfect sense. These rules are costless devices for offsetting externalities of individual behavior, and it is interesting that so large a share of what we call "pollution" can be prevented at almost no expense by the imposition of effective rules. By limiting the permitted use of the automobile horn, the noise level of the streets is markedly reduced. It costs almost nothing to put litter in a basket and really nothing to refrain from defacing walls or to turn one's radio down after 10 P.M. Contempt for society can be shown in other ways than by tossing garbage out the window. Advertising that is deemed to be against the public interest—for cigarettes or for doctor's services—can be kept out of the media quite easily.

What, indeed, does it cost to regulate traffic? If everyone knows that he is to drive to the right of a line running down the middle of the road (even if it's only an imaginary line), then traffic flows ever so much better than if individuals are left to decide for themselves which side of the road would be convenient to use. The functional efficiency of a shopping center parking lot depends not only on the few dollars worth of paint that goes into marking lanes and stalls, but also on the human courtesy of drivers who take no more than their share of space.

Restrictions on private behavior are thus feasible and nearly costless ways of controlling the waste that can occur in a dense city. In fact, they are thoroughly legitimized. An urban community is an ordered society by force of necessity, and the right of the city to say that some things may not be done or that other things must be done cannot really be challenged. Specifically what shall be banned and what required, though, is far from self-evident, and the tendency of the urban community, given power to legislate on the behavior of people, is to legislate its prejudices. There seems to be no way to separate anti-litter laws aimed at keeping the streets clean from anti-pornography laws aimed at keeping hearts pure. And if it is a good thing to have one-way streets, what can be wrong with one-race neighborhoods? If we are to keep our radio volume down to inoffensive levels, should we not keep disturbing ideas out of the newspapers as well? In principle, restrictions on behavior are in the general interest, but in practice they easily become invidious. The first use of zoning in California was to ban Chinese laundries from certain districts.[4] It was argued that they created fire hazards, but they were also a means of livelihood for the minority group which faced various forms of prejudice.

URBANIZATION AND THE "CLASS STRUGGLE"

It was the factory that provided the principal impetus to urbanization during the nineteenth century. Individual factories had to be large to make effective use of newly invented, power-driven machinery, and this required a labor force that was large enough to become quite an impersonal tool of production in the eyes of factory owners. Work was broken down into simple, repetitive tasks, and individual workers were paced relentlessly by lock-step organization of production. The ancient guild system and follow-on traditions of employer paternalism eroded under the intense competitiveness of manufacturing, so that the factory worker was left without much in the way of economic security or personal commitment to the company that paid him.

The urban factory worker was thus "on his own" in the economic system, subject to the worst consequences of fluctuation in the market for manufactured goods and almost desperately competitive with his fellow workers for the opportunity to earn a living. At the same time, the urban infrastructure—housing, sanitary facilities, transportation systems, schools, hospitals, and cultural facilities—grew only sluggishly and in a haphazard way to meet the needs of growing urban populations. Agglomerations of

4. Raleigh Barlowe, *Land Resource Economics* (Englewood Cliffs, N.J.: Prentice-Hall, 1958), pp. 495–496.

many factories in the same city, followed by the expansion of nonexport types of urban business, caused the urban labor force to swell and the sense of alienation and dissatisfaction within it to grow strong. Cities became the battleground in the classic economic struggle between "labor" and "capital." Labor unrest, with all that implies and led to, was a concomitant of urbanization in the industrial age, a profound and significant external cost.

Cities in the post-industrial age have labor problems, too, but they are of a fundamentally different sort. In most Western nations, collective bargaining became not only permissible but mandatory, and systems of social insurance (against unemployment or disability) were introduced, so that the workers as a group are shielded from the more extreme economic risks and able to negotiate with employers on a more nearly equal footing for a share in the earnings of business. There are still "factory strikes," where the issue is between an employer and the people who work for him—wages or working conditions—but these are not the source of general public concern at the present time.

Today the "labor problem" is epitomized by a dock strike, or a strike of schoolteachers or sanitation workers. The urban community is so interdependent that it has many strategic weak points. Most of these critical functions have actually been brought within the public sector, but public or private, a demand by labor in these areas is directed not against a specific employer but against the urban community as a whole. The labor problems of the post-industrial city are disputes for a larger share of the urban pie, carried on by threatening not the profits of an individual firm but the physical and economic viability of the city, the region, or sometimes the nation.

This is not to say that the demands by schoolteachers, firemen, or transit workers, for example, are unreasonable. Indeed, wage levels for public employees, in particular, have often lagged seriously behind wages in the private sector. Rather, the point is that a work stoppage by any one of certain categories of the urban labor force can cause major external costs to the community. This means that political pressure will be brought to bear, generally to comply with the demands of these strategic workers and to get them back to work. Though strikes by public employees and others in activities involving the "public interest" (especially the transportation industries) are generally less than completely legal, they are condoned by the philosophy that emerged from the industrial disputes of the nineteenth century.

Table 26

Inflation in a Two-Sector Urban Economy

Time period	Goods sector			Services sector			Total			Y/Q
	L	Q	Y	L	Q	Y	L	Q	Y	
t_0	60	60	60	60	60	60	120	120	120	1.0
								+ 25%		
t_1	30	60	60	90	90	180	120	150	240	1.6
								+ 10%		
t_2	15	60	60	105	105	420	120	165	480	2.9
			With "Balanced" Growth							
t_0	60	60	60	60	60	60	120	120	120	1.0
								+ 33%		
t_1	40	80	80	80	80	160	120	160	240	1.5

Source: Based on W. J. Baumol, "Macroeconomics of Unbalanced Growth," *The American Economic Review* (June 1967), 415–426.

Note: L = number in labor force.   Y = number of units of money.
        Q = number of units of output.

There is another aspect to the problem, which is illustrated by the numbers in Table 26. There is no satisfactory way to measure the "productivity" of most urban service workers—teachers, policemen, and barbers, to name just a few. This creates the impression that wage increases for these people are purely inflationary, and one leading economist has gone so far as to suggest that this factor is responsible for the fiscal problems of today's cities and their inability to cope with problems of pollution, congestion, crime, and housing.[5]

In Table 26 we start in time period t_0, with a labor force (L) of 120, divided equally between the goods sector and the services sector of the local economy. Each man produces one unit of output (Q) and is paid one unit of money (Y). In the next time period, there is a labor-saving innovation in the goods sector that cuts the labor requirement there in half and doubles the wage. The surplus workers move over to the services sector, and the

5. W. J. Baumol, "Macroeconomics of Unbalanced Growth," *The American Economic Review* (June 1967), pp. 415–426.

wage in that sector rises to remain in equilibrium with the wage in the goods sector. Services output rises only in proportion to the expanded labor force in that sector, and for the economy as a whole, the index of physical output (Y/Q) goes up to 1.6, which means that inflation has occurred. In the next time period, there is a further increase in productivity in the goods sector, more people coming into the services sector, another round of wage increases, and more inflation. The rate of increase in total physical output has slowed to 10 percent.

The lower portion of the table makes the alternative assumption that expansion of the economy is "balanced," that is, that the physical output in each sector grows by the same proportion. This means that the growth rate of total physical output is higher than in the unbalanced case, and the rate of inflation is somewhat less.

Obviously, these are hypothetical numbers and there are many implicit and explicit assumptions at work. They do illustrate the critical role of productivity measurements in the services sector and the presumption that technological innovation is not likely to occur in that sector. How could we say that a policeman who directed traffic eight hours a day in time zero is more productive doing the same thing in time one when his wage has doubled?

And, of course, service industry wages and the wages of public employees have risen sharply in recent years in North America.[6] So the hypothetical numbers seem to be related to a real-world problem. It is also true, however, that the shift away from blue-collar occupations in various nations does not seem to have been accompanied by declining economic growth rates, nor is the evidence concerning the causes of inflation very clear.

What we can say is that the economic structure of a modern metropolis creates conditions for a relatively new type of struggle over the distribution of income, one in which several service functions tend to be favored. But longshoremen are not service workers, and so the important dichotomy is "strategic-nonstrategic" rather than "goods-services." The "labor-capital" dichotomy is out of date, in any case.

The problem that cities have in meeting commitments for merit goods—welfare payments and subsidized housing, for example—from inelastic sources of public revenue are compounded by this new kind of struggle over wages. The more a social worker is paid, the less there is for

6. See Netzer, *Economics of the Property Tax.*

welfare checks. If carpenters' wages go up, it will be more difficult to provide public housing. If the city must subsidize or take over the transit system, it may be able to do less in the way of improving schools or hospitals.

DISCUSSION QUESTIONS

1. In your own opinion, what is the most important correlate of physical discomfort in a city? Its population size? Its density? Its heterogeneity? Its income level or distribution? Something else?

2. Could there be people or businesses in a city who contribute to urban dysfunction but who neither cause nor benefit from agglomeration economies? If so, what socioeconomic type are they likely to be? And what could or should be done about it?

3. If you see a "meter maid" approaching an expired parking meter, are you helping the community by putting a spare coin in the offending meter?

4. To what extent is the usefulness of zoning a function of city size?

5. What is the answer to the question: "Why doesn't everyone use public transit?" Is it a rhetorical question?

6. Refer to Figure 52(c). Is the ideal population level OA or OB?

7. "Real estate realities do not warrant slum-clearance subsidies." Discuss.

8. Suppose a subsidy of $10 million were required to fix up some old houses in the center of town. What alternative ways of spending the same amount to achieve improvement in the housing inventory might be considered?

9. What is your own principal complaint about the "quality of life" in your city? What things do you regularly do (or refrain from doing) solely out of consideration to strangers nearby? What potential civic restriction on your personal behavior would you find it most difficult to accept?

10. Should local public employees have the right to strike? If they should not, how should their wages be determined?

SELECTED REFERENCES

Blumstein, Alfred, *et al.* (eds.). *Systems Analysis for Social Problems.* Washington, D.C.: Operations Research Council, 1970.
Technical papers on problems and methodology of urban cost-benefit analysis, concerned primarily with external effects.

Detwyler, Thomas R., *et al. Urbanization and the Environment.* Belmont, Calif.: Duxbury Press, 1972.
Major elements of urban ecology, clearly illustrated.

Gordon, Mitchell, *Sick Cities.* New York: Macmillan, 1963.
A summary of salient statistical information about a wide range of urban problems from smog to public libraries, compiled by a freelance journalist.

Hunter, David R. *The Slums: Challenge and Response.* New York: Free Press, 1964.
A comprehensive essay on what is wrong about the slums of American cities, with a variety of suggestions for corrective action.

Lowe, Jeanne R. *Cities in a Race with Time.* New York: Random House, 1967.
Primarily a critical account of urban redevelopment efforts in a number of large American cities, based on extended research by a freelance journalist.

National Advisory Commission on Civil Disorders. *U.S. Riot Commission Report.* New York: Bantam Books, 1968.
A documented analysis of housing, employment, and other aspects of urban living conditions associated with the city riots of the late 1960s.

Netzer, Dick. *Economics and Urban Problems.* New York: Basic Books, 1970.
A compact review of urban problems such as housing, poverty, and transportation by a leading authority on local government finance in the U.S.

Schoenfeld, Oscar, and H. Maclean. *City Life.* New York: Grossman, 1969.
A collection of very readable autobiographical selections by well-known personalities—including Harpo Marx, Norbert Wiener, and Malcolm X—which convey the spirit and tempo of urban life in the recent American past.

Scientific American. *Cities.* New York: Knopf, 1966.

A set of essays by urban scholars, covering the origin of cities, problems of land use and transportation, and their internal economies.

Wilson, James Q. (ed.). *Urban Renewal: The Record and the Controversy.* Cambridge, Mass.: MIT Press, 1966.

A large, well-balanced collection of articles on the economics of urban land and housing markets in relation to the need for subsidized redevelopment, and the operation of the federal urban renewal program from its inception in 1949.

15

GOVERNING THE
POST-INDUSTRIAL CITY

IN 1953 the goods-producing sector of the United States economy—manufacturing—accounted for 32.1 percent of the national income. This was the largest proportion up to that time, and it may well be the high-water mark for all time.[1] The subsequent decline in this ratio led urban scholars to announce the emergence of the "post-industrial city," not only in the United States but very soon in many other nations as well.

The narrow interpretation of this turning point is that there will henceforth be more office jobs and fewer factory jobs in cities, the physical consequences of which could indeed be significant. Office functions may recentralize the city, since the suburban drift of factories had begun to scatter the workplace destinations of commuters. Only a few cities can play the role of major office centers, so there is likely to be burdensome growth in certain communities and relative stagnation in others.

In a broader sense, the decline in the relative importance of manufacturing per se signals an end to the concept of a city as merely an extension of the factory. When Gary, Indiana, was laid out in 1906, it was designed as a more or less self-contained facility for the production of

1. See John Friedmann, "Regional Development in Post-Industrial Society," *Journal of the American Institute of Planners* (May 1964), pp. 84–90.

steel.[2] Less explicitly planned cities that emerged in the nineteenth century were almost as explicitly thought of and administered as adjuncts to manufacturing. The housing supply, whether it was company housing or not, was a functional dormitory for workers, and retail stores were extensions of the factory canteen. Such public amenities as there were—parks, libraries, or hospitals—were in the nature of fringe benefits and part of the wage bargain. The success of the city was judged not by its liveability but by its physical output. It was a place to make money, not to spend it—a kind of urban plantation.

This is a caricature, of course. Some people built fine homes in town. Some wealth flowed back from the factories into civic programs that were not narrowly functional, such as schools and colleges. But manufacturing was where it all came from, and if civic leaders had to make choices about the way the city was developed or administered, the analogy of manufacturing efficiency came all too readily to mind. There was no discernable pay-off from street trees; it was cheaper to dump untreated wastes in any convenient stream or gully; drunkenness could cause industrial accidents; factory smoke and soot was a necessary price of progress—and so on. The conclusions were obvious. Environmental amenities cost money and they were not really necessary. Worse, they might interfere with volume production of manufactured goods.

THE CITY IS A CONSUMPTION GOOD

The regimen of an office economy is not so simple. The factory is essentially an environment for things, while the office—and the service sector as a whole—is much more an environment for people. The relationships are face-to-face and not side-by-side. Much more of the person than his manual dexterity or strength is called for in his work; the salesperson, the consultant, and (even) the accountant are constrained to be personable and considerate as well as quick-witted. The office and service environment is a community, an association of whole people, not an assembly line.

And it is very difficult to say just how much or what kind of "capital" is required to make the post-industrial economy work efficiently. Does the office building really need carpeting or a mural in the lobby? Will a civic

2. See R. A. Mohl and N. Betten, "The Failure of the Industrial City: Gary, Indiana, 1906–1910," *Journal of the American Institute of Planners* (July 1972), pp. 203–215.

aquarium or a sewage treatment plant help the city sell more insurance policies around the nation? Will bank employees make fewer mistakes if downtown traffic is unsnarled by the construction of expressways? Does a suburban, ranch-style home improve the judgment of a computer programmer who might just as well live in a downtown highrise?

The greater part of urban capital now in use is not an industrial investment that will pay off in terms of export-industry profits or sales. It is a way of spending money rather than a way of making it. The physical city is a consumption good.

This means that obvious or persuasive criteria for the way the city should be built and run are lacking. It makes little sense to say that mass transit is more efficient than the use of private vehicles, or that land proposed for shopping-center use is too valuable for use as a park—no more than it would to say that vanilla ice cream is more efficient than pistachio. It depends on what people want sufficiently to bear the opportunity cost. Consumption choices can only be evaluated in terms of psychological satisfactions—utility—for which there is not and probably cannot be any common yardstick. The fact that buildings, water mains, streets, and museums are durable, "investment" assets does not matter. There is no such thing as a rate of return on most of the things that we would call urban capital, any more than there is on a wristwatch or a refrigerator; we buy them because we want them, and that is the end of the story. Except, of course, to decide who "we" are—to say who has the power to control the use of community savings in shaping the physical urban environment. That is where community government comes in.

CONSERVATIVE, LIBERAL, AND RADICAL APPROACHES

Figure 55 is an overview of the options we have for controlling the development and use of the urban environment, conceived of as a consumption good. On the left-hand side are the physical resources, the first-generation know-how regarding their use (how to make plywood or generate electricity) and the environmental constraints such as the fact that the build-up of heat and waste products of a city may have biological effects that were not intended. On the right-hand side is the physical urban environment that we use these resources to create. Inside that box are listed some of the popular, catchword criticisms of the physical city and its functioning. The reader has every right to amend this list in any way,

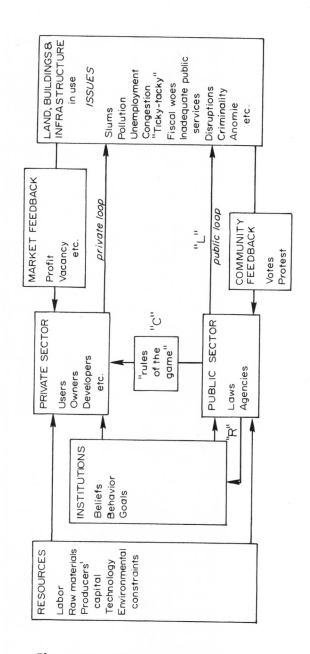

Figure 55. Urban management concepts.

because the hard fact is that these problems are subjective. If you choose not to worry about slums, then slums are not an issue for you.

People generally do think the city has problems, though, and want something to be done. This means influencing the process by which cities develop and are managed, a process that combines private and governmental activities. Within the diagram there is a "private loop" which represents responses by people who supply land, buildings, money, and services to demands for the use of real estate. If one developer makes a profit on new houses, another developer may decide to try his hand at it. If an apartment owner finds the neighborhood vacancy rate is very low, he may take the opportunity to raise his rents. If a leasing agent gets a number of inquiries from doctors who want to set up offices in a particular district, he may look around for an old house there that could be converted into a medical office. This information feedback from the market may be clear and quick or it may be sluggish and indistinct, depending on the sophistication of local real estate business.

Market feedback in the best of circumstances, however, ignores information that has no money content. A housebuilder can feel just as badly as social workers or their clients do about slums, but he probably can't do anything about it himself and break even. Smog and crime may help sell air conditioners and burglar alarms, and the market for good architecture in the suburbs may be stimulated by the drabness of housing in the central city, but the private sector is essentially unable to remove the source of the problem.

There is also a "public loop" in the figure. In a socialized economy, all the real estate in a city would be provided and administered by public agencies—houses and stores as well as streets and utility systems. Even in the most completely "laissez faire" urban economy, the public sector provides basic infrastructure, usually including schools, parks, and some hospitals. The public sector also regulates the private sector, by means of taxes, zoning, laws relating to private ownership of real estate and financial transactions, and procedural requirements for subdividing. People in the private sector may be restive under the "rules of the game" that emanate from the public sector, but they are generally constrained to play according to those rules. Yet it would be a mistake to suppose that the private sector is opposed to public regulation in general; there can be no real estate market without laws that define private property and ways in which it can be transferred; taxes to provide streets and schools are necessary if private property is to have substantial value.

The public sector takes its clues from "community feedback"—politically effective criticisms about the way things actually are. We have to make the public sector in this account stand for government in general, not just the government that happens to exist in the particular city. The powers of local government and the specific regulations that apply to private real estate business activities go back to fundamental national laws. Income taxes are designed at the national level, and development controls are usually worked up in intermediate levels of government. Problems that beset one city usually are common to many cities, however, so "community feedback" is not sterilized completely by the structure of government. For example, water-pollution problems that competitive cities are unable to deal with effectively can be referred to state or provincial governments.

The public and private sectors are both influenced by attitudes that prevail among the people in the community, and this is what the block labeled "institutions" means. In North America the great majority of people believe in and aspire to home ownership. Many oppose restrictions on the use of private automobiles. Some think that welfare assistance is a right, while others think indigent people should simply be excluded from the city. There are cities in the world where a man with long hair or a woman in a mini-skirt is subject to arrest. No more intense feelings are found than those concerning racial integration in the cities of the United States, involving as it does the school system, all forms of housing activity, the job market, and small business—and frequently the behavior and beliefs of policemen.

Suppose that community feedback demands that something be done about a particular problem—say, slums; what are the options and what is the best course of action? There are three symbols in the figure—C, L, and R, which locate the basic alternatives. People we can call "conservatives" respond to the problem by proposing a change in the rules that govern market activities—a tax benefit for people who increase the housing supply, perhaps. Others, whom we call "liberals," think it is self-evident that a public agency should be created to build and manage subsidized housing—that is, to socialize an economic activity where the market does not seem able to function effectively.

The *R* stands for radical, which means directing an effort at what seems to be the root of the problem. Why are there slums? Because there is poverty, some people will say. And why is there poverty? Well, perhaps it is due to racial discrimination in employment. If discrimination is rooted out of people's hearts, the reasoning goes, then the poverty that creates slums will disappear. Reform the spirit and the body will mend itself, so to speak.

All of these approaches are feasible, to some degree, and they are generally compatible, too. Tax allowances for accelerated depreciation have, in fact, stimulated housebuilding and indirectly improved the quality of the available housing supply. But, of course, so has publicly constructed housing—the effect of slum-clearance programs is a little more dubious. And almost any thinking businessman, when cornered by an effective moralist, will promise to hire and train a quota of now-impoverished slum dwellers, indirectly doing something in this way to ameliorate the slum problem.

All three of these approaches have limitations, or at least uncertainties attached to them. A recent mortgage-subsidy program in the U.S., FHA Section 235, designed to let low-income families become homeowners, was seriously abused by unscrupulous real estate people and corrupt government appraisers so that thousands of worthless dwellings were pawned off on hapless families. The FHA and veterans home loan programs in the United States certainly increased the post-World War II housing supply, but they filled up the suburbs with oceans of mediocre dwellings, choked the urban freeways, and may have driven up the general rate of interest as well. Canada's new tax law eliminates tax shelters and exemption of taxes on capital gains which, together, had stimulated apartment building; the apartments were wanted, but the price seemed too high and the benefit inequitable.

Public agencies have been established to perform functions that the market economy was discharging inadequately or not at all. Police and fire protection have been municipalized; schools and hospitals have become at least partly public functions; private utility and transit companies have been taken over; public parks have been provided and not a few public parking garages. Publicly owned housing is part of the residential inventory. Public efforts are often added to private ones in promoting new industry and in such things as tourism. Some cities have public marts for the sale of produce. But retail trade is generally left to private business, as is most housing and the provision of offices, factories, and warehouses—even though the land for them has been assembled through urban renewal and land banking.

On the other hand, public agencies such as these are often embarrassed by conflicting goals and undesired effects. The housing authority can stretch its subsidy to a larger number of units if it excludes the poorest of the poor from its clientele. Public property is removed from the tax rolls, which means that as the cost of it grows, the revenue base of the community shrinks. A parking facility or public mart can maximize its rental income or provide space at bargain prices, but not both. A fine park may raise nearby property values and eventually draw around it those people least in need of subsidized recreation. A user charge on municipal water, to support a sewage treatment plant, will become a very regressive tax. The free public library has no way to measure its demand, so it does not know when additional services to the community will be worth what they cost. The policeman has no way of knowing which laws most deserve to be enforced.

Many would scoff, perhaps, at the radical supposition that human behavior and attitudes can be changed by preachment and by laws. Sixty years of Marxism in the Soviet Union does not seem to have obliterated what Adam Smith called "the propensity to truck and barter." Religious leaders in California took an unprecedented, vehement stand against repeal of an open-housing law in 1964 and were soundly repudiated by voters. "You can't legislate morality," it was said.

But most people obey traffic laws; they stop for a red light even when there is no other traffic and no policeman in sight. They seldom nose into a parking space that someone else is trying to back into. Not many people drop their chewing gum on the sidewalk or puff cigars in elevators. Hardly anyone guffaws at a hunchback or stares at a disfigured face. When we push on a door, we usually allow for the fact that someone might be standing on the other side. The city itself is a civilizing force, a very good preacher.

It takes time for urban citizenship to sink in. People threw slops aimlessly into the streets of early London. When Tokyo began to revive after World War II, taxi drivers drove any whichway, but more recently the traffic in that city queues up almost spontaneously in lanes. Gradually, people internalize their own external costs and stop making an unnecessary nuisance of themselves. Maybe this is "greening" or becoming socialized or just growing up.

So it is not unthinkable that personal, moral discipline could eventually curtail the worst forms of pollution. Individuals, businesses, and communities may take it upon themselves to clean up the water, the ground, and the air they have used, without being punished if they don't and regardless of whether or not other people are showing as much consideration. One of the most encouraging things about the city is that self-control seems to evolve even in anonymity—when no one knows an offender well enough to be able to tell on him. This is a long step past village morality or the demeaning supervision of the Gauleiter, and it may understandably take several generations to mature.

A city full of "good guys" could still have a number of today's familiar problems, unfortunately. It may be self-evident that we should not spit on the sidewalk, but should we drive cars? Should we keep our hair trimmed short or our bosoms under wraps, as the case may be? Should the dockworker and the schoolteacher not ask for raises, or the landowner not ask for a higher price for his property than he himself paid? Should we expect school children to spend their Saturdays picking up dead leaves in the park or serenading an old folks' home? If we happen to want a community swimming pool, is it moral to ask help in paying for it from people who won't use it? Which living arrangement is better for the human spirit, the tower apartment or the garden city? To run a city, we need principles more complex than "love thy neighbor" or "do unto others, etc."

PUBLIC OWNERSHIP OF URBAN WEALTH?

What we are doing in this chapter is checking out nostrums, those simple prescriptions for utopia that keep popping up in conversations about urban problems. We know enough about cities now to understand why some ideas that sound very good won't really work, and this is a negative but necessary step along the way of finding ideas that do work.

The most ineffective chestnut is public ownership. Urban infrastructure, as we have noted, is already publicly owned for several practical reasons, and there are publicly owned housing units and commercial facilities. Why not socialize all the land and buildings?

Public ownership would certainly internalize all the externalities of a city, by definition. Community factories would pollute only community air and water. There would be no more Prisoner's Dilemma. New housing tracts would only overload the streets and schools of the same community that put up the housing. In principle, community administrators would take into account the total impact of any proposed development and shape it accordingly.

Public ownership would also bring in revenue from rents, in addition to or in lieu of various kinds of taxation. But any net improvement in revenue would rest upon monopoly restrictions in supply, as we have noted before.

Public ownership would not clarify the rights and wrongs of low-density housing, nor would it make the benefit-cost study for a subway system any simpler. Shopping center feasibility studies would have to incorporate a near-philosophical concern for the future of the city's older shopping districts. Criminals already make a living on public streets and there is no reason to think they would stay away from publicly owned stores or apartment buildings. A socialized city produces sewage and garbage, has to decide if bars will be open on Sunday, and has to get somebody to live in the least desirable part of the housing supply. Socialized land is not completely free of opportunity cost for use as open space. Public construction is not necessarily less drab than private buildings are.

Public ownership of the "means of production" supposedly leads to a more equitable distribution of income. But public ownership of consumption capital has no such implications. How can we treat people equally if some of them want to ban drag racing or tall buildings while others don't? There is no way to give everyone an equal view of the Golden Gate Bridge or equal parking. We might say in answer that in a socialized city people could decide these things in a democratic way, perhaps by choosing administrators; we ought to recall, though, that in 1933 the democratically elected government of Germany declared modern art to be "degenerate"—and implemented this decision very effectively. There is little if any pay-off from collectivizing consumption altogether, and there can be a lot of grief.

A NATIONAL SUBSIDY FOR CITIES?

New York City's mayor in the 1960s, John Lindsay, wrote a book in which he described the problems of that sorely troubled town. The message was, he said in the concluding chapter, that "our cities need help. They need money, desperately."[3] He meant money from the federal and state governments. A fat check from Washington to New York City would, of course, solve a lot of problems. The city of Calcutta has put in for help from the World Bank.

It is not unfair to Mayor Lindsay—who went on to say that the money had been taken away from New York in the first place—to observe that a nation of cities cannot subsidize cities. Most of the nation's income in Western countries is produced in cities, and that is where money for urban functions and urban development must come from. The urban population, taken together, must live within their own means.

Mayor Lindsay concentrated on two major problems in his book—welfare and crime. Many people would prefer not to think of crime as a money problem, but Mayor Lindsay does. A case can be made for manifold expansion of the New York City police force, and policemen's salaries have been rising sharply. More judges are needed, and more jails and rehabilitation centers and probation officers, to cope with an expansion in their loads that already seems way out of hand.

But lack of money did not create the problem. Any city must tax itself to support the police services it finds necessary, so if there is a runaway escalation of crime, there is something wrong with what the police are doing or with the people themselves, not with the fiscal system. It may take a literal army to make the streets of New York comparatively safe again, but sending the bill for that to the nation at large is a confession of terrible inadequacy in urban management. It cannot be the solution for all cities; something much more fundamental than money is needed.

Welfare is incontrovertably a money problem. It is also a most inappropriate function to finance by means of a local property tax, even in part, because people not on welfare can remove themselves and their businesses from communities where welfare costs are high. There is no way for any or all levels of government to pay out more money for welfare than taxpayers taken as a whole are willing to supply, but the arbitrary character of the intergovernmental fiscal system may result in the supply of something less. Federalization of welfare seems like a reasonable thing to try, yet the Mayor Lindsays of the world should prepare themselves for the possibility that the national citizenry may not really care how hungry the children in urban welfare ghettos are.

3. John Lindsay, *The City* (New York: W. W. Norton, 1969), p. 231.

In specifics, too, the welfare system is the source of some of its own worst money problems. New York's most troublesome aid category, money for families with young children, has been administered under rules that encouraged an underemployed or underpaid father to abandon his family.[4] It was a strong disincentive against taking the few jobs that were available.

The idea of revenue sharing, giving cities some share of national income tax revenues, is to be distinguished from subsidies for basic urban functions. There is some structure of intergovernmental fiscal arrangements that matches expenditure programs with sources of revenue, and we can hope that fiscal reforms will eventually search out that optimum arrangement. When the optimum is found that should be the end to appeals by cities for grants from the national government—for welfare, jails, subways, parks, or you-name-it. Urban governments that think they deserve a little bailing out or a little treat now and then from some other level of government don't understand the nature of cities.

CHECKING POPULATION GROWTH?

At several points in this book we have taken issue with the idea that urbanization is somehow inevitably detrimental to human beings. There is, we have pointed out, a positive correlation between urbanization and per capita income among nations, and there are several reasonable explanations for this (see Chapter Two). In so doing, we have made some implicit comments on the more general and now very popular idea that world population growth needs to be contained. But the relationship between "zero population growth" and the problem of urbanization is complex enough to be misunderstood; our handling of urban issues may be inadequate if that relationship is not made clear.

For we often see the problems of cities like New York and Tokyo cited as portents for the whole world if population growth does not cease. It is true of course, that exponential population growth would eventually bring the number of persons per square mile of land on the entire globe up to levels already reached in Tokyo, New York, and other giant cities. But it does not follow from this that problems now observed in these cities have been caused by growth in world population, nor is it correct to say that

4. *Ibid.*, pp. 154ff.

rising world population will inevitably spread the kinds of problems now seen in some of these large cities. Hence, the current plight of certain cities does not in any sense prove that world population must be held in check. Nor do extrapolations of world resource scarcity resulting from population growth imply that cities such as New York or Tokyo should be prevented from getting bigger than they are.

Tokyo certainly has its problems, but they are not due to excessive population growth in Japan. Between 1950 and 1970 the population of Japan grew by about 25 percent, while the real GNP per capita went up about 300 percent. Concentration of population in the Tokyo area at least facilitated the vast increase in national productivity and may have been an indispensable factor. The growth of Tokyo, with all its problems and its remarkable economic performance, is not really relevant to the zero-population-growth debate.

Urbanization does not contribute to resource shortages, except in-directly by helping to raise living standards and hence consumption. Demographers have not shown that human beings become more prolific when they migrate to cities and, indeed, there is some evidence that the opposite is true. Urban advantages can help to prolong life and thus contribute to national and world population growth, of course. Generally speaking, urbanization reflects the principle of comparative advantage —specialization by regions within a trading community of regions in those things each region does best—and therefore augments the effective supply of resources.

The observed diseconomies of urban scale, described in the previous chapter, are on the best evidence not net diseconomies. There are techno-logical and institutional ways to offset or prevent congestion, pollution, squatting, crime, disorder, and large-scale underemployment which seem to be the plagues of very large cities at the present time, at a cost that would leave room for increases in conventionally measured per capital real income. Tokyo's smog and New York's welfare ghettos are not basically the result of economic or natural laws but of human neglect or misun-derstanding.

Not long ago the author was on a bus in Seoul, Korea, on a Saturday afternoon, when a mile-wide traffic jam paralyzed the entire center of the city. Six lanes of busses, all heading into the center, crammed a four-lane, two-way main street, and it was more than two hours before the flow of traffic could resume. It was a warm day, and the exhaust from the bus motors did not make the air more agreeable. One might expect that this large population of immobilized passengers, their free time and their shopping excursions disappearing in the malfunctioning mechanism of the city, would have become irritable, but they did not. Ladies in their weekend finery gossiped and joked. Children exchanged cookies and toys through open windows with others in adjoining stalled busses.

This good humor seemed inexplicable, especially in a city that now boasts some of the most persistent and acrid smog, some of the largest and most unsightly swarms of squatter shacks of any city in the world, together with muddy, pot-holed streets and abundantly contaminated water supplies. The mystery was removed by a perceptive Peace Corps member who had been in Seoul long enough to appreciate its temper. This traffic jam, he explained, was the best problem these people ever had, the most promising thing in the history of a nation that for centuries had scratched a meager living from the rocky, dry, Korean earth. To lament that Seoul's present disorder and discomfort could have been avoided by creative planning, at no sacrifice to its economic effectiveness, would be to miss the point. The very hazards of the city made its vitality and its promise unmistakeable.

It would be worse than useless to shut down cities in the hope that a world Mathusian disaster can thus be avoided. It would be foolish to assume that by stopping the growth of world population we can make the air in Tokyo fit to breathe again or the streets of New York safe to walk on. Population growth and urbanization are separate matters.

METROPOLITAN GOVERNMENT?

There are more than 70 cities in Los Angeles County and over 600 distinct taxing jurisdictions.[5] Virtually all major urban centers are geographic amalgamations of once-distinct communities that gradually grew together in a functional and economic sense but retained separate political identities. The resulting patchwork of local government creates a number of problems in the effective management of metropolitan responsibilities and problems. Residents and businesses that want to escape the tax burden of one city where low-income population needs subsidized schooling and

5. For an interesting discussion of political fragmentation in metropolitan areas, see Mitchell Gordon, *Sick Cities* (New York: Macmillan, 1963), Chapter Twelve.

medical care can move to an adjacent town where these costs are less. Potential economies of scale in the provision of public services—such as fire protection and solid waste disposal—are lost if each small entity tries to go it alone. An area-wide public transportation system becomes almost impossible to organize. Affluent communities resist the intrusion of low-income housing. And each community is basically free to pollute the water and air of the metropolitan region because it can impose external costs on all the others.

So, many students of urban affairs believe that consolidation of local governments is an effective way to deal with several of the most significant problems that large cities seem to have. A form of metropolitan government was established in Toronto in 1953, and efforts along this line have been made in several U.S. areas, notably in Dade County, Florida. Relatively stronger central governments in Europe and Asia make metropolitan management somewhat easier than is the case in North America.

In a democracy, consolidation of governments cannot be achieved without the consent of the governed, and such consent for the purpose of taking a regional approach to metropolitan area problems has proved quite hard to come by.[6] It is perhaps obvious, for example, that effective air pollution control requires a regional approach. Studies have shown that air pollutants emanating from any one part of the San Francisco Bay Area will be carried by the wind to any other part. But it is also true that people who cause pollution may be different individuals from those who suffer from it, constituting different interests that are not reconciled merely by waving about an engineering study that shows how harmful soot can be to shade trees.

In Figure 56 there is a source of pollution—say, a smoky factory—at point X. Due to normal air currents, this smoke has an overspill effect in areas A and B. The circular area, $C+B$, around X is the economic radius of the factory, where factory workers and service industry workers dependent on this factory reside. If we feel that the answer to the smoke problem is to form a "smoke abatement" district including all that territory in which the smoke is produced and on which it falls, then our new governmental agency is $A+B$. Depending on the proportional significance of B, this limited-purpose regional government could decide to put factory X out of

6. For a good statement of this problem, see Stanley Scott and John C. Bollens, *Governing a Metropolitan Region: The San Francisco Bay Area* (Berkeley: Institute of Governmental Studies, University of California, 1968).

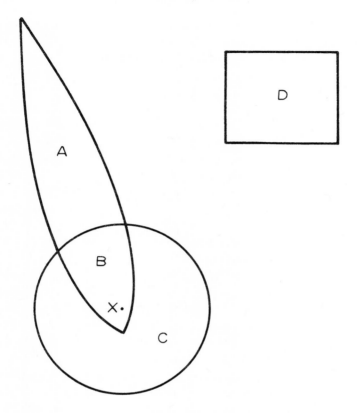

Figure 56.   The urban overspill problem.

business. This would be some sort of economic hardship for the people in
C and might be a net gain or a net loss to the people in *B*.

We might decide to solve this problem by defining the new jurisdiction to include *A* + *B* + *C*, hoping to capture all the people involved
one way or another and forcing them to deal jointly with their common
problem.

The people in *C* would probably drag their feet, however, having
something to lose and nothing to gain. The people in *A*, for their part,
might be frightened off by our proposal to consolidate the entire area, even
for an ostensibly limited purpose of air pollution control, for fear that it
might ultimately cost them control over their exclusive school system.

The people in area D are the consumers of factory X's product. In some sense, they too are involved in whatever decision is made about the smoke, but there is no obvious way to fit them into the scheme.

THE SENSE OF COMMUNITY

The problem is autonomy. There are various reasons why an individual might surrender his freedom to act and throw in his lot with a group of other people who then become the collective arbiter of how that individual will behave. There is the cultural pattern of choosing a mate and raising a family, which more or less consumes a person's identity. There is the expedient thing, like signing on with a corporation that will require some conformity of dress, speech, and personal behavior and spell out the limits of one's material aspirations. There is compulsion, like being drafted or annexed. Whatever happened to Latvia?

Living in a city means accepting the authority of the community with a small "c". To occupy premises we will pay rent. In driving a car we will keep to the right. We share the sidewalks and wrap our garbage. We do not sell liquor or real estate without a permit. We accept the premise that urban life is interdependent in many ways and that its opportunities are not available without a degree of conformity.

But that is a general premise. Unless we subscribe to a philosophy that denigrates the self, we are necessarily uncertain about the social and moral boundaries of our community and wary of giving away more of our autonomy than we need to. We do not know yet just how much diversity and nonconformity must be sacrificed for the sake of that community because we cannot be very specific about the community's goals.

We live in cities, just as we live in a world of many races, languages, convictions, and limitations—without having fully mastered the art of it.

DISCUSSION QUESTIONS

1.   Visit the newest office building in your community and find out, if you can, how much it cost per square foot to build. Do you believe that each extra dollar of construction cost was justified on the basis of increased efficiency of tenant firms? That is, is the design "functionally efficient" or a "consumption good" from the occupants' point of view?

2.   Is it more efficient to have a large area of common open space for a neighborhood than letting everyone have his own private back-yard? Does it matter?

3.   What aspects of community life does the urban land market (the "private loop" in Figure 59) ignore? How should this be remedied? Are there ways to improve market feedback and, if so, what are the practical limits to such improvement?

4.   What forms of "community feedback" exist in your community? Do they tell things "the way it is" to people in government? If not, is it because the feedback system is archaic?

5.   Why do you suppose the tradition of nonpartisan local government has appeared in North America? Does it help solve urban problems better than party government would, or does it stand in the way of solutions?

6.   What is the ideal way for a group of people to make joint decisions about the design or regulation of their urban environment? In particular, should the matter be left in the hands of "experts"? What criteria are available, and what should be done if a small group is intensely dissatisfied with a design and regulation scheme that the great majority have been able to agree on?

7.   Is the quality of community self-government reflected in the value of urban land?

SELECTED REFERENCES

Briggs, Asa. *Victorian Cities*. New York: Harper and Row, 1965.
A richly detailed account of rapid population growth in the manufacturing centers of late nineteenth-century England, emphasizing planning and infrastructure problems.

Dickens, Charles. *Hard Times*. London: Oxford University Press, 1955.
The renowned novelist's account of factory workers in a British manufacturing town hard hit by depression; the nineteenth-century class struggle is portrayed in vivid social literature.

Gans, Herbert J. *The Levittowners*. New York: Pantheon, 1967.
A sociologist's report on the attitudes, culture, and community

organization of American suburbanites, based on systematic observation over a period of two years.

Glazer, Nathan, and D. P. Moynihan. *Beyond the Melting Pot.* Cambridge, Mass.: MIT Press, 1970.
Two sociologists revisit ethnic communities of New York City to update their earlier description of several distinct patterns of social organization and the struggle for economic advancement.

Hadden, J. K., *et al.* (eds.). *Metropolis in Crisis.* Itasca, Ill.: F. E. Peacock Publications, 1967.
A collection of essays on the problems of American cities—race, poverty, pollution, schools, crime, housing, transportation, and government—responding mainly to the urban riots of the late 1960s and the Johnson administration's concern for the cities.

Jacobs, Jane. *The Death and Life of Great American Cities.* New York: Random House, 1961.
A city planner criticizes the planning profession for overlooking the vitality and cohesion of low-income urban neighborhoods in programs for redevelopment and subsidized housing.

Moynihan, Daniel P. *Maximum Feasible Misunderstanding.* New York: Free Press, 1969.
An outspoken Harvard sociologist, who served briefly as President Nixon's chief advisor on urban affairs, describes the origin of the War on Poverty concept of maximum feasible participation by low-income people in management of programs affecting them, what the concept was intended to mean, and how misunderstanding concerning it crippled the poverty program.

Warren, Roland L. (ed.). *Politics and the Ghettos.* New York: Atherton, 1969.
A collection of papers examining the black ghettos of American cities—why they exist, why they are apparently powerless to achieve economic improvement on their own, and why bureaucratic efforts to assist in this effort are ineffective.

APPENDIX

THE INCOME APPROACH

AND

INVESTMENT ANALYSIS

IN THEIR income approach to valuation, real estate appraisers must first project the earnings that a property will produce and then capitalize that projected stream of income at some discount rate that reflects the requirements of people in the market for such properties. It is natural, then, that investors often turn to appraisers for an answer to the question: "Is Property X a good investment for me?" In response, the techniques used by appraisers in their income approach have evolved in the direction of providing substantially more information than a simple prediction of selling price. A new analytical technique has been developed that improves the quality of the appraiser's basic work; it gives real estate investors a far clearer understanding of what may be anticipated from the purchase of a particular property, and it enables brokers to present income properties to the market in a manner likely to put each property into the hands of the investor who will derive maximum benefit from it. This technique is called "discounted cash flow analysis" or "internal rate of return analysis."

In Table 14 (Chapter Seven) the income approach is shown as a very simple process of multiplying net income by a capitalization factor. The factor (or its inverse) might seem to be essentially a "rate of return," and sometimes that term is used. But it is not a rate that the potential investor can compare directly with rates of return available from securities, thrift institutions, or other ventures; and it yields very little investment information. It is, in fact, a simple numerical relationship found by the appraiser in data on recently sold properties.

To illustrate this, and to show the progression from the very simplest income approach to discounted cash flow investment analysis, we must first back up one step to the concept of the "gross income multiplier" (GIM), which has been and still remains a popular valuation method. The GIM approach involves observing the ratio (M) of selling price (S) to gross possible income (GI) for many recently sold income properties, a ratio that seems to be fairly constant for any particular class of income properties in one community. "Gross possible income" is the total amount that could be collected in rents and other charges if a property were fully rented at rents normal for similar properties and if no tenant failed to pay his rent when due. It is usually measured on an annual basis, though monthly multipliers are sometimes used.

The market observations $(n$ in number) of selling price and gross income, or their ratios, are averaged as follows:

$$\frac{S}{GI} = M \quad \text{or} \quad M = \frac{m_1 + m_2 + m_3 + \ldots m_n}{n} \quad \text{e.g.,} \quad M = 7.$$

To estimate the selling price or market value (V) of some other property now being placed on the market, the appraiser need only obtain or forecast its gross income and multiply by this average ratio:

$$V = GI \cdot M \qquad \text{e.g., } \$140,000 = \$20,000 \cdot 7.$$

Now, if we think of V as the amount to be invested and believe that GI is the income that investment will provide each year, the reciprocal of M is our anticipated rate of return:

$$V \cdot \frac{1}{M} = GI \qquad \text{e.g., } \$140,000 \cdot \frac{1}{7} = \$20,000.$$

That is:

$$V \cdot f = GI \qquad \text{e.g., } \$140,000 \cdot (.143) = \$2,000,$$

where f is the reciprocal of M. For example, if we put \$140,000 in the bank and each year the bank sends us a check for interest in the amount of \$20,000, then our rate of return or rate of interest is 14.3 percent (rounding off).

Gross income from real estate, however, unlike interest paid by a bank, is not all spendable. Some of it must go for operating expenses—utilities, insurance, property taxes, regular repairs, payments to the manager, and some other items (but not including mortgage payments, "depreciation" charges, or income tax). There will also be some losses due to vacancy and collection problems. What remains is Net Operating Income (*NOI*), which the appraiser can usually obtain or estimate from his sample of recently sold properties, and which he can then divide by the selling prices of those same properties to get a *net* income factor (*R*) similar to the inverse of *M* in the *GIM* method:

$$\frac{NOI}{P} = R \qquad \text{or} \qquad P = \frac{NOI}{R} \qquad \text{e.g., } R = .10$$

R is sometimes called a "direct capitalization rate." Using it, together with the *NOI* of the property we are appraising, we can estimate the value of that property to be:

$$V = \frac{NOI}{R} \qquad \text{e.g., } \$140,000 = \frac{\$14,000}{.10}.$$

We could say the rate of return in our example is 10 percent, but this would assume that *NOI* continues unchanged forever. Money in the bank might draw interest forever, conceivably, but income real estate is a tangible commodity and is subject, in part at least, to deterioration and obsolescence. Thus part of *NOI* should be set aside each year to provide for the eventual replacement of the building or for some other way of making good this progressive decline in value. If we assume the economic life of the property to be fifty years, one method of allowing for this replacement would be to subtract from *NOI* 2 percent of the initial (present) value. However, the appraiser has not yet determined that value; we can achieve the same result algebraically, by subtracting the 2 percent from the term of the denominator, *R*. (For simplicity, we assume that the land, as well as the building, decline in value over the fifty-year span; the algebra is not affected by this assumption. We might also specify a sinking-fund allowance instead of our straight-line 2 percent recovery factor, but complication would not help at this point either.) The denominator is thus the sum of two rates—return *on* our investment and return *of* our investment:

$$V = \frac{NOI}{R_{on} + R_{of}} \qquad \text{e.g., } \$140,000 = \frac{\$14,000}{.08 + .02}.$$

The 8 percent figure might reasonably be regarded as *the* rate of return on this property, if it were not (primarily) for one further fact about the real estate market—namely, the existence of leverage, or the opportunity to borrow a substantial part of the purchase price. To most owners of income real estate, "return" means "return on equity" and that is the most important statistic a prospective purchaser of such property wants to know. If he can borrow two-thirds of the value of the property at 6 percent interest, he will not only need less equity to purchase it, but, in this example, the rate of return on equity will be greater than 8 percent. To find that equity rate, as a first approximation, we need only recognize that R_{on} is a weighted average of the mortgage interest rate (i) and the equity rate (r). The respective weights are the loan-to-value ratio (L/V) and the complement of that ratio (1-L/V). The concept is that part of the purchase price—say, two-thirds—is provided by the mortgage lender while the remainder is provided by the equity investor. Thus:

$$V = \frac{NOI}{[L/V \cdot i + (1-L/V) \cdot r] + R_{of}}$$

$$\text{e.g., } \$140,000 = \frac{\$14,000}{[2/3(.06) + 1/3(r)] + .02}$$

Solving for r in the example, since R_{on}, the total quantity inside the square bracket, is 8 percent, $r = .12$.

Note that this rate-of-return information has been derived from market data. It is implied by observed GIM's, normal operating expense ratios and leverage opportunities, and the projected gross income of the property in question. With such information, the appraiser is able to *deduce* the prevailing rate of return on equity as thus far defined.

Appraisers were making general use of this formula in their income approach when L. W. Ellwood pointed out an important conceptual error and provided a means of adjusting for it.[1] Normally, mortgage loans to finance the purchase of real estate are amortized over a term of years, so that the outstanding balance of the loan diminishes year by year; unless the property as a whole loses value at a corresponding rate, the fraction of total value represented by equity will thus increase, and the weights used in the above formula will have to change year by year. The end result is that the indicated return on equity is less than it appears without this adjustment.

Ellwood's new formula was fairly complex. To use it, appraisers had to rely on cumbersome and inflexible precalculated tables (limiting them to a loan-to-value ratio of exactly two-thirds in every case, and to only a few alternative mortgage interest rates, among other things); or they had to develop considerable skills in financial algebra and calculation.

One not very practical way to by-pass the problem is what appraisers call the "equity residual" method. This means assuming the dollar amount of the mortgage loan (Mtg) available on a property, subtracting the required payment (Pmt) on that mortgage from NOI for each year, finding

---

1. L. W. Ellwood, *Ellwood Tables for Real Estate Appraising and Financing* (Ridgewood, N.J.: the Author, 1959).

the present value of that net amount for every year, and summing up to equal the value of the equity (E). That is, property value is the sum of a dollar amount of mortgage that the appraiser knows or assumes at the outset, plus the value of the equity which he calculates:

$$V = Mtg = E$$

$$V = Mtg + \frac{(NOI-Pmt)_1}{(r+1.00)^1} + \frac{(NOI-Pmt)_2}{(r+1.00)^2} + \ldots,$$

where subscripts indicate particular years. The R_{of} rate in the denominator is 1.00 because the value of that year's net return to equity must be entirely recovered in that net return. The denominator has increasing exponents because the payments in the series are to be deferred for an increasing number of years.

Our latest formula would be tedious and perhaps impractical to apply, because it requires us to find the present value of varying amounts of cash return for each of an unlimited number of years. In fact, real estate investors normally hold a particular property for a limited time, after which it is sold, the remaining balance of the mortgage paid off, capital gain taxes and selling expenses paid, and the proceeds reinvested in some other property or a different type of asset. The lump sum net amount received by the investor upon disposition of the property is called the Reversion (Rev).

Before restating our formula to make use of this helpful new concept, there is one further step we can take that will greatly improve the significance of our calculations. The term in the numerator, which stands as NOI less mortgage payment, can be further amended to take account of income tax payments due each year because of ownership of the property—a negative expense if "tax shelter" is possible—and rental income itself can be allowed to vary if we believe that rents are likely to rise or fall during the time that the investor holds the property, or that operating expenses are likely to change. The numerator term is thus "cash flow to equity" (CFE), the amount an investor can spend at the end of the year. We then have:

$$V = Mtg + \frac{CFE_1}{(1+r)^1} + \frac{CFE_2}{(1+r)^2} + \ldots + \frac{Rev}{(1+r)^n}$$

for a holding period of n years. Recognizing that $V - Mtg = E$, we now have the formula given in this chapter for determining the "internal rate of return" on this investment. As Table 15 (Chapter Eight) shows, this formula is directly related to a "pro forma" accounting statement anticipating all the financial factors associated with the purchase of the specific income property—that is, its cash flows. This formula has three distinct uses:

1. Given the value of r, by virtue of knowing the rate of return that equity investors in his area generally expect, the appraiser can solve the formula for E and hence estimate the market value, V.

2. If the property in question has an asking price P, which in effect makes the market value V a known amount, it is possible to solve the equation for r, the yield, or true rate of return on equity, also called the "internal rate of return." It is not possible to solve for r algebraically, but computer programs to find the value of r in a different way are in wide use.

3. If the investor specifies the rate of return he requires, which may be different from the value of r used by the appraiser in use number 1 above, the formula can be solved for the value of the equity, and of the property as a whole, to that particular investor. The entire equation can be revised to take account of the particular situation of the individual investor—his tax bracket, expected holding period, and so on—to find a distinct "investment value" for each prospective purchaser. For example, the asking price for a property, based on use number 1 above, may be $140,000, while the investment value of the property to Mr. A may be only $130,000. The difference could be attributable to the fact that Mr. A's tax bracket is lower than that of other prospective buyers.

INDEX

375

103; plowed back, 102–103; sequestered, 102; squandered, 102
Listing agreement. *See* Broker
Listing, multiple. *See* Multiple listing
Loans, mortgage. *See* Mortgage loans
Location: and developer uncertainty, 244; of development, 146–148; of distribution centers, 58; economics of, 48–61, 72–75, 78; problems and public agencies, 153; of processing activities, 50; quotient of earnings for Denver, Colo., 92; requirements of tenants, 212; sold by real estate broker, 223; of trading businesses, 60; and transportation modes, 54; and urban land market, 170, 176–178, 185; and weight-gaining processes, 49–51; and weight-losing processes, 51–52
Locational constraints, 48, 114–118
Location quotient, 91–94
Los Angeles, industrial innovation in, 110

Marketability, 233–234. *See* Development
Market-comparison approach, 181
Market search, 210–225
Market, urban land. *See* Urban land market
Megalopolis, 14–18, 39
Merit goods, 304–319, 324–325, 346–347. *See also* Joint goods
Migration, 80–86
Minimum requirements method, 91
Mortgage insurance, 186, 190, 193, 249
Mortgage investor, 189, 196–207. *See also* Mortgage lender, Mortgage loans
Mortgage lender, 186, 189–196, 219. *See also* Mortgage investor, Mortgage loans
Mortgage loans, 189–207. *See also* Mortgage lender, Mortgage investor
Mortgage trader, 190
Multipliers: economic base, 64–78, 87–94; gross income, 370; and industry linkages, 115; input-output, 117; Keynesian investment, 65, 75–76

Negative exponential density theory, 143–146. *See* Clark, Colin
New towns, 248–252
New York City and subsidy issue, 359–361
Nonexport, 57–61, 63–78, 83, 86
Nonextractive occupations, 4

Optimum city size. *See* Size
Optimum maintenance level, 266
Ordered dense cluster, 27–28, 132. *See* Clustering

Pay-off matrix, 157–159
Planning. *See* Land planning
Police powers: and community operation, 268, 332; as joint good, 310, 315–316, 318; and private property, 175
Population: density, 3–4, 145, 333–335; effect of, on government processes, 84–85; growth, checking, 361–363; growth by replication, 328–330; size, 10, 12, 78–80, 256–257; supply, 80–86; urban, 6, 11, 361–363; world, 1–2
Port: attracts businesses, 54–55; city and hinterland, 101; exploitation, 100–105; and urban communities, 96–105
Post-industrial city, 350–366
Prisoner's Dilemma, 338–340, 358–359
Processing activities, 48–52, 106, 108
Promotion, 73, 79–80
Property tax. *See* Taxation
Property values, 179–186; and appreciation, 268; and the investor, 197, 207; and property tax, 217–218, 310–315; stability of, 129
Public goods, 315–319
Public services, 304–305, 312

Rank-size rule, 11–14
Real estate, 189–207: auction, 263–264; broker, 220–225; and building maintenance, 266; development, 228–259; investment return, 199, 201; mortgages, 168; users, 210–216